Media Ethics:

ISSUES AND CASES

SEVENTH EDITION

Philip Patterson
Oklahoma Christian University

Lee Wilkins
University of Missouri–Columbia

Connect
Learn
Succeed™

The McGraw·Hill Companies

Connect
Learn
Succeed™

MEDIA ETHICS, ISSUES AND CASES, SEVENTH EDITION

Published by McGraw-Hill, a business unit of The McGraw-Hill Companies, Inc., 1221 Avenue of the Americas, New York, NY 10020. Copyright © 2011 by The McGraw-Hill Companies, Inc. All rights reserved. Previous edition © 2008 and 2005. No part of this publication may be reproduced or distributed in any form or by any means, or stored in a database or retrieval system, without the prior written consent of The McGraw-Hill Companies, Inc., including, but not limited to, in any network or other electronic storage or transmission, or broadcast for distance learning.

Some ancillaries, including electronic and print components, may not be available to customers outside the United States.

This book is printed on acid-free paper.

2 3 4 5 6 7 8 9 0 DOC/DOC 1 0 9 8 7 6 5 4 3 2 1 0

ISBN 978-0-07-351194-8
MHID 0-07-351194-3

Vice President & Editor-in-Chief: *Michael Ryan*
Vice President EDP/Central Publishing Services: *Kimberly Meriwether David*
Sponsoring Editor: *Katie Stevens*
Manager Editor: *Meghan Campbell*
Executive Marketing Manager: *Pamela S. Cooper*
Senior Project Manager: *Lisa A. Bruflodt*
Design Coordinator: *Margarite Reynolds*
Cover Designer: *Mary-Presley Adams*
Buyer: *Kara Kudronowicz*
Media Project Manager: *Sridevi Palani*
Compositor: *Laserwords Private Limited*
Typeface: *10.5/12 Times Roman*
Printer: *R. R. Donnelley*

All credits appearing on page or at the end of the book are considered to be an extension of the copyright page.

Library of Congress Cataloging-in-Publication Data
Media ethics: issues & cases/[edited by] Philip Patterson, Lee Wilkins.— 7th ed.
    p. cm.
  Includes bibliographical references and index.
  ISBN 978-0-07-351194-8 (alk. paper)
  1. Mass media—Moral and ethical aspects. I. Patterson, Philip. II. Wilkins, Lee.
  P94.M36 2010
  175—dc22

2010016060

www.mhhe.com

To Amy, Andrew, Miranda and Joshua
Our equally bright and now-grown children,
unequally distributed between us

TABLE OF CONTENTS

FOREWORD

CLIFFORD G. CHRISTIANS
Research Professor of Communication
University of Illinois–Urbana

The playful wit and sharp mind of Socrates attracted disciples from all across ancient Greece. They came to learn and debate in what could be translated "his thinkery." By shifting the disputes among Athenians over earth, air, fire and water to human virtue, Socrates gave Western philosophy and ethics a new intellectual center (Cassier 1944).

But sometimes his relentless arguments would go nowhere. On one occasion, he sparred with the philosopher Hippias about the difference between truth and falsehood. Hippias was worn into submission, but retorted at the end, "I cannot agree with you, Socrates." And then the master concluded: "Nor I with myself, Hippias. . . . I go astray, up and down, and never hold the same opinion." Socrates admitted to being so clever that he had befuddled himself. No wonder he was a favorite target of the comic poets. I. F. Stone likens this wizardry to "whales of the intellect flailing about in deep seas" (Stone 1988).

With his young friend Meno, Socrates argued whether virtue is teachable. Meno was eager to learn more, after "holding forth often on the subject in front of large audiences." But he complained, "You are exercising magic and witchcraft upon me and positively laying me under your spell until I am just a mass of helplessness. . . . You are exactly like the flat stingray that one meets in the sea. Whenever anyone comes into contact with it, it numbs him, and that is the sort of thing you seem to be doing to me now. My mind and my lips are literally numb."

Philosophy is not a semantic game, though sometimes its idiosyncrasies feed that response into the popular mind. *Media Ethics: Issues and Cases* does not debunk philosophy as the excess of sovereign reason. The authors of this book will not encourage those who ridicule philosophy as cunning rhetoric. The issue at stake here is actually a somewhat different problem—the Cartesian model of philosophizing.

The founder of modern philosophy, René Descartes, preferred to work in solitude. Paris was whirling in the early 17th century, but for two years even Descartes' friends could not find him as he squirreled himself away studying mathematics. One can even guess the motto above his desk: "Happy is he who lives in seclusion." Imagine the conditions under which he wrote "Meditations II." The Thirty Years' War in Europe brought social chaos everywhere. The Spanish were ravaging the French provinces and even threatening Paris, but Descartes was shut away in an apartment in Holland. Tranquility for philosophical speculation mattered so much to him that upon hearing Galileo had been condemned by the Church, he retracted parallel arguments of his own on natural science. Pure philosophy as an abstract enterprise needed a cool atmosphere isolated from everyday events.

Descartes' magnificent formulations have always had their detractors, of course. David Hume did not think of philosophy in those terms, believing as he did that sentiment is the foundation of morality. For Søren Kierkegaard, an abstract system of ethics is only paper currency with nothing to back it up. Karl Marx insisted that we change the world and not merely explain it. But no one drew the modern philosophical map more decisively than Descartes, and his mode of rigid inquiry has generally defined the field's parameters.

This book adopts the historical perspective suggested by Stephen Toulmin:

> The philosophy whose legitimacy the critics challenge is always the seventeenth century tradition founded primarily upon René Descartes. . . . [The] arguments are directed to one particular style of philosophizing—a theory-centered style which poses philosophical problems, and frames solutions to them, in timeless and universal terms. From 1650, this particular style was taken as defining the very agenda of philosophy (1988, 338).

The 17-century philosophers set aside the particular, the timely, the local and the oral. And that development left untouched nearly half of the philosophical agenda. Indeed, it is those neglected topics—what I here call "practical philosophy"—that are showing fresh signs of life today, at the very time when the more familiar "theory-centered" half of the subject is languishing (Toulmin 1988, 338).

This book collaborates in demolishing the barrier of three centuries between pure and applied philosophy; it joins in reentering practical concerns as the legitimate domain of philosophy itself. For Toulmin, the primary focus of ethics has moved from the study to the bedside, to criminal courts, engineering labs, the newsroom, factories and ethnic street corners. Moral philosophers are not being asked to hand over their duties to technical experts in today's institutions, but rather to fashion their agendas within the conditions of contemporary struggle.

All humans have a theoretical capacity. Critical thinking, the reflective dimension, is our common property. And this book nurtures that reflection in communication classrooms and by extension into centers of media practice. If the mind is like a muscle, this volume provides a regimen of exercises for strengthening its powers of systematic reflection and moral discernment. It does not permit those aimless arguments that result in quandary ethics. Instead it operates in the finest traditions of practical philosophy, anchoring the debates in real-life conundrums but pushing the discussion toward substantive issues and integrating appropriate theory into the decision-making process. It seeks to empower students to do ethics themselves, under the old adage that teaching someone to fish lasts a lifetime, and providing fish only saves the day.

Media Ethics: Issues and Cases arrives on the scene at a strategic time in higher education. Since the late 19th century, ethical questions have been taken from the curriculum as a whole and from the philosophy department. Recovering practical philosophy has involved a revolution during the last decade in which courses in professional ethics have reappeared throughout the curriculum. This book advocates the pervasive method and carries the discussions even further, beyond freestanding courses into communication classrooms across the board.

In this sense, the book represents a constructive response to the current debates over the mission of higher education. Professional ethics has long been saddled with the dilemma that the university was given responsibility for professional training precisely at the point in its history that it turned away from values to scientific naturalism. Today one sees it as a vast horizontal plain given to technical excellence but barren in enabling students to articulate a philosophy of life. As the late James Carey concluded,

> Higher education has not been performing well of late and, like most American institutions, is suffering from a confusion of purpose, an excess of ambition that borders on hubris, and an appetite for money that is truly alarming (1989, 48).

The broadside critiques leveled in Thorstein Veblen's *The Higher Learning in America* (1918) and Upton Sinclair's *The Goose Step* (1922) are now too blatantly obvious to ignore. But *Media Ethics: Issues and Cases* does not merely demand a better general education or a recommitment to values; it strengthens the communications curriculum by equipping thoughtful students with a more enlightened moral awareness. Since Confucius we have understood that lighting a candle is better than cursing the darkness, or, in Mother Teresa's version, we feed the world one mouth at a time.

PREFACE

As you glance through this book, you will notice its features—text, illustrations, cases, photos—represent choices the authors have made. I think it's as important to point out what's missing as what's there, and why. I'll begin with what's been left out and conclude with what you'll find in the text.

First, you'll find no media bashing in this book. There's enough of that already, and besides, it's too easy to do. This book is not designed to indict the media; it's designed to train its future employees. If we dwell on ethical lapses from the past, it is only to learn from them what we can do to prevent similar occurrences in the future.

Second, you'll find no conclusions in this book—neither at the end of the book nor after each case. No one has yet written the conclusive chapter to the ethical dilemmas of the media, and I don't suspect that we will be the first.

What, then, is in the book?

First, you'll find a diverse, up-to-date and classroom-tested compilation of cases in media ethics. Authors from more than 30 institutions and media outlets contributed real-life and hypothetical cases to this text to help students prepare for the ethical situations they will confront in whatever areas of the media they enter. We believe case studies are the premiere teaching vehicle for the study of ethics, and this book reflects what we think are the best available.

Second, the text binds these cases together and provides a philosophical basis from which to approach them. While it intentionally has been kept succinct, the text introduces students to the relevant ethical theory that will help eliminate "quandary ethics," which often results when cases are used as a teaching strategy.

Third, you'll find built-in discussion starters in the questions that follow each case. The questions at the end of the cases were written by the authors of each case, with the instructions that they were to be like concentric circles. The tightest circle—the micro issues—focuses only on the case at hand and the dilemmas it presents. The next circle—midrange issues—focuses on the problem in its context and sometimes manipulates the facts slightly to see if the decisions remain the same. The most abstract level—the macro issues—focuses on issues such as truth, equity, responsibility and loyalty. Properly used, the questions can guide discussion from the particular to the universal in any case in a single class period.

The book may be used either as the main text for a media ethics course or as a supplementary text for ethics modules in courses on newswriting, media and society, advertising and public relations and photojournalism. The book works well for teachers who like to use the Socratic method in their classes or as resource material for lecture classes.

Our approach in this text is best illustrated by an anecdote from a class. One student had the last hand up after a particularly heated case study. When I called on her, she asked, "Well, what's the answer?" I was surprised that she asked the question, and I was surprised that I didn't have a ready answer. I joked my way out of the question by asking if she wanted "The Answer" with a capital "a" or a low-ercase one. If she asked today, I'd respond differently. I'd tell her that the answer exists within her, but that it won't emerge in any justifiable form without systematic study and frequent wrestling with the issues.

That's what this book is about. The chapters direct you in some systematic way through the philosophy that has explored these questions for centuries. The cases will make you wrestle with that knowledge in scenarios not unlike ones you might encounter while working. Together, they might not enable you to find "The Answer," but they might help you find *your* answer.

For the authors and contributors,

Philip Patterson

ACKNOWLEDGMENTS

The ethical dilemmas that challenge us require a "moral compass" to help us find our way down the winding paths of life. My compass was given to me by my parents at an early age, and it has worked for more than four decades. No one can ask for a better gift than that, and I thank them for their part in placing me where I am today.

No book of this type is a solo effort, and this book is certainly the result of hard work and encouragement by many people. To begin, each of the authors in the text has been a pleasure to work with. Lou Hodges, Cliff Christians, Ralph Barney, Jay Black, Deni Elliott and others listened patiently to the idea in its many stages and offered advice along the way. Over the years I have been privileged to attend workshops on ethics sponsored by the Poynter Institute, the Freedom Forum and the University of Nebraska. To Bob Steele, Ed Lambeth, Steve Kalish and Robert Audi I owe a debt of gratitude for helping me continue to learn about ethics as I seek to teach my students.

A special thanks goes to the Ethics and Excellence in Journalism Foundation and to McGraw-Hill Higher Education for grants to cover costs incurred in this edition of the text. Finally, I thank my wife, Linda, and my children, Amy, Andrew and Joshua: I love you all.

p.d.p.

When ethics entrepreneur Michael Josephson opens his public speeches, he asks audience members to think of the most ethical people they know. Those people set ethical standards for others, by who they are and by what they inspire. It's fair for readers of this book to know who's on my list.

First, my mother, whose sense of human connection and compassion has been only incompletely copied by her daughter. Second, my father, who is the most principled human being I have ever met. Third, my stepmother, Carrie, who's managed to love the family she's married into—a feat worthy of far more than a Kantian sense of duty. My dissertation advisor and friend, Jim Davies, affirmed for me the ethical connection between people and politics. My former colleagues at the University of Colorado, Russ Shain, Steve Jones, Sue O'Brien and Risa Palm, have proved that connection to be a very human one, as have my colleagues at the University of Missouri. They have also been willing to listen—*another ethical activity that too often goes unmentioned.* Barrie Hartman and the staff of the *Boulder Daily Camera* were wonderful reality checks.

I've received intellectual help as well. I've attended a number of conferences designed to teach me about ethics. The Hastings House, Gannett, the Poynter Institute and the University of Nebraska have done their best to educate me in this field. The people connected with those efforts deserve special mention. Among them, Ed Lambeth, Ted Glasser, Deni Elliott, Cliff Christians, Lou Hodges, Martin Linsky, Roy Peter Clark, Don Fry, Sharon Murphy, Jay Black, Ralph Barney, Steve Kalish and Robert Audi have helped most profoundly. Many of them you will find mentioned in various contexts on the pages that follow. All of them have a special place in my intellectual psyche.

Two sets of acknowledgments remain.

For the past 25 years, my students at the state universities of Missouri and Colorado have taught me much more about ethics than I have taught them. They have suffered through portions of this manuscript with me. Their questions and their insights are evident on every page of this book.

Then there are Miranda and David—my daughter and my spouse. For the smiles, the hugs, the reading of first drafts, the talking, the listening, the suggestions, the lecture about using "skin" names, the films and all of the rest that being a family means. Love and thanks. I could not have done this without you.

l.c.w.

1

An Introduction to Ethical Decision Making

By the end of this chapter, you should be able to:

- **recognize the need for professional ethics in journalism.**
- **work through a model of ethical decision making.**
- **identify and use the five philosophical principles applicable to mass communication situations.**

MAKING ETHICAL DECISIONS

Scenario #1: You work for a PR firm that represents pharmaceutical giant PharMedCo. The drug company has an herbal medicine used successfully in Europe to lower blood pressure. PharMedCo wants to sell it in the United States. They are planning a major national promotion, generating large fees for your firm. They want to use "third-party strategy," hiring key opinion leaders in the medical world to help get the word out and create a buzz by talking up the advantages of herbal products but they would not push PharMedCo's new herbal medicine directly. In doing some research, you discover a little-known piece of information: if the herb is used in combination with another over-the-counter drug, it can be abused to get high. You tell PharMedCo but they want you to go ahead without informing the third-party experts, who might possibly back out or even warn the public. What should you do?

    Scenario #2: The public high school in your local community is normally violence free, although police officers are stationed there by agreement with the city to help avoid problems. A reporter at your station gets a tip that a fight broke out and was broken up by an administrator. The fight was between two young women and the reporter is tipped that cell phone footage of it is on YouTube. The video shows the school official (but not the police officer) apparently throwing one of the young women to the ground in an effort to stop the fight while other unidentified people stand by, talking, laughing and screaming. The administrator is Caucasian; some of the students involved in the fight are African-American, including the young woman who is the focus of the YouTube footage. School officials maintain that no one was hurt and that the action taken by the administrator was necessary. The parents of the young woman say she was injured, but she does not receive medical treatment and is suspended from school for three days. At airtime, no other charges have been filed. Your reporter wants to incorporate the YouTube posting on the station's Web site as part of the coverage, and to include a few frames of it in her story. As the producer of the newscast, what do you advise?

Scenario #3: You are the producer for the nightly newscasts of the third-rated station in a Top-30 market. Poor ratings have caused the station to pay the lowest salaries in the market, meaning that most of the staff, like you, are relatively fresh out of college. Hoping to gain more market share, your station has formed an investigative team, and "I-Team" ads are airing throughout the day. Within weeks, they capture their first exclusive story. The I-Team has staked out the local airport— a medium-size facility with many domestic routes and four international flights daily. They have found several glaring security breaches. Running the story will expose the loopholes and possibly cause responsible parties to close them. However, the story could give important information to potential terrorists who might try to exploit other airports with your information. This story could give a big boost to your new investigative thrust. What do you do?

Scenario #4: You are the promotions director for a local television station that sponsors a large Christmas drive for all the charities that help the needy in your community. The station not only provides a large advance gift to start the campaign, but it also airs a feature story each night after Thanksgiving on a different charity receiving money. To avoid tying up staff, the station outsources the stories to a local public relations firm specializing in video news releases. About a week into this year's campaign you get a call from a woman who says that yesterday's video for the food bank where she works was staged. She also tells you off the record that the story stretches the truth of the amount of good the food bank does as well. You call a few of the other charities already profiled by the PR agency and detect a similar pattern: staged video and exaggerated stories. No one, however, wants to go on the record for fear they will be dropped from the list of charities receiving the funds. What do you do next?

The Dilemma of Dilemmas

The scenarios above are dilemmas—they present an ethical problem with no single (or simple) "right" answer. Resolving dilemmas is the business of ethics. It's not an easy process, but ethical dilemmas can be anticipated and prepared for, and there is a wealth of ethical theory—some of it centuries old—to back up your final decision. In this chapter and throughout this book, you will be equipped with both the theories and the tools to help solve the dilemmas that arise in working for the mass media.

In the end, you will have tools, not answers. Answers must come from within you, but your answers should be informed by what others have written and experienced. Otherwise, you will always be forced to solve each ethical problem without the benefit of anyone else's insight. Gaining these tools also will help you to prevent each dilemma from spiraling into "quandary ethics"—the feeling that no best choice is available and that everyone's choice is equally valid (see Deni Elliott's essay following this chapter).

Will codes of ethics help? Virtually all the media associations have one, but they have limitations. For instance, the ethics code for the Society of Professional Journalists could be read to allow for revealing or withholding the information in the airport scenario above, two actions that are polar opposites. That doesn't make the code useless; it simply points out a shortfall in depending on codes.

While we don't dismiss codes, we believe you will find more universally applicable help in the writings of philosophers, ancient and modern, introduced in this chapter.

This book, or any ethics text, should teach more than a set of rules. It should give you the skills, analytical models, vocabulary and insights of others who have faced these choices, to make and justify your ethical decisions.

Some writers claim that ethics can't be taught. It's situational, some claim. Since every message is unique, there is no real way to learn ethics other than by daily life. Ethics, it is argued, is something you have, not something you do. But while it's true that reading about ethics is no guarantee you will perform your job ethically, thinking about ethics is a skill anyone can acquire.

While each area of mass communication has its unique ethical issues, thinking about ethics is the same, whether you make your living writing advertising copy or obituaries. Thinking about ethics won't necessarily make tough choices easier, but, with practice, your ethical decision making can become more consistent. A consistently ethical approach to your work as a reporter, photographer or copywriter in whatever field of mass communication you enter can improve that work as well.

Ethics and Morals

Contemporary professional ethics revolves around these questions:

- What duties do I have, and to whom do I owe them?
- What values are reflected by the duties I've assumed?

Ethics takes us out of the world of "This is the way I do it" or "This is the way it's always been done" into the realm of "This is what I should do" or "This is the action that can be rationally justified." Ethics in this sense is "ought talk." The questions arising from duty and values can be answered a number of ways as long as they are consistent with each other. For example, a journalist and a public relations professional may see the truth of a story differently because they see their duties differently and because there are different values at work in their professions, but each can be acting ethically if they are operating under the imperatives of "oughtness" for their profession.

It is important here to distinguish between *ethics,* a rational process founded on certain agreed-on principles, and *morals,* which are in the realm of religion. For example, the Ten Commandments are a moral system in the Judeo-Christian tradition, and Jewish scholars have expanded this study of the laws throughout

A Word about Ethics

The concept of ethics comes from the Greeks, who divided the philosophical world into separate disciplines. *Aesthetics* was the study of the beautiful and how a person could analyze beauty without relying only on subjective evaluations. *Epistemology* was the study of knowing, debates about what constitutes learning and what is knowable. *Ethics* was the study of what is good, both for the individual and for society. Interestingly, the root of the word means "custom" or "habit," giving ethics an underlying root of behavior that is long established and beneficial to the ongoing of society. The Greeks were also concerned with the individual virtues of fortitude, justice, temperance and wisdom, as well as with societal virtues, such as freedom.

Two thousand years later, ethics has come to mean learning to make rational decisions among an array of choices, all of which may be morally justifiable, but some more so than others. Rationality is the key word here, for the Greeks believed, and modern philosophers affirm, that people should be able to explain their ethical decisions to others and that acting ethically could be shown to be a rational decision to make. That ability to explain ethical choices is an important one for media professionals whose choices are so public. When confronted with an angry public, "It seemed like the right thing to do at the time" is a personally embarrassing *and* ethically unsatisfactory explanation.

the Bible's Old Testament into the Talmud, a religious volume running more than 1,000 pages. The Buddhist Eightfold Path provides a similar moral framework.

But moral systems are not synonymous with ethics. *Ethics begins when elements within a moral system conflict.* Ethics is less about the conflict between right and wrong than it is about the conflict between equally compelling (or equally unattractive) alternatives and the choices that must be made between them. Ethics is just as often about the choices between good and better or poor and worse than about right and wrong, which tends to be the domain of morals.

When elements within a moral system conflict, ethical principles can help you make tough choices. We'll review several ethical principles briefly after describing how one philosopher, Sissela Bok, says working professionals can learn to make good ethical decisions.

BOK'S MODEL

Bok's ethical decision-making framework was introduced in her book, *Lying: Moral Choice in Public and Private Life.* Bok's model is based on two premises: that we must have empathy for the people involved in ethical decisions and that maintaining social trust is a fundamental goal. With this in mind, Bok says any ethical question should be analyzed in three steps.

First, consult your own conscience about the "rightness" of an action. *How do you feel about the action?*

Second, seek expert advice for alternatives to the act creating the ethical problem. Experts, by the way, can be those either living or dead—a producer or editor you trust or a philosopher you admire. *Is there another professionally acceptable way to achieve the same goal that will not raise ethical issues?*

Third, if possible, conduct a public discussion with the parties involved in the dispute. These include those who are directly involved such as a reporter or their source, and those indirectly involved such as a reader or a media outlet owner. If they cannot be gathered—and that will most often be the case—you can conduct the conversation hypothetically in your head, playing out the roles. The goal of this conversation is to discover *How will others respond to the proposed act?*

Let's see how Bok's model works in the following scenario. In the section after the case, follow the three steps Bok recommends and decide if you would run the story.

How Much News Is Fit to Print?

In your community, the major charity is the United Way. The annual fund-raising drive will begin in less than two weeks. However, at a late-night meeting of the board with no media present, the executive director resigns. Though the agency is not covered by the Open Meetings Act, you are able to learn most of what went on from a source on the board.

According to her, the executive director had taken pay from the agency by submitting a falsified time sheet while he was actually away at the funeral of a college roommate. The United Way board investigated the absence and asked for his resignation, citing the lying about the absence as the reason, though most agreed that they would have given him paid leave had he asked.

The United Way wants to issue a short statement, praising the work of the executive director while regretfully accepting his resignation. The executive director also will issue a short statement citing other opportunities as his reason for leaving. You are assigned the story by an editor who does not know about the additional information you have obtained but wants you to "see if there's any more to it [the resignation] than they're telling."

You call your source on the board and she asks you, as a friend, to withhold the damaging information because it will hinder the United Way's annual fund-raising effort and jeopardize services to needy people in the community because faith in the United Way will be destroyed. You confront the executive director. He says he already has a job interview with another non-profit and if you run the story you will ruin his chances of a future career.

What do you do?

THE ANALYSIS

Bok's first step requires you to *consult your conscience.* When you do, you realize you have a problem. Your responsibility is to tell the truth, and that means providing readers with all the facts you discover. You also have a larger responsibility not to harm your community, and printing the complete story might well cause short-term harm. Clearly, your conscience is of two minds about the issue.

You move to the second step: *alternatives.* Do you simply run the resignation release, figuring that the person can do no further harm and therefore should be left alone? Do you run the whole story but buttress it with board members' quotes that such an action couldn't happen again, figuring that you have restored public trust in the agency? Do you do nothing until after the fund-raising drive and risk the loss of trust from readers if the story circulates around town as a rumor? Again, there are alternatives, but each has some cost.

In the third step of Bok's model, you will attempt to *hold a public ethical dialogue* with all of the parties involved. Most likely you won't get all the parties into the newsroom on deadline. Instead you can conduct an imaginary discussion among the parties involved. Such a discussion might go like this:

EXECUTIVE DIRECTOR: "I think my resignation is sufficient penalty for any mistake I might have made, and your article will jeopardize my ability to find another job. It's really hurting my wife and kids, and they've done nothing wrong."

REPORTER: "But shouldn't you have thought about that *before* you decided to falsify the time sheet? This is a good story, and I think the public should know what the people who are handling their donations are like."

READER 1: "Wait a minute. I am the public, and I'm tired of all of this bad news your paper focuses on. This man has done nothing but good in the community, and I can't see where any money that belonged to the poor went into his pocket. Why can't we see some good news for a change?"

READER 2: "I disagree. I buy the paper precisely because it does this kind of reporting. Stories like this that keep the government, the charities and everyone else on their toes."

PUBLISHER: "You mean like a watchdog function."

READER 2: "Exactly. And if it bothers you, don't read it."

PUBLISHER: "I don't really like to hurt people with the power we have, but if we don't print stories like this, and the community later finds out that we withheld news, our credibility is ruined, and we're out of business." [To source] "Did you request that the information be off the record?"

SOURCE: "No. But I never thought you'd use it in your story."

REPORTER: "I'm a reporter. I report what I hear for a living. What did you think I would do with it? Stories like these allow me to support my family."

EXECUTIVE DIRECTOR: "So it's your career or mine, is that what you're saying? Look, no charges have been filed here, but if your story runs, I look like a criminal. Is that fair?"

PUBLISHER: "And if it doesn't run, we don't keep our promise to the community. Is that fair?"

NEEDY MOTHER: "Fair? You want to talk fair? Do you suffer if the donations go down? No, I do. This is just another story to you. It's the difference in me and my family getting by."

The conversation could continue, and other points of view could be voiced. Your imaginary conversations could be more or less elaborate than the one above, but out of this discussion it should be possible to rationally support an ethical choice.

There are two cautions in using Bok's model for ethical decision making. First, it is important to go through all three steps before making a final choice. Most of us make ethical choices prematurely, after we've consulted only our consciences, an error Bok says results in a lot of flabby moral thinking. Second, while you will not be endowed with any clairvoyant powers to anticipate your ethical problems, the ethical dialogue outlined in the third step is best when conducted in advance of the event, not in the heat of writing a story.

For instance, an advertising copywriter might conduct such a discussion about whether advertising copy can ethically withhold disclaimers about potential harm from a product. A reporter might conduct such a discussion well in advance of the time he is actually asked to withhold an embarrassing name or fact from a story. Since it is likely that such dilemmas will arise in your chosen profession (the illustration above is based on what happened to one of the authors the first day on the job), your answer will be more readily available and more logical if you hold such discussions either with trusted colleagues in a casual atmosphere or by yourself, well in advance of the problem. The cases in this book are selected partially for their ability to predict your on-the-job dilemmas and start the ethical discussion now.

GUIDELINES FOR MAKING ETHICAL DECISIONS

Since the days of ancient Greece, philosophers have tried to draft a series of rules or guidelines governing how to make ethical choices. In ethical dilemmas such as the one above, you will need principles to help you determine what to do amid conflicting voices. While a number of principles work well, we will review five.

Aristotle's Golden Mean

Aristotle believed that happiness—which some scholars translate as "flourishing" —was the ultimate human good. By flourishing, Aristotle sought to elevate any activity through the setting of high standards, what he called exercising "practical reasoning."

Aristotle believed that practical reason was exercised by individuals who understood what the Greeks called the "virtues" and demonstrated them in their lives and calling. Such a person was the *phrenemos,* or person of practical wisdom, who demonstrated ethical excellence in their daily activity. For Aristotle, the highest virtue was citizenship, and its highest practitioner the statesman, a politician who exercised so much practical wisdom in his daily activity that he elevated the craft of politics to art. In contemporary terms, we might think of a *phrenemos* as a person who excels at any of a variety of activities—cellist Yo-Yo Ma, poet Maya Angelou, filmmakers George Lucas and Steven Spielberg. They are people

CALVIN AND HOBBES © Watterson. Dist. By *UNIVERSAL UCLICK. Reprinted with permission. All rights reserved.*

who flourish in their professional performance, extending our own vision of what is possible.

This notion of flourishing led Aristotle to assert that people acting virtuously are the moral basis of his ethical system, not those who simply follow rules. His ethical system is now called *virtue ethics.* Virtue ethics flows from both the nature of the act itself and the moral character of the person who acts. In the Aristotelian sense, the way to behave ethically is that (1) you must know (through the exercise of practical reasoning) what you are doing; (2) you must select the act for its own sake—in order to flourish; and (3) the act itself must spring from a firm and unchanging character.

It is not stretching Aristotle's framework to assert that one way to learn ethics is to select heroes and to try to model your individual acts and ultimately your professional character on what you believe they would do. An Aristotelian might well consult this hero as an expert when making an ethical choice. Asking what my hero would do in a particular situation is a valid form of ethical analysis. The trick, however, is to select your heroes carefully and continue to think for yourself rather than merely copy behavior you have seen previously.

What then is a virtue? *Virtue lies at the mean between two extremes of excess and deficiency,* a reduction of Aristotle's philosophy often called the "Golden Mean" as shown in Figure 1.1. Courage, for example, is a mean between foolhardiness on one hand and cowardice on the other. But to determine that mean for yourself, you have to exercise practical wisdom, act according to high standards and act in accordance with firm and continuing character traits.

Unacceptable behaviors (deficiency)	Acceptable behaviors	Unacceptable behaviors (excess)
Cowardice	Courage	Foolhardiness
Shamelessness	Modesty	Bashfulness
Stinginess	Generosity	Wastefulness

FIGURE 1.1. Aristotle's golden mean

In reality, therefore, the middle ground of a virtue is not a single point on a line that is the same for every individual. It is instead a range of behaviors that varies individually, while avoiding the undesirable extremes. Candor is a good example of a virtue that is most certainly contextual—what is too blunt in one instance is kind in another. Consider two witnesses to a potential drowning: one onlooker is a poor swimmer but a fast runner, the other is a good swimmer but a slow runner. What is cowardice for one is foolhardy for the other. Each can exhibit courage, but in different ways.

Seeking the golden mean implies that individual acts are not disconnected from one another, but collectively form a whole that a person of good character should aspire to. A virtue theory of ethics is not outcome-oriented. Instead, it is agent-oriented, and right actions in a virtue theory of ethics are a result of an agent seeking virtue and accomplishing it. As Aristotle wrote in *Nicomachean Ethics:* "We learn an art or craft by doing the things that we shall have to do when we have learnt it: for instance, men become builders by building houses, harpers by playing on the harp. Similarly we become just by doing just acts, temperate by doing temperate acts, brave by doing brave acts."

Far from being old-fashioned, Aristotle's concept of virtue ethics has been rediscovered by a variety of professions. As Kenneth Woodward (1994) states in a *Newsweek* essay entitled "What is Virtue?" a call for virtue is still relevant today:

> But before politicians embrace virtue as their latest election-year slogan, they would do well to tune into contemporary philosophy. Despite the call for virtue, we live in an age of moral relativism. According to the dominant school of moral philosophy, the skepticism engendered by the Enlightenment has reduced all ideas of right and wrong to matters of personal taste, emotional preference or cultural choice. . . . Against this moral relativism, advocates of the "ethics of virtue" argue that some personal choices are morally superior to others.

Kant's Categorical Imperative

Immanuel Kant is best known for his *categorical imperative* which is most often stated in two ways. The first asserts that an individual should act as if the choices one makes for oneself could become universal law. The second states that you should act so that you treat each individual as an end and never as merely a means. Kant called these two rules "categorical" imperatives, meaning that their demands were universal and not subject to situational factors. Many readers will recognize the similarity between Kant's first manifestation of the categorical imperative and the Bible's golden rule: Do unto others as you would have others do unto you. The two are quite similar in their focus on duty.

Kant's ethical theory is based on the notion that it is in the act itself, rather than the person who acts, where moral force resides. This theory of ethics is unlike Aristotle's in that it moves the notion of what is ethical from the actor to the act itself. This does not mean that Kant did not believe in moral character, but rather that people could act morally from a sense of duty even if their character might incline them to act otherwise.

For Kant, an action was morally justified only if it was performed from duty—motive matters to Kant—and in Kant's moral universe there were two sorts of duties. The strict duties were generally negative: not to murder, not to break promises, not to lie. The meritorious duties were more positive: to aid others, to develop one's talents, to show gratitude. Kant spent very little time defining these notions, but philosophers have generally asserted that the strict duties are somewhat more morally mandatory than the meritorious duties.

Some have argued that in Kant's ethical reasoning consequences are not important. We prefer a somewhat less austere reading of Kant. While Kant's view is that the moral worth of an action does not depend on its consequences, those consequences are not irrelevant. For example, a surgeon may show moral virtue in attempting to save a patient through an experimental procedure, but the decision about whether to undertake that procedure requires taking into account the probability of a cure. This framing of Kantian principles allows us to learn from our mistakes.

The test of a moral act, according to Kant, is its universality—whether it can be applied to everyone. For instance, under Kant's categorical imperative, journalists can claim few special privileges, such as the right to lie or the right to invade privacy in order to get a story. Kant's view, if taken seriously, reminds you of what you give up—truth, privacy and the like—when you make certain ethical decisions.

Utilitarianism

The original articulation of *utilitarianism* by Englishmen Jeremy Bentham and later John Stuart Mill in the 19th century introduced what was then a novel notion into ethics discussions: *The consequences of actions are important in deciding whether they are ethical.* In the utilitarian view, it may be considered ethical to harm one person for the benefit of the larger group. This approach, for example, is the ethical justification for investigative reporting, the results of which may harm individuals even as they are printed or broadcast in the hope of providing a greater societal good.

The appeal of utilitarianism is that it has proven to mesh well with Western thought, particularly on human rights. Harvard ethicist Arthur Dyck (1977, 55) writes of Mill:

> He took the view that the rightness or wrongness of any action is decided by its consequences. . . . His particular understanding of what is best on the whole was that which brings about the most happiness or the least suffering, i.e., the best balance of pleasure over pain for the greatest number.

The benefit of utilitarianism is that it provides a principle by which rightness and wrongness can be identified and judged, conflicts can be resolved and exceptions can be decided. The utilitarian calculus also has made possible the "quantification of welfare" Dyck says, allowing governments to make decisions that create the most favorable balance of benefits over harms.

With its focus on the consequences of an action, utilitarianism completes a cycle begun with Aristotle (see Table 1.1). Aristotle, in developing the golden mean, focused on the *actor.* Kant, in his categorical imperative, focused on the *action,* while Mill, in his utilitarian philosophy, focused on the *outcome.*

Utilitarianism has been condensed to the ethical philosophy of the "greatest good for the greatest number." While this pithy phrase is a very rough and ready characterization of utilitarian theory, it also has led to an overly mechanistic application of the principle: just tally up the amount of good and subtract the amount of harm. If the remaining number is positive, the act is ethical. However, when properly applied, utilitarianism is not mechanical.

To do justice to utilitarian theory, it must be understood within an historical context. Mill wrote after the changes of the Enlightenment. The principle of democracy was fresh and untried, and the thought that the average person should be able to speak his mind to those in power was novel. Utilitarianism as Mill conceived of it was a profoundly social ethic; Mill was among the first to acknowledge that the good of an entire society had a place in ethical reasoning.

Mill was what philosophers call a *valuational hedonist.* He argued that pleasure—and the absence of pain—was the only intrinsic moral end. Mill further asserted that an act was right in the proportion in which it contributed to the general happiness. Conversely, an act was wrong in the proportion in which it contributed to general unhappiness or pain. Utilitarianism can be subtle and complex in that the same act can make some happy but cause others pain. Mill insisted that both outcomes be valued simultaneously, a precarious activity but one that forces discussion of competing stakeholder claims.

TABLE 1.1. The Shifting Focus of Ethics from Aristotle to Mill

Philosopher	Known for	Popularly Known as	Emphasized
Aristotle	Golden mean	Virtue lies between extremes.	The actor
Kant	Categorical imperative	Act so your choices could be universal law; treat humanity as an end, never as a means only.	The action
Mill	Utility principle	An act's rightness is determined by its contribution to a desirable end.	The outcome

In utilitarian theory, no one's happiness is any more valuable than anyone else's, and definitely not more valuable than everyone's—quantity and quality being equal. In democratic societies, this is a particularly important concept because it meshes well with certain social and political goals. In application, utilitarianism has a way of puncturing entrenched self-interest, but when badly applied, it can actually promote social selfishness.

Utilitarianism also suggests that moral questions are objective, empirical and even in some sense scientific. Utilitarianism promotes a universal ethical standard that each rational person can determine. However, utilitarianism is among the most criticized of philosophical principles because it is so difficult to accurately anticipate all the consequences of a particular act. Different philosophers also have disputed how one calculates the good, rendering any utilitarian calculus fundamentally error prone.

While utilitarianism is a powerful theory, too many rely exclusively on it. Taken to extremes, the act of calculating the good can lead to ethical gridlock, with each group of stakeholders having seemingly equally strong claims with little way to choose among them. Sloppily done, utilitarianism may bias the user toward short-term benefit which is often contrary to the nature of ethical decisions.

Pluralistic Theory of Value

Philosopher William David Ross (1930) based his ethical theory on the belief that there is often more than one ethical value simultaneously "competing" for pre-eminence in our ethical decision making, a tension set up in the title of his book: *The Right and the Good.* Commenting on the tension, ethicist Christopher Meyers (2003, 84) says:

> As the book title suggests, Ross distinguished between the *right* and the *good.*
> The latter term refers to an objective, if indefinable, quality present in all acts. It is
> something seen, not done. Right, on the other hand, refers to actions. A right action
> is something undertaken by persons motivated by correct reasons and on careful
> reflection. Not all right actions, however, will be productive of the good.

In acknowledging the competition between the good and the right, Ross differs from Kant or Mill, who proposed only one ultimate value. To Ross these competing ethical claims, which he calls duties, are equal, providing the circumstances of the particular moral choice are equal. Further, these duties gain their moral weight not from their consequences but from the highly personal nature of duty.

Ross proposed these types of duties:

1. Those duties of *fidelity,* based on my implicit or explicit promise;
2. Those duties of *reparation,* arising from a previous wrongful act;
3. Those duties of *gratitude* that rest on previous acts of others;
4. Those duties of *justice* that arise from the necessity to ensure the equitable and meritorious distribution of pleasure or happiness;
5. Those duties of *beneficence* that rest on the fact that there are others in the world whose lot we can better;

6. Those duties of *self-improvement* that rest on the fact that we can improve our own condition; and
7. One negative duty: the duty of *not injuring others.*

We would recommend two additional duties that may be implied by Ross's list but are not specifically stated:

1. The duty to tell the truth, *veracity* (which may be implied by fidelity); and
2. The duty to *nurture,* to help others achieve some measure of self-worth and achievement.

Ross's typology of duties works well for professionals who often must balance competing roles. It also brings to ethical reasoning some affirmative notions of the primacy of community and relationships as a way to balance the largely rights-based traditions of much Western philosophical theory.

Like Kant, Ross divided his duties into two kinds. *Prima facie* duties are those duties that seem to be right because of the nature of the act itself. *Duty proper* (also called actual duties) are those duties that are paramount given specific circumstances. Arriving at your duty proper from among the prima facie duties requires that you consider what ethicists call the *morally relevant differences.* But Ross (1988, 24) warns that:

> . . . there is no reason to anticipate that every act that is our duty is so for one and the same reason. Why should two sets or circumstances, or one set of circumstances *not* possess different characteristics, any one of which makes a certain act our *prima facie* duty?

Let's take an example using one of Ross's prima facie duties: keeping promises. In your job as a reporter, you have made an appointment with the mayor to discuss a year-end feature on your community. On your way to City Hall, you drive by a serious auto accident and see a young child wandering, dazed, along the road. If you stop to help you will certainly be late for your appointment and may have to cancel altogether. You have broken a promise.

But is that act ethical?

Ross would probably say yes because the specific aspects of the situation had a bearing on the fulfillment of a *prima facie* duty. You exercised discernment. You knew that your commitment to the mayor was a relatively minor sort of promise. Your news organization will not be hurt by postponing the interview, and your act allowed you to fulfill the prima facie duties of beneficence, avoiding harm and nurturing. Had the interview been more important, or the wreck less severe, the morally relevant factors would have been different. Ross's pluralistic theory of values may be more difficult to apply than a system of absolute rules, but it reflects the way we make ethical choices.

Ross's concept of multiple duties "helps to explain why we feel uneasy about breaking a promise even when we are justified in doing so. Our uneasiness comes from the fact that we have broken a *prima facie* duty even as we fulfilled another." (Lebacqz 1985, 27).

Communitarianism

Classical ethical theory places its dominant intellectual emphasis on the individual and individual acts by emphasizing concepts such as character, choice, liberty and duty. But contemporary realities points out the intellectual weakness in this approach. Consider the environment. On many environmental questions, it is possible for people to make appropriate individual decisions—today I drive my car—which taken together promote environmental degradation. My individual decision to drive my car (or to purchase a hybrid car) doesn't matter very much; but when individual decisions accumulate, the impact is profound not only for a single generation but for subsequent ones as well.

Communitarianism, which has its roots in political theory, seeks to provide ethical guidance when confronting the sort of society-wide issues that mark current political and business activity. Communitarianism returns to Aristotle's concept of the "polis"—or community—and invests it with moral weight. People begin their lives, at least in a biological sense, as members of a two-person community. Communitarian philosophy extends this biological beginning to a philosophical worldview. "In communitarianism, persons have certain inescapable claims on one another that cannot be renounced except at the cost of their humanity" (Christians et al. 1993, 14). Communitarians assert that when issues are political and social, community interests trump individual interests but does not trample them.

Communitarianism focuses on the outcome of individual ethical decisions analyzed in light of their potential to impact society. And when applied to journalism, you have a product "committed to justice, covenant and empowerment. Authentic communities are marked by justice; in strong democracies, courageous talk is mobilized into action. . . . In normative communities, citizens are empowered for social transformation, not merely freed from external constraints" (Christians et al. 1993, 14).

Communitarianism asserts that social justice is the predominant moral value. Communitarians recognize the value of process, but are just as concerned with outcomes. History is full of "good" processes that led to bad outcomes. For example, democratic elections led to the 1933 takeover of Germany by a minority party headed by Hitler. It was a democratically written and adopted Constitution which included the three-fifths clause where African-Americans were equal to three-fifths of a single Caucasian for purposes of population count. Under communitarianism, the ability of individual acts to create a more just society is an appropriate measure of their rightness and outcomes are part of the calculus.

Communitarian thinking allows ethical discussion to include values such as altruism and benevolence on an equal footing with more traditional questions such as truth telling and loyalty. Indeed, Nobel Prize winning work in game theory has empirically demonstrated that cooperation, one of the foundation stones of community, provides desirable results once thought to be possible only through competition (Axelrod 1984). Cooperation is particularly powerful when the "shadow of the future," an understanding that we will encounter the outcome of our decisions and their impact on others in readily foreseeable time, is taken into account.

Communitarian suffers from a lack of a succinct summary of its general propositions. But any notion of a communitarian community begins with the fact that its members would include, as part of their understanding of self, their membership in the community. "For them, community describes not just what they have as fellow citizens but also what they are, not as a relationship they choose (as in a voluntary association) but an attachment they discover, not merely an attribute but as a constituent of their identity" (Sandel 1982, 150). Communitarian community resembles family more than it resembles town.

Under communitarianism, journalism cannot separate itself from the political and economic system of which it is a part. Communitarian thinking makes it possible to ask whether current practice (for example, a traditional definition of news) provides a good mechanism for a community to discover itself, learn about itself and ultimately transform itself.

Communitarian reasoning allows journalists to understand their institutional role and to evaluate their performance against shared societal values. For instance, the newsroom adage "if it bleeds it leads" might sell newspapers or attract viewers, but it also might give a false impression of community and its perils to the most vulnerable members. Communitarianism would not ban the coverage of crime but would demand context that would help viewers or readers decide if they need to take action.

Thinking as a communitarian not only mutes the competition among journalistic outlets, it also provides a new agenda for news. Rape stories would include mobilizing information about the local rape crisis center. Political stories would focus on issues, not the horserace or personal scandals, and the coverage would be ample enough for an informed citizenry to cast a knowledgeable ballot. Writers have linked communitarian philosophy with the civic journalism movement. But like the philosophy of communitarianism, the practice of civic journalism has not yet been embraced by the mainstream of society.

THE "SCIENCE" OF ETHICS

Life in the 21st century has changed how most people think about issues, such as what constitutes a fact and what does or does not influence moral certainty. But ethical theory, with its apparent uncertainties and contradictions, appears to have taken a back seat to science. As people have become drawn to ethics they seek "the answer" to an ethical dilemma in the same way they seek "the answer" in science. Consequently, the vagaries of ethical choice as contrasted with the seeming certainty of scientific knowledge casts an unfair light on ethics.

We'd like to offer you a different conceptualization of "the facts" of both science and ethics. Science, and the seeming certainty of scientific knowledge, has undergone vast changes in the past 100 years. Before Einstein, most educated people believed that Sir Francis Bacon had accurately and eternally described the basic actions and laws of the physical universe. But Bacon was wrong. Scientific inquiry in the 20th century explored a variety of physical phenomena, uncovered new relationships, new areas of knowledge and new areas of ignorance. The "certainty" of scientific truth has changed fundamentally in the last 100 years, and there is every reason to expect similar changes in this century, especially in the areas of nano technology. Science and certainty are not synonymous, despite our tendency to blur the two.

Contrast these fundamental changes in the scientific worldview with the developments of moral theory. Aristotle's writing, more than 2,000 years old, still has much to recommend it to the modern era. The same can be said of utilitarianism and of the Kantian approach—both after 100 years of critical review. Certainly, new moral thinking has emerged—for example, feminist theory, but such work tends to build on rather than radically alter the moral theory that has gone before. Ethical philosophers still have fundamental debates but these debates have generally tended to deepen previous insights rather than to "prove" them incorrect. Further, thinking about global ethics uncovers some striking areas of agreement. We are aware of no ethical system, for example, that argues that murder is an ethical behavior, or that lying, cheating and stealing are the sorts of activities that human beings ought to engage in on a regular basis.

From this viewpoint, there is more continuity in thinking about ethics than in scientific thought. When the average person contrasts ethics with science, it is ethics that tends to be viewed as changeable, unsystematic and idiosyncratic. Science has rigor, proof and some relationship to an external reality. We would like to suggest that such characterizations arise from a short-term view of the history of science and ethics. In our view, ethics as a field has at least as much continuity of thought as developments in science. And while it cannot often be quantified, it has the rigor, the systematic quality and the relationship to reality that moderns too often characterize as the exclusive domain of scientific thinking.

Suggested Readings

ARISTOTLE. *The Nicomachean ethics.*

BOK, SISSELA. 1978. *Lying: Moral choice in public and private life.* New York: Random House.

BORDEN, SANDRA L. 2009. *Journalism as practice.* Burlington, VT: Ashgate.

CHRISTIANS, CLIFFORD, JOHN FERRÉ, and MARK FACKLER. 1993. *Good news: Social ethics and the press.* New York: Oxford University Press.

GERT, BERNARD. 1988. *Morality: A new justification of the moral rules.* New York: Oxford University Press.

MILL, JOHN STUART. *On liberty.*

POJMAN, L. 1998. *Ethical theory: Classical and contemporary readings.* Belmont, CA: Wadsworth Publishing Co.

ROSS, W.D. 1930. *The right and the good.* Oxford, England: Clarendon Press.

CHAPTER 1 ESSAY

Cases and Moral Systems

DENI ELLIOTT

University of South Florida—St. Petersburg

Case studies are wonderful vehicles for ethics discussions with strengths that include helping discussants

1. appreciate the complexity of ethical decision making;
2. understand the context within which difficult decisions are made;
3. track the consequences of choosing one action over another; and
4. learn both how and when to reconcile and to tolerate divergent points of view.

However, when case studies are misused, these strengths become weaknesses. Case studies are vehicles for an ethics discussion, not its ultimate destination. The purpose of an ethics discussion is to teach discussants how to "do ethics"—that is, to teach processes so that discussants can practice and improve their own critical decision-making abilities to reach a reasoned response to the issue at hand.

When the discussion stops short of this point, it is often because the destination has been fogged in by one or more myths of media case discussions:

Myth 1: Every opinion is equally valid.

Not true. The best opinion (conclusion) is the one that is best supported by judicious analysis of fact and theory and one that best addresses the morally relevant factors of the case (Gert 1988). An action has morally relevant factors if it is likely to cause some individual to suffer an evil that any rational person would wish to avoid (such as death, disability, pain, loss of freedom or pleasure), or if it is the kind of action that generally causes evil (such as deception, breaking promises, cheating, disobedience of law or neglect of duty).

Myth 2: Since we can't agree on an answer, there is no right answer.

In an ethics case, it may be that there are a number of acceptable answers. But there also will be many wrong answers—many approaches that the group can agree would be unacceptable. When discussants begin to despair of ever reaching any agreement on a right answer or answers, it is time to reflect on all of the agreement that exists within the group concerning the actions that would be out of bounds.

Myth 3: It hardly matters if you come up with the "ethical thing to do," since people ultimately act out of their own self-interest anyway.

Any institution supported by society—manufacturing firms or media corporations, medical centers, etc.—provides some service that merits that support. No matter what the service, practitioners or companies acting only in the short-term interest (i.e., to make money) will not last long. Both free-market pragmatism and ethics dictate that it makes little sense to ignore the expectations of consumers and of the society at large.

The guidelines below can serve as a map for an ethics discussion. They are helpful to have when working through unfamiliar terrain toward individual end points. They also can help you avoid the myths above. While discussing the case, check to see if these questions are being addressed:

1. What are the morally relevant factors of the case?
   (a) Will the proposed action cause an evil—such as death, disability, pain, loss of freedom or opportunity, or a loss of pleasure—that any rational person would wish to avoid?
   (b) Is the proposed action the sort of action—such as deception, breaking promises, cheating, disobedience of law or disobedience of professional or role-defined duty—that generally causes evil?
2. If the proposed action is one described above, is a greater evil being prevented or punished by allowing it to go forward?
3. If so, is the actor in a unique position to prevent or punish such an evil, or is that a more appropriate role for some other person or profession?
4. If the actor followed through on the action, would he be allowing himself to be an exception to a rule that he thinks everyone else should follow? (If so, then the action is prudent, not moral.)
5. Finally, would a rational, uninvolved person appreciate the reason for causing harm? Are the journalists ready and able to state, explain and defend the proposed action in a public forum or would a more detached journalist be ready to write an expose?

CHAPTER 1 CASE

CASE 1-A
How to Read a Case Study

PHILIP PATTERSON
Oklahoma Christian University

When you look at the photo on page 20, it stirs your emotions. It's the last moment of one girl's life (the younger survived). It's a technically good photo—perhaps a once-in-a-lifetime shot. But when you learn the "back story" of this photo, a world of issues emerge and the real discussions begin. And that's the beauty of cases as a way of learning media ethics.

For this case, here is what you need to know. One July afternoon, *Boston Herald* photographer Stanley Forman answered a call about a fire in one of the city's older sections. When he arrived, he followed a hunch and ran down the alley to the back of the row of houses. There he saw a 2-year-old girl and her 19-year-old godmother, on the fifth-floor fire escape. A fire truck had raised its aerial ladder to help. Another firefighter was on the roof, tantalizingly close to pulling the girls to safety. Then came a loud noise, the fire escape gave way and the girls tumbled to the ground. Forman saw it all through his 135 mm lens and took four photos as the two were falling.

The case study has several possible angles. You can discuss the gritty reality of the content. You can factor in that within 24 hours, the city of Boston acted to improve the inspection of all fire escapes in the city and that groups across the nation used the photos to promote similar efforts. You can talk about the ingenuity and industry of Forman to go where the story was rather than remain in front where the rest of the media missed it. You can critique his refusal to photograph the girls after impact. You can debate why the Pulitzer Prize committee gave Forman its top prize for this photo and add in the fact that more than half of the various "Picture of the Year" awards over decades are of death or imminent death. You can argue whether the *Boston Herald* profited off of the death and injury of the girls and what Forman's role was once he witnessed the tragedy. And you can ponder what happens when this photo hits the Web, stripped of context.

You can talk about any or all of these issues or imagine others. That's the beauty of a case study—you can go where it takes you. From this one case you can argue taste in content, media economics ("If it bleeds, it leads"), personal vs. professional duty, etc.

Perhaps you will want to role play. Perhaps you will ask yourself what Kant or Mill would do if he were the editor or whether a communitarian would approve the means (the photo) because of the end (better fire escape safety). Perhaps you want to talk about the "breakfast test" for objectionable content in the morning paper, whether it passes the test or whether the test ought to exist. Or what values led the paper to run the photo and the committee to give it an award.

During the semester, you can do more than just work through the cases in this book—you can find your own. All around you are cases of meritorious media behavior and cases of questionable media behavior. And, quite frankly, there are

Stanley J. Forman, Pulitzer Prize 1977. Used with permission.

cases where good people will disagree over which category the behavior falls into. Good cases make for good discussion, not only now but also when you graduate into the marketplace as well.

So dive in, discuss and defend.

2

Information Ethics:
A Profession Seeks the Truth

By the end of this chapter, you should be familiar with:

- **both the Enlightenment and pragmatic constructions of truth.**
- **the development and several criticisms of objective news reporting as a professional ideal.**
- **why truth in "getting" the news may be as important as truth in reporting it.**
- **how to develop a personal list of ethical news values.**

INTRODUCTION

Each traditional profession has laid claims to a central tenet of philosophy. Law is equated with justice; medicine with the duty to render aid. Journalism, too, has a lofty ideal: the communication of truth.

But the ideal of truth is problematic. We often consider truth a stable commodity: it doesn't change much for us on a day-to-day basis, nor does it vary greatly among members of a community. However, the concept of truth has changed throughout history. At one level or another, human beings since ancient times have acknowledged that how truth is defined may vary. Since Plato's analogy of life as experienced by individuals human beings as "truthful" in the same way as shadows on the wall of a cave resemble the physical objects that cast those shadows more than 3,000 years ago, people have grappled with the amorphous nature of truth. Today, while we accept some cultural "lies"—the existence of Santa Claus—we condemn others—income tax evasion or fraud. Most of the time, we know what the boundaries are, at least when we deal with one another face-to-face.

Compounding the modern problem of the shifting nature of truth is the changing media audience. When a profession accepts the responsibility of printing and broadcasting the truth, facts that are apparent in face-to-face interaction become subject to different interpretations among the geographically and culturally diverse readers and viewers. Ideas once readily accepted are open to debate. Telling the truth becomes not merely a matter of possessing good moral character but something that requires learning how to recognize truth and conveying it in the least distorted manner possible.

A CHANGING VIEW OF TRUTH

One pre-Socratic Greek tradition viewed truth—*alethea*—as encompassing what humans remember, singled out through memory from everything that is destined for *Lethe,* the river of forgetfulness (Bok 1978). Linking truth and remembrance is essential in an oral culture, one that requires information be memorized and repeated so as not to be forgotten. Repeating the message, often in the form of songs or poetry, meant that ideas and knowledge were kept alive or true for subsequent generations. Homer's *Iliad* and *Odyssey* or much of the Bible's Old Testament served this function.

This oral notion of truth, as noted in Table 2.1, was gradually discarded once words and ideas were written down. However, it has come to the fore with the advent of television and its computer cousins YouTube, etc., that allow viewers to hear the words of the president rather than wait for those words to be passed down to them. When we see something on television or our computer screen, we assume that it closely corresponds to reality. The maxim "Seeing is believing" reminds us that truth has become entangled with pictures, an oral concept of truth that has been a dormant form of knowledge for hundreds of years until technology made "seeing" events live worldwide possible.

While the ancient Greeks tied truth to memory, Plato was the first to link truth to human rationality and intellect. In *The Republic,* Plato equated truth with a world of pure form, a world to which human beings had only indirect access. In Plato's vision, there was an ideal notion of a chair—but that ideal chair did not exist in reality. What people thought of as a chair was similar to the ideal chair as the shadows on the wall of the cave are to the objects illuminated by the fire. To Plato, truth was knowable only to the human intellect—it could not be touched or verified. We're living in the cave.

Plato's metaphor of the cave has had a profound influence on Western thought. Not only did Plato link truth to rationality, as opposed to human experience, but his work implies that truth is something that can be captured only through the intellect. Platonic truth is implicit within a thing itself; truth defined the "perfect form." Plato's concept of the truth separated the concept from the external world in which physical objects exist.

Subsequent centuries and thinkers adhered to Plato's view. Medieval theologians believed truth was revealed only by God or by the Church. The intellectual legacy of the Reformation centered on whether it is possible for the average person to ascertain truth without benefit of a priest or a king. About 200 years later, Milton suggested that competing notions of the truth should be allowed to coexist, with the ultimate truth eventually emerging (see Table 2.1).

TABLE 2.1. A Philosophy of Truth Emerges

Source	Truth Equals
Ancient Greeks	What is memorable and is handed down
Plato	What abides in the world of perfect forms
Medieval	What the king, Church or God says
Milton	What emerges from the "marketplace of ideas"
Enlightenment	What is verifiable, replicable, universal
Pragmatists	What is filtered through individual perception

Milton's assertions foreshadowed the philosophy of the Enlightenment, from which modern journalism borrows its notion of truth. The Enlightenment cast truth in secular terms, divorced from the church, and developed a "correspondence theory" of truth still held today. The correspondence theory asserts that truth should correspond to external facts or observations. The Enlightenment concept of truth was linked to what human beings could perceive with their senses harnessed through the intellect. Truth acquired substance. It was something that could be known and something that could be replicated.

This Enlightenment notion of truth is essential to the scientific method. Truth has become increasingly tied to what is written down, what can be empirically verified, what can be perceived by the human senses. Enlightenment truth does not vary among people or cultures. It is a truth uniquely suited to the written word, for it links what is written with what is factual, accurate and important.

Truth and Objectivity

This Enlightenment view of truth is the basis for the journalistic ideal of objectivity. While objectivity has many definitions, at the least it is the requirement that journalists are to divorce fact from opinion. Objectivity is a way of knowing that connects human perception with facts and then knowledge. Objectivity is also a process of information collection (Ward 2004). Journalists view objectivity as refusing to allow individual bias to influence what they report or how they cover it. It is in journalism that all facts and people are regarded as equal and equally worthy of coverage. Culture, an individual sense of mission, and individual and organizational feelings and views do not belong in objective news accounts. An Enlightenment view of truth allowed objectivity to be considered an attainable ideal.

However, philosophy was not the only reason or even the most important reason, that objectivity became a professional standard in the early 1900s. The early American press was not really a mass press, and it garnered much of its financial support from political advertising and most of its readers through avowedly partisan political reporting. But America became more urban in the late 1800s, and publishers realized that to convince potential advertisers that their advertising would be seen by a large audience, they had to make certain their publications would be read. Partisan publications could not ensure that, for strong views offended potential readers. What publishers at the turn of the 20th century needed was a product that built on an Enlightenment principle that guaranteed that facts would be facts, no matter who was doing the reading. Opinion would be relegated to specific pages and both facts and opinion could be wrapped around advertising (Schudson 1978).

The normative ideal of objectivity came along at an advantageous time for yet another reason. The mass press of the early 1900s was deeply and corruptly involved in yellow journalism. Fabricated stories were common; newspaper wars were close to the real thing. Objectivity was a good way to clean up journalism's act with a set of standards where seemingly none had existed before. It fit the cultural expectations of the Enlightenment that truth was knowable and ascertainable. And it made sure that readers of news columns would remain unoffended long enough to glance at the ads.

The Enlightenment view of truth also was compatible with democracy and its emphasis on rational government. People who could reason together could arrive at some shared "truth" of how they could govern themselves. Information was essential to government, for it allowed citizens to scrutinize government. As long as truth was ascertainable, government could function. Under this view, *information provided the social glue as well as the grease of society.* Citizens and government needed information in order to continue their rational function. Information, and the notion that it corresponded in some essential way with the truth, carried enormous promise.

That changed when the 20th-century pragmatists—most notably Americans John Dewey, George Herbert Mead, Charles Sanders Pierce and William James— challenged the Enlightenment view of truth. They held that the perception of truth depended on how it was investigated and on who was doing the investigating. Further, they rejected the notion that there was only one proper method of investigation— that is, the scientific method. Borrowing from Einstein, pragmatists argued that truth, like matter, was relative.

Specifically, the pragmatists proposed that knowledge and reality were not *fixed by* but instead were *the result of* an evolving stream of consciousness and learning. Reality itself varied based on the psychological, social, historical or cultural context. Additionally, reality was defined as that which was probable, not as something intrinsic (the Platonic view) or something determined by only one method of observation (the Enlightenment view). Pragmatism found a comfortable home in the 20th-century United States. Under pragmatism truth lost much of its universality, but it was in remarkable agreement with the American value of democratic individualism. Soon pragmatism filtered through literature, science and some professions, such as law.

Pragmatism provided a challenge to objectivity. No sooner had the journalistic community embraced objectivity than the culture adopted more pragmatic notions of truth. That clash fueled criticism of objectivity. Several questions surfaced. If truth is subjective, can it be reported by an impassive, objective and detached reporter? Does such a reporter exist? Is truth a construct that relies on context?

Postmodern philosophy (see *The Matrix* that follows) has taken these questions to their logical extension, suggesting that the concept of truth is devoid of meaning.

Postmodernism asserts that context is literally everything, and that meaning cannot exist apart from context, which is directly opposed to fact-based journalism which assumed that facts were facts regardless of context.

The last 30 years have added yet another level of complexity to the problem: the information explosion. Facts and truth come to us quickly from all over the globe. Today, the Internet has removed the financial imperative of objectivity and made it once again financially viable to operate a partisan press, especially a virtual one. While objective reporting is still *one* standard, it is not the *only* standard. The recent ratings success of Fox News (higher in some ratings than CBS news programs) might indicate that the partisan press—Fox's claim of "fair and balanced" notwithstanding—can be made profitable. With the advent of blogs such as Huffington Post, which include not just words, but images, aggregated from many sources, yet a different notion of truth is emerging—what philosophers call the convergence or coherence theory of truth. Under this view, truth is discovered not through any single method of investigation but by determining which set of facts form a coherent mental picture of events and ideas investigated through a variety of methods. Convergence journalism—which uses sounds, images and words to cover stories—is one professional response to the coherence theory of truth and the technological possibilities of the Internet and the personal computer. Of course, convergence journalism requires an active audience. All too often, it is possible to be overwhelmed by the information available to us rather than devoting the time and effort required to make sense of it.

In short, objectivity has been deeply undermined by both philosophical shift and technological innovation (Christians, Ferré and Fackler 1993). Telling your readers and viewers the truth has become a complicated business as Sissela Bok points out:

> Telling the "truth" therefore is not solely a matter of moral character; it is also a matter of correct appreciation of real situations and of serious reflection upon them. . . . Telling the truth, therefore, is something which must be learnt. This will sound very shocking to anyone who thinks that it must all depend on moral character and that if this is blameless the rest is child's play. But the simple fact is that the ethics cannot be detached from reality, and consequently continual progress in learning to appreciate reality is a necessary ingredient in ethical action. (Bok 1978, 302–303)

WHO'S DOING THE TALKING ANYWAY?

The pragmatic's critique of objectivity has called attention to the question of who writes the news. Journalists—primarily male, Caucasian, well educated, and middle to upper class—are often asked to cover issues and questions that life experiences has not prepared them to cover. Stephen Hess (1981) noted that journalists (particularly the Eastern "elite" media), in terms of their socioeconomic status, look a great deal more like the famous or powerful people they cover than the people they are supposedly writing for. Work on the national press corps has shown similar results

The Matrix: A Postmodern Examination of Truth

"Do you ever have that feeling where you're not sure whether you are awake or still dreaming?"

"Yeah, all the time. . . . It just sounds to me like you might need to unplug, man . . . get some R&R?"

Thus begins Neo's journey down the rabbit hole (like Lewis Carroll's *Alice in Wonderland*) where reality literally turns inside out on itself. A computer wizard, and unknown genetic mutation, Neo—who is awakened to the possibilities courtesy of Morpheus—literally unplugs himself from the reality of a computer simulation where human beings serve as batteries for machines that run the world. Reality for most people is nothing more than a computer code invented by the artificial intelligence and inserted electronically into their neural systems from infancy onward. Neo is the person who has the capacity to crack and overcome the code.

The Matrix set the early standard for smart films about the potential of the computers that power the information age. The film was stylish. In fact, the long, black trench coats Keanu Reeves and Carrie-Anne Moss wore were eerily predictive of the attire worn by the Columbine High School shooters. The special effects and set design, based as they were on a comic book reality, gave form to one vision of hyper-reality, as did the film's otherworldly, violent content.

Besides being provocative, the film provides an accessible discussion of the postmodern approach to truth.

Postmodernism is a logical outgrowth of pragmatism. Instead of suggesting that truth varies with receiver, or sender or context, postmodernism suggests that truth—if it exists at all—is unknowable. Those who believe they know the truth, like Neo at the beginning of the film,

discover that their "reality" is false consciousness, founded on invalid assumptions that shift constantly in a chaotic environment.

Postmodernism rejects the correspondence theory of truth, or the Platonic ideal that truth is knowable only as an intellectual construct. In postmodernism, revealed truth does not exist, and the marketplace of ideas yields either falsity or babble. In the film, dreams are real, reality shifts and absolutely nothing is what it seems. Control, in the form of computer programs (malleable by both the programmers and the programmed), and death, in the form of biological waste, remain.

Most journalistic endeavors reject postmodern thinking on the grounds that the essence of humanity itself provides an irrefutable challenge to postmodernism's premise. Others have noted that postmodernism too easily falls into the trap of solipsism—the notion that it is impossible to know anything outside of one's individual thoughts and perceptions.

While traditional theory and theorists may reject postmodernism, contemporary culture sometimes embraces what Morpheus calls "the desert of the real." If postmodernism is an appropriate worldview, does that mean journalists and persuasion professionals should abandon their jobs or their ancient foundations?

We think not.

Neo and Morpheus still have to act. They learn to think in new ways, but their actions remain centered on their belief in human independence and the "rightness" of thinking about and connecting with others. Even in this postmodern vision, ethical thinking still has a place. Neo's goal, after all, is to dismantle one matrix so humanity can make its own choices.

(Weaver, Beam, Brownlee, Voakes and Wilhoit 2007). Journalists are better paid and better educated than the audience for their product, especially "legacy" media where the audience is aging every year.

In the past 30 years, almost every professional journalistic organization has developed programs specifically to attract and retain women and minorities with only incremental and sporadic success. This lack of access to the engines of information has not been lost on a variety of minority groups—from religious fundamentalists, who have in some cases established their own broadcasting networks, to racial minorities, who fail to find themselves either as owners or managers of media outlets. They argue that the result is news about middle-class Caucasians, for middle-class Caucasians. Perhaps the election of the nation's first African-American president will change media habits, but results to both employ and cover minorities have traditionally been slow and sporadic.

How individual journalists and the corporations they work for should remedy the situation is unclear. But as demographics changed us from a culture that is predominantly Caucasian to one that is not, the mass media, particularly newspapers, will play a decreasing role unless journalists find a way to report news that is of interest to the new majority of their readers. In the beginning of the 21st century, worldwide newspaper readership and broadcast viewership continued to decline. The winners: the Internet (including newspaper Web sites) and magazines that focus on celebrities rather than public affairs (Thorson, Duffy and Schumann 2007). Traditional journalists faced an audience in open rebellion with no clear strategy to regain the "eyeballs" advertisers desire or the public focus that civic engagement requires.

SEEING ISN'T BELIEVING

More than 80 years ago, journalist Walter Lippmann (1922) said, "For the most part, we do not first see, and then define, we define first and then see." He added that we tend to pick out what our culture has already defined for us, and then perceive it in the form stereotyped for us by our culture.

In one classic study (Rainville and McCormick 1977), a blind New York journalism professor claimed he could predict the race of football players being described in the play-by-play by what was said about them. Caucasian athletes were described as intellectually gifted while African-American athletes were described as physically gifted. In a culture that values brains over brawn, African-American football players were the subject of repeated stereotypical insults—all couched as praise. And even though the study is now more than 30 years old, the tendency to revert to these stereotypes continues on sports broadcasts today in which athletes are called "smart" and which are called "athletic." In the former, the quality was obtained by hard work; in the latter, it was a gift of genetics.

Women, the elderly and the gay community have conducted studies with similar results. Their conclusion has been that while journalists maintain that they are objective, they (like their readers and viewers) bring something to the message that literally changes what they see and what they report (Lester 1996).

In a *Columbia Journalism Review* cover story entitled "Rethinking Objectivity," author Brent Cunningham (2003) says that "objectivity can trip us up on the way to truth. Objectivity excuses lazy reporting. If you're on deadline and all you have is 'both sides of the story,' then that's often good enough." Cunningham cites numerous incidences of enterprising reporting spiked by editors. Cunningham points to a study of 414 Iraq war stories broadcast on ABC, CBS and NBC leading up to the 2003 conflict. All but 34 originated from the White House, the Pentagon or the State Department. The result: the "official truth" becomes the received truth, and only the bravest journalists dared depart from it. Timothy Crouse in his campaign memoir *The Boys on the Bus* reported the same phenomenon—stories outside the mainstream were not rewarded, they were spiked.

E. J. Dionne (1996) claims that the press is in internal contradiction. It must be neutral, yet investigative. It must be disengaged, but have an impact. It must be fair minded but have an edge. The conflicts make objectivity virtually impossible to define and even harder to practice.

DEFINING AND CONSTRUCTING THE NEWS

News reflects certain cultural values and professional norms. In a classic study, sociologist Herbert Gans (1979) studied how stories became news at *Newsweek* and CBS and found that almost all news stories reflected these six cultural values: (1) ethnocentrism; (2) altruistic democracy; (3) responsible capitalism; (4) individualism; (5) an emphasis on the need for and maintenance of social order; and (6) leadership. These dominant values helped to shape which stories were printed and what they said, what communication scholars call "framing."

Gans called these values the "para-ideology" of the media. He added that "the news is not so much conservative or liberal as it is reformist." Researcher James Carey (quoted in Cunningham 2003) says that it is this para-ideology that results in charges of liberal bias against the media. "There is a bit of the reformer in anyone who enters journalism. And reformers are always going to make conservatives uncomfortable."

News stories about middle-class or upper-class people, those who tend to successfully adopt the culture's values, made the American news "budget," according

1993, Washington Post Writers Group. Reprinted with permission.

to Gans. While Gans focused on journalism about the United States, other scholars have noted the same phenomenon, called *domesticating the foreign,* in international coverage (Gurevitch et al. 1991). Journalists working for U.S. media outlets tell stories about international events in cultural terms Americans can readily understand but which also sacrifice accuracy. For example, routine coverage of elections in Britain or Israel is conveyed in horse-race metaphors even though both countries employ a parliamentary system where governing coalitions are common and who wins the horse race not nearly so important.

PACKAGING THE STORY: NEWS AS MANUFACTURED PRODUCT

The goal of telling a "good story" also raises other ethical questions, specifically those that focus on packaging to highlight drama and human interest. Ethical questions about packaging began with newspapers but have intensified with television. Television demands video, and television's video imperative dominates both story selection and placement. For instance, when President Obama found himself in trouble for saying the Cambridge police "acted stupidly" in the arrest of Harvard professor and Obama friend Henry Gates, it was not the his verbal explanation that eased the tension. Instead, it was the made-for-television "beer summit" between Obama, Gates and the arresting officer that brought media closure to the situation and provided the lead story for the nightly news.

Journalists need something to package, which has led to a professional drive to find an "event" to report and to be there first. Few consumers realize it, but news is "manufactured" daily, just as surely as furniture, cars or the meal at your favorite fast food restaurant—and often the process can be messy. Journalists start the day with a blank computer screen and with press time or broadcast time looming. They end the day with a print story, a video package or a Web page—or often all three. And adding to the built-in tension of deadlines is the challenge to be fair, complete, accurate and, above all, interesting. Whole industries—particularly public relations or "strategic communications"—have emerged to help journalists package their daily stories on deadline.

The need to find an event has meant journalists have missed some important stories because they were not events but rather historic developments with both a past and a future. For example, major social developments such as the women's movement (Mills 1989), the civil rights movement and the anti–Vietnam War movement were under-covered until their leaders created events such as sit-ins and demonstrations for the media to report. Director Michael Moore said he began his career with the 1989 film *Roger and Me* about the devastation of General Motors layoffs on his hometown of Flint, Michigan, because he "didn't see on the silver screen or the television screen what happened to people like us. It was a story then (in the mid-1980s) and it's a story now and that's part of the reason I did the movie" (Smith 1992). This preoccupation with events affects coverage of science which is most frequently reported as a series of discoveries and "firsts" rather than as a process (Nelkin 1987). We are treated to stories about the new cures often without the necessary context—political, economic, etc.—to interpret the latest research results. Nelkin says that the twin dramas of "new hope" and "no hope" drive most science reporting. Former Vice-President and Nobel Laureat Al Gore's documentary *An Inconvenient Truth* was an example of making an "event" out of more than 50 years of science, all in an attempt to spur public debate.

Other stories are missed or misreported when they lack the easy "peg" editors look for. When thousands of lives were lost in Bhopal, India by a malfunctioning plant, coverage focused entirely on the event and not the socioeconomic, scientific and political causes that led to the disaster. Instead, news coverage focused on the picture-friendly event (Wilkins 1987). A deeper look at news coverage of the 1986 Chernobyl nuclear disaster, something Charles Perrow calls a "normal accident" in his book of the same title, found coverage echoed the stereotype of American superiority and Russian inferiority rather an approach focusing on science and risk (Patterson 1989).

Because of their nature, slow-onset disasters such as topsoil erosion, climate change and waste management have historically been under-reported. Phenomena not linked to specific events such as the growth of a permanent American under-class went unreported for years waiting for an appropriate news peg, such as the health care debate of 2009, to supply the needed event and photo opportunities required to make the news agenda.

Under event-oriented journalism, elections become horse races with "front-runners" and the "rest of the pack" counted and handicapped daily with each new poll. But reporting an election as a contest fails to focus on the policy issues, which is what democratic elections are supposed to be about. The quintessential example of this can be seen in the California election of Arnold Schwarzenegger where many said they voted for the actor simply because they deemed him "electable."

The phenomenon of "pack journalism" has been chronicled in several films, dating back to the classic *The Front Page* and later *The Boys on the Bus* (Crouse 1974) and the book *Feeding Frenzy* (Sabato 1992). All emphasize journalistic excesses and an unwillingness to engage in independent thought that would disturb enlightened and pragmatic philosophers alike. They also expose a system easily manipulated by politicians as editors remain skeptical of "scoops" that no other journalist has. This unwillingness to leave the "pack" with a break-out story led to many of the hottest political stories of the new century being reported first on the Web where these institutional pressures do not exist.

For instance, the *New York Times* resorted to quoting the supermarket tabloid the *National Enquirer* in its coverage of the O. J. Simpson murder case largely in an effort to keep up with media competition. Equally significant, the *Enquirer* had the story right. And, the entire Washington press corps was confounded when Internet gadfly Matt Drudge, who styles himself a political reporter, published what became the first mention of the President Bill Clinton/Monica Lewinsky scandal. Drudge has said that he prints rumor as well as fact; traditional journalists, who want to separate the two, remain deeply troubled by the impact of the speed of the Internet on the need to check facts before more traditional publication.

Journalists have also been cowed by the threat of litigation. The film *The Insider* presents a fictionalized but nonetheless fact-based account about the impact of litigation on reporting stories critical of big tobacco. Seymour Hersh's original reporting of the My Lai massacre during the Vietnam War, which eventually appeared in the *New York Times,* was held up because no other reporter had a similar story and a particular media outlet was afraid to stick its neck out.

Truth is more than just a collection of facts. Facts have a relationship to one another and to other facts, forming a larger whole. Yet analytic coverage of American institutions, of science and technology, of politics and of social movements is rare. What is more common—especially on cable news outlets—is to invite two or more parties with conflicting views, allot them too little time to discuss the issue at hand and then sit back and let the resulting heated exchange take the place of reporting. If the role of the mass media is not only to detail events and issues, but to make the relationship among them clear, is merely rounding up conflicting talking heads sufficient? Or do we need to do it better?

Stephen Hess (1981) has argued that journalists need to engage in reporting that looks more like social science than storytelling. Gans (1979) argues for news that is labeled as originating from a particular point of view. If readers and viewers are alerted to the worldview of those who have selected the news (as they were during the era of the partisan press) they would be better able to place news in context. Other scholars argue for news that is analytical rather than anecdotal, proactive rather than reactive and contextual rather than detached. On a practical level, working reporters and editors insist that individual journalists need to do a better job of understanding their own biases and compensating for them.

The accumulated evidence, both anecdotal and scholarly, today strikes at the core of objectivity and shows that intellectually, we are living in a pragmatic era, but professionally we seem to be unable to develop a working alternative to the Enlightenment's view of truth. Because of this, mainstream media are increasingly seen as irrelevant, particularly to a younger audience for whom truth is more likely to be a video on YouTube than a report on the network's dwindling nightly newscasts.

ON THE ETHICS OF DECEPTION

In a profession that values truth, is it ever ethical to lie? To editors? To readers? To sources, who may be liars themselves? Are there levels of lying? Is flattering someone to get an interview as serious a transgression as doctoring a quote or photograph? Is withholding information the same thing as lying? If you can only get one side of the story, do you go with it? Does it matter today if opinion mingles with news?

Crises of credibility have faced media outlets of all sizes including spectacular instances at both *USA Today* and the *New York Times* that resulted in front page editorial apologies and multi-page retractions. In the case of the *Times,* it started when a 27-year-old reporter, Jayson Blair, fabricated all or part of more than

Errors in Journalism: Inevitability and Arrogance

Confounding truth and deception in journalism is the problem of errors. Inadvertent mistakes in stories are common. One freelance fact checker (Hart 2003) wrote in the *Columbia Journalism Review* that she had not experienced an error-free story in three years of fact checking for *CJR,* one of journalism's leading watchdog publications. Her calls to fellow fact-checkers at other publications led her to believe that articles with errors are the rule, not the exception.

However, mistakes are different from fabrication and do not indicate a lack of dedication to the truth. Some, if not most, mistakes are matters of interpretation, but others are outright errors of fact. In her article, "Delusions of Accuracy," Ariel

Hart says that hearing journalists proudly claim to have had no errors or fewer errors than the *Times* found in Blair's writing is "scary, not the least because it encourages delusions of accuracy."

One problem seems to be audience members so disconnected from the media that they don't bother to correct our mistakes or, worse, assume as readers of the *Times* evidently did, that fabrication is *de rigueur* for journalists. "Journalists surely make mistakes often, but I think we don't—or can't—admit it to ourselves because the idea of a mistake is so stigmatized. . . . So mistakes need to be destigmatized or restigmatized and dealt with accordingly. They should be treated like language errors," Hart argues.

40 stories. After his resignation from the paper, the *Times* ran four full pages of corrections documenting every error discovered in Blair's reporting. The *Times'* correction made it clear that the *Times* had failed to correct the problem in earlier stages despite many opportunities to do so. In a subsequent analysis of the case, many at the *Times* and other places suggested that one reason Blair's actions had been unchecked for so long was because of his race. Blair was African-American, and he had been hired as part of the *Times'* diversity program. His mentors at the paper, Executive Editor Howell Raines and Managing Editor Gerald Boyd, who also was African-American, were among Blair's strongest supporters and both eventually resigned in the fallout. While the *Times* denied that race was the reason that Blair had been promoted, Blair himself did not.

PEARLS BEFORE SWINE © *Stephan Pastis/Dist. By United Feature Syndicate, Inc.*

However, Blair wasn't the only bad news for the *Times* during those weeks. Pulitzer Prize–winning reporter Rick Bragg also resigned from the paper after it became public that he, too, had published stories based largely on the reporting of stringers who did not receive a byline in the *Times*. Furthermore, some of his stories filed with non–New York datelines had been written on airplanes and in hotel rooms where Bragg was functioning more as a rewrite editor rather than doing actual on-the-scene reporting. Bragg said his practices were known at the *Times* and common in the industry. That comment aligns with one heard frequently in the Blair incident that sources did not complain to the *Times* about incorrect stories since they felt that fictionalizing stories was just the way things are done. This cynical appraisal of journalism threatens our credibility, which is the chief currency of the profession.

So, how do journalists feel about deception? A survey of members of Investigative Reporters and Editors (IRE) provides some insight into the profession's thinking (Lee 2005). Journalists think about deception on a continuum. At one end, there is almost universal rejection of lying to readers, viewers and listeners. IRE members regard such lies as among the worst ethical professional breaches. At the other end, more than half of the IRE members surveyed said they approved of flattering a source to get an interview, even though that flattery could be considered deceptive and certainly was insincere.

In the same survey, lies of omission—such as withholding information from readers and viewers and also editors and bosses—were considered less of a problem than fabricating facts in a story or fabricating entire stories, which was almost universally condemned. IRE members were more willing to withhold information in instances when national security issues were involved. The journalists also said some lies were justified; they approved of lying if it would save a life or prevent injury to a source.

The journalists surveyed also noted that there were outside influences on these judgments. Broadcast journalists were more accepting of hidden cameras and altering video than were print journalists, although that difference might be changing as more print journalists get video experience via their newspaper's Web sites. And, those who worked in competitive markets were more willing to accept deception than were those who saw themselves in less competitive environments. The more experienced a journalist was, the less likely he or she was to accept any form of deception. Finally, the survey revealed what journalists worry about is the impact such reporting methods have on the believability of news accounts and on journalists' ability to cover subsequent stories if caught in an ethical lapse.

Is it ethical to lie to liars? Is withholding information the same thing as lying? If not, under what circumstances might it be appropriate? If it is, are there ethically based justifications for such an act? Sissela Bok (1978) has written eloquently on lying to liars. She argues that such an act raises two questions. Will the lie serve a larger social good, and does the act of lying mean that we as professionals are willing to be lied to in return?

Bok suggests that most of the time, when we lie we want "free rider" status— gaining the benefits of lying without incurring the risks of being lied to. In other words, some journalists may believe it's acceptable to lie to a crook to get a story, but they professionally resent being lied to by any source, regardless of motive.

Lying is a way to get and maintain power. Those in positions of power often believe they have the right to lie because they have a greater than ordinary understanding of what is at stake. Lying in a crisis (to prevent panic) and lying to enemies (to protect national security) are two examples. In both circumstances journalists can be—either actively or without their knowledge—involved in the deception. Do journalists have a right to counter this lying with lies of their own, told under the guise of the public's need to know? Does a journalist have the right to print the truth when printing it will cause one of the evils—panic or a threat to national security— that the lie was concocted to prevent?

Then there is the "omission versus commission" issue. In the first, the lie is that some part of the truth was conveniently left out; in the latter, the lie is an untruth told purposefully. Bok asserts that a genuinely white lie may be excusable on some grounds, but that all forms of lying must stand up to questions of fairness and mutuality. According to Kant's categorical imperative, the teller of the white lie must also be willing to be lied to. Even lying to liars can have its downside as Bok points out in her book, *Lying.*

> In the end, the participants in deception they take to be mutually understood may end up with coarsened judgment and diminished credibility. But if, finally, the liar to whom one wishes to lie is also in a position to do one harm, then the balance may shift; not because he is a liar, but because of the threat he poses (Bok 1978, 140).

Reporting *via* the Internet has given new urgency to the issue of lying by omission. In most instances failing to identify yourself as a reporter when collecting information electronically from news groups, chat rooms or other modes of public discussion is considered problematic. Journalists, when pressed, note that the U.S. Supreme Court has ruled Internet transmissions are public. The ethical issue emerges when most of those involved in the discussion are not aware of the legal standards and expect, instead, the more ethically based relations of face-to-face interactions. Ethical thought leaves journalists with difficult choices.

Reporting *on* the contents of the Internet—and cable television—raises another series of challenges. How should journalist go about debunking rumors that circulate on the Internet? Conventional wisdom for the legacy media holds that re-printing or re-broadcasting rumors only furthers them. However, people seem to believe what they see on the Internet, no matter how implausible. News organizations in New Orleans covering Hurricane Katrina faced a series of difficult news decisions in face of the rumors sweeping the city. In some instances, they elected to print or broadcast that they could not substantiate rumors prevalent in the networked world. The same problems continue to plague journalists in stories as distinct as news of Michael Jackson's death or terrorist attacks in India.

Deciding how to handle rumors, however, appears to be only one challenge for journalists when the Internet is involved. A second, and perhaps more serious, challenge is how to treat information promulgated by well-known sources—information that is false. The best known example of this problem in former Alaska Governor and 2008 Vice-President candidate Sarah Palin's assertion on her Facebook page that the medical reform legislation moving through Congress in 2009 contained a provision for "death panels" for the elderly. While Palin's entry was not true, it was widely circulated through many media outlets—including FOX News—and left journalists with the almost impossible task of proving a negative. Calling someone a liar, at one level, seems the height of non-objective journalism. But, when the facts suggest that a source is lying—even if that source is not held to the same standards of truthtelling as journalists are—what becomes an acceptable professional mechanism to hold non-journalist sources to account?

ETHICAL NEWS VALUES

Most mass media courses present a list of qualities that define news. Most such lists include proximity, timeliness, conflict, consequence, prominence, rarity, change, concreteness, action and personality. Additional elements may include notions of mystery, drama, adventure, celebration, self-improvement and even ethics. While these lists are helpful to beginning journalists, they probably will not help you decide how to recount the news ethically.

We suggest you expand your journalistic definitions of news to include a list of ethical news values. These values are intended to reflect the philosophic tensions inherent in a profession with a commitment to truth. If news values were constructed from ethical reasoning, we believe the following elements would be emphasized by both journalists and the organizations for which they work.

> **Accuracy**—using the correct facts and the right words and putting things in context. Journalists need to be as independent as they can when framing stories. They need to be aware of their own biases, including those they "inherit" as social class, gender and ethnicity, as well as learned professional norms.
>
> **Confirmation**—writing articles that are able to withstand scrutiny inside and outside the newsroom. Media ethicist Sandy Borden (2007) refers to this as the "discipline of confirmation," a concept that reflects how difficult it can be to capture even a portion of the truth in sometimes complex news situations.
>
> **Tenacity**—knowing when a story is important enough to require additional effort, both personal and institutional. Tenacity drives journalists to provide all the depth they can regardless of the individual assignment. It has institutional implications, too, for the individual cannot function well in an environment where resources are too scarce or the corporate bottom line too dominant. In addition, news organizations need to trust journalists when they report independently rather than expect them to act as part of a pack.
>
> **Dignity**—leaving the subject of a story as much self-respect as possible. Dignity values each person regardless of the particular story or the particular role the individual plays. Dignity allows the individual journalist to recognize that news gathering is a cooperative enterprise where each plays a role, including editors, videographers, designers and advertising sales staff.

Reciprocity—treating others as you wish to be treated. Too often, journalism is "writing for the lowest common denominator." Reciprocity demands respect for the reader. It also rejects the notion of journalism as benevolent paternalism—"We'll tell you what we think is good for you"—and recognizes that journalists and their viewers and readers are partners both in discovering what is important and in gleaning meaning from it.

Sufficiency—allocating adequate resources to important issues. On the individual level, sufficiency can mean thoroughness, for example, checking both people and documents for every scrap of fact before beginning to write. On an organizational level, it means allocating adequate resources to the newsgathering process. With virtually every media outlet suffering from declining readers or viewers, thanks mainly to the Web, this is probably the central issue of the current media landscape.

Equity—seeking justice for all involved in controversial issues and treating all sources and subjects equally. Equity assumes a complicated world with a variety of points of view. Equity demands that all points of view be considered, but does not demand that all sides be framed as equally compelling. Equity expands the journalistic norms of "telling both sides of the story" to "telling all sides of the story."

Community—valuing social cohesion. On the organization level, a sense of community means that media outlets and the corporations that own them need to consider themselves as citizens rather than mere "profit centers." On the individual level, it means evaluating stories with an eye first to social good.

Diversity—covering all segments of the audience fairly and adequately. There appears to be almost overwhelming evidence that news organizations do not "look like" the society they cover. While management can remedy part of this problem by changing hiring patterns, individual journalists can learn to "think diversity" regardless of their individual heritages.

Like all lists, ours should not be considered inclusive or without some measure of internal contradiction. We believe those contradictions, however, provide an important continuum within which informed ethical choice can be made.

Suggested Readings

BENNETT, LANCE. 1988. *News: The politics of illusion.* Longman: New York.

BOK, SISSELA. 1978. *Lying: Moral choice in public and private life.* New York: Random House.

GANS, HERBERT. 1979. *Deciding what's news: A study of CBS Evening News, NBC Nightly News, Newsweek and Time.* New York: Vintage.

JAMIESON, KATHLEEN HALL. 1992. *Dirty politics.* New York: Oxford University Press.

LIPPMANN, WALTER. 1922. *Public opinion.* New York: Free Press.

PLATO. *The republic.*

WEAVER, DAVID H., RANDAL A. BEAM, BONNIE J. BROWNLEE, PAUL S. VOAKES, and G. CLEVE-LAND WILHOIT. 2007. *The American journalist in the 21st century: U.S. news people at the dawn of a new millennium.* Mahwah, NJ: Lawrence Erlbaum & Associates.

Cases on the Web

www.mhhe.com/mediaethics7e

"Columbine: News and community—A balancing act" by Lee Wilkins

"The doctor has AIDS" by Deni Elliott

"Taste in photojournalism: A question of ethics or aesthetics" by Lou Hodges

"Reporters and confidential sources" by Steve Weinberg

"Rodent wars and cultural battles: Reporting hantavirus" by JoAnn M. Valenti

"Too many bodies, too much blood: A case study of the 'family-sensitive newscast'" by Bill Silcock

"Nine days in Union: The Susan Smith case" by Sonya Forte Duhé

"SARS: The bug that would not go away" by Seow Ting Lee

CHAPTER 2 CASES

CASE 2-A

What's Yours Is Mine: The Ethics of News Aggregation

CHAD PAINTER
University of Missouri

In June of 2008, The *Hartford Courant* cut 95 jobs from its news department, roughly half of its news staff, in two rounds of layoffs. But within a few months, with an online news hole to fill and a reduced staff, the paper started aggregating local news from surrounding dailies.

In a search of the publication's Web site for Aug. 29–30, 2009, *Journal Inquirer* reporter Christine McCluskey counted 112 stories that were written by the *Courant*'s Connecticut competitors *Bristol Press, New Britain Herald, Torrington Register-Citizen, Waterbury Republican American* and her own paper (McCluskey, 2009). The stories were often—but not always—attributed to the original source, a practice Michael E. Schroeder, publisher of the *Bristol Press* and *New Britain Herald* called, "at best plagiarism, at worst outright theft" (McCluskey 2009).

Jeffrey S. Levine, the *Hartford Courant*'s director of content, explained his paper's position. "Aggregation is the process of synopsizing information from other news sources, most commonly by placing a portion of the information on your web site and linking to the original story" (McCluskey 2009). He cited a mistake in his paper's editing process that "inappropriately dropped the attribution or proper credit and in some cases credited ourselves with a byline to a *Courant* reporter" as the basis for the plagiarism claims.

The Society of Professional Journalists' code of conduct states "Never plagiarize" and the Associated Press code warns its writers: "don't plagiarize." Similarly, an ethics primer in online journalism from the University of Southern California's Annenberg School of Journalism states "Don't steal others' work. Such theft is plagiarism" (Niles 2009). Kovach and Rosenstiel call it a "deceptively simple but powerful idea in the discipline for pursuing truth: do your own work" (2007, 99).

However, aggregation is not a black-and-white issue. Is it acceptable to disseminate another news organization's work as long as that work is properly credited? Should the rules be the same for newspapers, broadcast outlets and online journalism? What about content-sharing organizations such as the Associated Press?

One of the core principles of journalism is the discipline of verification (Kovach and Rosenstiel 2007, 79). Aggregation violates that principle because it might not discriminate between rumor, fact and speculation (Kovach and Rosenstiel 2007) and because it doesn't allow for independent confirmation of facts. Falsehoods and rumor go unchecked even if the original source issues a retraction if the aggregators fail to correct or pull the offending story.

However, aggregation isn't a new concept in the news business.

Time magazine was a notorious aggregator. First published March 3, 1923, Henry Luce's flagship magazine aimed to summarize the news quickly, but few of its busy readers would have guessed that *Time* was digested entirely from the dozens of newspapers it subscribed to, "gaining its greatest free lunch from the opulent tables of the *New York Times* and *New York World*" (Swanberg 1972, 58).

Radio, at least in its infancy, relied heavily on newspapers for a steady supply of news reports. For their part, newspapers at first either cooperated with radio for increased exposure or completely ignored the new medium (Chester 1949). That changed with the rise of the CBS and NBC chain radio broadcasting networks, and increased advertising competition from radio. On April 24, 1933, the members of the Associated Press "passed a resolution directing the AP Board of Directors to refuse to give AP news to any radio chain" (Chester 1949, 255). State and national press associations "busied themselves with resolutions attempting to restrict news broadcasting, mostly because it was incongruous for newspapers to furnish free news" to their competitors in radio (Hammargren 1936, 93). Eventually the courts weighed in, punishing the most egregious uses of newspaper content on the radio airwaves as an unfair practice.

Currently, the Associated Press is battling aggregating Web sites such as Google News over use of unauthorized content. The Associated Press announced plans in July 2009 to create "a news registry that will tag and track all AP content online to assure compliance with terms of use." The proposed tracking system "will register key identifying information about each piece of content that AP distributes as well as the terms of use of that content, and employ a built-in beacon to notify AP about how the content is used" (AP.org 2009).

The Associated Press itself is a cooperative that supplies around-the-clock news content to its 1,500 U.S. daily newspaper members, as well as international subscribers and commercial customers (AP.org 2009). There is also a recent trend among formerly rival papers to form localized content-sharing arrangements (Ricchiardi 2009). The newspapers cite budgetary constraints and the cost of Associated Press content as the major reasons for the arrangements.

But Alan Mutter, a former editor in Chicago and San Francisco who currently writes the blog *Reflections of a Newsosaur,* speaks for those who regret the loss of diversity when he says: "Where there are multiple reporters covering the same beat or same event, you're going to get multiple views and everybody is going to try harder to go to a higher level of reporting. It's a fact of human nature that competition inspires better work" (Ricchiardi 2009).

Micro Issues

1. Does proper attribution solve the ethical problem of aggregation? If not, do you have an alternative idea?
2. If news organizations voluntarily agree to offer their content to be aggregated under specific conditions, does that eliminate the ethical issues?

Midrange Issues

1. Evaluate the following statement: Credibility, one of the foundations of journalism, is predicated on "The notion that those who report the news are not obstructed from digging

up and telling the truth" and that the journalists can tell "the news not only accurately but also persuasively" (Kovach and Rosenstiel 2007, 53). Can an aggregator be expected to be a watchdog over information that their media outlet did not create?

2. How are content aggregators such as the Huffington Post distinct, in an ethical sense, from long-standing cooperatives such as the Associated Press?

Macro Issues

1. Is aggregation an issue primarily of economics or ethics? If aggregators such as Google News paid for content, would that solve the problem?
2. Who "owns" the news? Does a media outlet have the right to require that a consumer pay for information that he or she needs to be a participant in a democratic society? Did the framers of the Bill of Rights give any clues in this area?

CASE 2-B

Is It News Yet?

MICHELLE PELTIER
University of Missouri

Every weekday afternoon he screams, pouts, whines, stomps his feet and throws things in rabid fits of frustration. It's Jim Cramer, the manic 54-year-old host of CNBC's "Mad Money" program. Cramer uses all the hyperkinetic bells, whistles and special effects of a television game show to showcase the non-stop onslaught of his latest buy and sell recommendations for stocks.

> "It occupies some sort of netherworld between sheer entertainment and useful financial advice," said *Washington Post* media writer Howard Kurtz, just a few months after the show began in 2005 (Farzad 2005).
>
> "This show is about making money and educating you while we entertain you. There's no bones about that," Susan Krakower, the Vice President of Strategic Development at CNBC who co-created the show with Cramer, told the *Hollywood Reporter* (Gough 2006).

Based on ratings, viewership rises along with the stock market's volatility, though it's difficult to know whether the people who tune in are more interested in entertainment or advice (Carr 2008). What is certain is that Cramer's over-the-top style appeals to viewers who might otherwise tune out the dense drone of financial news coverage. The information Cramer, a former hedge-fund manager, presents is both real and relevant. He reaches younger viewers than traditional financial shows; in fact, Cramer tours U.S. colleges on a regular basis.

However, during the financially disastrous year of 2008, the show's host made a number of high profile—and questionable—statements.

In March 2008, Cramer responded to a viewer who was tempted to sell his shares of struggling Bear Stearns stock.

> "No, no, no! Bear Stearns is fine," Cramer said on air. "Don't move your money from Bear! That's just being silly," (Cramer, "Mad Money" 2008).

When JP Morgan Chase took over the beleaguered investment bank less than a week later, the stock value plunged. Cramer justified his misplaced optimism, even suggesting that it was partly calculated, saying, "I guess I could have caused a run on the bank and said take your money out of Bear" (Cramer, "Street Signs" 2008).

In September 2008 Cramer interviewed the CEO of Wachovia and called the bank's stock one of only a few potential "winners" in the $700 billion bailout (Sorkin 2008). Two weeks later, a chagrined and sullen Cramer glowered an apology into the Steadicam, telling his viewers that he had "screwed up."

"I let you down 'cause I wasn't skeptical enough," he said. "I have to presume when it comes to banking right now there is no objective truth, just negative, just terrible things" (Cramer, "Mad Money" 2008).

Finally, in October, Cramer appeared on NBC's "Today Show" with a grim economic forecast. "Whatever money you may need for the next five years, please take it out of the stock market right now, this week," he advised viewers (Cramer 2008).

Amid accusations that such statements were akin to shouting "fire" in a crowded building, Cramer stood by his advice, emphasizing that he remained confident in the long-term investment potential of stocks (Carr 2008). "I am still committing for my retirement," he told Scott Collins of the *Los Angeles Times*. "I'm not backing away. Because, I have no intention of retiring in the next five years" (Collins 2008).

Legally, CNBC protects itself and its volatile show host with extensive disclaimers warning of the financial risk in the advice offered on the program. In part, the warning states viewers "should not take any opinion expressed by Cramer as a specific inducement to make a particular investment or follow a particular strategy" ("Mad Money" disclaimer 2008).

Micro Issues

1. How important is it that Cramer intends to entertain as well as inform in terms of the way he presents financial news?
2. Is the disclaimer that runs at the beginning of every show ethically defensible? How would you defend it?
3. How should a rational actor evaluate the claims of Cramer?
4. How is Cramer's show like and unlike what a public relations person for your local bank might do? Are there ethical distinctions between Cramer's approach and more traditional advertising or public relations?

Midrange Issues

1. What is the ethical role of CNBC in presenting a show like "Mad Money"?
2. Compare Cramer's brand of financial news with Comedy Central's Jon Stewart and his brand of fake news. Which is more ethically justifiable? Why?
3. Should a local newspaper's business or financial reporter treat Cramer's recommendations as a news story?
4. Do you think audiences are particularly vulnerable when it comes to complex topics such as financial news? Does that vulnerability result in any distinct ethical obligations?

Macro Issues

1. Are there some subjects that are too serious to be made entertaining in this way?
2. Cramer is an avowed capitalist. Can he also be trusted to be an objective critic of the capitalistic system—particularly considering the financial disasters of 2008? Is that his role?
3. Evaluate the usefulness of Cramer's show to individual viewers. Is he advisor or entertainer?

CASE 2-C

Visualizing September 11th

SARA GETTYS
University of Missouri

The morning of Sept. 11, 2001, AP photographer Richard Drew was covering a fashion show in downtown Manhattan. When two planes slammed into the World Trade Towers, the AP called Drew and sent him to the story (Cheney 2001). As people jumped, he photographed several of the jumpers, tracking one man in a white coat and dark pants in several frames. Drew remembers, "I've been at the AP for 32 years. I've covered my share of disasters and earthquakes and fires. . . . [So when], all of a sudden, people started falling out of the tower, I started photographing it" (Abransky 2002).

Papers across the country, including the *New York Times,* picked the photo to run as part of the coverage. The *Times* ran the photo above the fold on Page 7 of the A section in full color, the art for the lead story jump from Page A1. The photo ran alone surrounded by text that included a chronological accounting of the day's events.

That same morning, Milagros Hernandez received a frantic phone call from her brother Norberto Hernandez, who worked as a pastry chef at Windows on the World, a restaurant on the 107th floor of Number One World Trade Center. After speaking briefly with him, Milagros turned on her television set to watch coverage of the tragedy. She knew her brother worked above the burning floors, and she remembers her brother saying that if he ever were to be trapped, he would jump rather than burn to death.

Television coverage included pictures of people jumping, and one man in particular—wearing a white coat—caught her eye. But the fleeting image provided no clues as to the jumper's identity. When she opened the *New York Times* the next day, the victim's white jacket and dark complexion sent a shock of recognition through her. "Oh my God! That's my brother!" she remembers thinking.

Throughout the day on Sept. 11th, *Times* editors, along with their colleagues at other news organizations, worked to cover the attack. At the *Times,* staffers in the advertising and strategic planning departments worked the dictation desk, taking reports from reporters and eyewitness accounts (Tugend 2001). In an event where every aspect of coverage was graphic, violent and horrifying, the decisions about what to show to tell the totality of the story became the decisions that relied heavily on the standards of those working the desks. Stories from the Sept. 12th edition of the paper included photos of firefighters grieving for lost comrades, pictures and first-person accounts of the towers falling, and pictures of wounded victims waiting for help. There were no ads in the A section of the paper that day, with the exception of a full-page Verizon ad on the back cover.

When the photo ran, the *Times* started receiving calls from outraged readers who felt that this photo in particular was sensationalistic and exploited a man at the moment just before his death (Mitchell 2001). Papers nationwide that ran the photo

AP Photo/Richard Drew.

received similar calls. In Allentown, Pennsylvania, more than 60 people called the local paper to complain. The *Arizona Daily Star* posted the photo on its Web site but took it off in response to complaints.

In the midst of the tragedy and public outrage, Peter Cheney, a reporter for the *Toronto Globe and Mail,* was covering the attacks and cleanup and rescue attempts when he saw a missing person's poster of Norberto Hernandez and thought he might be the man in the photo. He contacted Milagros and decided to tell the story of the family who believed that the man pictured was their relative. In doing so, he addressed both the life of the victim the family believed was pictured and the grieving process of the survivors. He also included the family's response to the photo—from Milagros' belief that the man pictured was undeniably her brother, to Norberto's daughter, who didn't believe that the man in the photo was her father.

While the identity of the man in the photo remained uncertain, Cheney explored that possibility and allowed the family to express its grief and to celebrate the life of a loved one whose last moments may have been shared with millions of readers.

Micro Issues

1. Should AP photographer Drew have continued to "follow" the jumper once he realized what was happening?
2. Does it matter that it is difficult, some say impossible, to clearly identify the man in the photo?
3. Was it appropriate to place the photo on an inside page? Should it have run on Page A1? Should other publications in distant places have run the photo?
4. Was the story reporter Cheney wrote an invasion of privacy at this time of grief?
5. While Norberto Hernandez was included in a list of profiles that the *Times* ran on the victims, Hernandez's profile was only two paragraphs long and failed to mention the possibility that he was the man pictured on September 12th. Is this appropriate?

Midrange Issues

1. Does the placing of the photo on an inside page somehow mitigate what many concluded was an invasion of privacy?
2. How should the *Times'* editors have considered the fact that "the jumper" was alive when the photograph was taken?
3. Are the justifications for television running the video of the jumper somehow ethically distinct from those the *Times* adhered to? Should they be?
4. If the *Times* and other media outlets had failed to provide visual information about this element of the story, would those organizations have failed to recognize and report on the decisions these people made?
5. Compare this photo with the Pulitzer Prize–winning photo by Stanley Forman in Case 1-A of the girl falling to her death from a faulty fire escape in Boston. What are the differences? What are the similarities? Do you make the same decision for both photos? Justify your answer.

Macro Issues

1. Should the *Times* have altered the photo—or published a different one—where the individual jumper was less recognizable? Why or why not?
2. What values do you believe the *Times'* editors weighed as they arrived at their decision?
3. Because Sept. 11th was a horrific event, did coverage—in order to be accurate—have to picture some of the horror of that day? Would you apply the same reasoning to coverage of international events—say, conflict in the Middle East?
4. By publishing the photo, to whom or what is the *Times* being loyal?
5. Do the *Times* and other media outlets that published and broadcast such photos share any responsibility for the public emotion connected with the events of 9/11?

CASE 2-D

The Spouse Is Squeezed: A South Carolina TV Reporter's Attempt to Conceal Her Source

SONYA FORTE DUHÉ
Loyola University, New Orleans

It seems like a typical news day.

A man telephones WIS-TV Senior Reporter Heather Hoopes, claiming to possess a "bombshell videotape" that she must see.

The source tells the Columbia, South Carolina, NBC affiliate reporter the tape is available to her only if she comes to his house to get it. He says he won't mail it or drop it off at the station. If she wants it, she *has* to come and get it.

Concerned for her safety, Hoopes asks her husband, Jim Matthews—who for more than 20 years has worked with the Department of Justice's Drug Enforcement Administration (DEA) and now heads the local Columbia office—to drive her to the caller's home. He agrees.

Matthews has no idea that the videotape contains a privileged conversation between a murder defendant and his lawyer, secretly videotaped by a local sheriff's deputy. Hoopes isn't exactly sure what she is getting either.

After reviewing the tape, she broadcasts a story about the videotaping of the privileged conversation. To Hoopes and colleagues, the tape is a clear violation of the prisoner's rights. Hoopes's move to have Matthews drive her to retrieve the videotape from this confidential source leads to numerous court battles and thousands of dollars in legal costs for her, her husband and her employer.

CONTEXT

In 1995, Lexington County sheriff's detectives arrested B. J. Quattlebaum and charged him with the murder of William Swartz. Quattlebaum was taken to the Lexington County Jail, where he called his attorney.

The men used a small room to talk. Unknown to them, a deputy sheriff was secretly and illegally videotaping their meeting.

At a later time, the same confidential source, who was subsequently identified as Columbia attorney Jack Duncan, called Hoopes at WIS to alert her to this alleged wrongdoing. Hoopes, her news director and her editors decided to use a portion of the videotape to expose the illegal action. However, in an attempt to protect the arrested man's rights, the news team didn't use the audio portion of the tape.

The FBI attempted to obtain the name of Hoopes' confidential source but could not meet Justice Department protocol because of First Amendment questions. When the FBI's efforts to subpoena WIS ran into roadblocks, it attempted to make Matthews reveal the person's identity.

In a May 10, 1999, story in the *Washington Post,* Hoopes was quoted as saying, "I consider it a backdoor tactic. I don't understand why the Justice Department is doing this. It's very stressful for me and my husband. I carry an extra burden because I put him in the situation."

Prosecutors subpoenaed Matthews, and a federal grand jury demanded that the DEA agent testify about the case.

Matthews's lawyer, along with the WIS legal team, filed motions with U.S. District Court asking that Matthews not be forced to testify. Lawyers argued that forcing him to be a witness would violate his First Amendment rights. These motions were dismissed. Written pleas to Attorney General Janet Reno, FBI Director Louis Freeh and Justice Department official Beneva Weintraub also did not recuse Matthews from a court appearance.

The Radio Television News Director Association (RTNDA) is the world's largest professional organization devoted exclusively to electronic journalism. The organization represents local and network news executives in broadcasting, cable and other electronic media in more than 30 countries. In those letters, RTNDA President Barbara Cochran called on the Justice Department to end FBI attempts to force Matthews to testify. Cochran wrote:

> On behalf of the 3,400 members of the RTNDA, I am writing to express our grave concern about FBI attempts to force the husband of a South Carolina television station reporter to reveal to a grand jury what he knows about his wife's confidential source.
>
> Efforts to force Mr. Matthews to betray the confidence of his spouse not only raise compelling questions about marital privilege, but they represent a blatant attempt to circumvent the reporter's privilege recognized by the Constitution, the state, and the Justice Department.
>
> It is well recognized that news-gathering activities are protected under the First Amendment of the United States Constitution. This protection extends to information given in confidence to a reporter, including the source of that information. The South Carolina legislature has also expressed a strong public policy of protecting news-gathering activities, enacting a shield law whose aim is to protect the free flow of information to the public. Moreover, Department of Justice regulations expressly recognize that: Because freedom of the press can be no broader than the freedom of reporters to investigate and report the news, the prosecutorial power of the government should not be used in such a way that it impairs a reporter's responsibility to cover as broadly as possible controversial public issues.
>
> RTNDA is certainly aware of no case where a reporter's spouse has been ordered to disclose a confidential source. If prosecutors are allowed to obtain confidential news information from a third party where efforts to obtain the same information from the reporter have failed, then the protections afforded by the First Amendment and state press shield statutes would be meaningless.

Hoopes said, "I would have thought they [authorities] would have applauded the efforts of my source and WIS to bring this to light. Instead it seems like we're the criminals."

Quattlebaum was later convicted of first-degree murder and sentenced to death. In January 2000, the South Carolina Supreme Court overturned Quattlebaum's conviction, due in part to the videotape incident.

A federal judge ordered the deputy who videotaped the conversation to pay a $250 fine for civil rights violations. As for Hoopes's confidential source, he was sentenced to and spent several months in jail for lying to a federal grand jury and was disbarred.

Micro Issues

1. Should the reporter have taken the videotape? Why?
2. Should the reporter have asked someone to accompany her to pick up the videotape? If so, who?
3. Was it okay for the reporter to air the videotape?
4. Should the reporter have aired the audio from the videotape?

Midrange Issues

1. Does the reporter have the right to air videotape of an illegal act? When would it be inappropriate?
2. Was it the journalist's responsibility to expose this illegal taping of a privileged conversation?
3. Did the journalist breach her source's confidentiality by allowing her husband to accompany her to pick up the videotape?

Macro Issues

1. Should reporters be allowed to keep sources confidential if a criminal act has occurred?
2. What responsibilities do reporters have to law enforcement officials? Why?
3. Should spouses of reporters have the same First Amendment rights that reporters possess?
4. What role should nonjournalists play in the newsgathering process?

CASE 2-E

When Is Objective Reporting Irresponsible Reporting?

THEODORE L. GLASSER
Stanford University

Amanda Laurens, a reporter for a local daily newspaper, covers the city mayor's office, where yesterday she attended a 4:00 p.m. press conference. The mayor, Ben Adams, read a statement accusing Evan Michaels, a city council member, of being a "paid liar" for the pesticide industry. "Councilman Michaels," the mayor said at the press conference, "has intentionally distorted the facts about the effects of certain pesticides on birds indigenous to the local area." "Mr. Michaels," the mayor continued, "is on the payroll of a local pesticide manufacturer," and his views on the effects of pesticides on bird life "are necessarily tainted."

The press conference ended at about 5:15 p.m., less than an hour before her 6:00 p.m. deadline. Laurens quickly contacted Councilman Michaels for a quote in response to the mayor's statement. Michaels, however, refused to comment, except to say that Mayor Adams's accusations were "utter nonsense" and "politically motivated." Laurens filed her story, which included both the mayor's accusation and the councilman's denial. Laurens's editor thought the story was fair and balanced and ran it the following morning on the front page.

The mayor was pleased with the coverage he received. He thought Laurens had acted professionally and responsibly by reporting his accusation along with Michaels's denial. Anything else, the mayor thought, would have violated the principles of objective journalism. The mayor had always believed that one of the most important responsibilities of the press was to provide an impartial forum for public controversies, and the exchange between him and the councilman was certainly a bona fide public controversy. Deciding who's right and who's wrong is not the responsibility of journalists, the mayor believed, but a responsibility best left to readers.

Councilman Michaels, in contrast, was outraged. He wrote a scathing letter to the editor, chiding the newspaper for mindless, irresponsible journalism. "The story may have been fair, balanced and accurate," he wrote, "but it was not truthful." He had never lied about the effects of pesticides on bird life, and he had "never been on the payroll of any pesticide manufacturer," he wrote. "A responsible reporter would do more than report the facts truthfully; she would also report the truth about the facts." In this case, Michaels said, the reporter should have held off on the story until she had time to independently investigate the mayor's accusation; and if the accusation had proved to be of no merit, as Michaels insisted, then there shouldn't have been a story. Or if there had to be a story, Michaels added, "it should be a story about the *mayor* lying."

By way of background: The effects of pesticides on bird life had been a local issue for nearly a year. Part of the community backs Mayor Adams's position on the harmful effects of certain pesticides and supports local legislation that would limit or ban their use. Others in the community support Councilman Michaels's position that the evidence on the effects of pesticides on bird life is at best ambiguous and that more scientific study is needed before anyone proposes legislation. They argue that pesticides are useful, particularly to local farmers who need to protect crops, and because the available evidence about their deleterious effects is inconclusive, they believe that the city council should not seek to further restrict or prohibit their use. The exchange between Mayor Adams and Councilman Michaels is the latest in a series of verbal bouts on the subject of pesticides and the city's role in their regulation.

Micro Issues

1. Did Laurens do the right thing by submitting her story without the benefit of an independent investigation into the mayor's accusations about Councilman Michaels?
2. Is the mayor correct in arguing that Laurens acted responsibly by providing fair and balanced coverage of both sides of a public controversy without trying to judge whose side is right and whose side is wrong?
3. Is the councilman correct in arguing that Laurens acted irresponsibly by concerning herself only with reporting the facts truthfully and ignoring the "truth about the facts"?

Midrange Issues

1. Is it sufficient when covering public controversies to simply report the facts accurately and fairly? Does it matter that fair and accurate reporting of facts might not do justice to the truth about the facts?
2. Does the practice of objective reporting distance reporters from the substance of their stories in ways contrary to the ideals of responsible journalism?
3. If reporters serve as the eyes and ears of their readers, how can they be expected to report more than what they've heard or seen?

Macro Issues

1. What distinguishes fact from truth? For which should journalists accept responsibility?
2. If journalists know that a fact is not true, do they have an obligation to share that knowledge with their readers? And if they do share that knowledge, how can they claim to be objective in their reporting?
3. Justify or reject the role of objectivity in an era where more media outlets are available than ever before.

CASE 2-F

Monitoring *The Monitor:* Taste, Politics and an Explosive Photo

GINA BRAMUCCI, FREELANCE PHOTOJOURNALIST

The Monitor newspaper, launched in 1992, is the only independent paper in the small nation of Uganda in East Africa. The paper has an average daily circulation of 25,000, although it is estimated that at least 10 people read each paper in Uganda. Charles Onyango-Obbo, one of the paper's founding editors, is a high-profile critic of the government of President Yoweri Museveni. He has been imprisoned for what *The Monitor* has published, writes a weekly column for another paper, and is well known to the foreign media.

On April 28, 1999, an unnamed source brought a photo to *The Monitor*'s offices in Kampala, the Ugandan capital. The photo pictured a young woman, nude and pinned down by seven men. The men, wearing the uniforms of the Ugandan army, were shaving the woman's genital area with scissors. The photo is not printed in this book.

Deputy Editor David Ouma Balikowa received the photo, and shortly afterwards Ugandan security agents arrived to ensure that it would not be published. *The Monitor* editors wanted to talk with the security agents, but according to Ouma it was evident that if they shared the photo with the agents it would be confiscated. For the paper's editors, the attempt to suppress the photo was added incentive for publication. Gulu police confirmed that a case such as the one in the photo had been reported to them.

In his May 17, 1999, column on the incident Onyango-Obbo wrote: "The word was out that the paper had the picture. The paper's credibility as the country's only serious independent media voice was on the line. Here we were about to participate in what might seem like a cover up or take a risky plunge and get hurt."

The photo ran on May 11, 1999, on *The Monitor*'s back page with no accompanying story. The caption read:

> This picture was brought to *The Monitor* by someone who claimed to have taken it in Gulu barracks early this year without being noticed. Recent days have seen what locals say is renewed tension by state operatives to disrupt the calm that was returning to the region.

The northern barracks must be placed in context in order to grasp the significance of *The Monitor*'s claim. Since 1986, when Museveni first took power in Uganda, a small rebel insurgency in the north has plagued his presidency. The Lord's Resistance Army, or LRA, trumpets a pseudo-religious cause based on the premise of overthrowing Museveni and creating a utopian society that will be ruled by the Judeo-Christian Ten Commandments. To this end, the LRA targets its own people, the Acholi tribe, abducting children for soldiers, ambushing vehicles and killing and maiming haphazardly.

The LRA is not the only threat to civilians in northern Uganda, however. The U.S. State Department and nongovernmental organizations such as Human

Rights Watch and Amnesty International have regularly found government troops guilty of severe human rights abuses and have documented a pattern of looting, rape, torture and extrajudicial killings. The Gulu barracks, where *The Monitor* claimed the photo was taken, are the northern operational headquarters for these troops, the Ugandan People's Defense Force, or UPDF. It is in this context— a history of documented abuse—that *The Monitor*'s editors made the decision to publish the photo.

The publication of the photo caused immediate reaction from the media and civilians in Uganda. Reactions ranged from outrage to wholehearted support for *The Monitor.* Perhaps surprisingly, some of Uganda's women's rights groups criticized the paper's editors for their decision, as did Miria Matembe, the national minister of ethics and integrity. Matembe, who has been known for her advocacy on the part of women, felt that women and children would be disturbed by the graphic photo.

Arguments like Matembe's were countered forcefully by those in the media who felt that the photo's publication promoted basic equalities and liberties for women, the least advantaged party in Uganda's patriarchal society.

On the evening of May 12, with public discourse growing louder, Onyango-Obbo received a letter from the Criminal Investigation Department, or CID, of Uganda's police force. According to Onyango-Obbo, the editors spent six hours at CID before being taken to court. The state charged the men with sedition and publishing false news that could create "fear and alarm." The journalists pleaded not guilty of the charges and were released on bail of $63 each.

The UPDF released its own statement on May 12, denying that the photograph had been taken in Uganda and saying that "activities like rape as depicted in the picture cannot take place in any military barracks or for that matter in the UPDF operational zones." The army claimed that the fatigues worn by the soldiers pictured were not those used by the UPDF, and that the woman pictured has a West African hairstyle.

After a delay, the trial of *The Monitor* editors opened on Nov. 9, 1999, with Magistrate Pamela Mafabi hearing the case. In their testimony, UPDF officers repeated their claim that the uniforms of the soldiers pictured were not used in the Gulu barracks. But when presented with photos of well-known UPDF officers in uniforms similar to those pictured, one officer admitted that he wasn't familiar with all of the uniforms used. Although it's unclear when, at some point in 1999 northern UPDF officials also testified that women are regularly punished at army facilities by having their heads shaved with blunt razors.

After his first day in the courtroom, the defense lawyer for *The Monitor* editors, James Nangwala, was shot by unidentified gunmen in front of his home. He was hit in the shoulder, and Mafabi adjourned the trial until January 2000. The trial of 24-year-old Kandida Lakony, who came forward prior to the original trial and claimed to be the woman pictured in the photo, caused a further delay in *The Monitor* case. Lakony told officials the man shaving her was a former boyfriend and a soldier in the Gulu barracks. After a few days of protection in the state house of President Museveni, she was brought before a Ugandan court and accused of lying and giving misleading information to the police. The public was largely sympathetic to Lakony and her testimony was highly publicized, but the court found her guilty and she was sentenced to 12 months in prison. Lakony died shortly after her release.

Nearly two years after the photo's appearance in *The Monitor,* on March 6, 2001, Onyango-Obbo, Oguttu and Ouma were acquitted of the charges of sedition and publication of false statements. Another magistrate, Joshua Maruk, ruled that the state had failed to prove its case. "Looking at the caption of the photo, all that is indicated was a claim, the interpretation being that the publication was not vouching for the truth of the photo," Maruk wrote.

Micro Issues

1. Considering the circumstances, how should the paper have verified the photo's accuracy?
2. If it was impossible to verify the photo's accuracy, should the paper have published it?
3. Would your reasoning be different had the incident occurred in the United States?

Midrange Issues

1. Use utilitarian reasoning, and then the veil of ignorance, to analyze this case. How does the particular philosophical theory help you think through the issues?
2. How should journalists weigh their personal safety and well-being against their role as professionals?
3. Is this photo as described too offensive to be published in the United States? Are different standards appropriate in different cultures?

Macro Issues

1. What is the role of the media in developing nations? How might that role influence ethical decision making?
2. This case asks you to think about whether there is such a thing as universal ethical principles. Is there a universal standard you believe should be applied in this case?

3

Strategic Communication: Does Client Advocate Mean Consumer Adversary?

By the end of this chapter, you should be familiar with:

- how new technologies raise old ethical questions.
- the balance and cognitive dissonance persuasion theories and their role in persuasion.
- the amplified TARES test for evaluating the ethics of individual messages.
- why the relationship between the media and public relations is both symbiotic and strained.

REACH OUT AND TOUCH SOMEONE

Most of the readers of this book are in their early 20s, and are most often seeking *someone* in addition to the *something* of a college education. Many of you will conduct your search for friends and life partners online—and increasingly on sites such as eHarmony. Visitors to that site and others like it pay a subscription fee, complete various sorts of profiles and are linked with possible matches. The non-virtual world and that human thing called chemistry seem to take it from there.

Not much of an ethical issue involved—that is, until you learn how such Web sites really make their money. They do it not exclusively through the matching service they advertise, but more predominantly by attaching cookies to subscribers' computers, and then selling that information—willingly provided in the form of the profile—to marketers who seek a specific demographic, for example people of a certain age, or a certain income, and with specific likes and dislikes. Those electronic lists the Web sites sell—a process you must agree to in order to use the matching service—then allow marketers to push specific sorts of messages at you electronically and at times of their choosing, employing what the industry now terms behavioral marketing.

In addition to the technology of the cookie—which you can find and delete from your computer—marketers also are increasingly placing Web beacons—which can be neither spotted nor deleted by the average user—on your machine as part of the tracking process. While the marketers never know your specific identify—in other words your name—they know enough about you for selling purposes, right down to the fact that you like terrier dogs but not cats and that your favorite group is the Kings of Leon.

It's all part of the brave new world of strategic communication, or the seamless connections between what professionals used to refer to as advertising and public relations. And strategic communication, just like news, is facing a new economic reality: a business model that is no longer successful. What used to be the case, that entertainment or news content on either television or in a print medium was designed to deliver an audience to advertisers, is now increasingly problematic because people are finding ways to dodge persuasive messages as never before. Whether it's TiVo and skipping through commercials or getting news "for free" on the Web, strategic communication professionals are being forced to find novel ways to get their messages to "eyeballs"—or people acting in their roles as consumers.

These novel approaches can raise serious individual ethical issues—issues that once seemed more the realm of the journalist. Students who once said, "I went into advertising because I don't feel comfortable forcing people to talk to me and I don't have to think about invading people's privacy," are now facing decisions about whether and how to use computer-based technologies to do precisely these things—only this time to promote sales of various products and lifestyles as opposed to civil discourse or political involvement.

These facts of new media life also do not blunt some of the deepest continuing criticisms of persuasion, that the nature of the persuasive message itself—short, highly visual and intentionally vague—is overly reliant on stereotypes, spins the truth, glorifies consumerism at the expense of community and as an institution warps non-persuasive content in significant ways. The ease of bypassing persuasive messages also challenges one of the most significant justifications for advertising: that without the funding it provides, broad-ranging political discourse would not be possible in developed democracies such as the United States. These new economic realities have heightened the need for clear ethical thinking for those entering the persuasive end of the business.

TECHNOLOGY: A ROOM OF REQUIREMENT OR A SYSTEM OF VALUES?

Many of the issues raised by activities such as behavioral marketing or data mining for selling purposes arise because technology makes certain activities possible. Such activities, which most often require the enormous data processing capacities of the computer, also present professionals with two different ways of thinking about technology itself.

The first approach equates technology with efficiency. Those who subscribe to this school of thought assert that technology itself raises no ethical issues, but rather the ethical issues arise in how the technology is put to use. Think of the room of requirement in Harry Potter. In book five of the series, *The Order of the Phoenix,* Harry and his friends stumble on the room of requirement when they need a place to practice magic—specifically defense against the dark arts. (Professor Dumbledore apparently "found" the room during his student days when he was in desperate need of a "chamber pot.") The room of requirement is always equipped to fulfill the seeker's needs. Both Dumbledore's and later Harry's use of the room are done for "good" purposes.

Yet, in book six, *Harry Potter and the Half-Blood Prince,* the room of require-ment serves an evil purpose. Malfoy uses the room to repair the connecting closet that allows the death eaters to enter Hogwarts and kill Dumbledore. Same room—but in book six its use results in great evil. The room itself is not to blame; it is merely an efficient way of serving the needs of those who use it. It is in the intent of the user—not the existence of the room itself—that the capacity for ethical choice lies.

The second approach asserts that any technology is embedded with values. Think of the technology you are using right now: the written word and the printing press. What does writing value? A specific definition of truth, as reviewed in Chapter 2 of this book. A specific standard of evidence, for example written documents and sources for them are important. Some specific ways of organizing human community and of placing economic value on some activities. The act of writing and the tech-nology of the printing press have made much of contemporary human community possible—but those communities privilege some values while minimizing others.

In this view, articulated by French theologian Jacques Ellul, technology is at core a system of values that must be understood before any decision to adopt a tech-nology can be made. Failure to understand the values embedded in a technology can have many unintended consequences, some of them quite horrible.

Being a competent and ethical professional does not require you to resolve this deeply philosophical debate. But, it does require you to acknowledge that it exists, and to think clearly about whether, in the process of claiming efficiency, you have overlooked important questions of values.

THINKING ABOUT THE AUDIENCE: FROM PERSUASION THEORY TO PHILOSOPHICAL ANTHROPOLOGY

Psychologists first began to try to understand persuasion by working with a stimulus–response model. This early behaviorist approach led many to believe that the media could act as a "hypodermic needle" or a "magic bullet," sending a stimulus/message to an unresisting audience. These researchers, called "powerful effects theorists," found examples to support their theory in the public panic after Orson Welles's *War of the Worlds* broadcast on Oct. 30, 1938, and in the success of propaganda during both world wars.

But, the stimulus–response model proved a poor predictor of much human behavior. Later, communication theorists focused on cognitive psychology. Rather than analyzing persuasion as a simple behavioral reaction to a sufficient stimulus, these scholars theorized that how people think and what they brought to the per-suasive situation helped to explain persuasion. According to these theories, people

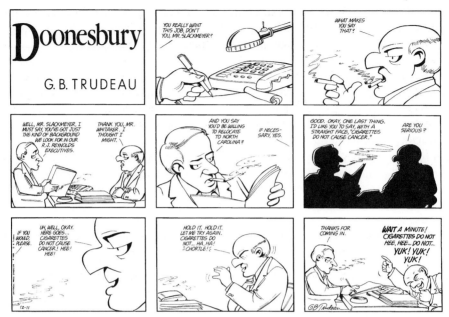

DOONESBURY © *G. B. Trudeau. Reprinted with permission by UNIVERSAL UCLICK. All rights reserved.*

strain toward cognitive balance. Simply put, we are most comfortable when all of our beliefs, actions, attitudes and relationships are in harmony, a state theorists called "symmetry."

Such theories have become known as "balance theories," since they stress the tendency of people to strive for cognitive balance in their lives. A person achieves balance only when his or her attitudes, information and actions are in harmony. Leon Festinger (1957) coined the term *cognitive dissonance* to describe the state where a message and an action give conflicting and uncomfortable signals. Think of it as knowing the hazards of smoking but choosing to smoke anyway, setting up a classic brain/action dissonance. The desire to eliminate that dissonance is a strong one, sometimes strong enough to influence purchasing behavior and voting habits—at least some of the time.

Advertisers use this theory. Knock a consumer off balance early in the commercial and to promise restoration of that balance through the purchase of a product. For instance, the opening scene of a commercial might suggest that your dandruff is making you a social outcast, and the subsequent copy promises you social approval if you use the correct shampoo.

Balance theories also explained why persuasive messages were sometimes quite effective while at other times inconsequential. No consequences to the problem, no lack of balance and subsequently no sale. This individually focused approach also provided the ultimate practical justification for advertising, the ancient Roman phrase *caveat emptor,* "Let the buyer beware." The creators of the ads were willing to assume little responsibility for the impact of their work, and academic studies gave them partial cover: if you can't prove that something's been effective, then it's unreasonable to suggest you take some responsibility for it. Even the FTC allows "puffery in advertising but not deception"—but they never tell you where they plan to draw the line.

Anthropologists assert that human rationality exists on equal footing with daily experience, language and symbols. Culture and our personal experience balance rationality (Wilkins and Christians 2001). If philosophical anthropology is correct, then ethical analysis of advertising founded in "Let the buyer beware" is morally unsustainable.

Instead, the ethical goal of advertising should be the empowerment of multiple stakeholders—from those who need to buy, those who need to sell, those who live in a community fueled by commerce and tax dollars and finally those who depend on advertising-supported news to be participatory citizens in a democracy.

If the concept of human being as creator of culture and then a dynamic user of symbols becomes an ethical foundation for thinking about the audience, advertising practitioners should be expected to operate within the following framework:

- Clients and the public need information that gives them "a good reason to adopt a course of action" (Koehn 1998, 106). The reason needs to be nonarbitrary and capable of helping people support one action instead of others.
- Rather than offering only expert opinion, advertising should foster ongoing discussion so that people can explore when options are sound and when practical knowledge (common sense) is superior.
- Advertising, just like news, can help foster reflective community, including the community of consumers. Just like the Super Bowl results are discussed at work the next day, often the creative ads that supported it are part of the social experience as well.
- Advertising needs to take seriously the role of culture in our lives. That means that advertising must authentically reflect the diverse voices that comprise our culture.
- Advertising will speak to the role of organizations in our lives. Questions of history and background can be conveyed in ads, but that must be done accurately and in context.

Given these general guidelines, let's explore a specific framework that puts ads to an ethical test.

THINKING ABOUT THE MESSAGE: A SYSTEMATIC TEST

The original TARES test is a checklist of questions the creators of every persuasive message should ask themselves to determine the ethical worthiness of the message (Baker and Martinson 2001). While the TARES test takes its inspiration from the "symbol formation" function of both advertising and news, public relations practitioners have added the significant element of advocacy to an ethical evaluation of public relations messages. Advocacy means "understanding and valuing the perception of publics inside and outside organizations" (Grunig, Toth and Hon 2000).

Advocacy also means communicating those perceptions to other publics, an effort that has become more complex because it involves relationships with multiple stakeholders "in a world of increasingly diverse and more active publics who are empowered by and connected through the Internet" (Fitzpatrick 2006, *x*).

Those who support the advocacy model argue that any misleading information put out by strategic communications professionals will be somehow "self-corrected" by the gatekeepers of the media or by the self-righting "marketplace of ideas." Those who reject the advocacy model do so on two grounds. First, they assert that advocacy too easily morphs into distortion and lies. Second, they argue that the long-term health of many enterprises, from business to government programs, is ill-served by "spin" and better served by honest, timely communication—even at the expense of short-term losses.

> Of course, public relations professionals do not enjoy the special status of the "Fourth Estate." Indeed, as representatives of *special* interests—as compared to the *public* interest—they and their clients and employers may have less protection from judicial forays into questions of ethics. Public relations professionals must consider both whether the special obligations associated with the freedom to communicate are being met and whether, in the absence of effective *self*-regulation, the government might step in to hold practitioners accountable for irresponsible behavior," (Fitzpatrick 2006, 16) [italics in the original]

To help you think through the ethical issues that persuasion raises—particularly in the world of strategic communication where most professionals will be asked to meld traditional advertising and public relations, we have connected the approaches in both fields through a single, ethically based test of specific messages.

The first element of the test—**T**—stands for **truthfulness.** Are the claims, both verbal and visual, truthful? If the message communicates only part of the truth (and many ads do this), are the omissions deceptive? Conversely, a message would pass the test if it meets a genuine human need to provide truthful information, even if some facts are omitted. Does the technology used to convey the message obscure or help to reveal the truth about the claims? In addition, practitioners should be able to verify with clients the truthfulness of client claims, and they should provide information to their audiences that will allow them to verify the truthfulness of claims in messages aimed at the public.

The Cheerios television ads that emphasize eating Cheerios as part of a heart-healthy lifestyle could easily pass the first element of the TARES test. People do have to eat, and the ads provide needed information. The ads also omit some

---

The Amplified TARES Test of Ethical Persuasion

T	Are the ad claims **Truthful?**	**E**	Is there **Equity** between the sender and the receiver?
A	Is the claim an **Authentic** one?		
R	Does the ad treat the receiver with **Respect?**	**S**	Is the ad **Socially** responsible?

information—for example, the other components of a heart-healthy lifestyle or the fact that other breakfast cereals also meet these requirements. But the omitted information does not lead the mature consumer to make false assumptions and bad choices.

In addition, telling the truth in times of crisis, such as becoming an advocate rather than an adversary in the long-term healthcare of a particular client, tests the foremost professional principles for public relations practitioners. The history of the field would suggest that businesses and agencies whose actions demonstrate that public health and safety are more important than short-term profits—telling the truth even when it hurts—are quite likely to profit and survive in the long term.

Step two in the amplified TARES test—**A** for **authenticity**—is closely linked to step one. Authenticity suggests that it's important not only to do the right thing, but also "to do it with the right attitude" (Pojman 1998, 158). We link this notion to the concept of sincerity. First, is there a sincere need for this product within the range of products and services available? Second, are the reasons given to the consumer purchasing the product presented in such a way that they also would motivate the person who developed and wrote the message? Simply put: would you buy your own reasoning about the uses and quality of the product advertised?

Authenticity, used in this way, is closely linked to disclosure, an important standard for public relations messages. The ethical end of disclosure is the generation of trust among and between various publics. "Ethical public relations professionals are forthright and honest and counsel clients and employers to adopt responsible communication policies built on principles of openness and transparency" (Fitzpatrick 2006, 13). Disclosure also demands providing information about who is paying for the message and who stands to profit from its success. Direct advertising of pharmaceuticals to consumers—once banned by law—often fail this part of the test.

Let's take a set of strategic communication messages about products designed to help elderly or infirm people live more independently. Although some of these products—for example, devices that turn on lights in response to a hand clap—may seem little more than high-tech toys, anyone with a grandparent in a wheelchair, a sibling crippled by an illness like rheumatoid arthritis or even a young person suffering from the imposed immobility of a broken leg can readily understand the need for such devices.

Others, such as advertisements for extended care facilities or supplements to existing insurance plans, attempt to focus on the human desire of independent living. But in making this point, if the messages stereotype elderly people as frail, helpless, weak or easily panicked, or if they knock otherwise healthy individuals off balance to sell a product based on fear, they do not authentically reflect the reality of life beyond age 65. The ad lacks authenticity based on an unrealistic stereotype of the early retiree. The TARES test would require rethinking the specific appeal in the ad to one that scares and stereotypes less and informs more. For creative people, such a switch is readily accomplished if they think about it. Just as important, a fresher approach might well sell more.

The **R** in the test stands for **respect,** in this case, respect for the person who will receive the persuasive message. However, as a shorthand way of thinking through this element of the test, it might be appropriate for advertising practitioners to ask themselves, "Am I willing to take full, open and personal responsibility for the content of this ad?"

Take the recent anti-texting-while-driving public service campaign that began with an ad of an actual car crash filmed from inside the car and its devastating aftermath. Even though the ad itself, which originated with a European government and went viral through YouTube, was filmed as a documentary, the campaign was criticized for its "scare" tactics. However, while the campaign relied on fear as a primary emotional tactic, it also provided rational reasons to not text and drive. Even though it was created by a government agency, the ad and its emotional appeal provide evidence of respect for human life.

The **E** in the amplified TARES test stands for **equity.** We conceptualize equity as follows: is the recipient of the message on the same level playing field as the ad's creator? Or, to correctly interpret the ad, must that person be abnormally well informed, unusually bright or quick-witted and completely without prejudice? Equity is linked to **access** for public relations professionals, and it takes its ethical power from the role of free speech in a democratic society. Free people are the autonomous moral actors that philosophers have long insisted must be the foundation of ethical choice and access to information equalizes an individual's ability to participate in the marketplace of ideas.

Think about this corporate image ad for Mobil Oil—the one with the pristine scenery, glorious sunset and an oil tanker. The ad claims that Mobil has the best interest of the environment at heart by building tankers with double hulls. While Mobil's claim—that it builds double-hulled tankers—is literally true, correctly interpreting the ad requires a recall of recent history. Mobil, and all other oil companies, were required by Congress to build double-hulled tankers after the single-hulled tanker, the *Exxon Valdez,* ran aground and spilled an enormous amount of oil in Alaska, an environmental disaster of the first magnitude. (See the Exxon case on the Web site for this book.) For the image ad to work, it counts on the average person not knowing—or not being able to connect—legal requirements with corporate behavior. The ad assumes (and actually depends on) an imbalance between the knowledge of the person who created the ad and the consumer. It flunks the concept of equity. Similarly, an airline company that brags about a point of customer service that has actually been codified by the Congressionally mandated passenger Bill of Rights, is relying on customer ignorance or forgetfulness to score points for behavior required by law.

Finally, the **S** in the amplified TARES test: Is the ad **socially responsible?** This is perhaps the most difficult element of the test for the simple reason that advertising practitioners have duties to many groups, among them their clients, the agencies for which they work, consumers, people exposed to the ad whether they buy or not and society at large.

Because this text emphasizes social ethics, we suggest interpreting this portion of the TARES test in the following fashion:

- If everyone financially able to purchase this product or service did so and used it, would society as a whole be improved, keeping in mind that recreation and self-improvement are worthy societal goals?

- If there are some groups in society that would benefit from using this product as advertised, are there others that could be significantly harmed by it? Are there ways to protect them?
- Does this ad increase or decrease the trust the average person has for persuasive messages?
- Does this ad take the notion of corporate responsibility, both to make money and to improve human life and welfare, seriously and truthfully?

For public relations practitioners, social responsibility also may be defined as **process,** whether public relations advocacy impedes or contributes to the robust functioning of the marketplace of ideas. An evenhanded process encourages both the journalists who use PR-generated information for news stories and various audiences who must rely on those stories as part of their decision making to use the information provided.

Using this concept of social responsibility should enable you to think ethically about television's decisions to air condom advertising. MTV, the network targeted at teenagers, chose to air such ads in 2000. More traditional network television outlets still do not. Which decision do you believe is more ethically justified? Why? Does the notion of social responsibility, and the process of democratic functioning, have any place in your analysis?

Or try this dilemma. With all the talk about global warming, there is one organism that thrives in a warmer subtropic environment—the mosquito that perpetuates dengue fever, a painful disease totally preventable by mosquito control. Does the "first world" have a right to advertise the comforts of energy consumption when a single degree's change in the world's climate allows more latitudes for the disease-bearing mosquito?

The amplified TARES test is a demanding one. But asking these questions, particularly during the process of creating an ad, can also be a spur to better, more creative execution and can be rewarded in the capitalistic marketplace. The TARES test may help advertising practitioners warn their corporate clients about the kind of advertising that could do them, as well as society at large, great long-term harm.

ADVERTISING'S SPECIAL PROBLEMS: VULNERABLE AUDIENCES

Advertising in a mass medium reaches large, heterogeneous audiences. Often, advertising intended for one group is seen by another. Sometimes the results are humorous, and maybe even a little embarrassing, as when ads for contraception or personal hygiene products make their way into prime-time programming.

However, in the case of Camel cigarettes' "Joe Camel" ads, this "confusion" of intended audience with actual recipients appeared quite deliberate. A few years ago, the Camel company agreed to withdraw the cartoon spokesperson "Joe Camel" from magazines and billboards after internal documents revealed the industry targeted underage smokers and sales figures bore out its success.

In other cases—for example, the beer industry—no such ban exists. Advertising intended for adults is often seen by those who cannot legally drink but do remember the catchy commercials and the presentation of drinking as something connected with fun and good times. Even young children remembered the recently used Budweiser talking bullfrogs and other creative beer ads. These ads air in a society when most adult alcoholics report having had their first drink when they were underage.

Are there certain types of audiences that deserve special protection from advertising messages? U.S. law says yes, particularly in the case of children. Legal restrictions on advertising targeted at children cover everything from Saturday-morning television programming to types of products and the characters that advertisers may employ. Children, unlike adults, are not assumed to be autonomous moral actors. They reason about advertising imperfectly, and in an attempt to protect them, American society has accepted some regulation of commercial speech.

However, the issue gets murkier when the target audience is formed of subgroups of adults—for example, ethnic consumers. Exactly when advertisers began to actively court ethnic consumers is uncertain. Brooks (1992) quotes a 1940 *BusinessWeek* article that reported an organization was established in Los Angeles to help guide advertisers who wished to garner the patronage of African-American consumers. Amazingly, the businesses were cautioned against using such words as "boss," "boy," and "darkey" in their ads. Instead, the advertisers were urged to refer to African-American consumers as "Negroes" who want the same things as other shoppers.

America is on its way to being a nation with no ethnic majority and the real attempt to court ethnic audiences began when those audiences acquired buying power. Hispanics are now the largest minority in the United States. The buying power of African-American consumers now tops more than $300 billion. The Asian-American market has also increased substantially.

Yet, a relative handful of advertisements reflect this emerging demographic reality, and commercials designed to appeal to this market segment sometimes employ troubling stereotypes or encounter other difficulties. For example, R. J. Reynolds Tobacco Company spent millions developing a cigarette aimed at African-Americans and put billboards in African-American neighborhoods to announce it, only to pull the product when consumer outrage caught up to Reynolds' plan.

Magazines pointed at teenage girls seldom reflect the reality of teenage bodies. Studies have shown that women who are exposed to such advertising images find their own bodies less acceptable. The same goes for facial features. Scholars have noted that the ideal image of beauty, even in magazines targeted at African-Americans, is a Caucasian one of small noses, thin lips and lighter skin tones. African-American women simply don't see themselves in these advertisements. Scholars in cultural studies argue that the impact of these repeated images is "cumulative." Ultimately, culture comes to accept without question what is nothing more than a gender or a racial stereotype and ultimately the stereotype becomes a "truism."

Few scholars have suggested that adults who are minorities need special protection from advertising. What they have noted is that ads that abuse the trust between consumer and advertiser have consequences. In the short term, products may not sell or may find themselves the target of regulation. In the long term, cynicism and societal distrust increases. People sense they are being used, even if they can't explain precisely how. The buyer may resort to avoiding advertising itself rather than to using advertising to help make better decisions.

JOURNALISM AND PUBLIC RELATIONS: THE QUINTESSENTIAL STRUGGLE

Public relations began as a profession in the late 19th century when newsmakers sought to find a way to get past journalism's gatekeepers to get their stories told from simple press releases to elaborate publicity stunts (such as the "torches of freedom" march for women smokers envisioned by Edward L. Bernays in the early years of the 20th century). For the client, PR practitioners offered free access to the audience; for the newspapers, they offered "free" news to publishers.

Despite the occasional animosity between journalists and public relations practitioners, the relationship is truly symbiotic—they simply could not live without each other. No news organization is large enough to gather all the day's news without several public relations sources. Business pages are full of press releases on earnings, new product lines and personnel changes, all supplied by writers not paid by the media. Travel, entertainment and food sections of newspapers would be virtually nonexistent if not for press releases. On the other hand, media outlets provide the all-important audience for an institution wanting the publicity.

With this common need, why are the two professions sometimes at odds? Much of the problem stems from how each of the two professions defines news. To the public relations professional, the lack of breaking news is newsworthy. Plants that operate safely and are not laying off any employees, nonprofit organizations that operate within budget and provide needed services, companies that pay a dividend for the 15th consecutive quarter are all signs that things are operating smoothly and make for a story that the public should hear. To the journalist, the opposite is true. Plants only make news when they endanger the public safety. Employees are at their most newsworthy when they bring a gun to work, not when they show up every day for 30 years.

The average news consumer rarely observes this constant struggle for control, yet he or she is affected by it. How should we evaluate a profession with the goal of persuading in a manner that does not look like traditional persuasion or the goal of preventing the dissemination of information that might harm the illusion that has been created? By undermining the concept of independent and authentic news messages accepted as credible by the public, are strategic communication practitioners undermining the central content vehicle for their messages? Doesn't persuasion need the contrast of news to succeeed?

More recently, the focus of animosity has centered on the concept of "synergy," or the notion that consumers should receive multiple messages for distinct sources, thereby increasing sales or public perception of particular issues. At the ethical core of synergy is the concept of independence—for the journalists who report on the news and for the consumers of both news and persuasive messages who need to make independent decisions about them. The current economic pressures on both strategic communication and journalism have intensified this tug-of-war over independence. Contemporary research suggests that synergistic concerns, particularly for those corporations that own both news and entertainment properties, is having an impact on soft-news program content (Hendrickson and Wilkins 2009).

PERSUASION AND RESPONSIBILITY

Hodges (1986) says that the notion of professional responsibility can be summed up in a single question: To what am I prepared to respond ably? In other words, what have my education and my experience equipped me to do and to assume responsibility for? Ask a strategic communications practitioner, "To what are you ably equipped to respond?" and he or she might answer, "To respond to a crisis for a client" or "To generate favorable media attention for a client" or "To generate increased sales for my client." However, there are greater responsibilities.

Hodges further states that responsibilities come from three sources. First, there are those that are *assigned,* such as employee to employer. Second, there are those that are *contracted,* where each party agrees to assume responsibilities and fulfill them. Third, there are the *self-imposed* responsibilities, where the individual moral actor takes on responsibilities for reasons indigenous to each individual. It is our contention that public relations, practiced ethically, will not only fulfill the assigned or contracted responsibilities with the employer or the paying client but also take on the greater calling of self-imposed responsibilities. These self-imposed responsibilities could include such constructs as duty to the truth and fidelity to the public good. The more self-imposed responsibilities the strategic professional assumes the more ethical the profession will become as practitioners see their personal good as being synonymous with the public good.

Suggested Readings

FITZPATRICK, K. and BRONSTEIN, C., eds. 2006. *Ethics in public relations: Responsible advocacy.* Thousand Oaks, CA: Sage Publications.

HODGES, LOUIS. 1986. "Defining press responsibility: A functional approach." In D. Elliott (ed.), *Responsible journalism.* (pp. 13–31). Newbury Park, CA: Sage Publications, Inc.

VONNEGUT, KURT. 1952. *Player piano.* New York: Dell Publishing Co.

BAKER, S. and MARTINSON, D. 2001. "The TARES test: Five principles of ethical persuasion." *Journal of Mass Media Ethics* Vol. 16, Nos. 2 and 3.

FESTINGER, L. 1957. *A theory of cognitive dissonance.* Stanford, CA: Stanford University Press.

LEISS, WILLIAM, STEPHEN KLINE, and SUT JHALLY. 1986. *Social communication in advertising: Person, products and images of well being.* New York: Methuen Publications.

O'TOOLE, JOHN. 1985. *The trouble with advertising.* New York: Times Books.

SCHUDSON, MICHAEL. 1984. *Advertising: The uneasy persuasion.* New York: Basic Books.

Cases on the Web

www.mhhe.com/mediaethics7e

"A case of need" by Deni Elliott
"Exxon's whipping cream on a pile of manure" by JoAnn M. Valenti
"A sobering dilemma" by Beverly Horvit
"Superman's Super Bowl Miracle" by Renita Coleman
"The Plagiarism Factory" by John P. Ferré
"Handling the media in times of crisis: Lessons from the Oklahoma City bombing" by Jon
    Hansen
"Public relations role in the Alar scare" by Philip Patterson
"Endowment or escarpment: The case of the faculty chair" by Ginny Whitehouse
"The gym shoe phenomenon: Social values vs. marketability" by Gail Baker

CHAPTER 3 CASES

CASE 3-A

Corporate Responsibility: Just Sales or Doing Well by Doing Good?

CHRISTINE LESICKO
University of Missouri

Being environmentally conscious is the wave of the present. In an effort to go green, top water purification system manufacturer, Brita, has launched a campaign Web site designed to influence people to stop using water bottled in plastic.

The Web site, filterforgood.com, includes statistics on plastic bottle waste, a pledge one can take, plus statistics of how many bottles have been saved by those who took the pledge. The Web site also includes links to the NBC show "The Biggest Loser," a weight-loss reality show, and where to buy Brita products. The site also promotes Nalgene reusable bottles, a bike race for the environmental cause and a college grant program.

Facts included on filterforgood.com are, "America used 50 billion water bottles in 2006 and sent 38 billion bottles to landfills, the equivalent of 912 million gallons of oil." The Web site reports, "The energy we waste using bottled water would be enough to power 190,000 homes."

If Web site visitors opt to pledge to reduce plastic bottle waste, they receive a coupon and more information about Brita filtration systems. Visitors can also purchase a "handy kit" to help become more eco-friendly which includes a Filter-ForGood Nalgene bottle, 10 On the Go sticks from Crystal Light, Kool-Aid and Country Time, along with other offers and coupons.

Brita's campaign is obviously not hiding its affiliation with sponsors. However, as a news article in the *New York Times* noted, Clorox—Brita's parent company— does not take back used water filters, which means there is no effective way to recycle them. Beth Terry, who developed the Web site TakeBacktheFilter.org, notes "in order to give up bottled water, you have to switch to another plastic product that's not recyclable."

The Web site includes a petition to Clorox to initiate a recycling program plus collecting used filters for recycling. The site also notes, "while the original European Brita GmbH Company has created a take-back recycling program for its filter cartridges, Clorox has no such program in place for reusing or recycling Brita cartridges." The site commends Clorox for what it is doing, but also notes the underlying irony of the campaign itself.

Micro Issues

1. Should those who developed the Brita campaign have investigated whether the filters could be recycled before they went public with the effort?
2. Should news journalists investigate campaigns of this sort and write about what they find?

3. How does this effort at corporate social responsibility seem like or unlike others—for example, turning in the tops of yogurt containers in exchange for corporate donations to breast cancer research?

Midrange Issues

1. Evaluate Brita's campaign using the expanded TARES test.
2. Evaluate the need for bottled water—which used to be uncommon in the United States—according to the expanded TARES test.
3. Should consumers base their purchasing decisions, in part, on efforts such as these?

Macro Issues

1. Take the notion of a campaign for a supposedly environmentally friendly disposable diaper, assuming there is one. What would a campaign like this look like from a communitarian philosophy? A utilitarian one? How would the campaigns be similar? How would they differ?
2. Does the concept of transparency apply to corporate social responsibility? If so, how? If not, why not?
3. In this and similar cases, to whom should the strategic communications professional be loyal? Why?

CASE 3-B

Tailgate Approved? The Rise and Fall of the Fan Can

ERIN SCHAUSTER
University of Missouri

Exposure to alcohol advertising is vast. According to the American Medical Association (AMA), the alcohol industry spends around $4.8 billion a year on advertising. In the United States, alcohol advertising is self-regulated with the general rule that such ads run only where the target intended audience is made up of at least 70% of those older than 21. However, the final decision about whether to run such ads is made by specific media outlets.

There are nearly 11 million underage drinkers in America, according to the AMA. Underage drinkers have a generous expendable income which contributes to the alcohol industry's yearly sales, now exceeding $22 billion. Underage drinking is arguably a result of several influences including peer pressure, product accessibility, and enticement from advertising and promotional efforts.

Despite industry self-regulation, alcohol messages and promotions reach underage drinkers nationwide. According to Janet Evans, senior attorney for the FTC, "When you've got a college campus audience you've got a very large number of persons who are below the legal drinking age there, and in addition, you've got a population that engages almost exclusively in binge drinking."

Near the end of the summer of 2009, Anheuser-Busch (AB) launched a unique Bud Light promotion, just in time for football tailgating season. The promotion consisted of beer cans color-coordinated to coincide with school colors from 27 colleges nationwide. Aside from color palettes identifiable to specific colleges, Bud Light cans were void of reference to college names, logos, or school mascots. Examples of product packaging can be seen at the promotional Web site, www.tailgateapproved.com.

According to Anheuser-Busch spokesperson Carol Clark, the promotion was planned to coincide with the launch of football season and baseball playoffs. Timing was an important tactic, which was developed in part to revive the suffering sales of the company's flagship brand, Bud Light. During the first two years of the 2007 deep recession, sales of the nation's biggest beer brand declined for the first time in 27 years.

The Fan Cans were a voluntary promotion for beer wholesalers and nearly half opted in, according to Anheuser-Busch's Carol Clark. With half of AB's wholesalers distributing promotional cans, college campuses and college towns became the new promotional distribution grounds for Bud Light just in time for tailgating season. The high levels of participation initially appeared to underscore acceptance within college markets nationwide.

However, it didn't take long for college administrators to notice. Many protested the promotion and those comments were reported as news in the *LA Times* and by the Associated Press. Through their administrations, colleges expressed concern over the distribution and promotion of Bud Light to underage drinkers, questioned whether the Fan Cans infringed on trademark rights, and expressed concern about the social responsibility of alcohol advertising. Schools objecting and requesting to have the promotion pulled from their markets included Boston College, University of Colorado, University of Michigan, Oklahoma State University, University of Wisconsin, Iowa State University, University of Minnesota and the University of Missouri, home state to Anheuser-Busch's corporate headquarters until the brewer was sold to a German firm in the middle of the decade.

According to a letter from University of Missouri to the corporation, Chancellor Brady J. Deaton said, "This is completely unacceptable and conveys the impression to the consumer that the University of Missouri is somehow supportive of this marketing effort for black and gold cans that were, in fact, never approved by MU." Boston College and the University of Colorado argued the colored cans implied colleges were endorsing the promotion through representation of school colors, even though no logo or names appeared on cans.

Anheuser-Busch agreed to drop the program within any college market that requested it. However, the company through its spokesperson insisted that its decision was not due to any agreement with the claims of irresponsible advertising. Anheuser-Busch maintained that it had neither infringed on any rights nor contributed to a socially irresponsible program. According to the firm's Customer Relationship Group, the promotion was neither college-specific nor team-specific, and the only correlation to sports was the promotion's launch time. Instead, the campaign was a promotion for the brand in general.

Anheuser-Busch promotes a high level of corporate social responsibility. At www.beeresponsible.com, which is also linked to the tailgate promotional Web site, the consumer is told, "Our message on college campuses is clear. If you're 21 and older and choose to drink, please drink responsibly. If you're under 21, respect the law; don't drink."

Despite abandoning some college markets, the promotion continued to run through summer into fall in some markets with continued promotional support online. The overall success rate is unknown. However, it could be safe to say that one clear result of the campaign is spiraling word-of-mouth for the Bud Light brand.

Micro Issues

1. Is it the college student's responsibility to abstain from underage drinking?
2. Do you accept Anheuser-Busch's claims that the campaign was not focused on markets with substantial underage drinking? Why or why not?
3. Should the media outlets in college communities have refused to run ads for the campaign?

Midrange Issues

1. Is the promotion in general and the news reporting after the complaints an example of the adage that any press is good press? How should journalists have covered the story to prevent giving Anheuser-Busch free media?
2. Do the Fan Cans resemble product placement? Do they raise the same sort of ethical concerns?

Macro Issues

1. Is self-regulation and social responsibility for spirits a concern for the alcohol corporation, wholesalers, distributors, media outlets or a combination of all involved parties?
2. Anheuser-Busch is now owned by a German conglomerate. Germany and much of the rest of the world have different standards when it comes to products such as alcohol and tobacco. Analyze the implications of culture in the creation of the Fan Can campaign.
3. Should alcohol advertising be regulated in the same way as tobacco advertising? Defend your answer.

CASE 3-C

Taking It for a Spin: Accepting Product Samples in the Newsroom

PHILIP PATTERSON
Oklahoma Christian University

To write an article on making the perfect "peartini" it helps to have the ingredients on hand. It's even more helpful if those ingredients come free—courtesy of a liquor company (Grey Goose in this instance) seeking publicity. The free ingredients and the story mix nicely (shaken, not stirred, perhaps?) at the Weatherford (OK) *Daily News.* That's because of a policy that asks supplicants looking for a free mention in a press release to submit samples for the staff to make up their own minds about the quality of the product and the newsworthiness of the story.

It began when publisher Phillip Reid decided the logical response to the more than 300 press releases daily (for a newspaper in a town of 10,000) was to ask the companies to put up or quit clogging up the fax machine. About half did, despite the lack of any promise of returns or reviews.

A wide variety of items have come into the newsroom, including the ingredients for a peartini, which Reid told the Oklahoma Press Association (OPA) made a "lovely story." Samples have included a scratch remover called "Applesauce," a concoction designed to clean the screen of your iPhone (it didn't), a robe and slippers, cell phones, candy, and coffee makers to presumably wake you after a night of drinking free bacon-flavored vodka. Dell sent a laptop computer.

Any reporter is free to pick up a product and try it out (though presumably some discretion was involved in the camouflage briefs with a built-in nightlight) with the clear understanding that no manufacturer is guaranteed a product review or favorable coverage. The decision, in effect, wrested control of the message away from the manufacturers with their carefully crafted press releases and back into the hands of journalists with their well-earned reputation for skepticism. When the product doesn't work, the paper is not afraid to name names. In the Applesauce story, the reporters sampled the competition until one worked as advertised.

Reid says he is motivated by a desire to change the habits of marketers who have little regard for the daily barrage of requests for what is essentially a request for free advertising. "Public relations agencies need to understand that we are not the free medium," Reid told the Associated Press. "We've had so much fun with this idea," said Reid, "but we want to get the point across that we're not free."

The mechanics are simple: the authors of unsolicited press releases received a return message asking for a sample. Mark Thomas, the executive director of the Oklahoma Press Association, said he sees nothing unethical about it.

> "Is it ethical to send people press releases and pretend it's news when it's advertising?" Thomas asks. ". . . If the person sending you a press release wants to convince you their product is really newsworthy, they ought to send you a sample and let you try it out."

But the idea has critics. Rick Edmonds of the Poynter Institute called the practice "dubious" and "horrendous" in an interview with the Associated Press. He likened it to "rolling the ethical clock back 40 years" to a time when deliverymen would roll in cases of liquor into the newsroom, particularly at the Christmas holidays.

On the other hand, Brenda Jones, the owner of an Oklahoma City–based PR firm (two hours from Weatherford), told the OPA that Reid has "every right" to ask for a sample to an unsolicited pitch."If you're promoting that product, then you better believe in it," Jones said."He's holding the fire to their feet and there is nothing wrong with that."

Some media organizations ban the practice of accepting samples or "gifts." The Associated Press directs employees to return items of more than a nominal value. The Society of Professional Journalists' Code of Ethics says reporters should "refuse gifts, favors, free travel and special treatment . . . if they compromise journalistic integrity," something Reid argues doesn't happen.

Of all the products sent to the *Daily News,* only Applesauce asked for the product back. Reid figured they wanted to test the sample to see if the consumer was getting what they paid for—something no press release can do.

Reid would like to see other papers try it, saying, "We've had so much fun with this idea. Now it's time to share our secret."

Micro Issues

1. Does this pass the "smell test?" If you are the competition to the *Daily News,* which are you more likely to do: try the practice or write an investigative article on it? Why?
2. Is the dollar value of the product a "morally relevant factor" (see Elliott essay after Chapter 1 for a discussion of this concept) in this practice? Could the paper accept a car, for instance? Defend your choice.
3. Does the company giving the product away have a reasonable expectation of coverage? Of favorable coverage? Does that expectation go up as the price of the free product goes up?
4. A few years ago, one athletic shoe company sent a single shoe to reporters at several media outlets. The second was promised—in the right size—if the reporter showed up at a press conference about the launch of the shoe. It was a record crowd. Would you accept the shoe if sports were your beat? If it were *not* your beat? Justify your decision.

Midrange Issues

1. How does this practice differ, if at all, from the media "junket" sometimes given to travel writers or film reviewers? From a press pass to watch a professional football game? Or a free ride on the team plan to cover the game? Does a poor economy factor in here?
2. According to Reid, the *Daily News* only mentions products when it's justified. Would it be more justifiable if the media outlet (newspaper, Web, television, etc.) had a regular consumer report with the story clearly identified as commentary?
3. Critique the statement of Edmonds when he accused the newspaper of "rolling back the ethical clock."
4. Is it fair to say a product doesn't work based on a one bottle sample? Justify your answer.

Macro Issues

1. Thomas implies that the reviewing of a donated item might be more ethical than running a press release without labeling it as such. Does he make a valid point? Justify your decision.
2. In the Applesauce case, journalists potentially saved consumers money by identifying a single product that didn't work. Does that "redeem" the entire practice?
3. If the practice of expecting freebies becomes as widespread as Reid says it should, can it be argued that the covering the cost of the freebies will outpace any potential savings from being warned of bad products?

CASE 3-D

Was That an Apple Computer I Just Saw? A Comparison of Product Placement in U.S. Network Television and Abroad

PHILIP PATTERSON
Oklahoma Christian University

Michael Scott, the buffoon-like office manager in the Emmy-award winning NBC comedy "The Office," shows up at casual Friday encouraging his shocked employees to check out his backside in his new Levi's jeans. In the wildly popular ABC drama/comedy "Desperate Housewives," Gabrielle (played by Eva Longoria) gets desperate enough for cash to model beside a Buick LaCrosse at a car show and for a mattress firm. In the now-cancelled "American Dreams," which portrayed American life in the 1960s, such American icons as Campbell's Soup and the Ford Mustang were woven into the show.

Hollywood calls it "brand integration." Its critics—some of them the very writers for shows using product placement—call it much worse. But by any name, the phenomenon is growing. During the 2004–2005 television season, more than 100,000 actual products appeared in American network television (up 28 percent in one year) according to Nielsen Media Research, generating $1.88 billion (up 46 percent in a year) according to PQ Media (Manly 2005). Advertising agencies have set up product placement divisions. Research organizations have cropped up to take on the task of measuring the effectiveness of product placement. And television shows in the United States seem to have an insatiable appetite for what they offer.

"The fact is, these brands are part of our lives, and brands exist in these television environments, so why not showcase them," said Ben Silverman, chief executive of the firm that produces "The Office" (Manly 2005, A14).

However, not everyone is pleased. In a 2005 meeting in New York during "Advertising Week," television writers protested outside a panel discussing the state of brand integration in television programming. Among their gripes: they want more of a say in how products will be placed and, inevitably, a share of the profits generated from writing a product into the script.

Most see the move as one of survival. Taking a cue from radio and its "soap operas," the original television shows were named for the sponsors ("The Colgate Comedy Hour" and "Texaco Star Theater"), and the audience had little option but to watch the ads. But while commercials undergirded the television industry for the first 50 years, the advent of the remote, and more recently TiVo have allowed consumers to avoid the very commercials that make the programming free.

"The advertising model of 10 years ago is not applicable today," according to Bruce Rosenblum, president of Warner Bros. Television Group. "At the end of the day, if we are unable to satisfy advertisers' appetites to deliver messages in new ways to the viewer, then we're destined to have a broken model" (Manly 2005, A14).

However, for government-sponsored television in Europe, the practice of product placement remains a sticky issue.

In a 2005 edition of "Spooks," a BBC drama, a logo for an Apple computer appeared in early airings of the show and then was removed in subsequent showings after British print media alleged that the Apple logo and others had slipped into BBC programming in exchange for cash and favors, which violates BBC rules. In Germany, firings occurred after public broadcaster ARD was found to have had shows full of illegal product placements for years (Pfanner 2005).

Not every European country has such a ban. In Austria, public broadcaster ORF airs more than 1,000 product placements a year on its shows and provides the ORF with about $24 million in funds to supplement its budget of approximately $1 billion. The ORF says that allowing the placements actually regulates what happens anyway. "If you don't regulate it, it exists anyway, in a gray zone," said Alexander Wrabetz, chief financial officer for ORF (Pfanner 2005, A15).

And even within the BBC, which has not announced any intent to change its ban on product placement, there are differing opinions. One BBC executive, speaking to the *International Herald Tribune* off the record said, "Back in the '50s, everything was called Acme, or we stuck stickers over all the brand names. There isn't a TV company in the world that does that now. Viewers don't find it convincing" (Pfanner 2005, A15).

Ultimately, success in product placement still comes down to whether the placement fits the plot. "The needle we have to thread," according to Johnathan Prince, creator of "American Dreams" and now working on Madison Avenue, "is to have brand integration that is effective enough to have resonance, but . . . subtle enough so that it doesn't offend" (Manly 2005, A16).

Micro Issues

1. Would you personally prefer to go back to the days where made-up names like "Acme" were placed on products to conceal the true brand names of the products?
2. Does the authenticity that real products such as name brand computers bring to a television show outweigh the intrusiveness of inserting a product into the plot of a show?
3. Are products placed into television shows the "price" you pay for free television, just as watching 30-second commercials were the "price" your parents and grandparents paid?

Midrange Issues

1. News magazines such as *Newsweek* will often run multi-page special sections on issues such as "Women's Health," and all of the ads within the section will be for products promoting women's health. What do you see as the difference between this practice and product placement on television shows?
2. Do you see a difference in whether product placement should occur in scripted dramas and comedies as opposed to reality television?
3. How does product placement in television shows differ from naming sports stadiums or college bowl games after corporate sponsors, where presumably they will be mentioned on air for free during newscasts? Should newscasters avoid the corporate names of these places and events?
4. When a news show ends with rolling credits that attribute the wardrobe of the anchor to a certain store, is that product placement? Is that an intrusion on the objectivity of the news? Justify your answers.

Macro Issues

1. If consumers are "zapping" and "TiVo-ing" through commercials in free television, what will happen to the medium if product placement fails to deliver the needed revenue to keep the programming free? What will happen to the United States if free television is eliminated?
2. In trying to "thread the needle" between effectiveness and offensiveness, what are some of the guidelines you would write for product placement?
3. Is the argument made by Wrabetz in this case an ethical one? Compare the argument to the five standards of the TARES test found in this chapter and see how it measures up.

CASE 3-E

Breaking through the Clutter: Ads That Make You Think Twice

FRITZ CROPP IV
University of Missouri

Controversial advertising campaigns were nothing new for Benetton when it unveiled its spring–summer 2000 worldwide communication campaign. In January 2000, "We, on Death Row," a statement against the death penalty featuring U.S. death row convicts, brought Benetton an unprecedented level of criticism, complete with an apology from its president and the loss of a potentially lucrative contract with a mainstream American retailer.

Benetton, the Italian clothing company, had a 15-year record of concerning itself with social issues, including peace, war, AIDS awareness and multiculturalism. Previous imagery featured a dying AIDS patient surrounded by his anguished family, a picture of a black horse and a white horse copulating, an unwashed newborn baby with an uncut umbilical cord, a buttock branded with an HIV-positive stamp, a priest and a nun kissing, the blood-soaked uniform of a dead Bosnian sniper, a white baby nursing at a black breast and the like.

Such ads invite controversy. The Vatican criticized the ad featuring a nun and priest kissing, and a French court ruled that the company had exploited human suffering in a campaign depicting dying AIDS patients and ordered it to pay damages to French citizens infected with the HIV virus. Yet Benetton seemed to invite the controversy, proclaiming its approach "looks reality in the face" (http://www.benneton.com) by tackling social issues. Company President Luciano Benetton said 10 years ago that "Our campaigns are an attempt to get away from traditional advertising in the belief that it has no power and no value any more." Adds Oliviero Toscani, Benetton's photographer and creative director, "My brief is not to concern myself with commercial images to sell more T-shirts but rather to create an image for the company that touches people in all of the countries in which Benetton is present" (Mundow 2000, 61).

While one cannot directly or singularly credit the advertising, Toscani's work has coincided with Benetton's worldwide growth. While critics decry the seeming vacuum between the provocative campaigns and the relatively mainstream Benetton stores and products, the company enjoyed a steady increase in worldwide sales and net profits through the 1990s. Benetton now sells clothes, accessories and sporting goods in more than 7,000 stores in 120 countries, with 70 percent of its sales originating in Europe (Conley 2000).

"We, on Death Row" began when Toscani began working with freelance journalist Ken Shulman to photograph and interview 26 U.S. prisoners on death row. The work culminated in a 96-page supplement in the January 11, 2000, edition of *Talk* magazine, followed by a series of individual pictures of the prisoners in selected U.S. magazines and on billboards in major U.S. cities.

"The campaign is about the death penalty," proclaims the Benetton press release on the company's Web site. "Leaving aside any social, political, judicial or moral consideration, this project aims at showing the public the realities of capital punishment, so that no one around the world will consider the death penalty neither as a distant problem nor as news that occasionally appear [sic] on TV." The *Talk* magazine supplement included pictures and comments from the prisoners, along with quotes from Pope John Paul II and the Dalai Lama. Questions were decidedly soft. Shulman asked inmates about their families, prison food, what they dream and what they miss, with no mention of the victims, no discussion of current feelings of remorse.

Given space limitations, the advertisements, which Benetton claims were decided upon after the pictures and interviews had been taken and completed, were limited to a picture of an inmate, a description of his crime, the method by which he would be killed, the words "Sentenced to Death," and the "United Colors of Benetton" logo. Seven inmates agreed to allow their photographs to be used for this campaign. Even less context is provided in this format. There was no warning for the victims' families that the pictures were about to appear.

When they did, criticism came from many angles.

Sears, Roebuck and Company canceled a franchising contract it had recently signed with Benetton. The contract was forged to help Sears with its declining clothing sales and help Benetton reestablish itself in the United States, which accounts for just 5 percent of the company's business. Further, Sears pulled from its shelves all brands owned by the global parent company.

California House leader Scott Baugh drafted a resolution urging all California residents to boycott Benetton until the campaign disappeared. The bill passed 59 to 8. Pennsylvania Attorney General Lynne Abraham called for a nationwide boycott. Activists from Parents of Murdered Children staged a protest outside Benetton's U.S. office in New York City. The company also was targeted in Texas by Justice for All, the New York group Center for the Community Interest and the International Union of Police Associations. Missouri Attorney General Jay Nixon filed a circuit court suit, saying that representatives from Benetton tricked their way into Missouri's jails by pretending to be journalists. "Selling sweaters on the backs of death row inmates is sick and wrong," he said.

Advertising critics were equally appalled. Bob Garfield, a columnist at *Advertising Age,* wrote, "There is no brand—not a single one—that has the right to increase its sales on the backs, on the misery, on the fates of condemned men and women, much less their slaughtered victims" (Steuver 2000, C01).

In April 2000, Benetton announced that Toscani, who once said there is no such thing as going too far (Hughes 2000), was leaving after 18 years. The company did not address whether the "We, on Death Row" campaign was a factor.

In the end, it is difficult to assess the cost or benefits to Benetton of "We, on Death Row." The $1.8 million in royalties to have been generated by the Sears deal represents a fraction of the company's $2 billion in annual sales. Similarly, the $15 million the company said it spent on global distribution, combined with the undisclosed production costs, may be balanced by the resulting publicity, which continues to build upon Benetton's edgy image among its young target as a socially conscious company. "A substantial number of consumers seem to sense genuine integrity and principle behind Benetton's actions," notes Patrick Allossery of the *Financial Post* (2000, C3).

Micro Issues

1. The 26 prisoners interviewed by Toscani and Shulman were convicted of 37 murders. Should Benetton have considered the victims' families before running its campaign? Should the company have given them advance warning that the images would appear?
2. Responding to 144 consumer complaints, the British Advertising Standards Authority accepted Benetton's explanation that the campaign was intended to encourage debate and remind people that even death row prisoners have human rights. Thus, it ruled that its duty was to uphold an advertiser's freedom of speech. When a clothing company exploits shocking issues in its advertising, is it an abuse of that freedom?
3. Was it okay for Benetton to expand its campaign to print advertisements and billboards without seeking the same type of permission it was granted prior to interviewing the prisoners for the *Talk* magazine insert?

Midrange Issues

1. It's been said that there's no such thing as bad publicity. Does the end of free publicity justify the means?
2. Does this type of campaign illuminate the issues or potentially trivialize them?
3. If the point of "We, on Death Row" was to raise awareness of issues surrounding the death penalty, is a one-sided approach appropriate? Should Benetton have sought opinions from people in favor of the death penalty?

Macro Issues

1. Should the definition of advertising be altered to include efforts such as "We, on Death Row," or should such campaigns be considered differently by review boards and by the media outlets that sell time and space?
2. Should standards be developed to prevent advertisers from insensitive or potentially irresponsible actions, or does paying for space or time supersede the need for balance, fairness or objectivity?
3. Benetton claims to "tear down the wall of indifference, contributing to raising the awareness of universal problems among the world's citizens." However, there are cultural chasms to be addressed. In this case, the company's belief that the death penalty is inherently wrong is consistent with European opinion on the issue but inconsistent with what many Americans believe. Should advertisers—or companies paying for space to espouse their own commentary—be sensitive to cultural differences? If so, what guidance should be provided for them?
4. Jim Faulds, an advertising executive in Edinburgh, says ads that go beyond the boundaries of good taste also push back those boundaries. People become numb to the shock tactics, and the only recourse is to shock further. Asks *Scotsman* reporter Michael Kerrigan (2000, 22), "As we recall the outrage that greeted those late 1990s campaigns we do indeed seem to be harking back to an age of innocence, long gone by. Have we, too, been implicated in Benetton's little habit?"

CASE 3-F

In the Eye of the Beholder: Dove's Campaign for Real Beauty

BRANDI HERMAN-ROSE
University of Missouri-Columbia

In the summer of 2005, Dove, a division of Unilever Corporation, launched its campaign for real beauty in the U.K. (see www.campaignforrealbeauty.com). This marketing campaign—initially to promote skincare products such as a firming lotion—has expanded to include public service ads and promotions that simply question what constitutes real beauty.

Dove's campaign has drawn extensive media attention because it features six very unconventional models. They range in dress size from 6 to 14 and have different body types. Some have tattoos. Others have larger thighs. Dove touts these models as "real women" with "real beauty."

To view a number of the ads that have run as part of this continuing campaign, go to the following Web sites: www.Dove.com or www.Campaignforrealbeauty.com.

These ads feature six women in no-frills white bras and panties. All six are in their 20s. They are of different races, sizes and shapes. One has a large tattoo on her thigh. They vary in height. One is lily white, others have curly hair.

Women are pictured large on billboards and print ads that ask about each woman's characteristics. One 95-year-old woman is pictured with the two words "Wrinkled or wonderful?" Another larger-than-average woman is pictured smiling broadly at the camera with the words "Overweight or outstanding?" Each ad features women who are outside the conventional modeling stereotype. Each image also asks whether the model should be described with a positive or negative word or phrase.

In an advertisement featured on TV for Dove's hair care products, women are seen walking the streets with identical blonde coifs. At a given point, these women pull off their wigs to reveal curly-, straight-, blonde-, brown- and black-haired women. This ad ran in multiple countries and emphasized the beauty found in each woman's unique hair type.

Other companies have tried to showcase real women in their ads without boosting sales or receiving the same recognition as Dove's real beauty campaign. So, how did Dove come up with this campaign idea? Did Dove push for this creative direction or was the idea the work of Ogilvy and Mather, Dove's advertising agency?

Dove's campaign for "real beauty" was the result of an extensive research initiative that studied 3,200 women in Argentina, Brazil, Canada, France, Italy, Japan, the Netherlands, Portugal, Britain and the United States. Of the women sampled, only 2 percent considered themselves "beautiful." Another 5 percent described themselves as "pretty" and only 9 percent described themselves as "attractive."

For the survey, Dove commissioned the services of StrategyOne and MORI International to ensure that the study met criteria and codes of conduct established by global research associations. In addition, Dove utilized leading independent thinkers and academic institutions for research design and data analysis. Finally,

Dove ensured that the study itself contained no reference to the brand or its parent, Unilever, and participants remained unaware of their sponsorship of the study (Lagnado 2004).

Dove, a company whose entire success is tied up in the actions and beliefs of women, is highly invested in research about women's belief systems. In a report entitled "The Real Truth about Beauty," the researchers (Etcoff et al. 2004) claim:

> Women's interest in and preoccupation with beauty, is not some easily dismissed concern. This study shows conclusively that women now judge beauty as important and even crucial as they navigate today's world. In attempting to democratize and make accessible to all the idea of beauty, women are eager to see a redefinition and expansion of the ideals, along the lines they see it and away from the limiting, narrowed and restricted body shapes and sizes we see in moving images and in print.

The campaign for real beauty launched in the summer of 2005 in the U.K. to wide acclaim in the British press, and that same media attention spread throughout the United States and worldwide. This global campaign has received a mixture of praise and ridicule.

Alicia Clegg, a writer for www.brandchannel.com, wrote about the real beauty campaign after its launch in the U.K. "By showing a wider range of skin types and body shapes, Dove's advertising offers a democratized view of beauty to which all can aspire. The campaign also has an implied moral purpose, one that takes on the ethical issues of consumerism" (Clegg 2005).

Despite the positive comments that Dove received, still others felt that the methods of marketing used for this campaign was nothing more than a veiled attempt to convince women of their imperfections. "Some people think that the ads were just a ploy for Dove to make money by trying to boost a woman's confidence, while at the same time catering to her insecurities by selling her a firming cream" (Marchese 2005). Still others (Gogoi 2005) have suggested that the only reason that this campaign showcasing "real women" works well at this time is because of the prevalence of reality television within the past few years.

When held up against other campaigns for beauty products, Dove is doing something considerably different. Campaigns for brands like Olay and Jergens, two of Dove's main competitors, feature long-legged, very thin women in sexy poses, choices that Ogilvy, with Dove's direction, avoided.

Dove's campaign has received more positive reception in the U.K. Citizens of the United States responded well to the ads for hair products, but getting U.S. women to see overweight women as beautiful has been a more difficult task.

Micro Issues

1. What about this ad represents an attempt to "cut through the clutter?"
2. Using the TARES test outlined in the chapter, how would you evaluate this ad?
3. What is the role of authenticity in getting consumers to buy products that make them look "better" than they really do?

Midrange Issues

1. The Dove campaign has been praised as an example of ethical advertising. Evaluate this statement.
2. What role does stereotyping—specifically about beautiful women—play in the creation of this ad? Is that use of stereotyping ethically distinct from ads that feature more traditional models?
3. To whom or what have the ads' creators been loyal?

Macro Issues

1. Examine the literature on eating disorders. What role do you believe ads play in the development of those disorders? How important is advertising compared to some other influences?
2. Since the population of the planet is aging, is what Dove is doing really just smart marketing? What role do you believe ethical thinking played in the campaign?

CASE 3-G

Quit, Blow the Whistle or Go with the Flow?

ROBERT D. WAKEFIELD
Brigham Young University

Anyone who spends sufficient years in public relations will face a crisis of conscience. Practitioners are trained for the tenuous task of balancing institutional advocacy with the "public interest" (Newsom, Turk and Kruckeberg 1996). Yet this role can lead to personal conflict, as it did in my case.

The setting was an urban school district with about 40 schools and more than 35,000 students. Its superintendent had a national reputation for innovative community outreach, and he was a media favorite. I worked with him for five years before he accepted a statewide position. His replacement was a quiet man with conservative views who, along with the administrative team he brought with him, believed that educators were trained to run the schools and could do so best with minimal interference.

Like most inner-city school districts, the system was losing students as people moved to the suburbs. In the previous decade, a student population that once filled four high schools could now fill only three.

The seven-member school board had approached—and then abandoned—the question of closing one of the schools because the proposal aroused such strong feelings among students, faculty and parents. However, the new administration, trying to balance those responses against the financial drain of supporting an additional high school on taxpayer dollars, decided to broach the question again.

Promised a tumultuous situation, the new administrators aggravated the problem by how they handled it. Rather than sharing the issue with the community or with school faculties to seek a mutually agreeable solution, they tried to resolve the entire problem behind closed doors.

I first learned about the closed-door approach at a "study meeting" with the school board. The new superintendent held these informal meetings during his earliest days in the district; they tended to be so boring and ambiguous that journalists seldom attended.

Before the meeting in question, the superintendent asked me whether any media would be present. I told him one reporter might come late. As the meeting began, I was surprised to hear him tell the board and the few staff members, "If any reporter shows up, I will change the subject—but today we're going to talk about closing a high school." He then outlined the results of meetings he had already held on the issue, discussed a proposal from a local community college to buy the building so it would not be abandoned and sought the support of the four high school principals.

Thus began my ethical conundrum. I agreed that the enrollment problem was serious and that closing a school was probably the best alternative, but I opposed the administration's method of resolving the issue. As public relations officer, I believed that public institutions must be open and that involving those affected by the closure in the actual decision-making process would eventually generate long-term support for whatever decision was made. I was appalled at the attempts to exclude the public; but I said nothing.

Closed doors can quickly swing ajar, and it took less than one day for news of the decision to leak. The school targeted for closure was one of the oldest in the state. It had recently received a U.S. Department of Education award as an exemplary inner-city school, but its community was the least affluent and arguably the least politically powerful.

The day after the "study session," and with a regular board meeting scheduled for the same evening, reporters called to verify what they were hearing. (Chief executives often forget that supervisors of individual units within the system have their own allegiances. In this case, one of the high school principals left the "study meeting" and informed his teaching staff that they would be receiving transfer students "from that inner-city school." The rumors began.)

After the phone calls, I asked the superintendent what he planned to say at the board meeting and was told, "We will discuss space utilization needs." I told him about the calls and that our jobs would be threatened if we were not truthful with the community. To his credit, he responded quickly and openly. The evening meeting unfolded as expected. The room was jammed with district patrons and with the media. The expected lines were drawn. Underlying the fervor was a common theme: closing a traditional high school was awful enough, but the secretive way in which the administration had reached its conclusions was unforgivable.

The next several weeks were an intense period of work for a young public relations officer. I did media interviews, talk shows and forums to explain the situation. I also met with dozens of teachers, parents and citizens, both to hear their comments and to take their suggestions. I had to be careful that my words represented the district instead of myself. I had worked with some local reporters for several years and felt comfortable giving them background so they could seek additional materials without revealing me as the original source. It was a personal risk, but the reporters never betrayed my trust.

Two additional incidents epitomized my ethical struggles. The first occurred after the initial board meeting, when a top administrator said the community misunderstood why decisions were made behind closed doors. I lobbied for openness. The administrator admonished me to remember who paid my salary, a rebuke that confirmed the new administration did not share my own values.

The second incident occurred when I was asked to meet with a man who had been chosen to speak on behalf of the community. I had taken only a few steps into his office when he said to me, "You don't agree with your administration, do you?" My response was silence while he explained his position.

For some reason, it was this encounter that forced my crisis of conscience: do I quit, blow the whistle or keep quiet? I had a wife and child to support; the employment picture at the time was not robust. Right or wrong, I surmised that the various relationships I had developed could appease many angry feelings. I also believed in the importance of education. So, I decided to stay through the crisis, then seek new employment.

About one month into the crisis, the board retained a consultant who, like me, believed in open communication. Two weeks later, four board members came to my office and requested a meeting. Because this constituted a majority of the board, such an assembly violated the law requiring the meeting be made public. I violated the law and invited them to stay. They said they were worn down by the constant tension and asked what I, as a public relations practitioner, thought they should do.

To me, the answer was straightforward. Relying on basic public relations formulas and common sense, I suggested that they could diffuse the tension by reverting to what should have been done in the first place: announce that selected representatives from throughout the city would form a committee to help review the situation and come to a decision that would then be discussed by the board.

To my surprise, the board members took this advice to the administration, and much of what I recommended was done. A few months later, the school was closed in a tearful farewell. And, five weeks after the school closed, I accepted a job with a local public relations firm.

Micro Issues

1. What sort of press releases or other talking points should Wakefield have prepared once the rumors began?
2. Should Wakefield have gone off the record with reporters he trusted?
3. Are there some sorts of decisions governmental bodies make that really should be kept from the media and hence the public? Is this one of them?
4. How should Wakefield have responded to the racial subtext of some of the protests about the closing of the school?

Midrange Issues

1. Should Wakefield have "blown the whistle" on the board members who requested an illegal meeting?
2. Was it appropriate for Wakefield to advise the board to take an approach different from that suggested by the superintendent?
3. How much does Wakefield's previous experience with a different superintendent influence his understanding of how the district works? How did this "workplace" socialization influence his ethical thinking?

Macro Issues

1. To whom should Wakefield be loyal?
2. Should he ever have told members of the community of his own personal views?
3. How does Wakefield's job compare with that of a press secretary for a political figure?
4. Is it ever appropriate to keep journalists in the dark about how political decisions are made?

CASE 3-H

Getting the Story, Getting Arrested: Photojournalism and Activism

LEE WILKINS
University of Missouri

British photojournalist Steve Morgan had worked as a freelancer for more than 20 years. Among his repeat clients was Greenpeace, an environmental organization that some characterize as radical, in part for tactics designed to stop various sorts of activities the group feels will degrade the environment. Supporters note that Greenpeace uses peaceful means to promote environmental change. However, the organization and its members have not shied away from direct confrontation, for example, attempting to physically prevent the killing of whales, when the environmental group and its members believe such action is warranted. All would agree that Greenpeace has a point of view.

On July 14, 2001, Morgan, along with Spanish videographer Jorge Torres, accompanied a group of 15 Greenpeace members as they protested a missile test off the coast of California, near Vandenberg Air Force Base. The protest involved boarding boats and sailing into the test path, an action that potentially could have stopped such a test. There had been previous protests at Vandenberg, but of the 50 people arrested as part of them, all had been charged with misdemeanors, which usually lead to a fine and probation.

Morgan's assignment from Greenpeace was to take pictures of the protest and to make certain those photos were circulated internationally by news services such as Reuters and Agence France-Presse (AFP). Greenpeace often employed the news media in this way to publicize its views. Morgan took a boat to the site of the protest, shot his photos and returned to shore. There he was arrested by the FBI, which charged him with trespassing, disobeying the orders of a federal officer and conspiracy—a felony.

Morgan's press credentials were examined and discarded by the FBI, Morgan said. He spent six days in the county jail, and then was allowed to fly home to Great Britain upon posting $20,000 bond, over protests of the prosecutor. About six months later Morgan returned to California with his wife and two children, where he was given probation by a U.S. court. The charges the journalists faced, and their sentences, were the same as those given to the protestors. "It was never my intention to go to the U.S. to break any laws," Morgan said. "I was attempting to document a protest, rather as I would if I were working for AP, Reuters, *The Guardian* or the *Independent,* and, as far as it's possible to be, I was there to be objective. As far as I was concerned, I was doing my job."

At the time of his sentencing, Morgan told the British newspaper *The Guardian* (which is considered the most left-of-center of the elite British print media), "As a photojournalist, my interpretation of events is shaped by my personal views and not by the persons or organizations who commission the assignments." A few months earlier, soon after his arrest, Morgan said that he would agree to work for Greenpeace again. "I would have no qualms about working for Greenpeace again—it would be determined by the kind of assignment offered. Greenpeace is an organization that in general I believe has done a lot of good. I may not agree with everything that they do, but agree in general as do most people that we all want to live on a clean and peaceful planet. But if I was asked to cover a demo involving the U.S., inflatables and the military, I think the answer would be pretty clearly: 'no, thanks.'"

Greenpeace saw the arrest as politically motivated and capable of setting a precedent for other photojournalists. "There is no question that there's some political motivation behind these charges," said Aaron Dyer, the group's lead attorney. "It doesn't appear to be related to Sept. 11, because it predates the attacks, but it does appear to be based on the desire of the Air Force to make a statement about these protests; and the government, the U.S. attorney general's office, seems to be assisting their efforts. It's inappropriate and it's unprecedented in U.S. jurisprudence."

Micro Issues

1. Should Morgan and the other journalist have been in the same boat as the protestors?
2. Does getting close enough to get a good picture—a professional necessity—lend some notion of support to the group?
3. Does the fact that Greenpeace hired Morgan constitute a real or potential conflict of interest for Morgan?
4. Should Morgan tell international news agencies that he is being paid by Greenpeace when he offers his work for sale?

Midrange Issues

1. How are freelance journalists like or unlike their salaried counterparts in terms of loyalty to their employers?
2. If you were a public relations professional, would you suggest that your organization hire its own photographer to cover events and provide the local media with the images? Does the kind of event matter?
3. Is Greenpeace's action in hiring a photographer ethically distinctive from political candidates who provide "photo ops"?

Macro Issues

1. In Europe, and in much of the rest of the world, news organizations are expected to have a point of view. How might that expectation change how editors would evaluate the newsworthiness of Morgan's pictures?
2. Was Morgan, a British citizen, ethically justified in relying on the U.S. First Amendment in his work? Should American journalists working in other nations rely on U.S. understandings of ethics and law, or should they adopt the local standards?

CASE 3-I

The *New York Times* Sudan "Advertorial": Blood Money or the Marketplace of Ideas?

HEATHER HOLLOWAY
University of Texas

The conflict in western Sudan began in February of 2003 when the Justice and Equality Movement (JEM) and the Sudan Liberation Movement (SLM), two local rebel groups, attacked government installations. The government was unprepared and responded with aerial attacks in Darfur. The attacks were carried out by Janja-weed, a militia group that recruited its members from local Arab tribes. According to the Save Darfur Coalition, the Janjaweed "received government support to clear civilians from areas considered disloyal to the Sudanese government." For its part, the government denies any connection to the militia group and issued statements calling them "thieves, gangs and crooks."

The conflict quickly took on ethnic dimensions based not only on race but also on economics due to the clash between farmers (primarily non-Arabs) and herdsmen (generally Arabs) for land and water. There are not any significant ethnic or religious differences between the two groups; both include Muslims, blacks and Arabs.

The tactics of the Janjaweed include indiscriminate killing and dismemberment of noncombatants, even young children and babies; systematically gang raping women; organized starvation and burning entire villages (Kristof 2005, Nov. 22). The people of Darfur live in fear of their village being attacked, their wives being raped, their children being brutally beaten to death or kidnapped and their homes and property being burned, leaving them to seek refuge in a nearby village where a similar fate may await them.

U.S. Secretary of State, Colin Powell, visited refugee camps of Darfur with the Sudanese foreign minister in the summer of 2004. He later testified before Congress that what was happening was genocide. The government of Sudan denied claims of their involvement, but Powell and his team of investigators "found that the government is clearly and directly involved in committing the genocide." Later, Congress, the Bush Administration and many others denounced it as genocide (Costello 2004).

Following Powell's visit, the conflict continued with failed attempts at compromise and a death toll that continued to rise. Save Darfur, a group organized to raise awareness of the conflict and to lobby for U.S. and U.N. intervention, claims that no one has been charged with any crime, and there remains a state of total impunity toward human rights violations. They compare Darfur to the Rwanda genocide of 1994.

According to reports by the World Food Program, the United Nations and the Coalition for International Justice, 3.5 million people are now hungry, 2.5 million have been displaced due to violence and 400,000 people have died in Darfur thus far. On April 30, 2006, Save Darfur led a rally in Washington, D.C. to raise awareness of the genocide in Darfur and to encourage the Senate to act.

As the conflict continued to escalate, militia attacks followed refugees over the border into neighboring Chad (Kristof 2006, March 7). The United States has had sanctions against Sudan since 1997. Initially the sanctions were because of Sudan's "support for international terrorism, efforts to destabilize neighboring governments and violation of human rights." More recently they are due to "allegedly encouraging genocide" (Weiss 2006).

Once the United States labeled the conflict in Darfur as genocide, the *New York Times* began covering the conflict intensely and has also covered groups like Save Darfur. Nicholas Kristof, a columnist at the *Times,* won the 2006 Pulitzer Prize for his commentary on the Darfur conflict. The Pulitzer board states he won "for his graphic, deeply reported columns that, at personal risk, focused attention on genocide in Darfur and that gave voice to the voiceless in other parts of the world."

Kristof spent a month in Sudan visiting refugee camps and destroyed villages and speaking with many who had suffered losses due to attacks by the Janjaweed. His reporting raised the public's awareness of the situation, and in later columns he urged the U.S. government and the United Nations to resolve the conflict. His proposals include sending troops and enforcing a no-fly zone from a French airbase in Chad (Kristof 2005, Nov. 22). Kristof has had the support of the *New York Times,* as evidenced by the editorials supporting his claims.

On March 20, 2006, the *New York Times* ran an eight-page "advertorial" supplement promoting the country of Sudan. The "Special Advertising Section" was written by Summit Communications, a public relations company that claims to hold an exclusive agreement with the *New York Times* to run ads for foreign governments (Salmon 2006). The advertorial looks more like a news page than an ad page, but it meets the requirements for advertorials set by the *Times* by being labeled as an "Advertising Supplement to the *New York Times*" in all caps and in an acceptable size. In addition, the insert does not use any style, layout or font of the *New York Times*. The cost of the insert was almost $1 million (Salmon 2006).

The lead story on the front page of the supplement was titled "The Peace Dividend" and promised that prosperity could lie ahead after years of conflict. The article quoted the Sudanese minister of investment saying, "The images that are being projected in the media do not present a coherent picture of Sudan in any way. Sudan is not only Darfur." The tone of the stories in the supplement was that the conflict in Darfur is minor compared to the prosperity of the rest of the country and that international media was blowing things out of proportion.

But the story reported in the editorial pages of the *New York Times* paints a different picture. According to Kristof, even getting an exact count of the number killed is impossible because of the government's attempt to cover up the atrocities.

There was an immediate reaction against the *Times* for accepting the advertorial. Activist groups claimed that the publication made the *Times* complicit in genocide. According to an article on the Pulitzer Prize Web site, Nicholas Kristof released a statement claiming that it "represents blood money" and "tarnishes a newspaper I love" (Chaffee 2006).

Catherine J. Mathis, spokeswoman for the *New York Times,* released this statement:

> The *Times* has vigorously reported on Sudan and our editorials have condemned the actions the Sudanese government has taken against its citizens. We accepted this special advertising section, however, in our strong belief that all pages of the paper's news, editorial and advertising must remain open to the free flow of ideas.
>
> In accepting it, we do not endorse the politics, trade practices or character in its leaders. Just as we print advertisements that rebut *New York Times* editorials, news articles or critical reviews, we print ads that differ from our editorial position. We do so in the belief that it is in the best interests of our readers for our pages to be as open as possible (quoted in Salmon 2006).

Because of the sanctions against Sudan, the State Department investigated the *Times* for publishing an advertisement encouraging investment there. This investigation focused on financial transactions between Sudan, Summit Communications and the *New York Times,* not on the content of the advertorial. According to a spokesperson from the Treasury Department, since the advertisement was published but not written by the *New York Times,* it is permissible under the sanctions (Weiss 2006).

During the controversy, Allen Siegel, the standards editor at the *Times,* claimed that "news and ads occupy opposite sides of a church–state wall. Newsroom editors don't approve or disapprove advertising, just as ad sales people don't pass upon the news content." However, the *Times'* relationship with Summit is an ongoing one. On their Web site (www.summitreports.com) Summit Communications states (italics added):

> Summit Communications is dedicated to raising the profile of the world's most dynamic emerging markets. *Through an exclusive arrangement with the* New York Times *Advertising Department, Summit Communications has published over 112 reports since 1999, reaching the most influential decision-makers in the American political, financial, and economic communities.*

The *Times'* argument for running the ads has been questioned by many. "In the face of genocide that has been documented, the defense of 'free flow of ideas' doesn't hold water," said Cheri Hadley (2006), Chairwoman of Sudan Peace and Justice Committee of Dallas in a personal interview with the author. "I believe that this being published in the *New York Times* makes this complicit with the whole genocide campaign. I know those are strong words, but I truly believe that. They need to do something to ameliorate being bought off."

Micro Issues

1. Should the *New York Times* have accepted the ad? Does it matter if the "facts" of the ad do not match those being reported by the news department?
2. Is the *Times* "complicit" in the genocide by deciding to run the advertorial?
3. Should Summit Communications have taken Sudan as a client?

Midrange Issues

1. If the advertorial had been written from the Janjaweed perspective, praising the work of the killers in driving undesirables out of the country, should the *New York Times* have rejected that ad? If so, who decides what views are acceptable in advertorials?
2. If Summit Communications had released the video on its Web site as a video news release (VNR) with similar content to the advertorial, should television stations have run it in their newscasts? Why or why not?
3. Does your answer change if the VNR is labeled as such? If Summit pays to have it run during commercial time?

Macro Issues

1. Are the advertising pages of a newspaper a part of the "marketplace of ideas"? Should they be reflective in any way of the editorial stances of the paper?
2. Should advertorials be subjected to the same standards of truth as a newspaper's editorial copy?
3. If you were one of the "reporters" for Summit, how important would it have been for you that you agree with the policies of the government you are touting in the pages of the advertorial? Could you have done the job regardless of whether you thought government-aided genocide had occurred?

4

Loyalty: Choosing between Competing Allegiances

By the end of this chapter, you should:

- understand why the articulation of loyalties is important in professional ethics.
- know Royce's definition of loyalty and at least one of the major problems with that conceptualization.
- understand how journalists' role in society provides them with an additional set of loyalties to consider.
- be familiar with and able to use the Potter Box as a justification model for ethical decision making.

LOYALTY AS PART OF THE SOCIAL CONTRACT

Decisions involving loyalty occur routinely for media professionals. When journalists make a decision to air or not to air a story, they have decided to whom they will be loyal. When recording executives cancel the contract of a controversial artist to avoid a boycott, they have chosen a loyalty. In fact, most ethical decisions come down to the question "To whom (or what) will I be loyal?"

The original discussion of loyalty in Western culture was written by Plato in *The Trial and Death of Socrates* (see Russell 1967). In Plato's *Phaedo,* Socrates bases his defense against the charges brought against him on his loyalty to divinely inspired truth. When asked by his accusers if he will stop teaching philosophy, Socrates responds:

> Men of Athens, I honor and love you: but I shall obey God rather than you, and while I have life and strength I shall never cease from the practice and teaching of philosophy, exhorting any one whom I meet. . . . For know that this is the command of God; and I believe that no greater good has ever happened in the State than my service to God.

While the word *loyalty* is not present in English translations of the *Phaedo,* the overall tone of the work is a tribute to loyalty, in this case a willingness to die for a cause.

Social contract theorist Thomas Hobbes was the first major Western philosopher to assert that God did not have to be the focus of loyalty. In his historic work, *The Leviathan,* Hobbes asserted loyalty is a social act (Socrates saw it as political) and asserted that the agreement allows people to form a "social contract" that is the basis of society. Unlike Socrates, Hobbes acknowledged that people could have more than one loyalty at a time and might, at certain times, be forced to choose among them—a notion most philosophers hold today.

Hobbes, unlike Socrates, also asserted that loyalty has limits. Loyalty to the ruler stops when continued loyalty would result in a subject's death—the loyalty to self-preservation being higher than loyalty to the ruler. The turmoil surrounding U.S. involvement in the Vietnam War is a classic example of this type of conflicting loyalties.

THE CONTRIBUTIONS OF JOSIAH ROYCE

American theologian Josiah Royce, who taught at Harvard in the early 1900s, believed that loyalty could become the single guiding ethical principle. In *The Philosophy of Loyalty* (1908), Royce wrote, "My theory is that the whole moral law is implicitly bound up in one precept: 'Be loyal.'" Royce defined loyalty as a social act: "The willing and practical and thoroughgoing devotion of a person to a cause." Royce would be critical, therefore, of the journalist who gets a story at all costs and whose only loyalty is to himself or the public relations professional who lets loyalty to an employer cause her to bend the truth in press releases or annual reports. To Royce, loyalty is an act of choice. A loyal person, Royce asserted, does not have "Hamlet's option"—or the leisure not to decide. For in the act of not deciding, that person has essentially cast his loyalty.

Loyalty also promotes self-realization. Royce spent much of his academic career fascinated with the new Freudian psychology and he viewed loyalty in its light. As a person continued to exercise loyalty, Royce believed, he or she would develop habits of character that would result in systematic ethical action. Like other aspects of moral development (see the last chapter of this book), loyalty can be learned and honed, Royce believed.

Loyalty as a single ethical guide has problems. *First,* loyalty, incompletely conceived, can be bias or prejudice thinly cloaked. *Second,* few people maintain merely a single loyalty and if loyalty is to become a guiding ethical principle, we need to develop a way to help distinguish among competing loyalties. *Third,* in a mass society, the concept of face-to-face loyalty has lost much of its power. *Finally,* is the most troubling question of whether it is ethical to be loyal to an unethical cause, for example racism or gender discrimination.

However, Royce suggested a way to determine whether a specific cause was worthy of loyalty. A worthy cause should harmonize with the loyalties of others within the community. For instance, the loyalty of the journalist should be in harmony with the loyalty of the reader. The loyalty of the advertising agency should not conflict with the loyalty of either its client or the consumer. Our loyalty to free and unfettered political discussion as the basis of modern democracy and journalism meets Royce's test of loyalty but has started much debate over campaign finance laws.

To Royce, the true problem of loyalty as an ethical principle was not the poor choice of loyalties but failure to adhere to proper loyalties: "The ills of mankind are largely the consequence of disloyalty rather than wrong-headed loyalty" (Royce 1908). Causes capable of sustaining loyalty, Royce noted, have a "super-individual" quality, apparent when people become part of a community. A spirit of democratic cooperation is needed for Royce's view of loyalty to result in ethical action. For instance, advertising agencies demonstrate an ethical loyalty when they view their role as providing needed information for intelligent consumer choice, but more often they opt for loyalty to the bottom line because they suspect that competing agencies do.

Royce's thought has been criticized on a number of grounds. First, some philosophers assert that Royce's concept of loyalty is simplistic and that the adoption of loyalty as a moral principle may lead to allegiance to troubling causes. For instance, the advertising copywriter who scripts distorted television spots about a political opponent in the belief that she must get her candidate elected is demonstrating a troubling allegiance to a politician over the democratic process. Similarly, a reporter who must get the story first, regardless of its completeness or accuracy, would be demonstrating a misplaced loyalty to beating the competition.

Second, others have noted that Royce provides no way to balance among conflicting loyalties. Media professionals such as journalists are faced daily with a barrage of potential loyalties—the truth, the audience, the sources, the bottom line, the profession—and choosing among them is among the most basic of ethical decisions. Other professions have similar dilemmas such as the documentarian who must be loyal to the truth in her art while at the same time being loyal to the producers who want large numbers of the ticket-buying public to see the final product.

Third, it is unclear how Royce's ethical thinking would balance majority notions against minority views. Strictly interpreted, Royce's notion of loyalty could inspire adherence to the status quo or strict majority rule. For instance, advertisements that stereotype groups of people despite evidence to the contrary help perpetuate incorrect images. The ads work because they appeal to the majority, but by stereotyping, they have crowded out more accurate impressions.

Yet despite these criticisms, Royce's thought has much to recommend it. First, Royce speaks to the development of ethical habits. Second, Royce reminds us that the basis of loyalty is social and loyalty requires we put others on an equal footing with ourselves. Most important is the overriding message of Royce's work: *when making ethical choices, it is important to consider what your loyalties are and how you arrived at those loyalties.*

JOURNALISM AS A PROFESSION

Loyalty is not a fixed point but a range within a continuum. In *Loyalty: An Essay on the Morality of Relationships,* Fletcher (1993) identifies two types of loyalty. The first is minimal: "Do not betray me." The second is maximal: "Be one with me."

Between these two poles is a range of possibilities for allegiance and for corresponding media behavior. The location on the continuum for YouTube will differ from that of *The Nation* magazine.

One of the problems modern news media face is that a large percentage of the U.S. public subscribes to the notion that if the media are not maximally loyal—that is, one with government, the military and so forth—then they are traitorous. The media have been called disloyal by politicians, often for no greater sin than fulfilling the watchdog role.

Loyalty can be linked to role. A role is a capacity in which we act toward others. It provides others with information about how we will act in a structured situation. Some roles are occupationally defined—account executive, screenwriter, editor. Others are not: mother, spouse, daughter. We all play multiple roles and they help us to define ourselves and to know what is expected of us and others.

When the role you assume is a professional one, you add the ethical responsibilities of that role. Philosophers claim that "to belong to a profession is traditionally to be held to certain standards of conduct that go beyond the norm for others" (Lebacqz 1985, 32) and journalism qualifies as one of those professions with a higher expected norm of conduct.

However, not all journalists agree in practice. Hodges (1986) makes the distinction in this manner: when asked what she does for a living, one journalist says, "I am a journalist" while another says "I work for the *Gazette.*" Hodges claims the first speaker recognizes her responsibility as a professional while the latter merely acknowledges her loyalty to a paycheck. The first would be expected to be loyal to societal expectations of a journalist, the second may or may not.

Journalists and their employers have debated whether journalism should be considered a profession. Advocates of professionalism assert that professionalism among journalists will provide them with greater autonomy, prestige and financial rewards. Critics see the process of professionalization as one that distances readers and viewers from the institutions that journalists often represent.

Despite these debates, we sense that journalists have two central responsibilities that are distinct in modern society. First, they have a greater responsibility to tell the truth than members of most professions. Second, journalists also seem to carry a greater obligation to foster political involvement than the average person.

Philosophers note that while ethical dilemmas are transitory, roles endure. Role expectations carry over from one situation to another. Loyalty to the profession means loyalty to the *ideals* of the profession. To Aristotle, loyalty to a profession also would mean maintaining high professional standards. The Aristotelian notion of virtue means being the best television producer or advertising executive you can be in the belief that you are being loyal to the profession and its ideals.

CONFLICTING LOYALTIES

As you can see, we are no longer talking about merely a single loyalty. We live in an age of layers of loyalties, creating added problems and complications.

Sorting through competing loyalties can be difficult, particularly when loyalties in one role appear to conflict with the loyalties of another. Much has been written about this issue and we have adapted one such framework from William F. May (2001), who outlined these layers of loyalties for college professors, but they are adaptable to those who work in the media. He offers four types of loyalty.

1. Loyalties arising from shared humanity:

   - demonstrate respect for each person as an individual.
   - communicate honestly and truthfully with all persons.
   - build a fair and compassionate environment that promotes the common good.

2. Loyalties arising from professional practice:

   - fulfill the informational and entertainment mission of the media.
   - understand your audience's needs.
   - strive to enhance professional development of self and others.
   - avoid the abuse of power and position.
   - conduct professional activities in ways that uphold or surpass the ideals of virtue and competence.

3. Loyalties arising from employment:

   - keep agreements and promises, operate within the framework of the law and extend due process to all persons.
   - do not squander your organization's resources or your public trust.
   - promote compassionate and humane professional relationships.
   - foster policies that build a community of ethnic, gender and socioeconomic diversity.
   - promote the right of all to be heard.

4. Loyalties arising from the media's role in public life:

   - serve as examples of open institutions where truth is required.
   - foster open discussion and debate.
   - interpret your professional actions to readers and viewers.
   - serve as a voice for the voiceless.
   - serve as a mirror of society.

The problem of conflicting loyalties is evident in reality that most media professionals work for a corporation. They owe at least some loyalty to their corporate employers. However, such loyalty seldom involves a face-to-face relationship. Corporations demand employee loyalty but are much less willing to be loyal in return. The fear is that one's allegiance to the organization will advance the interest of the organization without any reciprocal loyalty to the employee. This is particularly true in the first years of this century when many news organizations, particularly newspapers, are going out of business or facing severe economic cutbacks.

Most ethical decisions, however, are not about loyalties to corporations or loyalty to an abstract concept such as freedom of the press or the public's right to know. Most everyday loyalty decisions are about how you treat the subject of your interview or how you consider the consumer of your advertising. Such ethical decisions bring to the forefront the notion of *reciprocity.* Simply articulated, reciprocity requires that loyalty should not work against the interest of either party.

Ed Stein © The Rocky Mountain News/Dist. By Newspaper Enterprise Association, Inc.

Even in a time of shifting loyalties, there are some loyalties that should only be reluctantly abandoned such as loyalty to humanity and loyalty to truth. *Virtually no situation in media ethics calls for inhumane treatment or withholding the truth.* You can probably articulate other loyalties you would rarely, if ever, break. Even if you can't foresee every possible conflict of loyalty in your media profession, knowing where your ultimate loyalties lie is a good start to avoiding conflicts.

THE POTTER BOX

Ethical decision-making models, such as the one in Chapter 1 by Sissela Bok, help you make an ethical choice. In this chapter, you will learn a second decision-making model, one that incorporates loyalties into the reasoning process. The model was developed by Harvard theologian Ralph Potter and is called the Potter Box. Its initial use requires that you go through four steps to arrive at an ethical judgment. The case below will be used to help familiarize you with the model.

> You are the assistant city editor for a newspaper of about 30,000 circulation in a western city of about 80,000. Your police reporter regularly reports on sexual assaults in the community.
>
> While the newspaper has a policy of not revealing the names of rape victims, it routinely reports where assaults occur, the circumstances and a description of the assailant, if available.
>
> Tonight the police reporter is preparing to write a story about a rape that occurred in the early-morning hours yesterday on the roof of the downtown bus

station. Police report that the young woman who was raped went willingly to the roof of the bus station with her attacker. Although she is 25, she lives in a group home for the educable mentally handicapped in the city, one of seven women living there.

She could not describe her assailant, and police have no suspects.

Your reporter asks you for advice about how much detail, and what detail, he should include in the story.

The Potter Box has four steps (see Figure 4.1) that should be taken in order. They are (1) understanding the facts, (2) outlining the values inherent in the decision, (3) applying relevant philosophical principles and (4) articulating a loyalty. You proceed through the four steps in a counterclockwise fashion, beginning with the factual situation and ending at loyalties. We will examine each step individually.

Step One: Understanding the facts of the case. In the scenario, the facts are straightforward. As the newspaper editor, you have the information. Your ethical choice rests with how much of it you are going to print.

Step Two: Outlining values. Values is a much abused word in modern English. People can value everything from their loved ones to making fashion statements. In ethics, however, values takes on a more precise meaning. When you value something—an idea or a principle—it means you are willing to give up other things for it. If, as a journalist, you value truth above all things, then you must sometimes be willing to give up privacy in favor of it. In the foregoing case, such a value system would mean that you would print every detail, because you value truth and would risk invading the privacy of a person who is in some important ways unable to defend herself. If, as a journalist, you value both truth and privacy, then you may be willing to give up some truth, the printing of every detail, to attempt to preserve the victim's privacy.

Values often compete and an important element of using the Potter Box is to be honest about what you really do value. Both truth and privacy are lofty ideals. A less lofty ideal that most of us value is keeping our jobs. Journalists often value getting the story first or exclusively. A forthright articulation of all the values (and there will be more than one) in any particular ethical situation will help you see more clearly the choices that you face and the potential compromises you may have to make.

Step Three: Application of philosophical principles. Once you have decided what you value, you need to apply the philosophical principles outlined in the first chapter. For example, in the previous scenario, a utilitarian might argue that the

Facts	**Loyalties**
Values	**Principles**

FIGURE 4.1. The Four Steps of the Potter Box

greatest good is served by printing a story that alerts the community to the fact that some creep who rapes women who cannot defend themselves is still out there. Ross would argue that a journalist has duties both to the readers and to the victim and they must be weighed before making a decision.

Aristotle's golden mean might counsel a middle ground that balances printing every detail against printing no story at all. Kant would suggest that the maxim of protecting someone who cannot protect herself is a maxim that could be universalized, making a decision to omit some information justifiable. He would also argue to not use the woman as a means to your end—an exclusive story in this instance.

In this case, application of several ethical principles leads to the general conclusion that the newspaper should print some story, but not one that inadvertently reveals the victim's identity or that makes her out to be hopelessly naive in her trust of strangers.

However, you should be alert that while different ethical principles in this scenario lead to the same conclusion, many, if not most, ethical dilemmas may not produce such a happy result. The principles point to different and even mutually exclusive actions on your part, leaving you to decide your ultimate loyalty. But this is why the Potter Box demands that you apply more than one ethical principle, so that if (or when) they vary, you are able to explain why.

Step Four: Articulation of loyalties. Potter viewed loyalty as a social commitment and the results of using the Potter Box reflect that ethic. In the fourth step, you articulate your possible loyalties and decide whether they are in conflict. In the case above, you have a loyalty to the truth, to the community, to the girl and to your job—just for starters.

But, your loyalties are not in severe conflict with one another unless you adopt an absolutist view of the truth the community needs to know. It is possible to counsel your reporter to write a story that tells the truth but omits some facts (for example, the woman's residence in a group home and her mental retardation), alerts the community to a danger (there's a creep out there who police haven't caught), protects the victim's privacy (you won't print her name or where she lives) and allows you to take pride in the job you've done (you've told the truth and not harmed anyone).

However, use of the Potter Box often highlights a conflict between loyalties. In these instances, we refer you to Royce's concept: what you choose to be loyal to should be capable of inspiring a similar loyalty in others who are both like and unlike you. Journalists are often accused of being "out of touch" with their viewers or readers, a fact for which we are highly criticized.

Our experience with the Potter Box has been that the vast majority of ethical decisions will allow you to sustain a variety of loyalties—they are sometimes not mutually exclusive as we saw above. However, those decisions that are most troubling are ones where a loyalty becomes so dominant that you are forced to abandon other loyalties that once seemed quite essential.

While you may initially find the stepwise process of the Potter Box somewhat cumbersome, as you learn to use it you will become fluent in it. The following case study, "The Pimp, the Prostitute and the Preacher," illustrates how you might use the Potter Box when making an ethical decision.

The Pimp, the Prostitute and the Preacher

You are the court reporter for a daily newspaper in a city of about 150,000 in the Pacific Northwest. About a year ago, the local police force began to crack down on prostitutes working the downtown mall. However, the department sought to limit prostitution by arresting pimps rather than by arresting either the prostitutes or their customers. The first of those arrests has now come to trial, and your paper has assigned you to cover it.

In his opening statement, the local assistant district attorney tells the jury that in order to convict a person of pimping under state law, the state must prove first that money was exchanged for sexual favors, and second that the money was then given to a third party, the pimp, in return for protection, continued work, etc. During the first two days of the trial, he calls as witnesses four young women, ages 14 to 16, who admit they have worked as prostitutes in the city but are a great deal less clear on the disposal of their earnings. Your story after the first day of the trial summarizes the details without disclosing their names.

Near the end of the second day, the prosecutor calls as witnesses men caught paying one or more of the women to have sex with them. Among those who testify is a middle-aged man who in an almost inaudible response to a question lists his occupation as a minister at one of the more conservative Protestant churches in the city. He admits to having paid one of the young women for sex, and that day's portion of the trial ends soon after his testimony is complete.

About 45 minutes later you are back in the office to write the story when the newsroom secretary asks you if you have a few minutes to speak with "Reverend Jones." You look up and realize you are facing the minister who testified earlier. In the open newsroom he begs you, in tears and on his knees, not to print his name. He even holds out a copy of the story you wrote on page one of this morning's paper outlining why the names of the prostitutes had not been used. He asserts that, should a story with his name appear, his marriage will crumble, his children will no longer respect him and he will lose his job.

After a few minutes the paper's managing editor realizes what is happening and calls you, the minister and the news editor into his office for a conference.

Using the Potter Box, determine how you would report this story. Your decision will reflect a set of loyalties as well as the values and principles you have chosen. Others may choose differently. A justification model such as Potter's or Bok's does not eliminate differences. What it will do, ideally, is ensure that your choices are grounded in sound ethical reasoning and justifiable on demand.

When you are finished, the final casting of loyalties will inevitably create another fact for the first quadrant of the box. For instance, in this case, if the decision is to run the name, anything that might subsequently happen to the minister as a result—firing, divorce, even possible suicide—is now a hypothetical "fact" for the first quadrant of the Potter Box and you go through again. If you decide not to run the minister's name and his parishioners discover his actions, the newspaper loses credibility. This is also a "fact" to be entered into the first quadrant of the Potter Box. Considering these additional although hypothetical "facts," you may want to go through the process again to see if your decision will remain the same. (You might search the Web or see the Web site for this book for the story of Admiral Boorda, who committed suicide after it was revealed that he wore medals on his uniform he had not earned.) Regardless of your initial decision about the story, would the possibility of that subsequent "fact," obviously not known to the journalist at the time, make a difference in a later use of the Potter Box?

Now that you've made a decision about revealing the name of the minister based on the facts, we'd like to introduce additional facts. Read them and go through the Potter Box again focusing less on the minister and more on larger issues that affect how the story is written and how it is run in the newspaper. This time, think about the notions of stereotyping, how minorities are portrayed in news reports and what exactly we mean by "objectivity" and "truth."

> As the trial continues, it becomes clear that there are other factors at work. In your largely Caucasian community, the only people arrested for pimping have been African-American. All the young women who work as prostitutes are Caucasian, as are the customers who testify. As far as prostitution goes, your Pacific Northwest version is relatively mild. There are no reports of drug use among the prostitutes and their customers, and none of the prostitutes has complained of physical violence. Further, the prosecuting attorney cannot make any of the young women admit under oath that they ever gave the pimps any money. The jury verdict in this case is not guilty.

Do the new facts change your loyalties? Do they change the way you look at the trial? If so, in what way?

We recommend that you try using both the Bok and Potter justification models at various times in your ethical decision making. Becoming a competent practitioner of both methods will provide you with greater flexibility and explanatory power. We also recommend, regardless of the approach you use, that an unvarnished and critical discussion of loyalty become part of your ethical dialogue. We believe it will enable you to anticipate situations as well as react to them.

Suggested Readings

FLETCHER, GEORGE P. 1993. *Loyalty: An essay on the morality of relationships.* New York: Oxford University Press.

FUSS, PETER. 1965. *The moral philosophy of Josiah Royce.* Cambridge, MA: Harvard University Press.

HANSON, KAREN. 1986. "The demands of loyalty." *Idealistic Studies,* 16, pp. 195–204.

HOBBES, THOMAS. 1958. *Leviathan.* New York: Bobbs-Merrill.

OLDENQUIST, ANDREW. 1982. "Loyalties." *Journal of Philosophy,* 79, pp. 73–93.

POWELL, THOMAS F. 1967. *Josiah Royce.* New York: Washington Square Press, Inc.

Cases on the Web

www.mhhe.com/mediaethics7e

"She chose before losing the choice" by Tom Lyons
"Standing behind a reporter: The CBS/*News Journal* Controversy" by John Sweeney
"The anchor as activist" by Fred Bales
"The wonderful world of junkets" by Ralph Barney

CHAPTER 4 CASES

CASE 4-A

Twitter Ethics for Journalists: Can You Scoop Yourself?

CHARLOTTE BELLIS
TVNZ—Christchurch, New Zealand

Journalists in every developed nation are experimenting with using Twitter as a reporting tool. The site allows members to post searchable updates of fewer than 140 characters at a time about themselves and the world around them in updates called "tweets." "In countries all around the world, people follow the sources most relevant to them and access information via Twitter as it happens—from breaking world news to updates from friends," reads Twitter.com. One blogger on CisionBlog headlines, "Social media is a virtual Rolodex for journalists and media relations people." ReadWriteWeb.com believes Twitter helps them with quality assurance, discovering breaking stories, conducting interviews and promoting their work. A columnist on Poynter believes Twitter's ability to search updates "could make it easier for journalists to track beats, trends or issues." However, some have questioned whether the personal element Twitter invokes could result in a lack of vetting, unethical behavior or a blurring of traditional boundaries between journalist and citizen.

In January 2009, David Schlesinger, Editor-in-Chief at Reuters, published a blog entitled Full Disclosure: Twittering away standards or tweeting the future of journalism? after twittering from the World Economic Forum in Davos, Switzerland. Other journalists there joined @daschles in his Twitter experiment as they pushed to be the first to break developments, post comments on the behind-the-scenes experience and promote their stories. With '#davos' as the standard signoff for the attending journalists, any Twitterer could follow a continuous stream of comments from the ski resort.

However, the *Silicon Alley Insider* highlighted Schlesinger in a story headlined "Reuters Scoops Itself By Twittering From Davos." While at the meeting, Schlesinger—under his Twitter handle @Daschles—had tweeted comments like, "[Financial speculator George] Soros—financial industry has to shrink by half! #davos." And another: "Soros—new financial system needs to emerge before we can talk about length of recession." The *Insider* article asked Schlesinger "If a Reuters correspondent had done that, would you fire him/her?"

Schlesinger responded that Twitter is journalism and that it has the potential to be dangerous. He said he was not embarrassed that his tweets beat the Reuters newswire, adding he was not destroying Reuters standards by encouraging tweeting. "If great storytellers use [microblogging, macroblogging and social networking] platforms to display their knowledge, access, expertise and abilities, I think that is a marvelous advance."

In a follow-up interview Schlesinger said he encourages his reporters to experiment but understood how his tweets could stir debate, particularly because journalism is at an "inflection point" in history. ". . . A company like Reuters makes most of its money from being first, so by challenging our own systems and thus business model I became a legitimate target."

"Twitter is such a fast medium that it challenges our standards to always have, for example, two pairs of eyes on a story," said Schlesinger. "Do we have whole new standards for Twitter? Do we allow the unedited and unvetted?"

As journalism works to remodel itself for the 21st century, many believe the instantaneous nature of the Internet is a key element in the industry's viability. For journalists the problem becomes should they publish—via tweets—information as soon as it is known, even when the nature of the medium itself dictates that the information will lack context. Or should the journalist hold off and spend time getting the context of the story, vetting it through a more regular editorial process and publishing it in a more traditional, less instantaneous medium?

Another problem for journalists using Twitter is that the social networking site was built for instantaneous, personal thoughts. Twitter naturally lends itself to divulging information as if to a friend and results in tweets that have a personal tone. Twitter makes it easy to muddle the personal and the professional as Canada's *National Post* technology reporter David George-Cosh, known as @sirdavid on Twitter, learned. After declining an interview with reporter George-Cosh, a marketing professional twittered: "Reporter to me, 'When the media calls you, you jump, OK!?' Why, when you called me and I'm not selling? Newspapers will get what they deserve."

The reporter saw the tweet and responded with six heated tweets that included multiple expletives directed toward the marketing professional. MediaStyle.ca characterized @sirdavid's response with this headline: "*National Post* reporter has total Twitter meltdown." Hours later, the *National Post* apologized on their Editor's blog for the reporter's conduct on Twitter.

Micro Issues

1. Do you think it is important for journalists to distinguish their professional roles from their personal ones on social network sites? If you do, how might that be accomplished?
2. If you were Schlesinger's editor, how would you have responded to him "scooping" his own organization on the story? Does it matter that the organization paid him a salary to do this work?
3. If Schlesinger were a freelancer, do you think the same rules should apply? Why and why not?

Midrange Issues

1. Has the advent of Twitter or the Internet changed the nature of the "scoop" or of objectivity?
2. Should news organizations, or individual journalists, develop policies outlining how they will and will not respond to things that are written about them or their work online?
3. Is promoting a story an appropriate use of Twitter? Who should do it? Why?

Macro Issues

1. Does the personal nature of a social networking site make it an inappropriate place for journalism? Does the fact that tweets are so brief? How might your answers be supported by concepts such as Ross's duties?
2. Ask your friends how much it matters to them that the news and/or entertainment media they use get something first. What do you think hard news journalists should make of these responses? Feature reporters?

CASE 4-B

Where Everybody Knows Your Name: Reporting and Relationships in a Small Market

GINNY WHITEHOUSE
Whitworth University

Everybody is a source when you're covering an agricultural town with a population under 12,000.

But Sunnyside Police Sergeant Phil Schenck had not been a source for Jessica Luce when he asked her out for a date during a Halloween party in 1999. Luce had worked as a general assignment reporter at the *Yakima Herald-Republic* for almost a year. Sunnyside, Washington, was one of four communities she covered in this first job out of college. The two spent time together infrequently over the next two months.

"I was interested in him, we had fun, but if I had been asked what was going on I would have said we were friends," Luce said.

Nonetheless, a co-worker was incredulous. Luce remembers him saying, "You can't go out on a date with a source. It's one of the biggest taboos in journalism!"

The *Herald-Republic*'s four-page code of ethics advises staff to avoid conflicts of interest but offered no specifics on personal relationships that might cause conflicts of interest.

Luce decided to keep her relationship with Schenck quiet. She had never needed Schenck as a source and never thought the occasion would arise.

Schenck's boss, however, was another matter. Sunnyside Police Chief Wallace Anderson had been accused of shooting a great blue heron outside the police station, storing explosives at the station house and of having a threatening temper. Following a lengthy and expensive investigation, Anderson resigned in November.

By New Year's Day, Luce and Schenck decided they were definitely dating. "I kept my relationship under wraps save for a few confidants at work. I felt the relationship would be perceived as something wrong," Luce said. "But I didn't see it interfering with my job. Phil and I didn't talk about work as much as normal couples might. We knew it wasn't fair to either one of us."

In mid-February, Schenck was named acting captain, the number two position in the Sunnyside police department and the official media spokesman. Luce realized she needed to be pulled off the Sunnyside police beat immediately. Her editors agreed.

"It was hard to talk with them about my private relationship and I was forced to define things about the relationship that I hadn't even done for myself," Luce said.

Craig Troianello, her city editor, sat her down for a long conversation. "Jessica made it easy because she was straightforward. We didn't ask intimate questions—that's irrelevant in this case," Troianello said. "By taking the proactive ethical stand that she did, it was easy for us to deal with this."

Luce said Troianello emphasized that he was not questioning her integrity. However, he had to make sure he hadn't overlooked something that could be perceived as a conflict by readers.

"This was a lesson on perception versus reality," Luce said. Luce's reporting did not affect Schenck's promotion, nor had Schenck ever implied that a story should or should not have been covered. Nonetheless, Schenck benefited from the chief's departure.

Troianello said he was never worried that Luce's reporting was compromised, but he wanted to make sure the newspaper was above suspicion. "Issues involving the police department were in the forefront of the news," Troianello said. "People could read anything into it—that she was protecting the chief, that she was trying to bring the chief down. Those kinds of spins drove my concern."

On the other hand, Schenck questions whether a strict conflict-of-interest standard is realistic in a small town. "Everybody is a potential source—even the clerk at the grocery store. We eat food. If her husband or boyfriend is a farmer, you could say she is promoting eating. This is an ideal that might be somewhat impractical," Schenck said. "If you can't be a real person, how can you report on real people?"

Luce says if she had to do it all over again she would not have kept the relationship a secret as long as she did. Nonetheless, it would still be hard to talk to a supervisor about dating. Troianello said he understands the complexities of a journalist's personal life but would rather Luce had brought the relationship to the newspaper's attention by New Year's Day, when the two began dating.

However, he understands the dynamic of the situation. "She's in a small town where the number of people with four-year degrees and professionals is small," Troianello said. "It seems like there will be some mixing at some point. Relationships could occur as naturally as it does in the newsroom. I married a copy editor."

Once their relationship went public (they were later engaged), Luce was surprised at how supportive the community and city officials were, including the new police chief (someone other than Schenck). "What we as journalists see as an ethical problem and conflict of interest isn't necessarily going to be seen as an ethical problem by the public."

However, Luce never heard comments one way or another from the former chief or his supporters. On several occasions, city officials have questioned whether Schenck leaked information to Luce or *Herald-Republic* reporters. Schenck simply explained that he had not. "I deal with stuff every day that Jessica would love to get her hands on," Schenck said. "But we just don't talk about it."

Luce now covers education in the city of Yakima.

Micro Issues

1. Did Luce have a responsibility to tell her editors about her relationship with Schenck? If so, when should Luce have informed them?
2. What responsibility did the *Yakima Herald-Republic* editors have to explain expectations on conflicts of interest? Is spelling out those expectations necessary or appropriate in a code of ethics?
3. How would the ethical questions have changed if Schenck worked in another capacity for the city, such as being a teacher?
4. How would the ethical questions have changed if Luce and Schenck had remained only friends?

Midrange Issues

1. What aspects of their lives should journalists be able to keep private?
2. Is public perception of an ethical problem truly relevant?
3. Journalists spend most of their time with two groups: their sources and their co-workers. Considering those limitations, is dating possible or advisable?
4. Recently, NBC "Dateline" correspondent Maria Shriver took a leave of absence as her husband, Arnold Schwarzenegger, ran a successful race for governor of California. As she returns to her duties, what limitations, if any, should be imposed on her reporting? Justify your decision.

Macro Issues

1. Can journalists cover communities effectively if they are expected to remain remote and removed?
2. How specific should codes of ethics be on conflicts of interest?

CASE 4-C

A Question of Role: Is a Documentary Filmmaker a Friend, a Journalist or An Entertainer?

NANCY MITCHELL
University of Nebraska–Lincoln

In 1998, independent filmmaker David Sutherland wrote, produced, directed and edited a story about a young Nebraska farm couple, Juanita and Darrel Buschkoetter and their three daughters. It is a riveting story of the family facing the dual hardships of trying to keep the family farm and the family intact. With more than 200 hours of film shot over three years, Sutherland painted a portrait of the impact of the economic struggles of family life.

Sutherland interviewed 40 families before picking the Buschkoetters. Sutherland showed the couple examples of his work so they knew what they were getting into. During filming, neither Sutherland nor his crew ever became friends with the family. However, he said he did develop a friendship after the project wrapped up.

The series won critical acclaim. The documentary was nominated for four Television Critics Association awards, including Program of the Year. The project also was included in many critics' list for Best of TV for 1998, including the *Chicago Tribune, TV Guide* and the *Boston Globe.* Steve Johnson, critic for the *Chicago Tribune,* called it: "One of the extraordinary television events of the decade. 'The Farmer's Wife' is a breathtaking piece of work, a harrowing intimate love story set against an unforgiving physical and cultural landscape."

David Bianculli, *New York Daily News* said: "Watching 'The Farmer's Wife' is time very well spent: This is an honest, haunting, unflinching instructive and intimate study of a family that seems doomed to fail, but refuses to give up easily." Ron Miller of *The Oregonian,* wrote, "Not until this week's 'The Farmer's Wife' has any filmmaker probed so deeply into the heart of an American family with such gut-wrenching results."

The film attracted 18 million PBS viewers when it first aired, making it one of the most watched series in PBS history. The six and one-half–hour documentary aired in three segments. The first segment introduced viewers to the Buschkoetters, who tell the story (without the intrusion of a narrator) of the troubles they face both in their marriage and the risk of losing the farm after years of drought.

The second segment chronicles family life and the relentless challenge to make ends meet and the danger of losing the farm. The loan officer, Hoy Bailey of the USDA, tells the Buschkoetters to ask all the creditors for an extension. In one scene Juanita drives at night to the office of one of the creditors, where she asks for a two-year extension. The creditor, Rich Kucera, listens to her and eventually agrees. The next scene finds Darrel in the kitchen of their home and Juanita arrives home to tell Darrel that Kucera has agreed, reluctantly, to extend their agreement. Darrel comments that he can't believe that Kucera was nice:

DARREL: "He wasn't even nasty?"
JUANITA: "No."
DARREL: "Richard, not nasty? That's a first. . . . I couldn't even imagine that guy being nice."

In the ensuing scene, Darrel calls Hoy Bailey. The loan officer tells Darrel that all of the extensions have been granted except for one for $100 and without that, they'll lose the farm in a buyout.

DARREL: "You mean $100 would cause a buyout?"
HOY: "Yep."
DARREL: "Don't you think that's a little bit ridiculous? I mean, if it had to be, I could go out and sweep a street and make $100 and eliminate a buyout."

The last episode depicts the resolution of their problems. Darrel harvests a bumper crop but suffers the stress of working his farm and another to make enough money to feed the family. After Darrel lashes out, Juanita takes their girls to her sister and leaves him, but they return after a week or so. Darrel seeks counseling and the couple seems to be saving their farm and their relationship.

Sutherland describes himself as "a portraitist," not an investigative reporter. He said he crafted the film in such a way as to let interactions tell the story without a narrator. Sutherland described the approach as "third person, close up." Sutherland said he had no agenda for the film but added that he was concerned about those being filmed trying to use him to promote their agenda.

In answer to the question of how far he would go to not interfere with the story he said: "If someone's life were in the balance, I'd have come up with the money." Sutherland said Darrel and Juanita's dream of saving the family farm was parallel with his own dreams of creating a documentary that was an intimate portrait with a social issue as a backdrop. To Sutherland, it was important to "talk to them [the subjects] from your heart and not taking advantage of them."

In the final episode, when Juanita left Darrel, Sutherland chose not to follow her even though Juanita gave him permission. Sutherland trusted the story could be told in another way at another time and he eventually captured a summary of the event after the family was reunited.

Response to the series and the publicity led to opportunities for the Buschkoetters. They testified before Congress on the plight of the family farm, traveled on publicity tours and gave speeches. Sutherland stated that the Buschkoetters' girls gained more self-esteem. Sutherland said the project "made me fall in love with America again. It was about people who tried their best. What more could you ask for?"

Micro Issues

1. If you were the producer, would you have lent the Buschkoetters the $100 if doing so meant they wouldn't lose the farm? What does it do to the story if you lend the money? What does it do to the story if you don't lend the money? What does it do to the family?
2. Would you answer the question differently if you were a news journalist working on an in-depth piece on the same subject?
3. Did Sutherland make the right decision about filming the marital breakup? By not following her, do you think Sutherland helped or hurt the situation, or was there no effect?

Midrange Issues

1. When asked if he thought the personal rewards of creating a documentary might be construed as using people for personal gain, Sutherland responded: "I'm as uptight about

them [subjects of his documentaries] using me." Evaluate this statement. Is this same tension prevalent in news journalism?

2. Sutherland describes himself as a portraitist, not an investigative reporter (e-mail to author, September 7, 2003). Do you think this gives him freedom to make different choices than he would had he claimed to be an investigative reporter?

3. Does having a camera present change the story? Do you think filming the meeting when Juanita asks the creditor for the extension on the loan changed the creditor's behavior? Does that matter?

4. When, if ever, can a journalist or documentarian become friends with those he has written about?

Macro Issues

1. Is it possible to produce a documentary from an objective point of view? What should be a guiding principle in creating this type of work?

2. Does a documentary need to conform to different ethical understandings than other entertainment forms—for example, reality television or a prime-time magazine show? Why?

CASE 4-D

Conflicted Interests, Contested Terrain: The *New York Times* Code of Ethics

BONNIE BRENNEN
Marquette University

In January 2003, the *New York Times* broke a lengthy tradition and published its new ethics code on the Web. The *Times* decision was an important one, for ethics codes are often controversial in both their creation and their application. However, ethics codes can be an important marker of specific social practices created under particular social, economic and political conditions at distinct times in history.

For example, members of the American Newspaper Guild in 1933 crafted one of the first ethics codes developed by journalists rather than managers. That code suggested the "high calling" of journalism had been tarnished because news workers had been pressured by their employers to serve special interests rather than the public good. Conflict of interest was centered on the relationship between reporters and sources and the code made a particular point that business pressures were putting undue stress on newsrooms. The code recommended that to combat business pressures the news should be edited "exclusively in newsrooms."

Ethics codes in general are controversial among professionals and scholars. Some maintain that ethics codes are nothing more than generalized aspirations— too vague to be of any use when specific decisions must be made. Others insist codes can be helpful to beginning journalists, photographers and public relations practitioners; they provide some guidance in the form of rules that can be internalized as professional expertise and experience deepen. And still others see codes as a manifestation of the ideology of an era—more about power and politics than ethics.

The new *Times* code linked its creation to the public perception of the "professional reputations of its staff member(s)." The code was directed to "all members of the news and editorial departments whose work directly affects the content of the paper."

The code focused primarily on conflict of interest. In fact, the code did not mention accuracy and fairness and devoted only a single sentence to privacy. However, when addressing conflict of interest, the code was both specific and detailed. The *Times* code considered the impact that spousal relationships might have on news coverage. It also addressed whether journalists working abroad should abide by the ethics and mores of the countries in which they are stationed, most of which do not provide the equivalent of First Amendment protections.

The code required staff members to disclose yearly speaking fees in excess of $5,000 and prohibited staff members from accepting gifts, tickets, discounts or other "inducements" from organizations the *Times* covered. Staff members could not invest in companies they covered, and payment for favorable or altered coverage was specifically forbidden.

However, staff members were allowed to do certain sorts of unpaid work—for example, public relations for a child's school fund-raising event. But *Times* staffers were forbidden from giving money to candidates or causes, marching in support of public movements or appearing on radio and television shows to voice views that went beyond those of the paper. When family members, such as spouses, participated in such activities, *Times* staffers were required to disclose those activities to management and recuse themselves from certain sorts of coverage.

The *Times* code was protective of the newspaper's place in the marketplace. Staffers were prohibited from disclosing confidential information about the operations, plans or policies of the newspaper to other journalists. Such questions were to be referred to management. If readers asked such questions, *Times* staffers were encouraged to respond "openly and honestly." *Times* staff members also were prohibited from doing freelance work for any media outlet that competed with the *Times*. "Staff members may not appear on broadcasts that compete directly with the *Times'* own offerings on television or the Internet. . . . As the paper moves further into these new fields, its direct competitors and clients or potential clients will undoubtedly grow in number."

Micro Issues

1. Should managers and owners be subject to a code of ethics, particularly for publications as influential as the *Times?*
2. Why is the notion of perception—as opposed to action—important in considering the issue of conflict of interest?
3. Should the *Times* code have addressed a variety of common journalistic issues—such as accuracy, fairness and privacy?

Midrange Issues

1. Disclosure is often suggested as a remedy for conflict of interest. Evaluate this remedy.
2. Should conflict of interest rules be different at a small newspaper as opposed to the *Times?*
3. Does the *Times* code infringe on staffers' First Amendment rights? Do journalists give up some of their rights as citizens in order to do the work of journalism?
4. Are there instances when recusing oneself from an assignment is unsatisfactory? What should journalists do if such a case arises?
5. Should a conflict of interest extend as far as prohibitions against a journalist being an officer in the parent–teacher association (i.e., PTA or PTO) of his or her child's school? An officer in your local homeowners' association? Does the potential for those organizations to get involved in the news pages (i.e., teacher problems, zoning protests) influence your decision?

Macro Issues

1. What are the specific historical developments in the field of journalism that may have promoted the development of this particular version of the *New York Times* code?
2. Research indicates that codes that are developed by the newsroom have a much better chance of influencing behavior than codes that are superimposed by management. If the *Times* had used this approach, would it have "discovered" the actions of reporters such as Jayson Blair (details of the Blair case may be found on the Internet)?
3. Does the *Times* code place the organization's financial health on equal footing with the public trust? Is that appropriate?

CASE 4-E

Freebies and the Houston Rodeo

JIM MATHENY
WBIR—Knoxville, TN

The annual Livestock Show and Rodeo is a long-time civic tradition in Houston. Begun in 1931, it has grown into the largest livestock show and rodeo competition in the world. The three-week event draws championship athletes competing for some of the largest cash prizes in the sport. The rodeo features performances from popular singers and entertainers.

Expenditures on the rodeo approached $220 million in 2005, but show officials say the return on investment is about $345 million (http://www.hlsr.com, Economic Impact 2005). A portion of the revenue goes to the rodeo's scholarship program. In 2004, the rodeo spent 17 percent of its revenues on youth programs and scholarships for Texas high school students to attend in-state colleges and universities (Feldstein 2005a).

The 2005 edition of the Houston Livestock Show and Rodeo was considered by many to be the most successful in history, breaking prior records for attendance and revenue thanks to good weather and performances by superstar entertainers including Hillary Duff, Alicia Keyes and Gretchen Wilson. Paid attendance for all shows totaled $1,127,239 and topped 1 million patrons for the 11th consecutive year (Chow 2005). The festivities are hosted in Houston's Reliant Park, a property featuring several facilities with a combined capacity of more than 150,000 seats, so there are still many empty chairs during the 21 days of rodeo and music. Only the most popular individual performances sell out Reliant Stadium, home to the city's NFL franchise. With lots of leftover tickets unlikely to be sold, rodeo organizers have routinely donated these less-desirable tickets to other organizations in the community.

Recipients of free tickets include media and news organizations. A spokesperson for the rodeo told this author that virtually every news organization in Houston received free tickets to the 2005 Livestock Show and Rodeo. The rodeo has donated tickets to the press for more than 40 years. According to the *Houston Chronicle,* 1,700 free tickets were distributed to television stations and the *Chronicle* itself received 1,200 free tickets (Feldstein 2005b).*Chronicle* reporter Dan Feldstein says his paper's relatively new editor was actually unaware that the tickets were free and assumed the donated seats were somehow part of a "trade-out" for advertising space.

In addition to the donated tickets, reporters assigned to cover the event received other complimentary goods. According to Feldstein, those covering the event could ask for up to 10 "free alcoholic drink" coupons. Camera operators and on-air talent from local television stations, as well as photographers from the *Chronicle,* reportedly redeemed the coupons.

One station accepting alcoholic drinks free-of-charge was KTRK Channel 13, the local ABC affiliate that has televised the parade on opening day since 1959.

During the 2005 Houston Livestock Show and Rodeo, Wayne Dolcefino, a colorful KTRK investigative journalist, reported on the nonprofit's spending habits (Feldstein 2005b). Editors at KTRK killed the story and Dolcefino protested the decision by refusing to work for two weeks.

While no one other than employees of KTRK had seen Dolcefino's story, Feldstein's *Chronicle* article said the story apparently implied that the nonprofit spent funds on unusually expensive office furniture and other aesthetics unrelated to their philanthropic mission. Feldstein also said Dolcefino inquired about the nonprofit's distribution of free tickets, alcoholic beverages and catering services to event volunteers and news organizations. Dolcefino's inquiries into the amounts paid to entertainers resulted in a lawsuit by the rodeo against KTRK because payment amounts are considered to be trade secrets and potentially valuable information to competing national events bidding for the services of the same entertainers.

Concerning the freebie practice Feldstein said, "I don't think most people thought about it, or, they figured nobody ever covered the rodeo like a news event anyway" (Dan Feldstein, personal communication, November 4, 2005). Feldstein acknowledged the problems for the news organization's reputation due to negative public perceptions and thought the practice should be halted, but he does not believe the gifts influenced news coverage. "Although the public perception of freebies is bad, a few cameramen having free drinks or staffers going to the shows is not going to influence an editor's decision . . . the tickets just aren't that valuable. Nobody in the media is falling over themselves to see Clay Walker perform in a cavernous football stadium for the 10th year in a row" (personal communication, November 4, 2005).

Sports journalists are routinely offered, and sometimes come to expect, free food in the press box. The office spaces of many sports journalists are littered with freebies from prominent athletes displayed as a badge of honor touting prior work experience without considering the possible implication of unethical behavior. Entertainment features writers are frequently sent free CDs and DVDs from entertainment companies hoping to provide exposure for their product via the media.

The Houston rodeo is simply an extreme example, considering the massive quantities of free booze available to on-duty reporters. In the wake of Dan Feldstein's article, the rodeo's organizers said free tickets would not be distributed to the media in the future.

Micro Issues

1. Should newspaper and television reporters and crews covering the rodeo accept free tickets to the event?
2. Should media employees who are not covering the rodeo accept free tickets to the event?
3. What are the motivations of the Houston Rodeo to give free tickets to the media? Did they overreact by withdrawing the tickets in light of the *Chronicle* article?
4. Do sports or entertainment outlets that give tickets to the media have a right to expect publicity in return? Do they have a right to expect *favorable* publicity?

Midrange Issues

1. Do you see a difference between free tickets to a sporting event where news will be generated and a resort or theme park where presumably the only reason for the junket would be free publicity?
2. Is there a different standard for accepting freebies in news as opposed to sports? Entertainment? Travel?
3. Do you see a difference in accepting tickets to an event that might help you cover a story and accepting memorabilia from that event? In accepting alcoholic drinks from the event?

Macro Issues

1. Is this a credibility issue? Do you agree with Feldstein's statement that none of the freebies influenced coverage? Justify your answer.
2. Does the benefit to your audience from the coverage that freebies allow—especially for far-flung trips your budget would not allow or celebrities you would otherwise never meet—overcome the question of credibility if the subject of the story pays a significant amount for you to be there?

CASE 4-F

Can You Relate: Cross-Cultural Sensitivity and Reporting

ISABEL ORDOÑÉZ
University of Missouri–Columbia

Author's Note: *Sources used in this case study are personal, phone and e-mail interviews with Christina Tercero, Jim Larsen and Macarena Hernandez and a content analysis of stories in the Whidbey* News-Times.

"I want to see you in my office now," was the order that Jim Larsen, editor of the Whidbey *News-Times,* gave Jessie Stensland, a veteran police reporter and Christina Tercero, a general-assignment reporter and photographer for the Oak Harbor–based newspaper, which covers Whidbey Island, Washington. Elaine Sepulveda, 15, had vanished on the morning of Nov. 6, 2004. During the visit to the Sepulveda's house, Tercero had been expected to take some photos and learn from the experienced Stensland, but it had developed into more than that.

"The family said they want to talk just with you," Larsen told Tercero following a call from a spokeswoman for the Sepulveda family.

Tercero, 24, was born to Hispanic parents in Portsmouth, Virginia. She graduated from Western Washington University with a degree in journalism in 2003 and interned at the *News-Times* that summer. Tercero had worked for the Whibey *News-Times* since September of 2004. She had to write stories, take photos and help with the page layout. But she had not yet covered the police crime or court beats.

When both reporters arrived at the home of the Sepulvedas, a Hispanic family from Texas, Stensland immediately began asking cold and direct questions that made the family feel pressured. They soon asked the journalists to leave. Soon after, however, Stensland and Tercero decided to return and, through Tercero, the journalists apologized. After Tercero offered their apology, the family told her that they would be willing to talk, but just with her. During the conversation Tercero spoke Spanish and explained that she understood the pain this tragic event brought to the entire family.

The Sepulveda family's request put Larsen in an unexpected situation. How would the newspaper provide the best possible coverage if the family was only willing to talk with a reporter with no experience covering crime? Larsen decided that Tercero would cover the family side of the story and Stensland would follow the investigation. The family accepted the decision.

During the next few weeks Tercero wrote two stories about a candlelight vigil in which the family and other members of the Oak Harbor community prayed to find the girl.

"Elaine Sepulveda used to kiss her mother on the cheek every day before she would leave to school. That kiss has not come to her mother's cheek for two weeks, since Elaine's disappearance," wrote Tercero in her lead.

Meanwhile, Stensland wrote four stories on the search. Tercero's role was limited to contacting the family when Stensland needed comment or information from them. "Because I had the link with the family they asked me to call," Tercero said. However, she didn't receive credit in the stories for her help.

On January 16, after police discovered Elaine Sepulveda's body in a grave under a compost heap, they arrested Sepulveda's 18-year-old boyfriend.

In a feature story published on Jan. 19, Tercero painted a portrait of Sepulveda's life in a sensitive manner, loaded with details she gathered through interviews in Spanish with the family. Tercero's piece gained the respect of Larsen, who assigned her a beat. She also gained the family's gratitude.

Did Tercero succeed in her coverage thanks to her Hispanic background and fluency in Spanish or was it due to her personality? Was Stensland's problem one of her ethnicity or her approach to the story?

Those questions are floating not only at the Whidbey *News-Times* newsroom but also in many U.S. newsrooms where editors often make assignments based on reporters' ethnic or religious backgrounds. And as even more minorities continue to populate all corners of the United States and newsrooms compete to hire minority reporters, the assignments these reporters are given will come under even more scrutiny.

For Larsen, using ethnic criteria in deciding who covers what in a newspaper "seems like a bad idea" adding that "any journalist should be able to cover any assignment in a small community such as the one this newspaper covers." The only exception, Larsen said, should be "if there is a language barrier."

Larsen believes Tercero succeeded due to her empathy and because she is a person with whom people are comfortable talking. "Our more seasoned 'hard nosed' reporter had trouble getting access to the family, but Christina quickly established a trusting relationship with them. I think it's more a personality issue," he said.

Macarena Hernandez is an opinion columnist for the *Dallas Morning News,* where she writes about Hispanic issues and is an advocate for diversity in newsrooms. She agrees that the relevant criterion should be the reporter's ability to get information and communicate with sources, not their ethnic origin. "I don't agree with the idea of hiring journalists just because they are minorities," she said. "There are people who apparently belong to a minority, but they don't speak the language or understand the culture of the group they supposedly represent."

Hernandez described her experience working for the San Antonio *Express-News* where she was assigned the minority beat, including the Muslim community. "More than once, I felt that I was doing a bad job with them because I don't speak their language," Hernandez said.

Larsen and Hernandez agree that the principles that should guide every reporter's behavior are professionalism and responsibility. "A reporter's responsibility is to the facts and fairness; if both are achieved, any community should feel well served," Larsen said. "First I am a journalist and second, Latina," Hernandez said.

Micro Issues

1. Should Larsen honor the request of the Sepulveda family? Does it threaten the editorial independence of the *News-Times* to be told by the family which reporter to send?
2. Should Tercero decline the offer and return to the family explaining that the community would be better served if the regular crime reporter handled the story?
3. Should Stensland agree to the arrangement?

Midrange Issues

1. Critique the final statement of Hernandez. Do you agree that one can be a journalist "first" and a member of an ethnic community "second" or is it impossible to separate the two?
2. Critique the statement of Larsen that using ethnicity to determine who covers a story "seems like a bad idea." Is it always a bad idea? When, if ever, could it be a "good idea?"

Macro Issues

1. Hernandez says that she disagrees with hiring journalists "just because they are minorities." What role, if any, should race play in hiring journalists? What role, if any, should race play in assigning beats?
2. Does a diverse news staff ensure diversity of coverage in the pages of the newspaper or the minutes of a newscast? If not, what else must happen?
3. What ways should the media employ to ensure diversity in news coverage other than hiring practices?

5

Privacy: Looking for Solitude in the Global Village

By the end of this chapter, you should be able to:

- **appreciate the difference between the right to privacy and a need for privacy.**
- **distinguish between the law and ethics of privacy.**
- **understand the concepts of discretion, right to know, need to know, want to know and circles of intimacy.**
- **understand and apply Rawls's veil of ignorance as a tool for ethical decision making.**

WHY PRIVACY IN THE NEW MILLENNIUM?

If one area in media ethics has been stretched almost beyond recognition lately, it would be privacy. The rapid pace of change has highlighted one of the most enduring understandings of philosophy: new technologies sometimes raise old questions and often in novel ways.

Consider Facebook. For most college students, on most college campuses, Facebook has become *the* social networking site—a place to meet people, talk to friends, form interest groups outside of geographical constraints and beyond the prying eyes of parents and teachers. Many college students access Facebook multiple times daily.

Facebook has rules. Facebook members can build a personal profile, and then control electronic access to it. If a member wishes to join another member's network, they must be granted permission. It is a good example of control over your own circles of intimacy—a concept in law you'll learn more about in this chapter.

In September of 2006, Facebook made changes that automatically alerted everyone in a user's network any time any other member of that person's network updated anything. Users were flooded with minutia. Even more objectionable was that messages intended for one person, or one part of a network, were directed to *everyone* in a network (Stanard 2006). The furor was immediate and passionate:

> If you don't want this information to be out there, don't put it on Facebook. How did the news feed work any differently than the real-world gossip chain? . . . Eh, maybe this will convince people that they shouldn't put their whole lives on the Internet.
>
> It's not the fact that they can see it, it is the fact that it is "broadcast" that makes it bad. I don't care that people I know find out that I break up with a girl, but I don't want it to be sent RSS style to everyone I know.

In 2006, Facebook CEO Mark Zuckerberg apologized to Facebook users and relented on the policy change. In 2007, Facebook users protested again, this time over a feature called Beacon, which tracked user actions on dozens of outside Web sites and revealed information about users' actions and purchases to their Facebook friends ("Facebook Users Protest Online Tracking" Nov. 30, 2007). The Beacon feature was removed from News Feeds, and users now have opt-out control over whether their data is sent to third-party applications. The protest of Beacon is significant because the tracking feature was similar to tracking tactics often employed by online advertising, though usually without user awareness.

Behavioral advertising, which matches online ads to user interests, has sparked similar concerns. Behavior advertising employs cookies stored on the user's computer and transmitted to an ad network that tracks user behavior. Similarly but using a different mechanism, Gmail, Google's free e-mail service, targets advertising to users based on keywords appearing in users' e-mail messages.

According to the Center for Democracy and Technology ("Privacy Implications of Online Advertising" 2008), a Harris Interactive/Alan F. Westin study found that "59% of respondents said they were not comfortable with online companies using their browsing behavior to tailor ads and content to their interests even when they were told that such advertising supports free services. A recent TRUSTe survey produced similar results. It is highly unlikely that these respondents understood that this type of ad targeting is already taking place online every day" (p. 6). Because users are commonly unaware of this practice, they are unable to take action to protect their personal information if they wanted to. Although Web sites and advertisers sometimes offer opt-out options for users, few consumers "have been able to successfully navigate the confusing and complex opt-out process" (p. 13).

Many forms of technology seem to default to openness rather than privacy, and require some knowledge and action on the part of the user to enhance privacy and security. Twitter, the technological rage in 2008 and early 2009, allows anyone who is willing to share the details of their life ("I'm waiting in line at the Department of Motor Vehicles now . . . boring!") and who can gather readers who want to read the 140-character "tweets" is free to do so. In fact some stars have tens of thousands of followers of their every move as recorded on Twitter. And when Twitter was hit with a "denial of service" attack in the summer of 2009, the fact that the outage made national news validated the popularity and, some might say, the utility of the site.

The foregoing flap makes some important points. First, privacy on the Web is still important—even though the law considers Web content quite public. Second, the comments above reflect some sophisticated thinking about privacy—thinking that is philosophical even though the language of philosophy is never used, showing that the average person is capable of talking about privacy in both practical and theoretical terms. Third, these comments remind us that privacy isn't just about sex, it's about control over who we are and what we do as human beings living our everyday lives and who gets a "behind the scenes" look at our lives. Fourth, technology is implicated in our decisions about privacy at what is probably a novel level in human history.

Privacy is behind a number of news stories. Here are but a few of the most famous examples.

- The alleged liaison between President Bill Clinton and White House intern Monica Lewinsky came to symbolize the media's apparent inability to make distinctions between news and what one scholar called "mediated voyeurism" (Calvert 2000, 23). Calvert lists such diverse activities as hidden camera reports, the paparazzi phenomenon and video surveillance and suggests that such technology-based media content has forever changed journalism. "Our notions of news and human interest stories have shifted over time. Today, voyeurism passes as news" (Calvert 2000, 29).

- In 2006, the CEO of Hewlett-Packard attempted to spy on members of her own governing board, including having private investigators pose as journalists and collect their phone records—an investigative method called "pretexting." This made national news, provoked a Congressional hearing and resulted in the CEO's resignation.

- "Dateline" achieved ratings success in 2008 with a series of shows that lured unsuspecting men to a purported sexual hookup with a teenage woman only to be caught on camera (and in the front yard by the law) all in the name of news.

- "CBS Evening News" anchor Katie Couric had her own colonoscopy broadcast on national television two years after her husband died of the disease. Talk-show host Oprah Winfrey videotaped women having mammograms from carefully selected camera angles to demonstrate that routine medical screening exams don't hurt and can save a life. In these instances, Couric and the women in Winfrey's report gave up some element of privacy that most Americans continue to cherish for the greater good.

- After the 2000 election, Tim Russert of NBC noted in an interview with then-Vice President-elect Richard Cheney that he had asked for specific information regarding the health of Cheney's heart for months only to be stonewalled. It was only after Cheney had a mild heart attack that the public got an accurate and detailed response to Russert's questions and learned that Russert had asked them in the first place. Ironically, Russert would die of a heart attack not long after his victory in getting the information about the vice president's heart condition.

Domestic politics are not the only place where the lines between private and public have disappeared. Reality television treats us to "Survivor" and "Temptation Island" while the Internet brings us images of journalists and civilians being beheaded during the Iraq war. We watch in horror as the victims of Hurricane Katrina emerge and then flip the channel to "Real World" and "Road Rules." The travails of O. J. Simpson (accused of murder) or Mel Gibson (accused of DUI complete with an arrest that prompted an anti-Semitic diatribe) or Brooke Shields (postpartum depression and an ongoing battle with Tom Cruise, who publicly questioned Shields's illness on Oprah Winfrey's show) were good for cable ratings and became a sort of reality television for the all-news set.

THE NEED FOR PRIVACY

The so-called *right to privacy* has been widely debated and written about, but the arguments are made more problematic by the fact that the term never appears in the U.S. Constitution. Relatively little has been written about the "need for privacy." Philosopher Louis W. Hodges writes on the *need for privacy,* saying that "without some degree of privacy, civilized life would be impossible" (Hodges 1983).

Both a personal and societal need for privacy exists, Hodges claims. First, we need privacy to develop a sense of self. Constance T. Fischer (1980) states that people need privacy to "try out" new poses, future selves and so on, without fear of ridicule by outsiders. If we are to become the person we wish to be, we need a certain degree of privacy to develop that person apart from observation. Religious cults that seek cognitive control over their members do so in part by depriving the members of any real degree of privacy, restricting both growth and reflection.

Second, society needs privacy as a shield against the power of the state. As the state gains more information about its citizens, it is increasingly easy to influence, manipulate or control each one. Precisely because the state is feared, limitations on the power of the state, such as the Bill of Rights, were established to protect private life (Neville 1980). Throughout history, totalitarian regimes have used extensive government surveillance—the near absence of privacy—as a major component of any attempt to create a uniformly subservient citizenry, a subject that dominates Orwell's *1984.*

Therefore, while much of the debate focuses on the *right to* privacy, an equally compelling argument must be made for the *need for* privacy. Privacy is not a luxury or even a gift of a benevolent government. It is a necessary component of a democracy and the foundation of freedom, individual dignity and autonomy. But journalists have often been caught between what the law allows and what their consciences will permit. This confusion has led to ethical bungling on a scale that undermines the profession's credibility and feeds the stereotypical notions that journalists will do anything to get a story, and that audiences will willingly consume anything the journalist delivers. These images not only are at odds with reality but also make getting and understanding legitimate stories even more difficult.

PRIVACY AS A LEGAL CONSTRUCT

The legal notion of privacy began in 1890 with a *Harvard Law Review* article, written by Samuel Warren and Louis D. Brandeis (who eventually became a U.S. Supreme Court justice), calling for a constitutional right to privacy. Thanks to a taxonomy worked out by Dean Prosser in another influential law review article more than half a century ago, today the tort of privacy is manifest in four distinct ways:

1. Intrusion upon a person's seclusion or solitude, such as invading one's home or personal papers to get a story.
2. Public disclosure of embarrassing private facts, such as revealing someone's notorious past when it has no bearing on that person's present status.
3. Publicity that places a person in a false light, such as enhancing a subject's biography to sell additional books.
4. Misappropriation of a person's name or likeness for personal advantage, such as using Hollywood megastar Julia Roberts's image to sell a product without her permission.

While this four-part list is straightforward, problems exist. Not every state recognizes every tort—particularly "false light." Also, our notion of privacy is dynamic, subject to change. What once might have been an embarrassing, private fact—for example, that an unmarried woman is pregnant—is now commonplace knowledge and, quite often, cause for celebration. In the past, cancer was rarely mentioned in coverage of the famous. Today it is not only mentioned, it is often used to raise awareness of the disease. It even enters into the realm of public policy, as when cancer survivors Senators John McCain or Arlen Spector refer to their own medical struggles in the very public debate on national health care reform. Similarly, one's sexual orientation has increasingly moved toward commonplace knowledge. But at the same time, information once available for the asking, such as a student's telephone number or the address of an individual based on driver's license registration, is now closed by a maze of privacy legislation enacted at the end of the last century.

To further cloud the issue, the claim to privacy is different for different categories of people. Public figures, for example, are subject to a different standard than are others. There are "limited" public figures and even "accidental" public figures thrown into the spotlight by chance. Just exactly who the courts will consider a public figure fluctuates, leaving a journalist doing a story in a vulnerable position. As the newspaper lawyer in "Absence of Malice" told the young reporter played by Sally Fields, "They never tell us until it's too late."

When the media invade privacy, a huge verdict can make a plaintiff rich, but it cannot return that sense of control the initial invasion takes away. And interestingly, the courts have never awarded the same mega-verdicts for invasion of privacy as for libel on the theory that one's reputation is more valuable than one's privacy. So the law provides an unsatisfactory solution both for journalists and victims. Ethical thinking prior to broadcast or publication is preferable to a court battle.

PRIVACY AS AN ETHICAL CONSTRUCT

The ethical basis for privacy is much older than the legal one and appears throughout literature, asserting that privacy is a "natural right," that we possess by being human. Privacy is considered a need, a way of protecting oneself against the actions of other people and institutions. Privacy carries with it the notions of control and limited access. The individual should be allowed to control who may have certain sorts of information and, sometimes, the context within which that information is presented.

Communitarian thinking links privacy and community instead of seeing them as competing forces. "A credible ethics or privacy needs to be rooted in the common good rather than individual rights" (Christian 2010). "Communitarians see the myth of the self-contained 'man' in a state of nature as politically misleading and dangerous. Persons are embedded in language, history, and culture, which are social creations; there can be no such thing as a person without society" (Radin 1982). In the communitarian view, the community itself—the larger society— benefits from maintaining individual privacy. That maintenance, however, is in some modest tension with the needs of the community. In communitarian thinking, corporate demands would be every bit as subject to restriction as government for the same reason—the health of the community which, in turn, supports the flourishing of individuals. Christians considers control over commercial data banks, along with government surveillance and invasive news coverage of victims of tragedy, as the most important privacy questions emerging in the 21st century. Although privacy is related to human experience, the concept itself is not relative. Perhaps the best example of this is Article 12 of the Universal Declaration of Human Rights.

European scholars have linked privacy with a capitalist market economy on the one hand and the interventions of the welfare state on the other. "What does privacy mean to the homeless and the unemployed? . . . Is there a point to privacy if people do not have the means and the power to enjoy freedom?" (Gutwirth 2002, 52). The central role of technology also influences contemporary theory. Scholars note that individual control over the bits and bytes of private information is much more difficult to accomplish (some assert impossible) for the average individual, particularly if that person is coerced by economic or political necessity (Marx 1999). Some outside of academia have suggested that in modern society the very notion of privacy is impossible. "Privacy is dead" headlines have been appearing since the 1990s. In 1999, Scott McNealy, then CEO of technology developer Sun Microsystems, called consumer privacy issues a "red herring," according to *Wired Magazine.* "You have zero privacy anyway," he said. "Get over it." McNealy's company was and is a member of the Online Privacy Alliance, an industry coalition that campaigns for self-regulation rather than government-imposed privacy regulations. And Donald Kerr, deputy director of the U.S. Office of National Intelligence, told *Newsday* in 2007: "In our interconnected and wireless world, anonymity—or the appearance of anonymity—is quickly becoming a thing of the past."

In philosophy, the concept of privacy cannot stand apart from community. Responsibility for keeping things private is shared: individuals have to learn when to share or withhold information, while the community has to learn when to avert its eyes. Legal scholar Jeffrey Rosen notes that this attention to the role of the community in avoiding "the unwanted gaze" (the title of his book) stems from Talmudic law. He writes:

> Jewish law, for example, has developed a remarkable body of doctrine around the concept of *hezzek re'iyyah,* which means "the injury caused by seeing" or "the

injury caused by being seen." This doctrine expands the right of privacy to protect individuals not only from physical intrusions into the home but also from surveillance by a neighbor who is outside the home, peering through a window in a common courtyard. Jewish law protects neighbors not only from unwanted observation, but also from the possibility of being observed. . . . From its earliest days, Jewish law has recognized that it is the uncertainty about whether or not we are being observed that forces us to lead more constricted lives and inhibits us from speaking and acting freely in public (Rosen 2000, 18–19).

The last sentence is important: fear of being observed causes us to partially shut down our lives where we are celebrating, mourning or just going about our daily pattern. The law is detailed and strict. If your window looks into your neighbor's private courtyard, you must seal your window shut.

Taken into a media context, the "injury caused by being seen" gets thorny. Part of the problem with a "shoot first, edit later" philosophy for photographers and videographers at the scene of a tragedy is that the "injury caused by being seen" has already been exacerbated by the camera. The injury is something the Facebook protestors understood intuitively—they wanted only their closest friends to know about their breakups, hookups, etc. Like the philosophical approach developed by the Greeks, privacy is linked to our ability to "become" human and retain some element of dignity while doing it. "Only citizens who respect one another's privacy are themselves dignified with divine respect" (Rosen 2000, 19).

THE CONTINUING CONFLICTS

But privacy is a complicated matter; it doesn't trump every other right in every context. In practice, protection of privacy or what constitutes invasion of privacy is not always clear.

Grcic (1986) asserts that privacy can be negated by more compelling rights. In simpler times, the right to invade privacy belonged almost exclusively to the government. For example, an individual must relinquish control of a substantial amount of private information to complete federal and state income tax forms, and failure to provide such information makes one legally liable.

For the survival of the entire political community, the government demands that its citizens provide it with certain information that is otherwise private. However, specific rules govern such disclosure. The government cannot legally give your tax return information to other interested parties. Such a check on government power theoretically allows the maintenance of some level of individual privacy.

However, the government is not the only institution today that can demand and receive private information. Banks, credit companies, doctors and attorneys all request (and usually receive) a variety of highly private information, the bulk of it willingly disclosed. Inevitably, such disclosure is one-directional. While you are expected to provide your physician with your medical history to ensure proper treatment, your physician might be surprised if you inquired about her success rate with a particular surgical procedure, and she certainly is not required to give it to you. Doctors in states where laws requiring such information be made available to patients have been debated usually go on record as being against disclosure, saying that the information devoid of context can be deceiving or outright wrong.

Computers and databases have become tools for gathering and storing private information. Huge industries have cropped up selling private information. When you buy a house or apply for a job, the information industry disgorges huge amounts of legal and financial information about you with about a 40 percent chance of some error, according to some industry figures. The tensions over what should or should not remain private are not resolved; they are merely accounted for in today's complex society. And even when consumers are given a free chance to look at and correct their credit information, only a small percentage do despite the financial advantage to do so.

However, Warren and Brandeis had the press, not the government or financial institutions, in mind when they wrote their precedent-inspiring article more than 100 years ago. The pair developed their novel legal argument after a breakfast in celebration of Mr. Warren's wedding was covered by the press, an article that would be a benign social mention today if it made the press at all. Offended by this "outrage," Warren and Brandeis could not have anticipated trash television, "kiss-and-tell" books, computerized databases or the myriad other ways the mass media disseminate private information about people who are more or less willing to disclose it.

DISTINGUISHING BETWEEN SECRECY AND PRIVACY

People tend to think of private information as something they would like to keep secret, but such thinking confounds these two related but separable concepts.

Secrecy can be defined as blocking information intentionally to prevent others from learning, possessing, using or revealing it (Bok 1983). Secrecy ensures that information is kept from *any* public view. Privacy, however, is concerned with determining who will obtain access to the information. Privacy does not require that information never reach public view, but rather who has control over that information which becomes public.

Secrecy often carries a negative connotation. But secrecy is neither morally good nor bad. Privacy and secrecy can overlap but are not identical. "Privacy need not hide; and secrecy hides far more than what is private. A private garden need not be a secret garden, a private life is rarely a secret life" (Bok 1983, 11).

The law has given us an interesting metaphor for the ethics of privacy. In *Dietemann v. Time,* jurist Alan F. Westin viewed privacy as the ability to control one's own "circles of intimacy." In the case, two reporters for the former *Life* magazine lied to Dietemann to enter his California home and later expose him as a medical quack practicing medicine without a license. While the courts saw some social utility in exposing such behavior, Dietemann had a reasonable expectation of privacy in his own home, and ruled against the media in the civil suit that followed.

Philosopher Louis W. Hodges has used the concept of circles of intimacy to develop a working concept of privacy for journalists and other professionals. If you

PUBLIC   PUBLIC

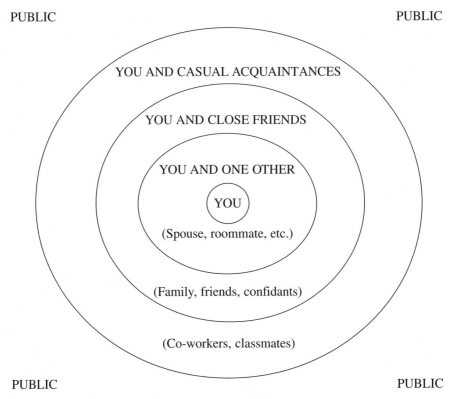

PUBLIC   PUBLIC

FIGURE 5.1. The concept of circles of intimacy

conceive of privacy as a series of concentric circles, as Figure 5.1 illustrates, in the innermost circle you are alone with your secrets, fantasies, hopes, reconstructed memories and the rest of the unique psychological "furniture" we bring to our lives.

The second circle you probably occupy with one other person, perhaps a sibling, a spouse, a parent, roommate or loved one. You might hold several "you plus one" circles simultaneously in life and the number and identity of these you plus one circles might change at various times in your development. In that circle, you share your private information, and for that relationship to work well, it needs to be reciprocal—based on trust.

The third circle contains others to whom you are very close—probably family or friends, perhaps a lawyer or clergy member. Here, the basis of relationships is still one of trust, but control over the information gets trickier. This circle was probably the issue in the Facebook controversy—information the sender thought would be known by a few became known by many. It's the nature of information. As the ripples in the pond of intimacy continue to spread, what you reveal about yourself becomes progressively more public and less intimate, and you lose progressively more control over information about you.

Using this model, privacy can be considered control over who has access to your various circles of intimacy. Invasion of privacy occurs when your control over your own circles of intimacy is wrestled from you by people or institutions. Rape victims who unwillingly see their names in print or their pictures broadcast frequently speak of the loss of control they felt during the experience as being similar to the loss of control during the rape itself.

Journalists sometimes invade circles of intimacy either accidentally or purposefully. Awareness of the concept will allow you to consider the rights and needs of others as well as the demands of society, particularly when the issue is newsworthy. Under at least some circumstances, invasion can be justified, but under other circumstances it's not. Part of the ethical growth of a journalist is to know when the rule applies and when the exceptions should occur.

DISCRETION: WHETHER TO REVEAL PRIVATE INFORMATION

With the distinction between privacy and secrecy in mind, the next problem confronting the ethical journalist is "discretion"—a word not usually associated with journalism. Bok (1983, 41) defines discretion as "the intuitive ability to discern what is and is not intrusive and injurious."

We all decide at times to reveal private information, and doing so wisely is a mark of moral growth discussed in the final chapter of this book. Discretion demands moral reasoning. Once a source decides to reveal private information, a reporter's discretion remains the sole gatekeeper between that information and a public that might need the information or might merely want the information. The journalist is forced to rely on moral reasoning to decide if he is feeding the voyeur or the citizen in each of us.

What is a journalist to do with information resulting from another's indiscretion? Kantian theory would suggest that the journalist treat even the indiscreet source as the journalist herself would wish to be treated, making publication of the indiscretion less likely. Yet many journalists claim that, in practice, everything is "on-the-record" unless otherwise specified. In situations like these, a return to Ross's list of prima facie duties could be helpful. What is my duty to an often vulnerable and sometimes unwitting source? To a curious readership or viewership? To a media owner who wants (and pays for) my story?

Returning to the issue of Facebook, it seems that many 18- to 22-year-olds have yet to learn discretion in their postings. And the problem is even greater on MySpace, which draws an even younger crowd. Indiscreet postings have led to numerous problems including sexually predatory behavior by some adults and even stalking or cyber-bullying by peers. And reality television—which is usually anything but real—is an almost textbook case of persons willing to endure or divulge almost anything to get a chance at fleeting fame. In the summer of 2009 consider these facts from reality television:

- One young lady had her criminal probation revoked because of a scene on "Bridezilla" where she was seen fighting with another person. Her defense: it was only acting, it wasn't really her at all.

- The entire nation was fascinated by the divorce of the title characters from TLC's "Jon and Kate Plus Eight" as it played out in celebrity-oriented magazines.
- Susan Boyle, a surprised finalist on "Britain's Got Talent" (an amateur talent show that gave birth to "American Idol"), was hospitalized from exhaustion soon after her plunge into instant fame, including millions of hits on YouTube postings as well as coverage in the British tabloid media.
- Numerous participants on reality shows told news sources that producers routinely picked winners and losers to promote a "story line" contrary to the stated rules of the competition—charges eerily reminiscent of the quiz show scandals of the 1950s where producers fed answers to contestants deemed popular by the audience.

WHEN THE RIGHT TO KNOW IS NOT ENOUGH

Just as the distinction between secrecy and privacy is easily confused, there is also a misconception on the part of both journalists and the public among the concepts of "right to know," "need to know" and "want to know." However, the three concepts are distinct and not interchangeable.

Right to know is a legal term often associated with open-meeting and open-record statutes. These laws are a legal, not ethical, construct. Journalists have a legal right to the same information that other members of the public may obtain—for example, the transportation of hazardous materials through their communities.

Ethical problems can emerge from right-to-know information. Is it ethical to print everything a journalist has a legal right to know? For instance, police reports routinely carry the names of suspects, victims and witnesses to a variety of crimes. If a reporter has information that might harm, on the local level, the right to a fair trial or, on the national level, national security, should it be withheld?

Need to know originates in the realm of philosophy. One function of the mass media is to provide information that will allow citizens to go about their daily lives in society, regardless of political outlook. Providing information the public needs to know includes within it the concept of journalistic tenacity and responsibility.

Too often, when journalists assert the public has a "right to know" what they mean is that citizens "need" the information to get along in their daily lives. For example, the average citizen cannot examine bank records—they're specifically excluded from the Freedom of Information Act. That duty is left to auditors and the government. But what happens when government fails? With the recent turmoil in the financial sector, including those who lost billions in a New York-based Ponzi scheme, journalists could reasonably argue that at least some information about the health of financial institutions and the character of those who run them is needed by the public to make informed economic decisions. Need to know requires a tenacious journalist, as the law is not a tool for such stories.

Need to know is the most ethically compelling argument of the three. Need to know demands that an ethical case be constructed for making known information that others wish to keep private. Need to know also means that a case be made that the journalism is not engaging in mere voyeurism. When an argument is framed in terms of right to know, it reduces the journalist to ethical legalism: I will do precisely what the law allows. When an argument is framed in terms of need to know, however, it means that counterbalancing forces have been weighed and that bringing the information to light is still the most ethical act.

Finally, there is the issue of **want to know,** which speaks to the curiosity in all of us. Want to know is the least ethically compelling rationale for acquiring and disseminating information. We all want to know a lot of things—what our neighbors do in the evening hours, how much money other people earn and who in Hollywood is sleeping with whom. While we may want that information, however, we don't really need it and most certainly have no right to it.

Journalists—especially bloggers—have become sources for much "want to know" information. A number of media outlets have been founded on the public's desire to know about celebrities, criminals and even common folk. Nearly a century ago, *Police Gazette* titillated its readers with information they wanted to know that no other media outlet provided. Today that function is filled by slick Web sites and syndicated television shows such as "TMZ." In the mainstream media, it is "want to know" print magazines and video magazines that are the only growth area in the entire industry.

Consider the world of YouTube, where anything you "want to know" is probably available. Have a blooper at your wedding? There's an entire category for that. Getting irritated in public? There's a category for that. Thanks to the ubiquitous cell phone camera, bad public behavior once limited to a small group of strangers around you, might go "viral" like the four million viewers on YouTube who watched Chan Yuet-tung have a bad day (Boulware 2006).

It started when Elvis Ho Yui Hei, a 23-year-old rider on a Hong Kong motor bus, tapped Yuet-tung on the shoulder and asked him to please speak more softly on his cell phone, addressing him with the culturally-respectful term of "Uncle." The request prompted a six-minute, sometimes profane and always loud verbal harangue by the 51-year-old Yuet-tung while Hei sat mostly silent. Across the aisle, however, a student held up his camera phone to capture the moment. It quickly made its way to YouTube, where millions saw the meltdown that only a few had witnessed on the bus.

In an article about YouTube entitled "Everybody's Watching," author Jack Boulware (2006, 100) stated:

> We've all been privy to a moment like this at one time or another—a rare window of real life that you might see and tell your friends afterward; another little anecdote from the daily pageant of human beings trying to share space on the planet. . . . What began as a simple, weird altercation on a Hong Kong bus has turned into a worldwide phenomenon. And all because of a small company [YouTube] in an office above a pizza parlor in San Mateo, California.

In the world of YouTube and its competitors, everyone can get the 15 minutes of fame predicted by pop artist Andy Warhol. And if you need to be reminded what the "want to know" market is worth, in 2006, Google purchased YouTube for $1.6 billion.

JOHN RAWLS AND THE VEIL OF IGNORANCE

Preserving human dignity in times of crisis is a difficult task. Political philosopher John Rawls, an articulate proponent of the social contract theory of government, has provided a helpful exercise to make decisions about particularly thorny privacy issues (Rawls 1971).

Rawls's theory of "distributive justice" takes the best from utilitarian theory while avoiding some of its problems. It begins with the premise that justice should be equated with fairness. In order to achieve fairness, Rawls suggests an exercise he calls the "veil of ignorance." In the exercise, before a community can make an ethical decision affecting its members, the community must consider the options behind a veil of ignorance. Behind the veil, everyone starts out in an "original position" as equals who do not know whether they will be powerful or powerless when they emerge from behind the veil.

Rawls suggests that rational people would be willing to make and to follow decisions when individual distinctions such as gender or socioeconomic status are laid aside. For example, if the issue is whether to photograph or interview survivors at the scene of an airline crash, you could gather many people with diverse views behind the veil. Among them could be a reporter, a photographer, a survivor, a victim's family, an average reader or viewer, the management or owner of the media outlet, the owner of the airline, paramedics at the scene, the flying public and others. Behind the veil, in the original position, none of the participants would know what their status would be when they emerged. *Their arguments would then be free of bias that comes from points of view.* The participants would argue the pros and cons of the public's need to know and the victim's right to privacy without knowing whether they would emerge as a reporter, a reader or a victim.

When people begin their deliberations behind such a veil, Rawls suggests that two values emerge. We will first act so that *individual liberty is maximized;* however, we will also act so that *weaker parties will be protected.* We will look at each concept separately.

First, Rawls suggests the liberty of all will be valued equally. Behind the veil, freedom of the press (a liberty journalists cherish) becomes equal to freedom from intrusion into private life (a liberty readers cherish). How you retain both becomes a debate to be argued from all points of view, free of bias.

Second, behind the veil, the weaker party is usually protected. Few participants would make an ethical decision that might not be in the interest of the weaker party unless the evidence was overwhelming that it would better the lot of the entire group. Behind the veil participants would be forced to weigh the actual and potential harm that journalists, as powerful people representing powerful institutions, could inflict on people who are less powerful.

It is important to note that consensus is not required, and maybe even not expected, behind the veil. The veil of ignorance is designed to facilitate ethical discussions, not stymie them from lack of unanimity. Using the veil of ignorance, the ethical decision maker arrives at what Rawls calls "reflective equilibrium," where some inequalities are allowed. However, they will be the inequalities that contribute in some significant way to the betterment of most individuals in the social situation. For instance, the consensus of the group behind the veil might be to run a photo of a victim of tragedy if it might prevent a similar tragedy from occurring.

Reflective equilibrium summons what Rawls calls our "considered moral judgment." Balancing the liberties of various stakeholders, while protecting the weaker party, allows for an exploration of all of the issues involved, which utilitarianism sometimes fails to address.

Using the concepts of right to know, need to know, discretion and circles of intimacy, along with Rawls's concept of distributive justice, will provide you with the ethical tools to begin the work of balancing conflicting claims of privacy. These tools will enable you to better justify your choices, to make decisions systematically and to understand what went wrong when mistakes occur.

Selected Readings

ALDERMAN, ELLEN, and CAROLINE KENNEDY. 1995. *The right to privacy.* New York: Alfred A. Knopf, Inc.

BOK, SISSELA. 1983. *Secrets: On the ethics of concealment and revelation.* New York: Vintage.

GRCIC, JOSEPH M. 1986. "The right to privacy: Behavior as property." *Journal of Values Inquiry* 20, 137–144.

HIXSON, RICHARD F. 1987. *Privacy in a public society.* New York: Oxford University Press.

HODGES, LOUIS W. 1983. "The journalist and privacy." *Social Responsibility: Journalism, Law, Medicine* 9, 5–19.

ORWELL, GEORGE. 1949. *1984.* San Diego: Harcourt, Brace, Jovanovich.

RAWLS, JOHN. 1971. *A theory of justice.* Cambridge, MA: Harvard University Press.

ROSEN, JEFFREY. 2000. *The unwanted gaze: The destruction of privacy in America.* New York: Random House.

SCHOEMAN, FERDINAND D., ed. 1984. *Philosophical dimensions of privacy: An anthology.* New York: Cambridge University Press.

Cases on the Web

www.mhhe.com/mediaethics7e

"Naming names: Privacy and the public's right to know" by John B. Webster

"Public grief and the right to be left alone" by Philip Patterson

"A reporter's question: Propriety and punishment" by Stanley Cunningham

"Computers and the news: A complicated challenge" by Karon Reinboth Speckman

"Honor to die for: *Newsweek* and the Admiral Boorda case" by Philip Patterson

"Culture, law and privacy: Should ethics change in a cultural context?" by Lee Wilkins

"Arthur Ashe and the right to privacy" by Carol Oukrop

CHAPTER 5 CASES

CASE 5-A

Funeral Photos of Fallen Soldiers: Public Interest or Public Outrage?

PENNY COCKERELL
Daily Oklahoman

PHILIP PATTERSON
Oklahoma Christian University

On May 11, 2004, an improvised explosive device struck the vehicle in which Army Spc. Kyle Adam Brinlee, 21, was riding in Iraq. He was killed in the explosion, the first combat-related death of an Oklahoma National Guard member since the Korean War. On May 19, more than 1,000 people gathered in the Pryor (OK) High School Auditorium for his funeral. Guests included the governor of Oklahoma, who spoke at the ceremony. Members of the media were allowed to attend but confined to a sectioned-off area. Most of the media were reporters from Oklahoma City and Tulsa media outlets.

In attendance also was photographer Peter Turnley, who was shooting a photo essay for *Harper's Magazine.* It was to be the first of four "major eight-page photo essays" of Turnley's work that *Harper's Magazine* would showcase in the coming year (2004), according to a press release on the National Press Photographers Web site **(www.npp.org).** Turnley was a well-known photographer whose work had been on the cover of *Newsweek* more than 40 times, according to Turnley's own Web site **(www.peterturnley.com).** He also had had photos appear in such publications as *Life, National Geographic, Le Monde* and *The London Sunday Times,* among others. He also had covered wars in such locations as Rwanda, South Africa, Chechnya, Haiti, Afghanistan and Iraq.

In August 2004, three photos from Brinlee's funeral appeared in *Harper's* in a photo essay entitled "The Bereaved: Mourning the Dead in America and Iraq." The essay focused on both American and Iraqi funerals with several pictures of grieving families, a photo of doctors unable to save a 10-year-old Iraqi boy and a stark scene of Iraqis passing by a corpse lying on the street in Baghdad. In an interview given before the essay was published (Winslow 2004), Turnley said, "This first essay speaks in images about a very important theme touching our world today in a way that I don't think has been seen much before elsewhere."

One of the photos shows Brinlee in an open casket at the rear of the auditorium with several mourners still seated in the background. As of the spring of 2007, this photo does not appear on a Web site of all the Turnley photo essays for *Harper's Magazine.* It was not available for printing in this book, but can be found on page 47 of the August 2004 edition of the magazine.

Brinlee's family filed suit against Turnley and the magazine claiming a variety of torts including intentional infliction of emotional distress, invasion of privacy and unjustly profiting from the photos. In their filing, the family claims that despite the large crowds in a public school, the funeral was a "private religious ceremony." They added that the photos went "beyond all bounds of decency."

The family claimed that Turnley had been told by the funeral director to abstain from photographing the body of the soldier. In a response to the court, Turnley denied he had received the instructions, and claimed the body was placed near the media section for access. In a later interview with CNN, Turnley claimed: "It seems to me that the responsibility of a journalist today is to tell as much as possible about the true realities of what is taking place in the world. My desire is to simply try to dignify the reality of what people experience in war by showing the public what does happen there."

"The casket was open for friends and family—not to gawk at and take pictures and publish them. Not for economic gain," the lawyer for the family argued in an interview with the Associated Press.

The family sought $75,000 in actual damages on complaints including publication of private facts, appropriation of Brinlee's photo for commercial purposes and intrusion. In December 2005 a federal judge ruled that the family privacy was not invaded by the photos. "[P]laintiffs appear to have put the death of their loved one in the public eye intentionally to draw attention to his death and burial," Judge Frank Seay ruled in granting summary judgment to the media defendants. Elsewhere in the ruling, Seay pointed out that the plaintiffs lost their right to privacy during the funeral by choosing to publicize the event.

Harper's Magazine publisher John R. MacArthur echoed the ruling of the judge. "For me, from the beginning, it was a First Amendment issue and it was also a matter of our integrity. I have not met anyone yet who thought that photograph was disrespectful in any way."

Micro Issues

1. Can a funeral that is held in a public place be considered a private event?
2. Does it make a difference that Turnley and other media were given permission to attend the funeral?
3. Does it make a difference that the photos taken were of images in plain view of those attending the funeral?

Midrange Issues

1. Is newsworthiness a legal defense to the claim of invasion of privacy? Is it an ethical defense?
2. Does the fact that the family allowed media coverage of the funeral prevent them from suing for the distress that the Turnley photos allegedly caused? If the family had not allowed media coverage of the funeral, would your opinion of Turnley's photos be different?
3. In what way, if any, would video of the funeral differ from the still photographs of Turnley?
4. Are open-casket photos of soldiers a reality that journalists should be covering as Turnley contends or "beyond all bounds of decency" as the family contends? Can the two sides be reconciled?

Macro Issues

1. Is this a First Amendment issue as the judge and the media maintain? When other rights, such as the right to privacy, come into conflict with the First Amendment, how is the conflict best resolved?
2. What is the role of the media in covering conflicts such as the war in Iraq? Do wounded soldiers or those attending them have any privacy rights that trump the public's right to know?

CASE 5-B

A Person of Interest

CARA DeMICHELE
University of Missouri

Scarcely a week after America was attacked on Sept. 11, 2001, terrorism took a different twist—letters tainted with deadly anthrax. The first such letters were post-marked from Trenton, New Jersey, on Sept. 19, 2001, and sent to the *New York Post* and "NBC Nightly News" anchor Tom Brokaw. A New Jersey letter carrier began to show symptoms of an unusual illness on September 27, but it wouldn't be identified as anthrax exposure until after the death of Bob Stevens, a photo editor at American Media, Inc., in Boca Raton, Florida. Stevens died of inhalation of anthrax. By the end of November, five people would die from the disease, and 17 more would be infected, while nearly 30,000 others would be given antibiotics. Congress shut down for two days after contaminated letters were mailed to Senators Tom Daschle and Patrick Leahy.

Multiple agencies tried to trace the infection, and by October 2001 it became clear that the anthrax had originated in the United States, from a strain grown at Iowa State University in Ames. Tests also showed not only that some of the anthrax was very refined but also that some had been "weaponized," making it more likely to be inhaled. There were at least 200 people in the United States who were thought to have the expertise to be capable of such a crime, but only 30 to 40 of them had access to the Ames anthrax strain.

Careful not to label anyone a "suspect" prematurely, the FBI spent months repeatedly interviewing and investigating 20 to 30 "persons of interest" who had worked or did work for federal laboratories on contract. Media outlets worldwide followed the investigation. Part of that reporting process demanded that journalists keep an eye on discussion boards and statements coming from the Federation of American Scientists (FAS) on the Web. Dr. Barbara Hatch Rosenberg, a molecular biologist at the University of New York at Purchase and chairwoman of a biological weapons panel at FAS, is familiar with the work of scientists in the close-knit biological weapons community and had been acting as advisor to the FBI.

On Feb. 19, 2002, Rosenberg made a statement at Princeton University claiming that the FBI had identified and twice questioned the man responsible for the anthrax attacks but was "dragging its feet" because the man was a former government scientist. In her comments, which also had been the subject of discussion at the FAS Web site for months, Rosenberg stated that many scientists in the field knew of the suspect, who may have formerly worked at the U.S. Army Medical Research Institute of Infectious Diseases at Fort Detrick, Maryland, and was currently working as a contractor in the Washington, D.C., area. Her comments were first reported in the *Trenton Times* newspaper and then were slowly picked up by other U.S. media outlets.

The news coverage died down in the ensuing month until early June, when news organizations were tipped that the FBI would be searching the Maryland apartment and Florida storage locker of a bioweapons expert on June 25, 2001.

Dr. Steven J. Hatfill, a former Fort Detrick scientist, was first interviewed by the FBI in December 2001. Like some of the other 20 to 30 scientists who were deemed "persons of interest," Hatfill consented to the searches. At that time, the agency had searched the homes and offices of 25 other scientists with little to no media coverage. Just like the other searches, the FBI found nothing in the Hatfill searches but chose to keep him as a "person of interest." And, unlike the other searches, the Hatfill investigation received extensive and ongoing media coverage.

It is likely that some news organizations had been aware that Hatfill was a possible target since December 2001 because his name and gossip about him had appeared on the FAS Web site. According to the articles and transcripts that covered the Hatfill case, there was plenty about his past that made him a likely suspect. ABC News, among others, reported that the FBI was interested in Hatfill partly because in the late 1970s Hatfill attended medical school in Zimbabwe near a Greendale elementary school. "Greendale School" appeared as the phony return address on one of the tainted letters sent to the Senate. In the early 1990s, Hatfill worked as a researcher for the National Institutes of Health (NIH). During this time he was widely quoted in newspaper articles as a bioterrorism expert and often gave lectures on the dangers of biowarfare.

After leaving the NIH, Hatfill had worked in the virology division of the Army's biodefense laboratory at Fort Detrick from 1997 to September 1999. A Fort Detrick spokesman told the Associated Press that the virology division studies how to protect military personnel from biological weapons. The spokesman stated that while Hatfill probably had access to labs that contained the Ames anthrax strain, it wasn't part of his primary duties. In 1999, however, Hatfill commissioned a report that describes placing 2.5 grams of a simulated form of anthrax into a business envelope, which only fueled speculation.

On March 4, 2002, Hatfill was fired from his job at Science Applications International Corporation, a Pentagon and CIA contractor that helps the government with biological defenses. Hatfill told the *Baltimore Sun* that he had been fired because journalists were constantly pursuing him. Most recently, Hatfill lost his research job at Louisiana State University as a result of the investigation.

On Aug. 1, 2002, the FBI performed a second search of Hatfill's apartment and again found nothing. By the time of Hatfill's Aug. 11 press conference to again deny any involvement with the anthrax attacks, the FBI had searched his home twice, his car, his storage facility in Florida and his girlfriend's apartment with no success. Despite not being able to place Hatfill in New Jersey when the letters were sent, the FBI decided not to change Hatfill's "person of interest" status. Now years later, out of about 20 to 30 "persons of interest" investigated by the FBI, Hatfill's name was the only one to have been released publicly. He was never formally charged with any crime or officially named a "suspect."

Micro Issues

1. When, if ever, did Hatfill become news? When, if ever, did the case cease to be newsworthy?
2. When the original allegations surfaced, what sort of questions, if any, should journalists have asked Dr. Rosenberg, who made the original allegations?

3. When should Hatfill have been contacted to respond to the suspicions? How should his responses have been reported?
4. Would legal action on Hatfill's behalf be a better remedy than an ethical one? Why or why not?

Midrange Issues

1. Journalists covering this beat almost certainly knew about Hatfill but did not report what was being said about him until Dr. Rosenberg's comments were made in public. Evaluate this news judgment.
2. Should journalists have attempted to obtain the names of other "persons of interest"? Should they have published those names?
3. Are journalists responsible for Hatfill losing his job?
4. Do you think the FBI used the news media to try to pressure Hatfill? If you do, how should the journalists have responded?

Macro Issues

1. When, if ever, did the FBI's failure to solve the anthrax case become news?
2. How do you think the fact that journalists themselves were the targets of some of the anthrax letters figures into the media accounts of the investigation?
3. Using both utilitarian theory and Kant's categorical imperative, develop a newsroom policy that provides guidelines for covering "persons of interest."

CASE 5-C

Blind Justice? On Naming Kobe Bryant's Accuser after the Rape Charge Is Dropped

PATRICK LEE PLAISANCE
Colorado State University

In June 2003, Los Angeles Lakers star Kobe Bryant was recovering from medical treatment at the exclusive Lodge and Spa at Cordilera in Colorado. Bryant asked the resort's 19-year-old concierge, whom he had met earlier, up to his room, and the two had intercourse. Bryant insisted the sex was consensual, but the woman claimed she was forced against her will. After a weeklong investigation, Bryant was arrested and prosecutors filed a rape charge against him. A national media frenzy ensued.

Mainstream news outlets, however, scrupulously avoided identifying the woman in their coverage—even when Eagle County court officials mistakenly released documents containing some of her personal information. Colorado is one of several states with so-called rape shield laws, which prohibit authorities from disclosing the identity of victims in rape cases to spare them the additional trauma of public—and possibly unfair—scrutiny. Most news organizations themselves also have policies against naming assault victims on the theory that the social stigma that continues to be attached to sexual assault merits special treatment in coverage. So these mainstream news organizations never disclosed the woman's name to their audiences.

But anyone with Internet access and a few minutes to spare could quickly learn quite a bit about her. Her name, photos, e-mail address, cell phone number and even details about rumors surrounding her sexual and mental history were instantly made available—mostly on Internet sites created by fans of Bryant. A Los Angeles–based sports radio talk-show host, Tom Leykis, began referring to her by name on the air soon after the rape case was filed. His show is heard on 60 stations across the country.

Fifteen months later, the high-profile case presented a second ethical challenge for journalists. Just as a jury was being selected for the trial, the woman decided to back out as a witness for the state prosecution's case. The criminal case against Bryant was dropped. But at the same time, his accuser filed a civil lawsuit against him in federal court in Denver. The switch in courts posed the question of whether the playing field had changed for journalists who, since that point, had protected her identity in their coverage. Denver's two competing metropolitan daily newspapers, the *Rocky Mountain News* and the *Denver Post*, reacted in diametrically opposite ways.

John Temple, editor and publisher of the *Rocky Mountain News*, said the paper decided to reverse its policy and name the woman once she filed her civil suit because the issue changed. It was no longer a story about the state pursuing a sex-assault charge based on her evidence and testimony. By continuing to press her case on her own in civil court to seek monetary damages, the notion of fairness obligated journalists to treat all civil plaintiffs the same, Temple said—especially after a federal judge denied the woman's request to file her civil suit anonymously. "In the criminal case, we did not name the accuser because it was the state of Colorado prosecuting the case. The state . . . was attempting to vindicate a state interest," Temple said in an interview. "In the civil matter, the woman is pursuing an individual monetary interest. She is using the public courts in what is essentially a personal injury case.

"She had the choice not to go forward after Judge Matsch said she couldn't proceed anonymously. As a general rule, the *News* names plaintiffs in civil suits. Here, both sides' personal integrity and credibility are at issue and the *News* believes fairness requires that both parties be named in reporting on this civil suit. . . . In a case where there is no state interest involved and the complaint doesn't address a larger public interest, it's unfair for the accused to be treated differently from the accuser."

The *Denver Post* editors, however, reached the opposite conclusion and argued that naming her in coverage of her civil suit would be unethical. In a letter published for readers explaining their decision to continue to withhold the woman's name, *Post* editor Gregory L. Moore and managing editor Gary R. Clark argued that the potential harm to the woman created by naming her far outweighed any disadvantage for Bryant in granting her anonymity. "It is clear from the Bryant case—and from similar cases—that a stigma remains and that rape provokes a unique set of questions and blame that does not apply to victims of other crimes," Moore and Clark wrote. "It is our hope that societal attitudes toward alleged rape victims would mirror the treatment afforded alleged victims of other violent crimes. But judging from the reaction to the accuser of the Kobe Bryant case, whose life has been threatened, we don't believe that to be the case just yet. Though her identity will be available to anyone who attends the federal trial or reads court documents, and many in her community know her name, it is not the same as publishing her name and photograph day after day in hundreds of thousands of newspapers."

In March 2005, six months after Bryant's accuser initiated her civil suit, she and Bryant reached a monetary settlement involving a payment to her of an undisclosed amount, and the suit was dismissed.

Micro Issues

1. Is rape just like any other crime, or should it be treated differently by the news media?
2. The name of the alleged victim is not used in this case study. Should her name be used in the context of a robust ethics debate?

Midrange Issues

1. Temple of the *Rocky Mountain News* relies on claims of "fairness" to make his case for publishing her name. How might this notion of fairness be considered differently to argue that it would serve "fairness" *not* to name her?
2. Moore and Clark of the *Denver Post* rely on claims of minimizing harm to defend their decision to withhold her name. How might you argue that potential "harm" to Bryant may be as great or greater than the harm to the woman in allowing her to maintain anonymity?

Macro Issues

1. How would you say the two decisions of both newspapers reflect philosophical principles? In what ways do either draw from a Kantian notion of *duty* to respect human dignity in all our dealings? How do they draw from utilitarian thought in their assessment of the consequences of naming or not naming the woman?
2. In 1991, the *Des Moines Register* won a Pulitzer Prize for a series that documented one woman's journey through the court system after her rape, and she consented to be named throughout the stories. Geneva Overholser, editor of the *Register* at the time, has since argued that the journalistic practice of withholding the names of rape accusers and victims actually reinforces the social stigmatization of rape victims that editors and reporters claim to be fighting. Is she correct?
3. Should this perceived stigma be considered a factor in the decision whether to name the woman in this case?

CASE 5-D

Children, Privacy and Framing: The Use of Children's Images in an Anti-same-sex Marriage Ad

YANG LIU
University of Wisconsin

The brief ballot measure read, "Only marriage between a man and a woman is valid or recognizable in California" (www.votergide.sos.ca.gov 2008) but it was packed with potential for conflict. So when the parents of some San Francisco first graders recognized their sons' and daughters' faces in a advertisement promoting California's controversial 2008 Proposition 8, which successfully sought to outlaw gay marriage in the state (www.protectmarriage.com 2008) they were shocked.

The ad picked up two scenes from a Web site news video clip originally produced by the San Francisco *Chronicle* for a news story that described 18 students attending their lesbian teacher Erin Carder's wedding (www.sfgate.com 2008). The newspaper story was a feature piece that took no position on Proposition 8. The story included an account of the wedding, which was held on October 10, 2008. In the newspaper piece, and on the 80-second accompanying video, the children's participation was described as "tossed rose petals and blow bubbles . . . giggling and squealing as they mobbed their teacher with hugs" (www.sfgate.com 2008). The story noted that it was a parent who suggested the trip and that because every student needed parental permission to attend, two students did not accompany their classmates to the wedding.

However, the central message of the advertisement was, "children will be taught gay marriage unless we vote Yes on Proposition 8" using two scenes with the children's images. The first showed the children in a group, and their faces are somewhat difficult to distinguish. The second showed a single child looking into the camera. The ad did not include the scenes of the children hugging their teacher that were part of the original news story. In addition, the creators of the ad altered the color tones in the scenes with children to be somewhat darker than the original news story as posted on the *Chronicle* Web site. The ad featuring the video clip of the wedding was one of several similar ads run in support of Proposition 8.

After viewing the ad, four of the parents of the children involved wrote a letter to the Yes-on-Proposition-8 campaign, demanding that the campaign stop running the ad. Their request was denied. The *Chronicle* did not question the use of the copyrighted material in the ad nor did it make a request that the ad be discontinued.

Micro Issues

1. How would you evaluate the truthfulness and accuracy of the video accompanying the political advertisement?
2. Three days after the ad began airing, law Professor Lawrence Lessig said in a National Public Radio interview that the law "should not stop the ability of people to use material that has been publicly distributed." Evaluate this statement using ethical theory.
3. Do children constitute a vulnerable audience when it comes to privacy?

Midrange Issues

1. All advertisements, by virtue of their brevity, engage in selective use of facts. Evaluate whether this ad is within that professional mainstream in an ethical sense.
2. What should the Chronicle do about the use of news material for the purpose of political persuasion, regardless of the specific issue?

Macro Issues

1. How would you evaluate the statement that this ad constitutes protected political speech?
2. It has been argued that the children do not have the ability to reason about the politics of same-sex marriage in this wedding, so they were not expressing consent to the same-sex marriage, but only expressing affection for their teacher. Is their participation in the wedding a private matter without political meaning or not? Justify your answer.

6

Mass Media in a Democratic Society: Keeping a Promise

By the end of this chapter, you should be familiar with:

- many of the criticisms leveled at the way the U.S. media cover government and elections.
- the special problems of reporting on terrorism and hate.
- why the media should be concerned with social justice for the powerful and the powerless alike.
- evaluating all forms of political communication through a single, ethically based framework.

INTRODUCTION

Americans view the written word as essential to political society. The First Amendment to the U.S. Constitution states:

> Congress shall make no law respecting an establishment of religion, or prohibiting the free exercise thereof; or abridging the freedom of speech, or of the press; or the right of the people peaceably to assemble, and to petition the government for a redress of grievances.

Scholars such as John C. Merrill (1974) assert that the First Amendment should be interpreted purely as a restriction on government, emphasizing freedom of expression and downplaying any notion of reciprocal journalistic responsibility. But others, including Alexis de Toqueville (1835), who studied our democracy about 150 years ago, viewed the press of the day as an essential antidote to a culture that valued liberty over community. The press, de Toqueville said, was an incubator of civilization, an idea that political philosopher John Dewey would further for the mass media of his day just under a century later.

MOTHER GOOSE&GRIMM-(NEW) © 1999 GRIMMY, INC. KING FEATURES SYNDICATE.

Madison, Hamilton and Jay in the *Federalist Papers* expected citizens to be informed and to participate in politics. They knew that political debate, including what was printed in the press, would be partisan and biased rather than objective, but they also believed that from this "noisy" information the rational being would find the truth. Unfettered communication was essential to building a new nation. Citizens had an obligation to read such information; the press had an obligation to provide it. Tucked within all of this, we believe, is a promise that the mass media, both in 1791 and now more than 200 years later, will provide citizens with what they need to know to get along in political society, an analysis now called the "social responsibility theory" of the press. However, assuming such a responsibility is becoming progressively more difficult because of the increasingly complex structure of the contemporary American political system.

EVALUATING POLITICAL COMMUNICATION

For the Greeks, where democracy was born, the art of politics was considered a gift from the gods, who provided men with *adios,* a sense of concern for the good opinion of others, and *dike,* a sense of justice which makes civic peace possible. In the ancient myth, these gifts were bestowed on everyone, not just some elite. All men were able to exercise the art of politics through rhetoric and argument in the assembly, a form of direct democracy that survived for only a few years in Athens. No newspapers, no television, just in-person debate. The Greeks called it *polity,* which translates as community, one of the Greeks' highest ethical constructs. Greece was also the last place that direct democracy was practiced.

Considering the contemporary cacophony, that's not such a big surprise. It's not just the negative campaign commercials. It's the barrage of opinion masquerading as analysis on cable television, the thousands of blogs available on the Internet, the candidate campaign Web sites—including entries into domains such as Facebook— the late night comedians, "Comedy Central" and all the rest. One study by the Pew Charitable Trusts in 2004 found that more than half of Americans under age 50 get their news about politics "regularly" or "sometimes" from late-night comedians. But these respondents were also among the least likely to know basic facts about candidates. Even on the lowest level, politics, for most, is a mass-mediated event.

Evaluating all this political information is a problem for both media consumers and for journalists. Furthermore, as news blends into entertainment and persuasion leaches into both genres, providing a consistent way of examining every political message becomes essential in ethical analysis. Political scientist Bruce A. Williams (2009) has begun this process with a four-part test he believes will help you determine when information has political relevance:

- First, is the information **useful**—does it provide citizens with the kind of information that helps individual and collective decision making?
- Second, is the information **sufficient**—is there enough of it and at enough depth to allow people to make informed choices?
- Third, is the information **trustworthy?**
- Fourth, **who is the "audience"**—the political "we" on which the ancient Greeks placed so much emphasis?

Information that meets these criteria should be considered politically relevant, mediated information regardless of genre or source, Williams says. Under this test, a Jon Stewart show or a Stephen Colbert monologue would be considered politically relevant communication every bit as much as a campaign ad or an investigative piece. Under this sort of analysis, cable news programming, which often features dueling opinions by talking heads talking over each other, often unsubstantiated by evidence, would actually fare less well than the comedy monologue. In a famous dustup between cable news personality (now CATO Institute fellow) Tucker Carlson, "Comedy Central" comedian Jon Stewart took on the entire genre of punditry, suggesting that his show was more truthful and politically relevant.

Putting all political communication into the same arena also has another virtue—every message can be evaluated along the same standard. Here, again, Williams (2009) suggests four criteria.

- **Transparency**—Does the audience know who is speaking? This has become a major problem in recent elections with the rise of PACs and groups not bound by campaign finance rules and rarely bothered with the total accuracy of their claims, something seen on both sides in the 2009 debate over health care reform.
- **Pluralism**—Does the media environment provide an opportunity for diverse points of view, either in different messages that are equally accessible or within a single message? Does every side have access to the engines of information that are now the modern equivalent of the face-to-face rhetoric of ancient Greece?
- **Verisimilitude**—Do the sources of the messages take responsibility for the truth claims they explicitly and implicitly make, even if these claims are not strictly verifiable in any formal sense?
- **Practice**—Does the message encourage modeling, rehearsing, preparing and learning for civic engagement? Does it encourage activities like voting or less direct forms of political activity like thinking about issues, looking at Web sites, blogging or talking to neighbors face-to-face? Is the ad or article empowering or does it contribute to the cacophony that has dominated recent political campaigns?

While this puts all political messages on a level and ethically based play-ing field, contemporary democratic politics still produces some morally relevant variations—at least when it comes to news and persuasion. We will review some of the most commonly acknowledged issues now.

GETTING ELECTED

For any politician to enact change, he or she must first be elected, and in our mass society, that means turning to the mass media to reach the electorate. In one clas-sic study, voters admitted learning more about candidates' stands on issues from advertising than they did from news (Patterson 1980). And considering that modern presidential campaigns place ads only in contested states, many voters get little exposure to even the limited and one-sided information coming from ads. In the past decade, campaign Web sites have become increasingly important. But since they are under the control of the candidate and not bound by any constraints of objectivity or completeness, they too qualify as advertising. So today, more than 30 years after the first studies indicated this, advertising is still the leading source of information for most people in most campaigns.

Because ads are a leading source of campaign information, factual accuracy, therefore, must be the starting point for ethical political advertising. As philosopher Hannah Arendt has noted, "Freedom of information is a farce unless factual infor-mation is guaranteed and the facts themselves are not in dispute" (Arendt 1970).

News stories about elections emphasize strategy and tactics rather than stands on issues, forcing voters who want to become informed about the candidate's policy choices to get their information from ads, often "negative" or "attack" ads framed by the other side. They do this in part because policy information is largely missing from news stories which tend to focus on polls, who's hot and who's not, electabil-ity and character, but usually only the search for flaws.

Contemporary voters can discern the various types of political ads, according to election studies. Comparative ads, ones that contrast candidate positions on spe-cific issues, were viewed as information rich, and voters view them as an appropri-ate part of political discourse. Attack ads, ones that are personal and negative, that contain no "positive" or "issue-oriented" information, were disliked and distrusted in the studies. A few years ago, a majority of political ads were either positive or contrasted stances of the candidates (Benoit 1999). Another study from the same time showed that voters were able to distinguish among negative, comparative and positive or biographical ads (Jamieson 2000). Studies provide ample evidence that it once is possible to create ethical political advertising on the local, state and national levels and win.

However, in just a decade, the tide has turned, and "going negative" is now seen as the only route to victory for candidates at all levels. And as an added inducement to create negative ads, candidates see them run repeatedly, for free, as the negative charge is debated on cable news over and over. It was perceived negative coverage and a slew of ethics complaints that Sarah Palin blamed for her

Ed Stein © The Rocky Mountain News/Dist. By Newspaper Enterprise Association, Inc.

failure to finish her term as Alaska's governor following her unsuccessful stint on John McCain's ticket.

Today, political advertising is a news beat. These news stories, often called "ad watches," put the claims in political ads to the tests of truthfulness and context. Anecdotal evidence suggests that aggressive journalism focusing on attack ads and negative campaigning can have an impact on the voters' knowledge of particular candidates. Under the social responsibility of the press, it is the responsibility of journalists to evaluate political advertising as legitimate news and to hold candidates publicly accountable for the advertising sponsored by a campaign or, in the grayer areas, advertising paid for by political action groups, even those disavowed by the candidate.

Ideally, political advertising would be factual and rational. The use of emotional arguments designed to stir listeners or viewers "to set aside reason" is a "violation of democratic ethics" (Haiman 1958, 388). There may, however, be times when valid issues have strong emotional content, such as the ongoing debate over abortion or immigration. The melding of emotion and issue in such cases is not unethical. Totalitarian regimes have historically used emotional rather than rational appeals to either gain or retain power.

However, such ads usually lack any evidence to support the claims. Seeking the evidence behind political assertions has historically been the role of the news media. When this sort of journalism is lacking, it begins a cycle that was foreseen by Walter Lippmann: "In the absence of debate, restricted utterance leads to the degradation of opinion . . . the more rational is overcome by the less rational, and the opinions that will prevail will be those which are held most ardently by those with the most passionate will" (Lippmann 1982, 196).

If political advertising is indeed a special case (Kaid 1992), then journalists and their audiences should demand higher standards, more regulations or both. While some of the solutions to the current problems have both First Amendment and financial ramifications, they are worthy of discussion. They include the following:

- Allot limited amounts of free time to qualified candidates for major office to level the playing field for candidates;
- Strengthen state regulations against corrupt campaign practices and find ways to enforce those regulations;
- Encourage journalists to stop covering the "horse race" aspect of campaigns and focus on problems and solutions;
- Hold candidates accountable for their ads and for the ads of political action committees or other groups such as moveon.org;
- Teach journalists to read and report on the visual imagery of a campaign, and to ask candidates questions about it;
- Allow attack ads only if they include the image of the candidate directing the attack;
- Reject unfair or inaccurate ads created by political action committees;
- Conduct ad watches as part of media coverage of a campaign, analyzing the ads for omissions, inconsistencies and inaccuracies.

It takes money to buy ads, and in contemporary democratic societies that means the candidate with the most money often has the loudest voice. Many argue the influence of money in the political system is pervasive and corrosive, and bills have been introduced to limit the power of money in politics only to die in the political process or be ignored in the real world by substituting "soft money" for restricted money.

The issue came to the forefront in the 2008 campaign. Barack Obama changed his mind about accepting public funding for his campaign when he realized that he could easily raise more money than the amount allotted by law, while John McCain accepted the public funds. The huge "money gap" that resulted played a role in the election (and was a much discussed topic on news shows) though it is debatable how much of a difference it made. While it can be argued that money buys elections, especially in the light of evidence that the most heavily-funded campaign wins more often than not, it can also be argued that monetary gifts are merely precursors to votes and the most popular candidate in gifts is often the most popular in votes as well.

How to deal with the influence of money in elections is an important policy question, but there seem to be few effective mechanisms for curtailing its influence. Politicians are too entrenched in the existing system to be objective, and the media that could presumably investigate political money and its negative influence are compromised by the act of receiving so much of the cash. The problem cannot be "solved" in this brief chapter, but it is worth considering whether a media system in a democracy might not be able to be a part of the solution rather than a part of the problem.

LEARNING ABOUT LEADERS
AND THEIR CHARACTER

Today, a pressing political issue is whether people can become acquainted well enough and deeply enough with any candidate to acquire an opinion. After all, a representative democracy rests on the Greek concept of *adios,* a concern for the good opinion of others. Except for a small group of insiders, the mass media have become the primary source of political information, including information about character. In addition to providing voters with facts, something that is generally assumed to be the role of news, the media also provide citizens with a framework to understand those facts.

Candidates have been quick to utilize a variety of media outlets. California Governor Arnold Schwarzenegger announced his candidacy on the "Tonight Show." Because journalists cover national campaigns in a pack, there is seldom any really distinctive political reporting during elections (Crouse 1974; Sabato 1992). However, for journalists, campaign assignments hold the opportunity for personal prestige. The person who covers the winning candidate for a network will almost assuredly become the White House correspondent for the next four years, a guarantee of celebrity status, increased income and, many would argue, real political power by setting the agenda of coverage. Journalists covering a national election have almost as much at stake as the candidates they cover.

Further, journalists treat front-runners differently than they do the remainder of the candidate pack (Robinson and Sheehan 1984). Front-runners are the subject of closer scrutiny, but those examinations are seldom about issues. When Secretary of State Hilary Clinton was running for President in 2008, her front-runner status resulted in coverage that nearly everyone, including the journalists producing it, felt was subtly sexist. Clinton maintained that she had to campaign as much against the stereotype as she did against her opponents. Candidates and their paid consultants have developed strategies that will allow them either to capitalize on front-runner status and image or to compensate for a lack of it. Free media—synonymous with a positive story on the 5:00 p.m. news—has become the watchword of most state and national political campaigns. Candidates have mastered the "photo opportunity" and, for incumbents, the "Rose Garden strategy" designed to thwart anything but the most carefully scripted candidate contact with the voting public.

At the same time candidates try to script their every move, the media have the right, and the responsibility, to get "behind the curtain" (Molotch and Lester 1974) to the real candidate. What happens after the curtain is down often makes news in ways the candidates could not have foreseen. Often it is sexual scandal or financial wrongdoing that brings down the carefully crafted veil that major politicians erect. Journalists face a number of questions in cases such as these. Just because the information is available and even accurate does not automatically mean that it is relevant.

Conceptualizations of character have changed significantly since the founding of the republic, when character was defined in Aristotelian terms—an observable collection of habits, virtues and vices. Freudian psychology has altered that definition to include motivation, the subconscious and relationships that help to form all of us as people. What journalists cover is "political character," the intersection of personality and public performance within the cultural and historical context. Character is dynamic—the synergy of a person within an environment (Davies 1963). Journalists who explore character often do so for an ethical reason, despite apparent invasions of privacy.

Political figures are powerful people. Ethicist Sissela Bok (1978) has noted that when an unequal power relationship is involved, it is possible to justify what would otherwise be considered an unethical act. To paraphrase Bok, investigation of the private character of public people is validated if the person investigated is also in the position to do harm. In those cases, invading privacy in an attempt to counter that threat is justified. However, that invasion also needs to meet some tests (Schoeman 1984):

- The invasion must be placed in a larger context of facts and history and must include context to provide meaning;
- The revelation of private facts about political figures should meet the traditional tests of journalism and needs to be linked to public, political behaviors before publication or broadcast becomes ethically justifiable;
- The invasion of privacy must further the larger political discourse and must meet the most demanding ethical test: the "need to know."

Careful reporting on character can pass these tests. However, journalists must also weigh the harm done to others, particularly family members, who have not sought the public limelight. In the campaign of 2008, one of the ethical quandaries reporters faced is whether the pregnancy of vice-presidential candidate Sarah Palin's unmarried daughter was news. Arguments can be made for both sides of the controversy, but eventually virtually every media outlet ran the story, including many who did so after determining the story was already "out there."

Even reporting that passes the three tests above must be filtered through discretion— a word usually used in moral development theory. In ethics, discretion means having the practical wisdom not to reveal everything one is told, even if facts or events would be of casual interest to many. Journalists have the difficult problem of being discreet in their news coverage, even when candidates, their handlers or supporters and opponents have been indiscreet—sometimes deliberately so. Discretion prevents mainstream media from slipping into "tabloid journalism" or the domain of gossipy blogs that cast doubt on our journalistic motives and credibility.

Reporters covering political character should be aware that there are several building blocks of character, including the:

- politician's development of a sense of trust;
- politician's own sense of self-worth and self-esteem;
- development of a politician's relationship to power and authority;
- early influences on adult policy outlook;
- way a politician establishes contact with people;
- flexibility, adaptability and purposefulness of mature adulthood;
- historical moment.

The media's current emphasis on covering political character provides the best illustration of the need to balance the demands of governing with privacy. No culture has ever expected its leaders to be saints; in fact, some cultures have prized leadership that is decidedly unsaintly. In American culture, the concept of public servant—which is the work of politics—has been replaced by the epithet "politician"— synonymous with "crook," or "liar," a caricature reinforced in popular culture by iconic films such as *Mr. Smith Goes to Washington* or *All the King's Men.* However, Americans were reminded that public service can be a high calling, as shown by the first responders to the 9/11 tragedy, many of whom lost their lives. The late Senator Edward Kennedy described his job as public service. Such service, dating as far back as Athens, was considered the mark of a life well lived.

THE PROPER ROLE OF THE MEDIA— GUARD DOG OR LAP DOG?

One of the ironies of democratic politics is that, in order to accomplish something, you first have to get elected, but it is accomplishing something, not getting elected, that is the major work of politics. Journalists fuel the irony by covering politicians more at the time of their elections or re-elections and paying much less attention to their policy making in between elections. Regulatory agencies, cabinet offices and the courts are not considered glamour beats by the national press corps. Annual surveys by journalism watchdog groups show a dwindling number of reporters on the regulatory beat, which accounts for the late start the media had on a story like global warming until it was forced to the forefront by former Vice President Al Gore in his award-winning documentary. A similar decline in coverage has been noted for years in state legislatures as well.

Yet the national press corps, particularly, is often a player in the policy process by reporting "leaks" and granting "off-the-record" interviews. Political scientist Martin Linsky (1986) describes how leaks have become part of the Washington policy-making process. Government officials, both elected and appointed, use the mass media to leak a story to find out how others will react to it—floating a "trial balloon" in the press. Other times, policymakers will leak a story because they wish to mount support for or oppose a cause.

Sometimes leaks take the form of whistle-blowing when a government employee honestly believes the public good is not being served by the system. Watergate's famed (and now named) source, "Deep Throat," apparently was so motivated when he leaked key parts of the government investigation into the Watergate break-in to *Washington Post* reporters Bob Woodward and Carl Bernstein, who wrote a set of stories that ended in the resignation of President Richard Nixon. More recently, the initial information about the Abu Ghraib prison abuse scandal in Iraq came to journalists in e-mails from service men and women who were alarmed at the treatment of Iraqis held at the prison and of the military command's unwillingness or inability to change the system.

More than two decades ago, Linsky (1986) wrote about the role of the media in the policy-making process and raised two important points regarding ethical journalistic practice still relevant today. First, leaks are an acceptable way of doing government business and policymakers are using them skillfully. Second, leaks can alter the outcome of the policy process itself, and much anecdotal evidence exists to support this conclusion. Of fundamental importance for journalists is the question of whether reporters, editors and their news organizations should become consciously involved in the process of governing by participating in the leaking process, and if so, in what manner? Recent scandals involving faked stories have caused most national media to tighten their regulations on when they grant "off-the-record" requests and when they use the information. But still the practice is common.

Most ethicists agree that the media's primary function is to provide citizens with information that will allow them to make informed political choices (Hodges 1986; Elliott 1986). Media organizations are expected to act as a watchdog on government. Edmund Burke, in a speech in Britain's House of Commons during the late 1700s first called the media the "Fourth Estate" (Ward 2004). In the United States, the Founders protected the press in the Bill of Rights. Thomas Jefferson saw the press as the guardian of the public's interest despite the bitter, partisan nature of the press of his day.

The watchdog media, set apart by custom and by law, also have a "guide dog" function to help citizens make their way through the political process. However, when the press covers politics as a constant "food fight" by competing interests, both journalists and citizens are soured to the process. Political reporter E. J. Dionne in *Why Americans Hate Politics* (1991) argues that defining news as conflict (as virtually every journalism text does) inevitably reduces political debate into a shouting match. And, post-9/11 there is always the chance that critical coverage of government, especially the Pentagon, will be labeled "unpatriotic" by critics, including many in political power. This is not a problem exclusively confined to the U.S. system, as documentaries such as *Control Room*—in an in-depth look at the al-Jazeera newsgathering operation—make clear.

Dionne agrees with Plato, who said that democratic politics, while a "degenerative" form of government, was probably the best available system considering that human beings were its primary components. And the same can be said of the humans who cover the governing process. Media critic James Fallows (1996, 7) goes one step further. He holds journalism directly responsible for voter apathy, congressional gridlock and government via opinion polls rather than political leadership. In a quote that rings just as true today as it did when he made it before the turn of the century, Fallows claims:

> The harm actually goes much further than that, to threaten the long-term health of our political system. Step by step, mainstream journalism has fallen into the habit of portraying public life in America as a race to the bottom, in which one group of conniving, insincere politicians ceaselessly tries to outmaneuver another. The great problem for American democracy in the 1990s is that people barely trust elected leaders or the entire legislative system to accomplish anything of value. . . . Deep forces in America's political, social and economic structures account for most of the frustration of today's politics, but the media's attitudes have played a surprisingly important and destructive role.

Media critic Katherine Hall Jamieson (1992) has suggested that, when it comes to politics, journalists should get themselves a new definition of news. Instead of emphasizing events and conflict, Jamieson believes news stories could equally revolve around issues and multiple policy perspectives. Fallows and others insist that implicit in the right to report on politics is that successful governing is an outcome for which the media are partially responsible. The cynical assumptions that government can never act for the public good, and that journalists and the media are somehow outside and perhaps even above the political system, are almost nihilistic. Ethical practice allows journalists and their media consumers to become more conscientiously involved in the American democratic political system.

MODERN PROBLEMS: TERRORISM AND HATE

Terrorism is, at its most fundamental level, an act of communication; it communicates hatred toward the target. Scholars suggest that terrorism was not possible (or effective) before the modern mass media was capable of amplifying the message of hate. Terrorists and the media have a symbiotic relationship: terrorists need the media to communicate their messages, and the media garner ratings and increased readership when terrorism is in the news, even while deploring the violence. Simultaneously, the media must perform a dual role: acting as filters of the terrorists' message and as watchdogs of government response.

Terrorism presents journalists with what philosophers call "hard questions." Terrorism is news, but news coverage furthers terrorists' ends and makes more terrorism likely. How to break that cycle has been the subject of much professional anguish throughout the world, with some governments resorting to censorship of news. And objectivity is often antithetical to the situation. In the face of some forms of terrorism such as genocide, journalists must take the side of humanity, even if it means abandoning objectivity. CNN correspondent Christiane Amanpour argued on air with former President Bill Clinton about America's reluctance get involved in the racial and civil war after the former Yugoslavia disintegrated. Amanpour was not alone in her views, and after extensive debate the United States and NATO did engage in the conflict.

Terrorism also presents nation-states with hard problems. Nations under attack almost reflexively clamp down on their citizens—particularly those who question or dissent. Democracies pass laws, for example the PATRIOT Act, that enhance government's powers over its citizens. The PATRIOT Act not only increased the government's powers of search and seizure (unchecked by the courts), but also allowed incarceration of suspected terrorists without bail or public notification. What made the Act more devastating was the inclusion of a provision that made it impossible for journalists to get information needed to evaluate the effectiveness of the Act. If truth is the first casualty of war, then independence of thought and action is the first casualty of terrorism.

Journalists perform another role in such historic times—that of moral witness. Ethicist Patrick Plaisance (2002) suggests that when journalists report on such

events as terrorism, its causes, its execution and its results, the journalist functions as a "moral witness" because such news stories cannot be understood or reported outside of a moral framework. Plaisance and others assert that to be detached and objective about genocide and hate is to condone it. When journalists write the first draft of history of the early part of this century, they must deal with competing claims about justice, community, truth and power. Such reporting requires excellence in both ethical reflection and professional technique. It has seldom been more difficult—or more important—to do both well.

SOCIAL JUSTICE IN A DEMOCRATIC SOCIETY

Just as there are members of a power elite, there also are those who feel excluded from political society. One popular interpretation of U.S. history has been to track the gradual extension of power to ever more diverse publics. But the process has been uneven and contentious. All minority groups seek access to the political process and, since the mass media have become major players in that process, they seek access to media as well.

Media ethicists suggest these political and social outgroups provide the mass media with a further set of responsibilities. They assert that the mass media, and individual journalists, need to become advocates for the politically homeless. Media ethicist Clifford Christians suggests that "justice for the powerless stands at the centerpiece of a socially responsible press. Or, in other terms, the litmus test of whether or not the news profession fulfills its mission over the long term is its advocacy for those outside the socioeconomic establishment" (Christians 1986, 110).

This socially responsible view of the media suggests that journalists have a duty to promote community and the individuals within it. Those who are in significant ways outside the community—economically, socially or culturally—need a voice.

Christians's argument can be amplified beyond democracy's racial, ethnic and economic outgroups. In contemporary democratic society, clearly some "things" also are without political voice. The environment, ethnic issues, poverty and human rights violations beyond American shores all have difficulty finding a powerful spokesperson. These issues cross traditional political boundaries. Those who will be affected by them also need a voice.

Communitarian thinking takes social responsibility to the next level. It urges that justice is the ethical linchpin of journalistic decision making. If justice becomes the fundamental value of American journalism, then the media have the goal of transforming society, of empowering individual citizens to act in ways that promote political discussion, debate and change (Christians et al. 1993).

What makes journalists uneasy about either the communitarian or social responsibility approaches is that they smack of a kind of benevolent paternalism. If individual human beings carry moral stature, then assigning one institution—in this case the mass media—the role of social and political arbiter diminishes the moral worth of the individual citizen. The mass media become a kind parent and the citizen a sort of wayward child in need of guidance. Such a relationship does not promote political maturity.

While the weight of recent scholarly opinion sides with Christians, the view is not without risk. If accepted, it means a thorough change for the mass media in the U.S. political system. That change would bring about other changes, some of them not easy to anticipate. But whether change is what's needed, or merely a return to the strict libertarian view, both call for some sophisticated ethical reasoning. As Thomas Jefferson said, being a citizen of a democracy is not easy—to which journalists might well add, neither is covering one.

Suggested Readings

CHRISTIANS, C., T. GLASSER, D. MCQUAIL, and K. NORDENSTRENG. 2009. *Normative theories of the media: Journalism in democratic societies.* Champagne, IL: University of Illinois Press.

DIONNE, E. J., JR. 1991. *Why Americans hate politics.* New York: Simon & Schuster.

FALLOWS, JAMES. 1996. *Breaking the news: How the media undermine American democracy.* New York: Pantheon.

FRY, DON, ed. 1983. *The adversary press.* St. Petersburg, FL: The Modern Media Institute.

JAMIESON, K. H. 2000. *Everything you think you know about politics . . . and why you're wrong.* New York: Basic Books.

LINSKY, MARTIN. 1986. *Impact: How the press affects federal policymaking.* New York: W. W. Norton.

MADISON, JAMES S., ALEXANDER HAMILTON, and JOHN JAY. *The Federalist papers.*

WARD, STEPHEN. 2004. *The invention of journalism ethics.* Montreal: McGill-Queen's University Press.

Cases on the Web

www.mhhe.com/mediaethics7e

"The David Duke candidacy: Fairness and the Klansman" by Keith Woods

"Whose abuse of power: The *Seattle Times* and Brock Adams" by Lee Wilkins

"Denver's Rocky Flats: The role of the alternative press" by Lee Wilkins

"Terrorist use of the news media: News media use of terrorists" by Jack Lule

"Singapore: Balancing democracy, globalization and the Internet" by Seow Ting Lee

CHAPTER 6 CASES

CASE 6-A

Cable News: 24/7 Political Speech or Something Else?

SU JING
University of Missouri

Jack Cafferty is a CNN commentator whose provocative style sometimes results in a negative public and political response. On the April 9, 2008, broadcast of *The Situation Room,* Cafferty was asked to comment about the U.S.–China relationship. Cafferty opened with the statement that he does not know whether China as a nation is different than it was decades ago, but added that the U.S. relationship with China is.

"We're in hock to the Chinese up to our eyeballs because of the war in Iraq, for one thing," Cafferty said. "They're holding hundreds of billions of dollars worth of our paper. We are also running hundreds of billions of dollars worth of trade deficits with them as we continue to import their junk with the lead paint on them and the poisoned pet food and export, you know, jobs to places where you can pay workers a dollar a month to turn out the stuff that we're buying from Wal-Mart." Cafferty was referring to a series of scandals in 2007 and 2008 where Chinese imports were contaminated with toxic substances, including lead on children's toys.

"So, I think our relationship with China has certainly changed," he continued. "I think they're basically the same bunch of goons and thugs they've been for the last 50 years."

Two days later, the Xinhua News Agency, China's official press agency, reported that the Legal Immigrant Association (LIA), an organization of legal immigrants, most of them Chinese, started an online petition calling for a formal apology. They allege that Cafferty's remark was racist and exacerbated negative attitudes Americans hold about the Chinese and Chinese Americans.

It's not common to witness such a blatant discrimination against an ethnic group of people with such a derogatory connotation in a national TV program," the petition read. "We believe his remark clearly exposed his hatred and bigotry against Chinese people as a whole. Without doubt, many people feel hurt, especially, the Chinese people, by this shameless assault."

On April 14, 2008, Cafferty clarified his remarks saying his earlier comments referred to China's government, not the people themselves. That same day, CNN issued the following statement: "It was not Mr. Cafferty's nor CNN's intent to cause offense to the Chinese people, and we would apologize to anyone who has interpreted the comments in this way."

Not satisfied, the Chinese Foreign Ministry demanded an apology on April 15, saying that Cafferty's comments reflected his "ignorance and hostility toward China."

In a *Times* of London report, CNN continued to maintain that it is "a network that reports the news in an objective and balanced fashion." The statement added,

"As part of our coverage we also employ commentators who provide robust opinions that generate debate. It should be noted that over many years, Jack Cafferty has expressed critical comments on many governments, including the U.S. government and its leaders."

For weeks after the comments, protests against CNN and Cafferty were held outside the CNN offices in Atlanta, San Francisco and Hollywood. Thousands attended and demanded that Cafferty be fired. Two Chinese citizens sued CNN for violating the dignity and reputations of the Chinese. The suit has since been dropped.

According to Chinese Foreign Ministry spokesman Quin Gang, CNN President Jim Walton sent a May 15, 2008, letter to Zhou Wenzhong, Chinese ambassador to the United States stating: "On behalf of CNN I'd like to apologize to the Chinese people for that. CNN has the highest respect for Chinese people around the world and we have no doubt that there was genuine offense felt by them over the Jack Cafferty commentary."

Micro Issues

1. Cable news often employs commentators who make outrageous statements. What ethical guidelines should govern commentary and commentators?
2. If Cafferty's comment referred to the Chinese government and not its citizens, does that change your view of his comments?
3. Should Cafferty's comments have been more specifically tied to concrete examples, even though he is a commentator?

Midrange Issues

1. What is the most effective way for the public to respond to statements on cable news with which they disagree?
2. What is the appropriate policy to deal with such protests?
3. Who is responsible for this problem: Cafferty or CNN? Who can best solve it: Cafferty or CNN?

Macro Issues

1. John Stewart Mill noted, even if "opinion be in error, it may, and very commonly does, contain a portion of truth; and since the general or prevailing opinion on any subject is rarely or never the whole truth, it is only by collision of adverse opinions that the remainder of the truth has any chance of being supplied." How do you evaluate this statement in light of the current environment of 24-hour cable news?
2. Does the fact that CNN prides itself on its international coverage figure into the network's decision to apologize? Discuss the ethics of issuing an apology not because of an inaccuracy but in order to maintain an image. Is it ethical to apologize in order to maintain access for future stories?
3. As an American-based network CNN operates under a U.S.-centric understanding of unfettered political discourse. How do you think news journalists should explain that tradition to nations that do not share this legal or cultural heritage?

CASE 6-B

Victims and the Press

ROBERT LOGAN
National Institute of Medicine, Washington, D.C.

Alice Waters' daughter, Julie, seven, has leukemia. Her illness was diagnosed in its early stages in March 2000. Julie's physicians believe her condition can be successfully treated.

Ms. Waters, 37, lives in a mobile home in an unincorporated area a few miles from Metroplex, a city of 1.5 million. Ms. Waters' street is the only residential section in the area. At the north end of the street—which has 12 mobile homes on each side facing one another—are four large gas stations that catch traffic off the interstate that runs a quarter mile away to the west. At the south end of the street (about a quarter mile away) are two large tanks that are a relatively small storage facility for Big Oil, Inc. Next to this—starting almost in her backyard—is the boundary of a successful, 700-acre grapefruit orchard, which borders on a municipal landfill. About a quarter mile away are large well fields that are the principal source of drinking water for Metroplex.

In July 1999, a 6-year-old boy in the household two doors down from Ms. Waters was diagnosed as having leukemia. He was not as lucky as Julie; his diagnosis was late in the progression of his disease, and he died in December 2000. In 2001, an infant girl became the second baby born with birth defects in the neighborhood within seven years. Both families moved before Ms. Waters came to the neighborhood in 1999. Internal medicine specialists Dr. Earnest and Dr. Sincere met Julie soon after she was admitted to the hospital in October 2000. They were instrumental in getting funding for Julie's care when her mother was unable to pay. They are members of Worried M.D.s for Social Responsibility, a self-proclaimed liberal, national public interest group that gets actively involved in national political issues.

The physicians told Ms. Waters that they were suspicious about the causes of Julie's illness. Three cancer and birth-defect incidents on the same street, the physicians said, were not a coincidence.

In November 2001, they began to collect water samples from the wellhead at Ms. Waters's house. They sent the samples to a well-regarded testing lab in another city. Since then, they have tested the water at a professional lab every four months. Every test revealed traces of more than 10 human-made and natural chemicals often associated with oil storage tanks, pesticides, grapefruit orchards, gas station leaks, lead from automobile emissions and a large landfill.

However, each chemical occurs consistently at 6 to 15 parts per billion, which is considered safe for drinking water based on standards set by the U.S. Environmental Protection Agency (EPA). At higher levels these chemicals are associated with carcinogenic risks or increases in birth defects, but the levels found at Ms. Waters' wellhead are within safety thresholds set by the EPA. There is no evidence the chemicals are associated directly with the health problems found in Ms. Waters' neighborhood.

At a fund-raising party last night for mayoral candidate Sam Clean, Drs. Earnest and Sincere privately told Clean what they had found. Clean is a well-known public figure, has a reputation as an environmentalist, owns a successful health food restaurant chain, is media wise and looks good on television. He is a long shot to become mayor and needs fresh issues to draw attention to his candidacy.

At 11:00 a.m. today, KAOS news radio begins running as the top story in its 20-minute news rotation "Clean Attacks City Lack of Cleanup." In the story, Clean gives a sound bite attacking city officials for "ignoring cancer-causing agents in water in a neighborhood where children have died, which is next door to the city's water supply." He describes the neighborhood's medical problems and describes (without naming) Julie and Alice Waters. The news report explains that water from the neighborhood has several "toxic agents believed to cause cancer at higher levels" and points out that the city's water wells are within a quarter mile of oil tanks, gas stations, a grapefruit orchard, a landfill and septic tanks. County officials are said to be unavailable for comment. The report runs throughout the day at 20-minute intervals.

By 2:30 p.m., calls to the switchboard have jammed the newsroom. The callers who get through are frightened about their drinking water. City Hall's switchboards are jammed. The callers sound upset and ask whether their water is safe to drink.

By 4:00 p.m., reporters from the local ABC affiliate are already knocking on doors in the trailer park and sending live reports from the scene. Neighbors tell them where Alice and Julie Waters live.

At 4:15 p.m., your managing editor gives you the story. You are an ambitious reporter for *Metroplex Today,* the only morning newspaper in Metroplex. Both of you realize this is clearly Page 1 potential, but you have only a few hours before deadline for the next morning's edition. After a few phone calls, you discover that the mayor, the city council and most city and county officials are all out of town at a retreat and are unavailable for comment. The regional EPA office is not answering the phone.

A trusted spokesperson for Regional Hospital tells you that Drs. Sincere and Earnest are furious at Clean for releasing the story and have no comment. She fills you in with all of the above information. The same Regional Hospital spokesperson says Ms. Waters does not want to be interviewed. She suddenly realizes that her husband, whom she walked out on several years before, might see the story and return to town.

Sam Clean is more than happy to talk to you.

Micro Issues

1. Is Clean a reliable enough source for KAOS radio to base its reports on?
2. Should KAOS have broadcast the story?
3. Should you respect Ms. Waters' wishes and leave her and her daughter out of the story?
4. Are Dr. Earnest and Dr. Sincere reliable sources?
5. What do you tell the public about whether the water supply is safe?

Midrange Issues

1. Would you be working on the story if KAOS and ABC had ignored it?
2. Would you be working on the story if there was little public reaction after the KAOS broadcast?
3. If Ms. Waters decides to do an interview on ABC later today, do you then include her in your story?
4. If city and county officials remain unavailable, how do you handle their side of the story? Does that delay publication until you can get more information, or do you go with what is available?
5. Are there unbiased sources you can contact about risk assessment? Who?

Macro Issues

1. How do you handle the discrepancy between the information from the EPA and the skeptical scientists and environmentalists?
2. What is the public's probable reaction to reporting this story? Should your newspaper take any precautions to prevent public panic? If so, what should they be?
3. How risky is the water compared to risks we take for granted, such as traveling by car? Can you think of a relevant comparison for your article comparing the relative risk of the water to a well-known risk?
4. Is it the media's role to speak for a society that is averse to many risks? How might the media accomplish this function?

CASE 6-C

Painful Images of War: Too Painful for Whom? When?

BEVERLY HORVIT
University of Missouri

On March 23, 2003, in the first few days of the second Gulf War in Iraq, U.S. troops traveling in a six-vehicle convoy made a wrong turn and were ambushed by Iraqi forces. Six of the U.S. troops were captured, and nine were killed. That news was confirmed when the Qatar-based satellite network al-Jazeera rebroadcast Iraqi television footage of five captured soldiers—four men and one woman—as well as images of slain soldiers. Pfc. Jessica Lynch was among those captured but was not interviewed by Iraqi state television.

The bodies of four of the dead soldiers were filmed as they lay on the floor of a makeshift morgue. Two of the dead soldiers appeared to have been shot in the head. A fifth body was shown lying on the road behind an ambushed U.S. military truck. The tape also showed five of the captured Americans being interviewed by Iraqi officials, who were off-screen.

U.S. officials, including Defense Secretary Donald Rumsfeld, immediately criticized the Iraqi government for allowing those interviews to be recorded and broadcast. By doing so, Rumsfeld argued, the Iraqis had violated the 1949 Geneva Conventions, which mandate how prisoners of war are to be treated. Article 13 states, in part, that "prisoners of war must at all times be humanely treated" and "must at times be protected, particularly against acts of violence or intimidation and against insults and public curiosity."

The International Committee of the Red Cross concurred.

The Geneva Conventions mandate that prisoners only be asked their name, rank and serial number and that they not be subjected to "degrading and humiliating treatment." The al-Jazeera footage shows the U.S. soldiers—some visibly nervous—being asked additional questions about their hometowns and their reasons for coming to Iraq.

Immediately after al-Jazeera began broadcasting the footage, Rumsfeld told reporters, "Needless to say, television networks that carry such pictures are, I would say, doing something that's unfortunate" (Reid and Doran 2003). Lt. Gen. John Abizaid of the U.S. Central Command went further: "We will hold those [in charge] accountable for their actions" (Reid and Doran 2003).

After the Pentagon said the interview footage violated the Geneva Conventions, al-Jazeera pulled the interviews but temporarily continued to broadcast images of slain soldiers (Hamilton 2003). Similarly, although CBS News briefly showed a clip of the al-Jazeera tape, it stopped after the Pentagon complained and e-mailed U.S. news organizations asking them not to use the tape.

The late Peter Jennings, then the anchor of ABC's nightly news show, told viewers that pictures of the captured soldiers and probably slain soldiers "have been seen widely throughout the world, including in Iraq. The Bush administration has said very forcefully this violates the Geneva Conventions governing the

US MILITARY
IRAQ WAR POW

Edgar Hernandez

**Army Spc.
Shoshawna Johnson**

**Army Spc.
Joseph Hudson**

Pfc. Patrick Miller

AP Photo/Iraqi TV via APTN.

Sgt. James Riley

treatment for prisoners of war, and the president of ABC News has decided not to broadcast the pictures at this time."

In a "Nightline" edition the next night, Dave Marash of ABC News said "one simple rule" at ABC and other networks is not to use such pictures "until we know that families have been informed that their soldier has been captured." And, even when ABC knew the families had been notified, Marash noted there were other limitations on what ABC would show: "Pictures of dead soldiers, in which their wounds are grotesquely obvious, and their faces, perhaps, identifiable. And the real-time depiction of clearly frightened soldiers being asked questions that go well beyond the name, rank and serial number approved by the Geneva Conventions rulebook."

Newspaper editors around the United States also had to grapple with deciding which images, if any, to publish. Some U.S. newspapers chose to publish neither still photographs from the footage nor the soldiers' names. Others opted to run mug shots of the soldiers that had been cropped from the video footage but not still photographs of the slain soldiers. In many cases, the newspapers felt compelled to explain their rationale to their readers.

The *Orlando Sentinel, Atlanta Journal-Constitution,* Portland *Oregonian* and *Nashville Tennessean* are examples of papers whose editors decided not to use any of the still photographs from the al-Jazeera tapes on the first day. Dan Hortsch, public editor of the *Oregonian,* which published mug shots after the soldiers' names were released, told readers that although the Geneva Conventions applied to governments and not the news media, "the media must consider whether their actions further the intent of the captors" (Hortsch 2003).

In its story for March 24, the *Washington Post* told readers it was "not publishing the names of some of the soldiers because they had not been officially released by the Pentagon." The *Post* and *USA Today* did, however, use the name of Army Spc. Joseph Hudson, 23. Hudson was the second soldier to be questioned. When asked why he was in Iraq, Hudson replied: "I follow orders." Similarly, the *Orlando Sentinel* and *Constitution-Journal* ran a mug shot of Hudson.

Other newspapers, including the *Fort Worth Star-Telegram, Hartford Courant, Salt Lake Tribune* and *Sacramento Bee,* ran photos of the five captured soldiers cropped to mug shots. The *Star-Telegram* and *Sacramento Bee* published the mug shots on their front pages. In a Page 1 note to readers, *Star-Telegram* editors said, "We believe it is important for our readers to know their condition after capture, so we have chosen to run photos of their faces." Their actions and explanation did not impress some readers, many of whom sent angry letters to the editor.

A *Star-Telegram* (2003) editorial argued that publishing the photos would hold the Iraqis accountable for the POWs' well-being:

> The photographs . . . make it impossible for Iraqi officials to deny that they have these brave Americans in custody or to explain away possible injuries after their conditions have been documented. . . . Should the unthinkable happen—that they die after appearing in the news—then it will be clear that the soldiers were mistreated as prisoners. . . . Many families of prisoners held during the Vietnam War said that the media reports at least let them know their husbands, fathers, sons and brothers were still alive.

By the time the Pentagon had notified Spc. Shoshana Johnson's family of her capture, her parents already knew: they "had stumbled across it on their own—on a Spanish-language television station they had tuned in so that their granddaughter could watch cartoons" (Kenworthy, Willing and Cauchon 2003).

Complaints of media coverage of POWs cut both ways. One al-Jazeera employee told the *Los Angeles Times,* "Everyone showed footage of Iraqi prisoners of war just a day ago, and no one said a thing about that" (Pasternak 2003). Likewise, a Red Cross spokesman said, "Images being shown of POWs on both sides are a cause for concern" (Neuffer 2003).

Gina Lubrano, readers' representative for the *San Diego Union-Tribune,* said readers complained when the newspaper published a photograph of a dead Iraqi soldier, a photograph similar to one that appeared on the front page of the *New York Times.* She told readers (Lubrano 2003):

> The reason photographs of prisoners are permissible in the *Union-Tribune* and other newspapers and suspect when supplied by the Iraqis has to do with who is behind the camera and the intent behind the photo. Government-run Iraqi television represents the government holding the prisoners. Photographing them being questioned can be interpreted by some as an attempt by the Iraqi government to ridicule them and hold them up to public curiosity. . . . The photos of the Iraqi prisoners and the dead published in the *Union-Tribune* and other newspapers have been taken by independent photojournalists, not the government, and are an attempt to show the events of war, not *to ridicule them.*

Micro Issues

1. Critique the *Star-Telegram*'s argument that publishing the photos would make the Iraqis more accountable for the welfare of the soldiers.
2. How should American media respond to the threat by the U.S. Central Command officer to hold those in charge "accountable for their actions"?

Midrange Issues

1. Lubrano makes a distinction between the independent U.S. press and the state-owned Iraqi press in justifying her paper's action while condemning a similar action by al-Jazeera. Is the distinction valid? Justify your answer.
2. Is there a difference between film and still photography of the dead soldiers, and does that difference, if any, justify handling the images differently?

Macro Issues

1. Should the press acquiesce to the government's request to not show photos of the war based on:
   a. notification of families?
   b. taste?
   c. the Geneva Conventions?
   d. national security? Justify your answers.

CASE 6-D

For God and Country: The Media and National Security

JEREMY LITTAU
Lehigh University

MARK SLAGLE
University of North Carolina—Chapel Hill

The ethical issues involving the intersection of the media and national security typically revolve around the question of duties and loyalties. Those questions, as the following three-part case demonstrates, are long standing. They also allow journalists to evaluate the consistency of their reasoning over time—something good ethical thinking is supposed to promote. How journalists respond to these cases also may depend on the differing philosophies individual journalists and their news organizations adhere to.

With this introduction, decide each of the following three cases, all of which have an important role in the history of journalism ethics. As you resolve the various issues in each case, ask yourself whether you have been consistent in your decision making and what philosophical approach or approaches best supports your thinking.

Case Study 1: The Bay of Pigs

In 1961, an anti-communist paramilitary force trained and supplied by the CIA was preparing to invade Cuba and topple Fidel Castro. Although the desire of the American government to overthrow Castro was no secret, the specifics of the invasion plan were not known to the public. On April 6, a *New York Times* reporter filed a story with his editors that declared the invasion was "imminent." The paper prepared to run the story with a page-one, four-column slot using the word "imminent" in the text and the headline.

After much discussion, *Times* managing editor Turner Catledge and publisher Orvil Dryfoos decided to remove the word "imminent" from the story and shrink the headline to a single column. These changes were made, in part, in response to a phone call from President John F. Kennedy, asking the paper to kill the story. On April 17, the anti-Castro forces landed at Cuba's Bay of Pigs, where all group members were either taken prisoner or killed. The botched invasion was a major embarrassment for Kennedy, who later told Catledge that if the *Times* had run the story as planned it might have prevented the disastrous invasion (Hickey 2001).

Micro Issue

1. Did the *Times* act ethically in downsizing and downplaying the story?

Midrange Issue

1. Are there certain categories of information, for example troop movements or the development of new weapons, which journalists as a matter of policy should either downplay or not publish as all?

Macro Issue

1. How should journalists respond if government officials request that specific "facts" (which are not true) be printed as part of a disinformation campaign to confuse our enemies?

Case Study 2: Osama Bin Laden

Since the attacks of Sept. 11, 2001, Osama bin Laden and his deputies have released a series of video and audio tapes containing speeches about their ongoing operations. Many of them have first aired on al-Jazeera, the Arab-language news channel that broadcasts in the Middle East but also can be received in many American and European markets. The U.S. government, specifically President George W. Bush, urged the U.S. media not to rebroadcast these tapes, arguing that they might contain coded messages to al-Quaeda "sleeper cells" and could result in more attacks. Most broadcast networks acquiesced to the request, although it was never made clear whether any of the tapes, in fact, contained such messages (Spencer 2001).

Micro Issue

1. How is this request like and unlike President Kennedy's request to the *New York Times?*

Midrange Issues

1. Does the fact that other news agencies in other countries broadcast the tapes have any bearing on what U.S. broadcasters should do?
2. Should U.S. broadcasters have agreed to this request in October of 2001? Should they agree to the request today? Why or why not?

Macro Issue

1. How would you respond to a viewer who says that broadcasting the tapes is unpatriotic and puts American lives at risk?

Case Study 3: Make News, Not War?

In 1991 CNN correspondent Christiane Amanpour arrived in the Balkans to cover the breakaway of Slovenia and Croatia from Yugoslavia. After witnessing several brutal battles, including the siege of Dubrovnik, she moved on to Bosnia to cover the hostilities there for almost two years. Troubled by the lack of coverage the war was receiving, Amanpour encouraged her editors to devote more time to the issue. In 1994, Amanpour appeared via satellite on a live television broadcast with President Bill Clinton. She asked the president if "the constant flip-flops of your administration on the issue of Bosnia set a very dangerous precedent." Amanpour's pointed questions embarrassed the administration and generated more coverage of the war and of American foreign policy. Amanpour later admitted she wanted to draw more attention to the plight of the Bosnian Muslims (Halberstam 2001).

Micro Issues

1. Should Amanpour consciously have tried to influence U.S. foreign policy in this way?
2. If she had not tried to influence U.S. policy, would she have been complicit in the genocide that followed?

Midrange Issues

1. Are some issues, such as genocide, so ethically reprehensible that journalists should speak out as citizens in addition to fulfilling their professional responsibilities?
2. Is it appropriate for journalists to testify at war crimes trials when they have witnessed and reported on atrocities?

Macro Issue

1. Is it naive for journalists to continue to say that "we just let readers make up their minds" on these issues? If you answer yes, what does that say about the ethical dilemmas that come with the power we have as journalists?

CASE 6-E

Mayor Jim West's Computer

GINNY WHITEHOUSE
Whitworth University

The quiet, conservative city of Spokane, Wash., woke up to a surprise on Thursday, May 5, 2005, as residents opened their newspapers. They discovered that Mayor Jim West had used his city computer to solicit young men in gay chat rooms and that two men claimed West had sexually molested them as children.

In the months prior, West had been e-chatting on *Gay.com* with someone he believed to be an 18-year-old recent high school graduate, and offered him a city hall internship, sports memorabilia, help getting into college and excursions around the country. In reality, he had been corresponding with a forensic computer expert hired by the *Spokesman-Review*.

Reporter Bill Morlin had spent two years along with Reporter Karen Dorn Steele tracking down allegations from the 1970s that West had sexually molested boys while he was a county sheriff's deputy and a Boy Scout leader. West had been close friends with fellow deputy David Hahn and fellow Scout leader George Robey, who both committed suicide after sexual abuse allegations were brought against them in the early 1980s.

In 2002, the reporters discovered links to West while investigating abuse by local Catholic priests. West was at that time Republican majority leader in the Washington state senate and was considering running for what he called his "dream job"—being mayor of his hometown, Spokane. During the campaign, the reporters did not believe they had enough information to confirm any allegations. Eventually, they received tips from both anonymous sources and sources who would later go on the record and swear in depositions that West had abused them. One man, Robert Galliher, said West molested him at least four times as a child and that he was assaulted repeatedly by Hahn. Galliher, who says he has struggled with drug addiction as a result of the molestations, said he was in prison in 2003 when West visited him and sent him a message to keep his mouth shut. In addition, other young men reported that they had had sex with West after meeting him on gay chat lines and had been offered favors and rewards.

Spokesman-Review Editor Steven Smith and his staff spent days agonizing over creating a fictional character to go online at Gay.com and consulted with ethics experts at the Poynter Institute and elsewhere as they considered options. Smith told Spokane readers that the newspaper would not ordinarily go to such lengths or use deception, "But the seriousness of the allegations and the need for specific computer forensic skills overrode our general reluctance." Most important, Smith said the *Spokesman-Review*'s decisions were based on concerns about abuse of power and pedophilia, and not whether the mayor was homosexual.

The forensic expert, who previously worked for the U.S. Customs Office, followed strict guidelines. The expert posed online as a 17-year-old Spokane high school student and waited for West to approach him. The expert did not initiate conversation about sex, sexuality or the mayor's office. In the months that followed, the high school student supposedly had an 18th birthday. West then requested meetings with the fictional young man and arrived in a new Lexus at an agreed-upon spot—a golf course. His picture was taken secretly and the forensic expert broke off contact.

West was told about the forensic investigator in an interview with *Spokesman-Review* staff the day before the story broke. He admitted to the offers made within the chat room but denied abusing or having sex with anyone under age 18. When asked about the abuse allegations from the two men, West told the *Spokesman-Review* editors and reporters, "I didn't abuse them. I don't know these people. I didn't abuse anybody, and I didn't have sex with anybody under 18—ever—woman or man."

West insisted that he had not abused his office and that he was not gay. After the story broke, local gay rights advocate Ryan Oelrich, a former member of the city's Human Rights Commission, told the newspaper that he had resigned after coming to the conclusion West appointed him in an effort to pursue a sexual relationship. Oelrich said West offered him at one point $300 to swim naked with him in his swimming pool. Oelrich declined.

A conservative Republican, West blocked antidiscrimination provisions in housing for homosexuals, and voted against health benefits for gay couples while he served in the Washington state legislature and as mayor. He supported legislation barring homosexuals from working in schools or day care centers and called for bans on gay marriage. He told "The Today Show" that he was merely representing his constituents' views.

West asserted a message that he would repeat eventually on CNN, MSNBC and in a host of other national broadcasts: "There is a strong wall between my public and my private life."

Many political scientists disagreed with West's interpretation. Washington State University Political Science Professor Lance LeLoup said using an elected position for personal benefit is both unethical and "a misuse of power." Gonzaga University Political Science Professor Blaine Garvin told the *Spokesman-Review,* "I think it's a pretty bright line that you don't use your command over public resources to earn personal favors. That's not what those resources are for."

At the same time, some media critics criticized the newspaper's choice to use deception. The public cannot be expected to believe journalists and the veracity of their stories if lies are told to get at information, said Jane Kirtley, director of the Silha Center for Media Ethics and Law at the University of Minnesota. Speaking at a Washington News Council Forum on the *Spokesman-Review*'s coverage, Kirtley asserted that police officers can practice deception as part of their jobs, but journalists should not.

"It's one thing for the police or the FBI to pose as a 17-year-old boy," William Babcock, journalism department chair at California State University–Long Beach, told the *Seattle Post-Intelligencer.* "It's another for a journalist to take on the role of junior G-man and do something that essentially is considered police work." Babcock insists that the *Spokesman-Review* should have gotten the information through traditional reporting methods, but he agreed that no one, particularly a city mayor, should expect privacy in an online chat room.

Poytner Ethicist Kelly McBride, who previously was a reporter at the *Spokesman-Review,* said deception should not be normal practice but that the newspaper considered key ethical obligations: that the issue is grave and in the public interest, alternatives are explored, the decision and practice are openly shared with readers and the mayor is given the opportunity to share his story.

Jeffrey Weiss, a religion reporter for the *Dallas Morning News,* said he rarely believes the ends should justify the means, "but some do."

The FBI investigated West on federal corruption charges but did not find his actions warranted prosecution. Special Counsel Mark Barlett said in a media conference, "Our investigation did not address whether Jim West's activities were ethical, moral, or appropriate. . . . We did not attempt to determine whether Jim West should be the mayor of Spokane."

In December 2005, Spokane voters ousted the mayor in a special recall election. West later said the newspaper had created a "mob mentality" and that considering the accusations, even he would have voted against himself. On July 22, 2006, West died following surgery for colon cancer, a disease he had been fighting for three years. He was 55.

Micro Issues

1. Do you agree that police officers are ethically permitted to use deception but journalists are not?
2. Was the *Spokesman-Review* justified in using deception? Under other what extreme circumstances do you believe deception might be justified?

Midrange Issues

1. Some critics claimed that West's story only would come out in a provincial, conservative community, and that his story would not have been news had he been the mayor of Chicago or Miami. Do you agree?
2. Sissela Bok says deception might be permitted if the act passes the test of publicity. Does the *Spokesman-Review* meet that standard?
3. Should the use of a forensic computer expert in this case be characterized as the ends justifying the means? Why or why not?

Macro Issues

1. Should there be a wall between the public and private lives of public officials? At what point do public officials' private lives become public concern? Is public officials' sexuality always part of their private lives?
2. The *Spokesman-Review* is locally owned by the Cowles Publishing Company. The family business includes a downtown mall with a parking garage, which was developed in financial partnership with the city of Spokane. The garage has been subject to repeated lawsuits and controversy. Some critics believed that the *Spokesman-Review*'s delay in reporting about the mayor was due to a conflict of interest. Editor Steve Smith insists that the story was reported as the facts became evident. How do locally owned media companies manage covering their own communities without incurring conflicts of interest?

CASE 6-F

Journalists or Jokesters: The Pimp, the Prostitute and an ACORN That Fell away from the Tree

PHILIP PATTERSON
Oklahoma Christian University

The editors of the Columbia Journalism Review (cjr-study-guide 2009) called it a rare news story that was both "overplayed and ignored." Fox News claimed that only they cared about the story while other media accused Fox of lying. And in the end charges and counter-charges—possibly heading for court—surrounded the story.

It began when two conservative activists, James O'Keefe and Hannah Giles, approached several offices of ACORN—a politically-liberal advocacy group that was instrumental in the voter registration drives that led to the election of Barack Obama. In the hidden video shot at the Baltimore office of ACORN, O'Keefe claims to be a pimp, Giles a prostitute and they have large ambitions for their enterprise that would require a home where allegedly underage girls would be imported to act as prostitutes. Their multi-city tour of ACORN offices posing as a pimp and prostitute cost them about $1,300 out of their own pockets, they claimed in later interviews after they made their video public.

Although later facts showed that they were thrown out of some ACORN offices and the police were called in Philadelphia, the reception was warmer at a couple of offices and outright cordial at the Baltimore office where an African-American woman is seen giving the couple advice on everything from establishing their illegal enterprise to hiding their assets from the IRS.

The fallout was almost immediate. ACORN employees were fired and Congress voted to eliminate certain funding for ACORN, particularly in the matter of the 2010 census, but the total amount was debatable since many of the dollars were grants for which ACORN had not yet applied. However, others were looking into the possibilities that O'Keefe and Giles broke several laws in getting their story.

The hidden camera video and the story of how the young pair got the interviews was the star of most Fox News shows for more than a week in the fall of 2009. And while other media did cover the story—despite FOX on-air claims to the contrary—none had the enthusiasm for the story that Fox exhibited. This fact earned Fox support from strange quarters when Jon Stewart, host of his own self-proclaimed "fake news" show on "Comedy Central" asked, "Where are the *real* reporters on this story?"

The debate began almost immediately about whether the two young activists were just the latest in a long line of investigative journalists dating back to Upton Sinclair and Ida Tarbell or the political "hitmen" that others made them out to be.

Less than two weeks after the incident, the *Columbia Journalism Review* weighed in with two online articles about the sting. In an interview with Mark

Bowden (Fenwick 2009) who wrote about smear tactics in the Sonia Sotomayor Supreme Court confirmation hearing for *The Atlantic,* he told *CJR:*

> The young woman and filmmaker who visited those ACORN offices were political activists, and they put together what is, in essence, a very effective political protest against an organization they would like to damage. And they've done a very effective job of doing that.

The author of the *Review* article, Alexandra Fenwick, called the pair "political hitmen" and not journalists, but then asks, "Does it matter?" Her conclusion: "So ACORN got caught on candid camera, and they got caught good. Does it matter who shot the video and what their motivations were? Maybe not. Just don't call it journalism."

In a companion story, *Columbia Journalism Review* author Greg Marx (2009) had this to say:

> Of course, most of O'Keefe's conservative audiences won't view the videos as simple "information," anyhow. Instead, they'll likely see them as Michael Moore's liberal fans see his documentaries—as confirmations of their own worldview. And, with coverage of the ACORN story coming mostly from conservative-leaning outlets, it seems likely to perpetuate a troubling trend: *the sorting of the public into different fact universes.*

Marx also quotes *Outside the Beltway* writer James Joyner, who says: "It's simply unwise for large media outlets that claim to deliver 'all the news that's fit to print' to ignore big political stories when millions of people are talking about them."

Micro Issues

1. Is this journalism or not? Critique the claim of Fenwick that this is not journalism. Is "gothcha journalism" unethical in every case?
2. What are the ethical implications of encouraging someone to give illegal advice?
3. The ACORN employee giving the "advice" was African-American, as are many of their clients; the pair was Caucasian. The network that gave the tape the most exposure was Fox Network, with a mostly-Caucasian, mostly-conservative demographic. Is race a factor in this story and if so, how?

Midrange Issues

1. What is the difference between the hidden camera techniques of O'Keefe and Giles and the confrontational techniques of Michael Moore's documentaries or Bill O'Reilly's news show?
2. What do you see as the praiseworthy aspects of their reporting? What do you see as the blameworthy aspects of their reporting?
3. Critique the Joyner quote that it is unwise for mainstream media to ignore stories like this. Does this negate the traditional gatekeeper role that media have traditionally played?

Macro Issues

1. Are O'Keefe and Giles journalists? Should they be given press credentials to a legitimate news event like a political convention or a Presidential press conference? Is a blogger a journalist?
2. Should bloggers be allowed the privileges of mainstream journalists? Who decides?
3. What does Marx mean when he says these issues put audiences in "different fact universes." Do stories like this that divide rather than unite have a place in mainstream media?

7

Media Economics: The Deadline Meets the Bottom Line

By the end of this chapter you should be familiar with:

- **the economic realities of the social responsibility theory of the press.**
- **the economic and legislative initiatives that have combined to place control of information in the hands of fewer and larger corporations.**
- **how various mediums have coped with the current economic and technological realities of media.**
- **the "stakeholder" theory of economic success.**

INTRODUCTION

In the summer of 2009, one of the nation's leading media companies, the *Washington Post*, tarnished its reputation with an idea quickly labeled "pay for play" by critics. In a story broken by Politico.com, the *Post* printed a brochure advertising a series of *Washington Post* "salons" where for the price of $25,000 interested parties could spend an evening with lobbyists, lawmakers and White House officials, along with *Post* reporters. The salons—which were cancelled within days of the revelation of the idea—were to be held in the home of *Post* publisher Katharine Weymouth and the conversations led by the editor of the *Post*. The first proposed session was to be on health care.

Critics came from everywhere. White House press secretary Robert Gibbs joked at a press conference that he might not be able to afford to take a question from a *Post* reporter. Weymouth, who had been on the job for only 17 months with no prior newsroom experience, took the blame after initial releases blamed the marketing department for issuing an unapproved brochure. She wrote a front page apology.

The media firestorm was reminiscent of the *L.A. Times*/Staples Center scandal (see the case on the Web site for this book) where that paper became a financial partner of the new downtown arena at the same time it was covering the opening with a special section. Reporters for that paper were taken by surprise by the financial arrangement, just as the *Post* newsroom knew nothing of the proposed salons until the story broke on a Web site founded by ex-*Post* writers. Another similarity in the two scandals is that in each case the problem arose on the watch of a new publisher with no formal journalism background.

Within a week, the salon affair became just one more anecdote to be added to newspaper closings and mass layoffs to reveal an industry in peril. About a decade earlier, newspapers had jumped to the Web with no real financial model other than the hope that advertising would eventually catch up, and customers were resisting any retroactive attempt to pay for news content they were habituated to enjoying for free. Only the *Wall Street Journal* seemed capable of holding the line on charging readers for content. In one of the ironies of the situation, more readers than ever before were going to a "newspaper" for information, but most of them were Web readers paying nothing for the service. And since most newspapers were part of chains and those chains part of media conglomerates, the perils of the daily paper threatened even the few healthy parts of the media economy.

The *Post* controversy is a microcosm of the problems facing the industry today. The media are in a financial meltdown, a problem that began with the newspaper industry but which, by the time you read this book, is expected to have migrated to television. In 2009, the magazine industry appeared to be taking the brunt of the financial changes with industry standards such as *Newsweek* shedding both pages and staff while other venerable publications, such as *Gourmet,* closed entirely. Indeed, the only circulation growth in the magazine industry was in celebrity and gossip magazines. But whether the communications channel was newspapers, magazines or television, the financial strain affected and is affected by the governments news organizations cover, the stockholders those same organizations answer to and the bureaucracies that makes the rules. In this chapter we will look at one theory that has guided the press for more than half a century and then look at how individual media are fulfilling their promise envisioned by the theorists. We will then conclude with an alternate view of accountability in the new millennium.

A LEGACY OF RESPONSIBILITY

The *social responsibility theory of the press* was developed in the 1940s by a panel of scholars, the Hutchins Commission, with funding from Henry Luce, the conservative founder of *Time* magazine. The social responsibility theory envisioned a day when an active recipient of news and information was satisfied by a socially responsible press. According to the Hutchins Commission, media have the following five functions in society:

1. To provide a truthful, comprehensive and intelligent account of the day's events in a context that gives them meaning.
2. To serve as a forum for exchange of comment and criticism.
3. To provide a representative picture of constituent groups in society.
4. To present and clarify the goals and values of society.
5. To provide citizens with full access to the day's intelligence.

But social responsibility theory has a fundamental flaw: it gives little attention to modern media economics. This omission occurred in part because multinational corporations and chain ownership were still on the horizon when the Hutchins Commission worked. Because the theory was developed early in the McCarthy period, there also was an unwillingness to link economic and political power for fear of being labeled Marxist. This omission means that *the social responsibility theory does not deal with the realities of concentrated economic power,* particularly in an era when information has become a valuable commodity.

As the mass media became enormous, economically powerful institutions, they joined what political scientist C. Wright Mills (1956) called the "power elite," a ruling class within a democratic society. Time has proved Mills right. Power is found not only in the halls of government but also on Wall Street. And power is found not only in money or armies, it is also found in information. Media organizations, precisely because they have become multinational corporations engaged in the information business, are deeply involved in this power shift.

Today the media are predominantly corporate owned and publicly traded, with media conglomerates among the largest (and until recently, the most profitable) of the world's corporations. The corporate owners of the average news operation are more insulated from contact with news consumers than virtually any other business owner in America. And, there are fewer of them. Most local media outlets in the world were owned by six multinational corporations and each has become increasingly large in an attempt to gain market efficiencies.

This emergence of media as economic and political power brokers leads to the question of how a powerful institution such as the mass media, which traditionally has had the political role of checking other powerful institutions, can be checked. Can the watchdog be trusted when it is inexorably entwined with the institutions it is watching? For instance, when a media outlet is owned by a corporation such as General Electric, can it cover the health care debate objectively when the parent company might have a stake in the outcome through inventions and patents?

Similarly, what news organization can be trusted to take a critical look at the FCC's consideration of loosening the ownership rules when the conglomerate that owns individual outlets stands to profit from the changes? As media corporations expand exponentially in the pursuit of profit, who will watch the watchdog?

When the social responsibility theory was framed in the 1940s, the primary informational concern was scarcity: people might not get the information they needed for citizenship, and until recently, government agencies such as the FCC were still basing policy decisions on the scarcity argument when any consumer with cable or a satellite dish knew otherwise. Today, however, the primary informational concern is an overabundance of raw data: people might not filter out what they need through all the clutter. Media and their distribution systems changed, but the theory remained silent, especially about the role of profit.

The clash of large, well-financed institutions for control of information is a modern phenomenon. Classical ethical theory, which speaks to individual acts, is of little help in sorting out the duties and responsibilities of corporations larger than most nations that control the currency of the day: information. Americans are unwilling to accept government as the solution to counter the concentrated economic power of the media, and government has been hesitant to break up the large media conglomerates. Europeans have taken a different view, in many cases using tax dollars to support a government controlled broadcast system. In some cases, such as the Scandinavian countries, tax dollars also support newspapers—with the goal of sustaining multiple, distinct voices in the public sphere (Picard 1988).

HYPER-COMPETITION AND ITS IMPACT ON NEWS

Legacy journalists, those journalists who did not come of age as "digital natives," and the news organizations that employ them, face a huge shift in the assumptions about what makes news media profitable and praiseworthy. Legacy journalism emerged from an era of low-to-moderate economic competition. Even though specific rivalries were often intense, they were local and definitely not across media platforms. Individual organizations competed for consumer satisfaction and time, consumer spending, content, advertisers and employees. More than 15 years ago, media scholar Steve Lacy (1989) predicted these low-to-moderate competitive environments would produce a quality news product based on individual organizations' financial commitment to news, which in turn was perceived useful by audience members and sustained by a journalistic culture that valued excellence and public service.

But, low-to-moderate competition no longer exists in the contemporary media marketplace. Instead, you now live in an era of hyper-competition, much of it provided by Web access. In hyper-competition, supply substantially exceeds demand so that a large percentage of the producers in the market operate at a financial loss. Classical economic theory holds that hyper-competition cannot exist permanently. However, news and information are not traditional economic commodities; they are called "experience and credence" commodities, meaning that a consumer cannot judge whether the product actually meets individual needs until he or she has invested in and spent time with the product. News also is linked to social welfare, a category of products with significant external values not readily captured by price point or profit margin.

Media economists Ann Hollifield and Lee Becker, based on evidence collected in multiple nations as well as the United States suggest that the current media marketplace is a hyper-competitive one (Hollifield and Becker 2009). The results are predictable.

First, markets fragment. Fragmenting markets drive down profits because access to everything from advertisers to readers/viewers to workers declines. Then, as profits decline, content quality also declines. News organizations will increasingly

implement low-cost strategies. These low-cost strategies will drive down wages for professionals, journalists will have to produce more in less time and with fewer resources and news organizations will begin to rely on un-paid, non-professionals to provide some content. As competition intensity reaches hyper-competition, profits for most media organization will disappear or nearly disappear.

Hollifield and Becker note that as a result of the financial stress, both news organizations and individual journalists will become more susceptible to influence peddling from such activities as bribery, monetary subsidies, information subsidies and the trading of editorial content for advertising or other sources of revenue. "Hyper-competition unchecked will create conditions that increase the likelihood that journalism ethics will be violated at both the organizations and individual levels" (Hollifield and Becker 2009, 67).

Some scholars have referred to this era as one of "liquid journalism" where "traditional role perceptions of journalism influenced by its occupational ideology—providing a general audience with information of general interest in a balanced, objective and ethical way—do not seem to fit all that well with the lived realities of reporters and editors, nor with the communities they are supposed to serve" (Deuze 2008, 848).

Before you dismiss this as mere theory, think back to the anecdote that opened this chapter. When news organizations, and even individual journalists, worry about their "brand" rather than the public they serve, something essential has been lost or at least downgraded. Perhaps the most troubling element in this strand of research in media economics is that the public appears not to value—or even sometimes recognize—that quality is declining. In hyper-competitive situations, ethics takes a back seat to survival and the common good becomes the loser in the process.

TELEVISION: CONGLOMERATION, CONSOLIDATION AND SURVIVAL

Television, a medium that began its existence as a free service brought to the public by willing advertisers has morphed into something that nine out of ten Americans now pay for twice—once with their cable or satellite bills and, for most, twice with their attention to advertising. Yet television, particularly at the network or cable level where programming is produced, is always in search of more efficiency and revenue streams.

Take the two entities that are the original television networks: NBC and CBS. In the past decade, both have acquired more assets from publishing houses to cable networks to content distributors. The goal of all this financial activity is not only to find profit centers but also to create vertically integrated companies with diverse sources of income. Consider this scenario:

- By acquiring production facilities, networks can now own the shows they broadcast, a new phenomenon cutting deeply into the old system of buying programs from independent producers who took the risks to reap the possible rewards if shows were picked up.
- By acquiring cable stations such as USA, networks control outlets for their shows as they go into the lucrative phases of syndication, taking advantage of legislation that ended the FCC's old "fin-syn" rule prohibiting networks from being syndicators.
- By acquiring the maximum number of local television stations owned by law, networks can reach up to 35 percent of the population with their own O&O's (owned and operated stations) and have a built-in network for uploading news when it happens in a market where they own a station.
- By acquiring after-market distributors, networks make money on rentals and sales of boxed DVD sets of popular series.

The result is a pair of companies that have survived in the broadcasting industry for nearly a century and that can now control a product from the filming of the pilot episode to the last airing of the syndicated show or personal download, sometime decades from now. And it must be emphasized that much of what is now possible in the bullet points above has only recently been made possible by FCC and court rulings as well as generous anti-trust rulings. And NBC and CBS are but two "legacy" media corporations to have acquired their way to financial success.

Media consolidation allows for a diversification of income. In the case of NBC, after the acquisition of Universal, revenues went from 90 percent advertising-based to 50 percent, with the remainder coming from subscriptions, admissions, licensing and other ancillary income. By weaning away from advertising, media companies have hedged against the vagaries of recession. The strong showing of theater ticket sales in the summers of 2008 and 2009 have proved that consumers will pay for content, and television, by owning its product and making it increasingly easier to access, is following that model.

Conglomeration, consolidation and the aftermarket added more revenue streams and made things more predictable for stockholders. But not everyone is happy with the direction media ownership is taking. Groups as diverse as the National Organization for Women and the National Rifle Association criticized and challenged recent changes in ownership limits proposed by the Federal Communications Commission (FCC). FCC Commissioner Michael Copps, in a minority dissent to the loosening of ownership restrictions, called the changes another step in the "Clear Channelization" of American media, a reference to Clear Channel, a media company that had benefited from earlier relaxation of ownership limits in radio, only to become a lightning rod for consumer complaints about nonlocal ownership of radio stations. *Columbia Journalism Review* Editor at Large Neil Hickey (2003) summed up the fears of many when he concluded,

> What we risk over the long haul is ownership creep that may eventually see the end of the few remaining rules, and with them, the public's right to the widest possible array of news and opinion—at which point, robust, independent, antagonistic, many-voiced journalism may be only a memory.

Soon after the new ownership rules were proposed, they were challenged in court and in Congress. Consumers—organized on the Internet—objected so vigorously that Congress ultimately rejected the changes. One particularly contentious proposal would have allowed newspapers to own local television stations in the market where they published. Critics claimed that when the local newspaper is allowed to own two or more television stations and up to eight radio stations in the nation's largest markets (the amount allowed by FCC regulations), competition in news would no longer exist and the public would lose important viewpoints.

Ironically, the critics got their way and newspapers were enjoined (again) from owning television stations in their local market based largely on the argument that the ban would ensure more diversity in the market. The irony is that the net result might be that the critics of newspaper ownership of television outlets might have hastened the death of the local paper in several communities where readership was drastically declining.

MOVIES AND MUSIC: BLOCKBUSTERS AND PIRATES

While digital technology sent shock waves throughout all media industries, the strongest tremors were felt in the entertainment business. There, digital technology arrived at the same time a handful of global companies took control of about 85 percent of the record industry. The rationale for the consolidation in the music industry was that profits from established labels and artists would be used to promote new talent. However, the corporate approach meant that managers now focused on quarterly profits and selling records rather than making music and promoting art.

Corporations wanted blockbuster hits. They were difficult and expensive to make and promote and impossible to predict. Wal-Mart, the largest retailer of music in America, wanted to make its profits from the industry while carrying only about 2 percent of all releases available in a single year (Anderson 2006).

Chris Blackwell, who began a small record label in the 1970s and sold it to Poly-Gram in 1989, said, "I don't think the music business lends itself very well to being a Wall Street business. You're always working with individuals, with creative people, and the people you are trying to reach, by and large, don't view music as a commodity but as a relationship with a band. It takes time to expand that relationship but most people who work for the corporations have three-year contracts, some five, and most of them are expected to produce. What an artist really needs is a champion, not a numbers guy who in another year is going to leave" (Seabrook 2003, 46).

Other industries are affected by the new economic realities as well. Major studios no longer want to make medium-budget films—from $40 million to $80 million. Instead, they prefer smaller films for $10 million or less and "blockbuster" films with budgets of $100 million or more. Films in the middle—particularly the $40 to $60 million range—are now considered too risky to make by many producers and some studios. Plus, investors want films with a built-in audience, so a huge percentage of the nation's screens are filled with sequels, comic book heroes and action-adventure movies known to be big in foreign distribution. Advertising budgets became bloated, creating large opening weekends that are typically followed by dropoffs in attendance of up to 70 percent as the word of mouth got out that some films were not that good.

The effect of this trend was that midpriced, independent films, with fewer explosions and with no-name actors, have less chance of being made than ever before. True, there was the occasional medium budget breakout but the entertainment industry, focused as it was on the "blockbuster" business model, continued to play it safe. The same mentality is true of music and book publishing as well, where fewer producers meant fewer outlets for artists and a dumbing down of content to please a mainstream audience.

Meanwhile, another threat to the digital entertainment industries emerged. Piracy and sharing of digital files sent music CD sales plummeting and threatened movies as download speeds and storage space allowed for the transfer of very large files. Those who did buy their music legally through iTunes, Rhapsody or some other source, opted to pay less than a dollar for a tune they like instead of nearly twenty dollars for the corresponding CD. In 2002, the industry shipped 33.5 million copies of the year's 10 best-selling CDs, barely half the number it had shipped in 2000. Today, that number has been halved again, with a "best-selling" CD often registering sales in the tens of thousands compared to chart-topping "albums" in the early rock era that routinely sold half a million copies.

The music industry—from producers to radio station owners—was slow to realize that consumers had forever changed the way they would buy and listen to their music. Sir Howard Stringer, the chairman of the Sony Corporation of America, called downloaders "thieves" and compared them to those who shoplift from stores. The recording industry initially filed suit against some select downloaders and was successful in shutting down the very popular, but ultimately illegal, file-sharing site Napster. But, eventually, a pricing structure that made downloading inexpensive, combined with the emergence of popular devices to play it on such as the iPod, seemed a more effective—and more profitable—remedy. But recording's gain was radio's loss as iPods became the equipment of choice for the under-40 audience to access music. A look at the top 10 formats in radio, available at several industry Web sites, validates the fact that it is a medium with an aging audience.

Meanwhile the movie industry, not yet hurt as deeply as the music industry, raced to find its own equivalents of the dollar download, especially after the DVR made high quality copying easy. By making legal movies readily available through retail kiosks at as low as a dollar per night or easily available through the mail with services like Netflix, the industry got at least some money from the movie after-market at the same time that domestic and foreign box office held strong.

The ethical implications are obvious. As you read this section, ask yourself these questions:

- When was the last time you bought a CD or DVD as opposed to burning one belonging to a friend?
- Have you ever loaned out a CD or DVD to be copied by a friend?
- Do you agree that person-to-person music sharing or video sharing constitutes theft?
- Is file sharing a good way to register a protest about the impact of profit?
- Is Sir Howard Stringer right that it is equivalent to shoplifting?
- Would you feel the same way if someone shared *your* work?

On an industry-wide level, new artists, especially those who don't fit the corporate view, will find the Internet to be a two-edged sword. It will give them the publicity they need at an affordable cost, but it will allow for file sharing or dollar downloads that make it virtually impossible to make significant sums of money. As is often the case in the mass media, the development and adoption of a new medium or delivery technology has unanticipated consequences for existing media and formats. For music, the solutions are elusive and the stakes are high. Will creative people, who find their energies unusable in the music industry, turn to other mediums, or will the industry—and most importantly—consumers find a way to reward the creators of this most personal of medium?

NEWSPAPERS: LOSING THE PENNY PRESS REVOLUTION

Financing the American media through advertising is so deeply ingrained in the system that it is hard to imagine any other way. Yet newspapers in America were supported solely by their readers for more than a century. Incidentally, in 1920, then-Secretary of Commerce Herbert Hoover argued for commercial-free radio, a funding formula that would have likely failed or at the least, changed the medium entirely.

The legacy funding formula for most newspapers was created more than 170 years ago when Benjamin Day, publisher of the *New York Sun,* started the "penny press" revolution by lowering the price of his newspaper to a penny at a time when his competition was selling newspapers for a nickel. He gambled that he could overcome the printing losses with additional advertising revenue—if circulation increased. When his gamble paid off, virtually every publisher in town followed his lead.

What Day did was farsighted. By pricing their products at or below the cost of printing, publishers cast their economic future with their advertisers. But advertisers demand "eyeballs" and paid circulation, guaranteed by the Audit Bureau of Circulation, was the standard. The system worked as long as circulation increased to cover the increasing costs of covering the news. But readership peaked more than two decades ago, and newspapers began shedding costs. Some sold to chains. Others combined with rivals in "joint operating agreements "(JOA) which were, in effect, a congressionally-approved exception to anti-trust laws. Under a JOA, rival papers could combine press operations, billing operations, etc. but act as rival newspapers in their quest for news. However, with more than 30 years of history to evaluate the impact of the JOA legislation, what scholars and stockholders now know is that no joint operating agreement has allowed both newspapers to survive under the new financial arrangement for longer than a decade.

Such consolidation efforts were not nearly enough to survive the onslaught of the Web and a business model that provided news—a expensive commodity to produce—for free online. Layoffs and hiring freezes became a fact of life at large and award-winning papers such as the *Los Angeles Times,* the *Chicago Tribune* and the *New York Times* and smaller community papers as well. No one has found a way to "monetize" the Internet operation, and an attempt to gain more readers by being more convenient eventually had become a way for many to not pay for news content at all. Although ads were possible and even populous on newspaper Web sites, advertisers were loath to pay the same amount that audited readership had commanded. Major newspapers such as the *Rocky Mountain News* in Denver folded. Some, like the *Wall Street Journal,* decreased their page size while most decreased their page count beginning a cycle where smaller "news hole" required fewer journalists. Other papers went to less-than-daily circulation in an attempt to survive. A summer 2009 *Columbia Journalism Review* article called for major papers and wire services to all go to a paid model on their Web sites simultaneously while admitting in the same article the anti-trust implications of their suggestion.

But no other good ideas emerged, and at the time this book went to press, newspapering remained in serious trouble. The local newspaper in most communities had long been a monopoly operation with returns of greater than 20 percent annually common before the bleeding of circulation and advertising. Even after cutbacks, newspapers still boast a "name brand" in most communities and the largest reporting staff in any given local market. With readers decreasing, some newspapers are increasingly putting video segments on their Web sites in an attempt to siphon viewers from local nightly newscasts. How this even more expensive use of the Web will play out is unknown, however, but it does demand that journalists be cross-trained for the new media reality as newspapers add video and sound and television stations add print stories to their Web sites.

THE MODERN DILEMMA: STAKEHOLDERS VS. STOCKHOLDERS

The current state of media financial affairs can be summarized as an emphasis on corporate responsibility to the stockholders of publicly traded corporations—including the six media behemoths. In stockholder theory, corporations and their leaders have a single, overriding and legally binding promise to those who purchase stock: increase the share price. Milton Friedman, who first articulated the theory, suggests that increasing the share price is *the* promise that managers make. Whatever is legally done to promote that end is ethically right.

In every key media format—radio, television, newspapers, magazines, cable television and motion pictures—more than half of the gross revenues are concentrated in a handful of corporations—what media economics researcher Ben Bagdikian (1990, 5) has called "a de facto ministry of information within a democracy." If decisions are made to release only CDs that have a chance to go platinum, the will of one stakeholder—new or emerging artists—bends to the will of the corporation that can scarcely afford to foster unknown talent on the shareholder's dollar. The same can be said of new filmmakers, authors or any other would-be artist wanting to reach mass audiences.

Business ethicist Patricia H. Werhane (2006) has a different vision of the traditional stakeholder map. She says that some sorts of businesses—such as health care—have a public responsibility that extends beyond individual stockholders. These companies, she says, should operate from an "enriched stakeholder" model as opposed to a "profit-driven stockholder" model. The enriched stakeholder model puts something other than the corporation at the center of the "stakeholder" map (for health care, she suggests the patient) and rings that central stakeholder with government, investors, the court system, medical professionals, insurance companies, managed care plans and others. By changing the stakeholder map, Werhane suggests that other "promises" surface and that other measures of success emerge. Recent suggestions for fixing the nation's health care crisis have included paying doctors for outcomes rather than procedures—a form of practicing stakeholder ethics.

Werhane says that this way of thinking can result in some extraordinary outcomes. The Grameen Bank model pioneered the concept of "micro loans" to fight poverty in Bangladesh. The notion of lending very small amounts of money to individuals with good ideas was a way to leverage the "borrowers" (more than 90 percent of them women) and their families out of poverty. The micro loan concept and its inventor, Muhummad Yunnus, were awarded the Nobel Peace Prize in 2006. And, the bank itself remains both solvent and profitable, with a loan repayment rate of more than 98 percent.

The stakeholder model of media economics has much to recommend it. At the center of the map are citizens and community. Around the center is a ring including audiences, creative artists, stockholders, governments, nongovernmental organizations, journalists, strategic communication professionals, corporate managers and employees. By asking what benefits citizens living in communities the most, media corporate managers would begin to use a different gauge of success that does not place profit first in every situation. Media corporations would no longer search for a one-time "hit" that can be packaged, imitated (think reality television) and mass reproduced (think movie sequels). Instead, they would make smaller investments in a variety of experiments, allowing creativity and connection to community to help determine what works for both stakeholders and stockholders and what does not.

SOCIAL RESPONSIBILITY IN THE NEW MILLENNIUM

But stakeholder theory is far from a reality in the media universe. Good journalism is expensive, and in an era of declining subscriptions and ad revenues, few newsrooms enjoy budgets as large as in past years. The television networks have closed entire bureaus, and many newspapers have pulled back on overseas correspondents, leaving coverage of foreign news to the wires and CNN. The current era of cutbacks and consolidations has been noted by media researcher Robert McChesney (1997), who makes this analogy:

> Imagine if the federal government demanded that newspaper and broadcast journalism staffs be cut in half, that foreign bureaus be closed, and that news be tailored to suit the government's self-interest. There would be an outcry that would make the Alien and Sedition Acts, the Red Scares and Watergate seem like child's play. Yet when corporate America aggressively pursues the exact same policies, scarcely a murmur of dissent can be detected in the political culture.

The effect of cutbacks is lost news for the consumer. One photojournalist, Brad Clift, told the authors that he went to Somalia months before U.S. troops were dispatched, using his own money because he felt the starvation there was an underreported story. Only an occasional network crew and a handful of newspapers pursued the Somalia story before former President George H. W. Bush committed U.S. troops to the region in December 1992. Most news organizations, like this photojournalist's employer, declined to cover the emerging story, pleading that they had depleted their international budgets by covering Operation Desert Storm.

In reading the code of ethics of the Society of Professional Journalists, two of the "guiding principles" of journalism speak directly to the ethics of media economics: (1) seek truth and report it as fully as possible and (2) act independently. Seeking the truth can be personally and financially expensive, something that stakeholder theory demands and stockholder theory avoids.

Some media companies *have* learned the lesson. McKinsey and Company (National Association of Broadcasters 1985) studied 11 of the nation's great radio stations, such as WGN in Chicago and reported what made an excellent radio station. Their findings were:

- The great radio stations were audience oriented in their programming; and
- The great radio stations were community-oriented in their promotions.

Great radio stations had a knack for becoming synonymous in their communities with charitable events and community festivities even without an immediate return on investment. The attitude is summed up by WMMS (Cleveland) General Manager Bill Smith:

> If you want a car to last forever, you've got to throw some money back into that car and make sure that it's serviced properly on a continual basis. Otherwise, it's going to break down and fall apart. We know that we're constantly rebuilding the station one way or another. We throw the profit to the listening audience . . . to charities, to several nonprofit organizations, to free concerts or anything to affect the listeners of Cleveland as a whole . . . because they identify us as being community-minded.

Uplifting examples are far too rare. Entry-level salaries for journalists in both print and broadcast are far too low—under $28,000 in one survey, draining the industry of the talent that might solve some of the seemingly insoluble problems. But a strong democracy requires a strong media and valid solutions must be found. The stakes could not be higher.

Suggested Readings

AULETTA, KEN. 1991. *Three blind mice: How the TV networks lost their way.* New York: Random House.

BAGDIKIAN, BEN H. 2000. *The media monopoly.* 6th ed. Boston: Beacon Press.

CRANBERG, GILBERT, RANDALL BEZANSON, and JOHN SOLOSKI. 2001. *Taking stock.* Ames, IA: Iowa State University Press.

MILLS, C. WRIGHT. 1956. *The power elite.* New York: Oxford University Press.

MCCHESNEY, ROBERT W. 1991. *Rich media, poor democracy: Communication politics in dubious times.* Urbana: University of Illinois Press.

Cases on the Web

www.mhhe.com/mediaethics7e

"Union activism and the broadcast personality" by Stanley Cunningham

"A salesperson's dilemma: Whose interests come first?" by Charles H. Warner

"Turning on the *Light:* The San Antonio newspaper war" by Fred Blevins

"Calvin Klein's kiddie porn ads prick our tolerances" by Valerie Lilley

"*Ms.* magazine—No more ads!" by Philip Patterson

CHAPTER 7 CASES

CASE 7-A

Crossing the Line? The *L.A. Times* and the Staples Affair

MEREDITH BRADFORD AND PHILIP PATTERSON
Oklahoma Christian University

The *Los Angeles Times,* in a "special report" on December 20, 1999, called attention to an event its editors perceived as a breach of journalism ethics. The multistory report was entitled "Crossing the Line." What made this report extraordinary is that it was the *Times* itself that had crossed the line that triggered this journalistic exposé.

A few weeks earlier, the Staples Center, a $400 million sports and entertainment arena in downtown Los Angeles, had opened to great fanfare. Most observers shared the hope that the facility, which would house two basketball franchises and one hockey team, would spark a revitalization of downtown. Staples Inc. had won the naming rights to the arena by paying $116 million.

Tim Lieweke, president of the Staples Center, left with $284 million more to raise, had initiated talks with McDonald's, Anheuser-Busch, United Airlines, Bank of America and others to become "founding partners." He was eager to have the *Los Angeles Times* as a founding partner because of previous joint successes and because he thought the paper could contribute value beyond cash.

The Staples arena already had a promotional arrangement with the *Los Angeles Times* in exchange for cash payments from the *Times* and free advertising in the paper. "The arrangement is similar to that many big-city papers have with their local professional sports teams," said David Shaw, the *L.A. Times* Pulitzer Prize–winning media critic, in an investigative piece on the controversy (Shaw 1999). "But for the Staples Center, Lieweke wanted more. He wanted the *Times* as a founding partner."

Since the Staples Center could be a major contributor to the revitalization of downtown Los Angeles, *Times* executives were "eager to participate," Shaw said. The price for founding partners ranged from $2 million to $3 million per year for five years. Jeffrey S. Klein, then senior vice president of the *Times,* who supervised early negotiations on the Staples deal, "didn't think it was worth what they were asking." Negotiations stalled for several months in 1998 until a "Founding Partner Agreement" was accepted on December 17, 1998, between the L.A. Arena Company and the *Los Angeles Times.* Part of the language in the agreement stated the two companies "agree to cooperate in the development and implementation of joint revenue opportunities."

"Although all of the principals in the negotiations say that the precise terms of the Staples deal are confidential," Shaw reported, "information from a variety of sources shows that in effect the *Times* agreed to pay Staples Center about $1.6 million a year for five years—$800,000 of that in cash, $500,000 in profits and an estimated $300,000 in profits from what Lieweke had called 'ideas that would generate revenue for us.'"

This latter part of the deal was clarified in a clause of the final contract that said, in part, that the *Times* and the L.A. Arena Company would agree to cooperate in the development and implementation of joint revenue opportunities such as a special section in the *Los Angeles Times* in connection with the opening of the arena, or a jointly published commemorative yearbook, Shaw said.

These "joint opportunities" were to create $300,000 of net revenue for each party annually. According to the contract, these opportunities would be subject to the mutual agreement of both parties.

On Oct. 10, 1999, the *Times* published a special 168-page issue of its Sunday magazine dedicated to the new Staples Center sports and entertainment arena.

Only after the section was published did most of the paper's journalists learn that the *Times* had split the advertising profits from the magazine with the Staples Center. Feeling that the arrangement constituted a conflict of interest and a violation of the journalistic principle of editorial independence, more than 300 *Times* reporters and editors signed a petition demanding that publisher Kathryn Downing apologize and undertake a thorough review of all other financial relationships that may compromise the *Times'* editorial heritage.

The petition, in part, stated "As journalists at the *L.A. Times,* we are appalled by the paper entering into hidden financial partnerships with the subjects we are writing about. The editorial credibility of the *Times* has been fundamentally undermined."

Less than two years before the episode, Downing had been named publisher by Mark Willes, the new chief executive of Times Mirror Corporation, parent company of the *Los Angeles Times,* despite having no newsroom background. Her previous experience had been as a legal publicist. Willes had moved from General Mills to Times Mirror in 1995. Willes had made no secret of his desire to "blow up the wall between business and editorial" (Rieder 1999). He was also on record as telling *American Journalism Review* in 1997 that "[the] notion that you have to be in journalism 30 years to understand what's important, I find rather quaint" (Rieder 1999).

Downing did apologize, calling it a "major, major mistake." After taking questions at a two-hour staff meeting on October 28, she admitted that she and her staff "failed to understand the ethics involved" (Booth 1999). Downing meanwhile canceled all future revenue-sharing deals with Staples, promised to review all contracts with advertisers and ordered up awareness training for the ad side.

For his part, Willes seemed to reverse his earlier stance when he said, "This is exactly the consequence of having people in the publisher's job who don't have experience in newspapers" (Rieder 1999).

On the business side of the paper the arrangement was widely known and discussed openly for most of 1999. Downing says she deliberately withheld the information from Michael Parks, the paper's editor, but did not direct her subordinates on the business side not to talk about it to him or to anyone else in editorial, according to several reports.

Shaw reports that Willes argued that the absence of such discussion only shows the need for "more communications, not less. . . . The profit-sharing deal happened not because the wall came down," Willes says, "but because people didn't talk to one another when they should have."

In an interesting argument, Downing claimed if the editorial side of the paper did not know about the profit-sharing deal with the Staples Center before printing, then the Sunday magazine devoted to the Staples Center would be unbiased. The un-informed editorial staff would have no reason to be biased.

Many critics from inside and outside the newspaper agree with Shaw that "readers have no reason to trust anything the *Times* wrote about Staples Center, or any of its tenants or attractions, anywhere in the paper, now or in the future, if the *Times* and Staples Center were business partners." He adds that readers will wonder whether other improper arrangements, formal or informal, might also exist or be created in the future with other entities, agencies and individuals covered by the *Times*.

Whether connected to the Staples affair or not, massive changes were in store for Willes, Downing, Parks and the *Times*. The newspaper was bought by the Tribune Company, publisher of the *Chicago Tribune*, in March 2000. All three employees were gone within a year.

Micro Issues

1. Critique Willes' early and late statements about journalistic experience in newspaper management positions.
2. Is the actual loss of credibility as disastrous as the reporters felt, or does the public really have the same sensibilities as those in the profession?
3. How does entering into the contract with the Staples Center differ from the sports department accepting press passes for the events held in the arena?

Midrange Issues

1. If one acknowledges that "the wall" is good and necessary, how does that affect media engaged in advocacy journalism?
2. Shaw entitled his article "Journalism Is a Very Different Business." In what ways do you think journalism differs from other businesses?

Macro Issues

1. In the new information age, where so many competing views can be found on most issues, is "the wall" still relevant?
2. When a newspaper is a publicly traded company, do the loyalties of the paper shift from the public to the shareholders? If not, how can you justify a move that might be counterproductive to profits?
3. After you read the next case, determine if the episode above is a factor in the recent decline in circulation of the *Los Angeles Times*.

CASE 7-B

Profit Versus News: The Case of the *L.A. Times* and the Tribune Company

LEE WILKINS
University of Missouri

Editor's note: *In April of 2007, the entire Tribune Company was sold to entrepreneur Sam Zell for a reported $8.2 billion. He reported he will break up the media conglomerate, including selling off the Chicago Cubs to help pay for the acquisition. The case below is still an excellent example of what publicly owned newspapers across America face in an era of rising costs and declining revenue sources.*

In October 2006, management of the Chicago-based Tribune Company, the relatively new owners of the *Los Angeles Times,* fired Jeff Johnson, publisher of the newspaper. The reason: Johnson had objected publicly to newsroom staff cuts ordered by the parent corporation.

"Jeff and I agreed that this change is best at this time because *Tribune* and *Times* executives need to be aligned on how to shape our futures," said Scott Smith, president of Tribune Publishing, a subsidiary of the Tribune Company (Seelye 2006). A memo to the staff distributed at the paper added: "Sorry to tell you that we are told that Jeff Johnson is out as publisher of the *Los Angeles Times.*"

Johnson had not gone quietly. Faced with corporate instructions to boost earnings by 7 percent, which was to be accomplished in part by cutting newsroom staff as well as utilizing increased technological efficiency, Johnson went to the community for support and got it. Twenty Los Angeles civic leaders, among them former U.S. Secretary of State Warren Christopher, the Los Angeles County Federation of Labor chief Maria Elena Durazo, L.A. Police Commission Chairman John Mack and Geoffrey Cowan, dean of the University of Southern California's Annenberg School of Communication, protested, noting, "All newspapers serve an important civic role, but as a community voice in the metropolitan region, the *Los Angeles Times* is irreplaceable" (Rainey 2006).

Instead, they urged the parent corporation to put more money into the paper, not less. In the six years of *Tribune* ownership, the paper had lost more than 200 journalists, moving from a staff of about 1,200 to about 940.

At issue was one central question with a multitude of implications: was the *Los Angeles Times* contributing enough to the bottom line of its parent corporation—a contribution that was reflected in the price of *Tribune* stock? In the 21st century, with chains and conglomerates, media finances are complicated, and those affecting newspapers are no exception.

The Tribune Corporation purchased the paper and its other substantial holdings from the Chandler family in 1999, an indirect result of the turmoil at the paper that erupted after the Staples Center problems (detailed in the previous case). The *Tribune* owned additional newspapers, 26 television stations (including Los Angeles' KTLA) and the Chicago Cubs baseball team. Despite this diversity of holdings, the stock price of the Tribune Company had remained relatively stagnant. In the same month as the firing, the Tribune Company announced that its third quarter operating revenues for the entire conglomerate were down 2 percent from the previous year, but publishing profits were off 17 percent. This was attributed to declines of both advertising (down 2 percent from 2005) and circulation (down 8 percent in a year).

In order to boost the price, the corporation had engineered a $2 billion buyback of company stock. The *Tribune* also set a target of $200 million in companywide cost cutting over a two-year period. The company was also selling some of its media holdings but had no plans to sell the baseball team because it would have adversely affected the corporation's synergistic media strategy in its hometown, Chicago.

However, Tribune Corporation stockholders, including the Chandler family—with multiple seats on the Tribune Board of Directors—remained unsettled about their investment. This was despite the fact that the *Times* continued to make a substantial profit. Its operating profit margins were at about 20 percent—ahead of most big metropolitan newspapers. However, its cash flow had declined, according to sources inside the paper (Rainey 2006).

During the same time period, the *Times'* photo department staff had decreased by about a third and the graphics and design department had lost about 40 percent of its staff. Large daily operations in Ventura County and the San Fernando Valley, which had been scaled back previously, had shrunk again to just a handful of reporters. The paper had won 13 Pulitzer Prizes in the previous five years but had lost former editor John S. Carroll, who resigned about a year before Johnson was fired. The pressure to slash newsroom staff had played a role in his decision to leave (Rainey, Sept. 14, 2006).

"This newspaper does so many things well," Dean Baquet, the news editor said. "It is one of only three or four papers in the country with really robust foreign bureaus and that cover the war in Iraq in depth. . . . We have a D.C. bureau that competes on every big story. We cover the most complicated urban and suburban region in America. We do a lot of other things. You can't continue to do that if [staff reductions] keep up" (Rainey 2006).

In response to the newsroom turmoil, Smith affirmed the national stature of the paper but added, "There is a misperception that counting numbers of people is the right way to measure the quality of a great newspaper. You are mixing quality and quantity" (Rainey 2006).

Micro Issues

1. What should individual reporters and editors at the paper do? Should they cooperate with the new editor? Strike?
2. Assuming some cuts will have to be made, which of the activities outlined in Banquet's quote—or others you might think of—do you think the editors should relinquish?

Midrange Issues

1. Was it appropriate that this dispute go public? Who should cover the news of large media organizations?
2. Is the *Los Angeles Times* a national media resource? Should that make any difference—to the staff, to the corporate owners?
3. How might someone like John Stuart Mill, in light of his essay "On Liberty," evaluate this situation?

Macro Issues

1. Several Los Angeles billionaires, including David Geffen, expressed an interest in buying the *Times*. What might local ownership mean to the paper? Are there down sides to local ownership?
2. Would an owner like Geffen, with deep financial and creative ties in the entertainment industry, present important conflicts of interest for any staff? If so, how might they be handled?
3. What is the impact of a "synergistic media strategy" on the way a local newspaper covers its community?
4. Ask your parents about their retirement accounts. Would they be willing to take a lower return on investment in a situation like this to ensure a robust local newspaper? If you have a retirement account, would you?

CASE 7-C

"Bonding" Announcements in the News

JOANN BYRD
Seattle Post-Intelligencer

The "Wedding Book" in the Sunday "Northwest Life" section of the *Herald* in Everett, Washington, includes weddings, engagements and 25th and 50th wedding anniversaries. Each event submitted is reported with a one-column picture and about 2 inches of copy. People who want a more detailed announcement or their own language can buy a reduced-rate display ad, for which they write the copy.

In the fall of 1990, a lesbian couple filled out the form used to collect information and submitted it for the "Wedding Book" page. The women wanted to announce they had made a lifetime commitment to each other in a bonding ceremony attended by family and friends in a local park.

The *Herald* serves an area combining the suburbs of Seattle and surrounding rural communities. Many in the core communities had made it clear over the years that they expected the paper to reflect and reinforce conservative family values. The county had grown 36 percent in the previous decade and showed an increasing diversity of races, cultures and lifestyles. Other institutions, including the state's biggest bank, had adopted policies recognizing unmarried relationships, and the city of Seattle had recently been involved in a visible campaign to have domestic partners of city employees declared eligible for medical insurance.

The decision to accept the announcement was made almost instantly. Simultaneously, Stan Strick, the paper's then-managing editor, suggested expanding the page to include, as the in-paper announcement put it, "significant personal milestones in people's lives, everything from adoptions to retirements."

Readers were notified of the change Sunday morning, Nov. 25, 1990, in a story alongside the jumps of section-front pieces about gay couples who had exchanged vows and ministers discussing church positions on gay commitment ceremonies. The paper, with its page renamed "Celebrations," would be "one of the first in the nation to accept bonding ceremonies other than weddings," said the announcement.

The decision was condemned from pulpits in the county that morning, and people in the community began to protest. The women's announcement ran on the revamped page Dec. 2, under a standing head, "Bondings," that matched the labels for "Weddings," "Engagements," "Anniversaries" and "Birthdays."

The community reaction became intense. Hundreds of angry subscribers canceled their subscriptions (as did some people who didn't have subscriptions). Letters and phone calls flooded the newsroom; a local businessman organized a protest group and visited the *Herald* advertisers, urging, although unsuccessfully, a boycott of the paper. Delegations from the conservative Christian community came to the paper to demand that the policy be rescinded. Seattle television covered the debate, and national media interviewed Strick. The storm continued for months. Letters to the editor and organized letter-writing and telephoning campaigns followed national news stories. As other newspapers across the country were approached to publish gay bonding ceremonies, editors phoned for details of the *Herald*'s experience.

Most of the complaints centered on Biblical interpretations condemning homosexuality. Those callers and letter writers felt the *Herald* was endorsing sin, and giving to homosexual relationships the sanction that should be reserved for heterosexual marriages, engagements and wedding anniversaries.

The *Herald*'s position was that sexual orientation was not a morally relevant basis for refusing to accept the announcements, that a page of reader-generated "significant personal milestones" simply had to give people equal access.

The policy has not been changed, but no other gay couple in the county submitted an announcement in the years following. One advertiser quit advertising for several weeks. Many of those who canceled subscriptions have not returned.

Micro Issues

1. Should the paper have accepted the announcement?
2. What options could you imagine? (Should the paper, for instance, have treated it as a news story rather than institutionalizing gay commitments on its announcement page?)
3. Some critics thought the *Herald* was bragging about being "one of the first" to accept gay bonding announcements. Would it have been better to skip the advance notice and simply publish the bonding ceremony and the new publication procedures for the page?
4. Some defenders likened the paper's decision to publishing mixed-race marriages before such notions were thought "socially acceptable." Is that a legitimate parallel? Are there others?

Midrange Issues

1. Gay commitments are not recognized by most state laws. Should the paper publish any arrangements that do not have legal status?
2. This case arose on a page where "news" is defined by people who want to make the announcements, not by reporters working a beat. Does that raise different ethical questions in the newsroom?
3. How far should the newspaper go in giving people equal access to its pages? Is anything anybody wants to announce okay?

Macro Issues

1. Offending people and their most deeply held beliefs is not morally justified unless there is an overriding moral obligation. How much should the paper weigh the probability of offending a large portion of its audience by doing what it considers morally correct in this case?
2. Chances are that there would have been less dispute if the change had occurred at a paper in a big city. Are the values at stake here different from community to community, and should all newspapers' decisions recognize that?
3. How much should a secular entity like a newspaper reflect religious beliefs?
4. The women involved in this case were harassed by conservative groups for months afterward. Does a newspaper have an obligation to censor news that may harm those submitting it? If so, what are the criteria?

CASE 7-D

Punishing the Messenger: The Tobacco Industry and the Press

STEVE WEINBERG, FORMER ASSOCIATE EDITOR
Columbia Journalism Review, University of Missouri—Columbia

When ABC News, under the cloud of a $10 billion libel suit, apologized to Philip Morris in August 1995 for an award-winning investigation entitled "Smoke Screen," most journalists were stunned. The network's action damaged the credibility of a top-notch news organization, perhaps undermined investigative reporting as a journalistic genre, and encouraged lingering questions about the impact of the bottom line on corporate decision making regarding news stories.

The two-part investigative piece reported by Pulitzer Prize winner Walt Bogdanich stated that tobacco companies, including Philip Morris and others, added nicotine to cigarette tobacco with the purpose of keeping smokers hooked on the drug. The story itself had been exhaustively researched for more than a year, and all of the sources but one—"Deep Cough"—had agreed to go on the record with their comments. In the process of researching the story, Bogdanich learned that during the manufacturing process, nicotine is actually removed from tobacco at one point only to be added back into the tobacco later.

Less than a week before the show aired on the news magazine "Day One," the U.S. Food and Drug Administration (FDA) issued a letter stating that it believed there was mounting evidence that nicotine is "a powerfully addictive agent" and that "cigarette vendors control the levels of nicotine that satisfy this addiction" (Weinberg 1995, 27).

Spokespersons for the tobacco industry were quoted in the segments, and Philip Morris, just days before the show was to air, sent ABC News a two-paragraph statement that said, in part, "Nothing done in the processing of tobacco or manufacture of cigarettes by Philip Morris increases the nicotine in the tobacco blend above what is naturally found in the tobacco." The investigative report never made the allegation that nicotine levels were increased beyond those that occur naturally; rather it suggested the tobacco companies had the ability to remove some of the drug from cigarettes and had chosen not to do so.

Controversy erupted after the first part of the story aired on Feb. 28, 1994. A second segment, which aired one week later, focused on the list the tobacco companies had supplied to the federal government of 700 cigarette ingredients. Thirteen of those ingredients are banned in food. Philip Morris was not mentioned at all in the second segment.

Journalists applauded the work. The coverage won a George Polk award and a DuPont/Columbia University award. Congressional hearings into the tobacco industry were called as a result of the story. One day before those hearings were to begin, Philip Morris sued for libel, asking for $5 billion in compensatory damages and $5 billion in punitive damages, despite the fact that Virginia law capped punitive damage awards at $350,000. The story about the libel suit ran nationally, often without the notation about the award restriction. In addition, the tobacco giant gave every indication that it would pursue the suit vigorously, spending more than $1 million per month for more than a year on the litigation.

At ABC, newspeople saw what they perceived as an immediate chilling effect. The day Philip Morris filed the lawsuit, two independent producers were notified by a producer at ABC's program "Turning Point" that their documentary on the tobacco industry's advertising tactics and production transfers to overseas sites was being shelved, despite the outlay of about $500,000.

Legally, the going was equally difficult. Although the network gave every indication that it intended to fight and win the libel suit, discovery tactics by Philip Morris bedeviled the process. Documents that normally would have been public were marked as trade secrets, thus sealing them and making them impossible to report on. Worse yet, from the journalists' point of view, Philip Morris attempted to unearth Deep Cough's identity by subpoenaing records of reporters' phone bills, credit card purchases and travel in an attempt to retrace the journalist's footsteps to Deep Cough's door. A judge initially approved of the subpoenas in the discovery process but later reversed himself after the network contested the decision.

As in many expensive lawsuits, talk about a settlement surfaced from time to time, starting in the summer of 1994, just three months into pretrial discovery—and just as rumors began that Disney might make ABC part of its entertainment empire. Insiders weren't surprised. But it wasn't until almost a year later, on June 30, 1995, that *The Wall Street Journal* reported that settlement talks had begun anew. By that time, and despite assurances from ABC's trial lawyers, other lawyers and some ABC managers had decided that portions of the investigative report would not withstand trial scrutiny.

It turned out that the trial lawyers had been kept away from the settlement negotiations. In-house lawyers, who were joined in the final days by renowned First Amendment lawyer Floyd Abrams, worked with Philip Morris's litigators on the language of an apology to the two tobacco companies. (Abrams had been involved in the case briefly, before the settlement talks began.) The network's statement ultimately ran in more than 700 publications under the headline "Apology Accepted." Philip Morris dropped the suit.

The apology was clearly a victory for Philip Morris, but was it a sellout for ABC? If "Smoke Screen" contained one or more factual errors, it might be possible to consider the extremely limited language of the apology and the absence of any monetary awards (ABC did agree to pay the other side's legal fees, at least $15 million), a victory of sorts for the network. ABC's assertion in the apology letter that it stands behind the show's intended principal focus and the signing of the reporter and producer to new long-term contracts with substantial raises—even though both refused to sign the settlement agreement—are a vindication of sorts for the show.

ABC was purchased by Disney after the suit was settled.

Micro Issues

1. Should Deep Cough have been allowed to remain off the record?
2. What standards of evidence should journalists doing investigative work demand from their sources and documents?
3. How should other news organizations that covered the libel suit have reported it?

Midrange Issues

1. Should journalists work out agreements about legal liability with their editors in advance of broadcast or publication?
2. Should the journalists have been willing to wait on the story and work with government regulators on the issue?
3. What professional values are served by stories such as "Smoke Screen"?
4. Does reporting on undesirable products or issues—toxic waste or tobacco, for example— demand a different professional standard than reporting on city government?

Macro Issues

1. What is the responsibility of "corporate ownership" to encourage and protect investigative reporting?
2. Do journalists, who increasingly work for large corporations, have a responsibility to the public to find mechanisms to counter the demands of the bottom line?
3. Do journalists have a watchdog role when it comes to covering corporations and economically powerful interests?
4. Compare "Smoke Screen" to Upton Sinclair's classic *The Jungle*. Would such a treatment of the tobacco industry be possible today?

CASE 7-E

Paying the (Newspaper) Bills

IVY ASHE
University of Missouri

The official announcement was short, consisting of just 235 words in the "News in Brief" section of the *Rice Thresher,* the student-run weekly newspaper at Rice University. After four years of providing its student body with subscriptions to both the *New York Times* and the *Houston Chronicle,* the Office of the Dean of Undergraduates had decided to cut the newspaper expenses from its budget.

"The decision is not that the colleges will not get newspaper subscriptions. The decision is that I cannot afford to pay for them," the Dean's office told the campus newspaper. Indeed, even as the $30,000 normally allocated to periodical subscription costs was eliminated from the yearly budget sheet, Dean Forman observed that Rice's residential colleges still had "as much control over their spending as possible."

The residential college system, much like those in place at institutions such as Yale, Harvard, and Oxford, or, in the literary world, Hogwarts of *Harry Potter,* serves as the major organizational hub for campus life at Rice. Students are assigned to one of nine dorms and remain members of this community for their entire undergraduate career. Each college is a self-governing unit, run by a body of peer-elected students, and is provided with a budget by the Dean of Undergraduates, which they allocate as deemed necessary. Despite the overall cutback to the Dean's spending, these individual college accounts remained untouched, so students could "choose to use their own money to continue to provide newspaper subscriptions."

The shift in responsibility troubled some, including the news editor of the campus newspaper, *Thresher,* Catherine Bratic. In an opinion piece published in both the campus paper and, two weeks later, the *Chronicle,* Bratic decried the university's decision, stating that leaving the subscription power in the hands of the residential colleges would be the beginning of an "uphill battle," stemming largely from the very nature of residential life.

According to the Rice Web page, the colleges are the "primary place for dining, studying, and socializing."

These overall functions, writes Bratic, lead to a "design [that] does not easily accommodate educational priorities." Although a print newspaper arguably carries both social (because the *Chronicle* and *Times* were delivered to the college dining halls, reading the newspaper became a community mealtime activity) and educational value, most emphasis for the purpose of a newspaper tends to fall on the side of information acquisition and augmentation of a basic classroom curriculum:

> Contemporary research on the rationale for using newspapers in education still validates . . . the value of newspaper-based instruction for building students' learning and thinking skills, growing their knowledge base, stimulating their interest in reading, and developing the tools for good citizenship.

In contrast to the basic educational nature of newspapers is the residential colleges' role as "essentially social institutions." As social institutions, their fiscal priorities might place spending on subscriptions relatively low on the list. In a particularly dramatic example of her point, Bratic noted one college, immediately following the announcement of the canceled subscriptions, proposed spending $2,000 on "a new 66" television for the game room." While proposed expenditures are not as extravagant, the bulk focus on social needs (common costs include those of hosting a late-night study break or paying for new intramural sports equipment), as opposed to with the academic ones. For Bratic, and for the 224 signees of an online petition asking the Rice administration to reconsider its decision, "students should not be forced to choose between their social life and academic lives" when making residential budget decisions.

Such thinking, however, runs counter to Forman's goal of providing a relatively high degree of autonomy for Rice students. "I believe in the value of having students make these decisions, and my goal is to make as few . . . for them as possible. They have the responsibility to make important decisions that affect the future of their college experience."

Forman, then, called upon the colleges to step forward and help support their own out-of-classroom education. Several letters to the editor and blogs about the subscription cancellations pushed the same point. Other online commentators raised the issue of the importance of subscribing to a print newspaper in the first place, since the same resources are available online. In response to this argument, Bratic observes that "having the newspapers in common . . . enormously increases the chance that students will read them. Furthermore . . . they at least cannot help but see the day's headlines."

Micro Issues

1. Should students, either through their mandatory fees or other means, be required to support campus media? Justify your answer.
2. Would you make the same argument in favor of textbooks? Laboratory equipment? Tickets to athletic events?
3. How would you define the purpose of the campus newspaper?

Midrange Issues

1. As a part of the educational experience, should campus media ever reduce staff? Cut budgets? Decrease circulation?
2. Scholars suggest there is a digital divide—particularly by social class. What is a university's obligation with regard to universal Web access being included in tuition?

Macro Issues

1. Return to the discussion of social responsibility of the press in this book. What is the remaining role of newspapers today? Do you have those same expectations of Web-only news sites, such a Politico?
2. Is it the business of a university to assist students in acquiring the habit of consuming the news? If so, on what basis? Does the venue (print vs. Internet) matter?

8

Picture This: The Ethics of Photo and Video Journalism

By the end of this chapter, you should be familiar with:

- the legal and ethical issues involved in photojournalism in the area of privacy.
- the technology available for altering photos and the ethical and epistemological issues those possibilities raise.
- the legal and ethical problems of file footage and "eyewash."
- the conundrum of open source journalism.

INTRODUCTION

Nowhere is the concept of citizen-journalist more accepted than in photography, where devices like cell phones have made virtually everybody a photographer and most a videographer. Add in the hundreds of thousands of video cameras that businesses employ for security, and virtually no event—from one child stomping on another in a soccer match to a would-be terrorist buying household chemicals to make a bomb—falls outside the realm of cameras. Today's editorial question is rarely "Do we have art?" It's more likely "Do we use this photo or that one?", often from sources outside the employment of the media.

Decades of technological developments have dramatically shortened the time between the occurrence of a news event and the dissemination of photos or video of it to the public. Digital photos can be posted to the Web almost instantaneously. Video is routinely beamed live into television homes across America and posted to the Web in seconds. Once, the most instantaneous ethical decisions in photography was: "Shoot or don't shoot?" Today the question has added layers: "Post or don't post?" Or: "Go live or not?" Or: "Do we use this amateur video?"

Decisions that once could be made in the relative calm of the newsroom after a dramatic tragedy now must be made in the field in an increasingly competitive media environment. And making the right decision can be the difference in being applauded for ingenuity or being criticized for insensitivity.

PROBLEMS IN THE PROCESS

Age-old axioms assure us that "The camera never lies" and that "Seeing is believing." Yet as Arthur Berger (1989) points out in *Seeing Is Believing,* because of the many variables in photography—camera angles, use of light, texture and focus—a picture is always an *interpretation* of reality, not reality itself. He adds that a dozen photographers taking pictures of the same scene would produce different views of the reality of it. The story below illustrates that.

Only one photographer, Nat Fein, won the Pulitzer Prize for photography while taking a picture that dozens of other photographers were shooting—the retirement of Babe Ruth's number by the New York Yankees. You can easily find this photo on the Internet, and when you do, notice that by moving to the rear of his subject, Fein captured a different angle and told a different and more dramatic story with his photo. Not only did the photo win journalism's top prize, it has been called the iconic sports photograph of the 20th century—all by manipulating the angle of the photo and capturing not only Babe Ruth, but, off the to right of the photo, all the photographers who had shot the cliché shot for their newspapers.

Not only does the camera differ from the eye in its ability to manipulate angle, light and focus, but cameras also capture an isolated reality by presenting us with a slice of life, free from context. In *About Looking,* John Berger (1980, 14) says:

> What the camera does, and what the eye can never do, is to fix the appearance of that event. The camera saves a set of appearances from the otherwise inevitable supersession of further appearances. It holds them unchanging. And before the invention of the camera nothing could do this, except in the mind's eye, the faculty of memory.

The role of journalism is to place context back into the ubiquitous images created by professionals and amateurs alike. It's not enough, from an ethical standpoint, to say, "Here's what happened" to an audience who probably knows the news before the newscast airs or the newspaper hits the street. They also know that photos are easily manipulated on any laptop computer and video is only marginally harder to change, but not by any means impossible. Because of those two facts, journalism must say: "Here's why we believe this happened the way you are seeing it." Otherwise, the nightly news does nothing for the consumer that YouTube can't do better.

TO SHOOT OR NOT TO SHOOT?

Arriving on the scene of a newsworthy event, the photographer must make several decisions. The most basic is whether or not to shoot the photo of a subject who is in no position to deny the photographer access to the event. Often these vulnerable subjects are wounded, in shock, or grief-stricken. In that newsworthy moment, the subject loses a measure of control over his or her circles of intimacy (see Chapter 5 for a description of this concept). That control passes to the photographer, who must make a decision.

Goffman (1959) claims people possess several "territories" they have a right to control. Included in Goffman's list are two territories that are: the right to a personal space free from intrusion (i.e., by a camera lens) and the right to preserve one's "information," such as a state of joy, or grief, from public view.

By its very nature, photojournalism is intrusive and revealing—two violations of Goffman's sense of self. Someone else's misfortune is often good fortune for the photojournalist. In the last century, more than half of the winning images in top photography contests were pictures of violence and tragedy. And most of the amateur images that make the news are of violence and tragedy. So eventually every photojournalist happens on an assignment that intrudes on a subject's privacy. Garry Bryant (1987), a staff photographer with the *Deseret News* of Salt Lake City, offers this checklist he goes through "in hundredths of a second" when he reaches the scene of tragedy:

1. Should this moment be made public?
2. Will being photographed send the subjects into further trauma?
3. Am I at the least obtrusive distance possible?
4. Am I acting with compassion and sensitivity?

To this list Bryant adds the following disclaimer (1987, 34):

> What society needs to understand is that photographers act and shoot instinctively. We are not journalists gathering facts. We are merely photographers snapping pictures. A general rule for most photojournalists is "Shoot. You can always edit later."

The line between newsworthiness and intrusiveness, between good pictures and bad taste, is often blurry. Donald Gormley, the general manager of the *Spokane Spokesman-Review,* offers some insight into the difference between photos that are universally offensive and photos that are simply tough to view:

> Compassion is not the same as good taste. If a reader knows the person pictured in a very dramatic photograph, he may find it offensive. That's a sin against compassion. If he is offended whether he knows the person or not, the sin is probably one against good taste. (1984, 58)

Editors argue that decisions cannot be made concerning photos that do not exist. Not every picture of grief needs to be ruled out just because the subject is vulnerable or grieving. Where to draw the line is a decision best made in the newsroom rather than at the scene. The photographer who attempts to perform a type of ethical triage at the scene of a tragedy might find his career in jeopardy if the assignment fails to capture the pathos of the event when all other photographers succeeded. In addition, the photographer who fails to capture some of the event, for whatever reason, fails to capture some of the truth for the reader or viewer.

However, the window of time for deciding later is closing. Today's technology means that television is often live at the scene of a tragedy, broadcasting footage even before the immediate family is alerted. Scenes that might once have been edited now go straight on the air. An important stage in the ethical decision-making process is bypassed. And with the advent of camera phones, even more events are being captured and offered to the media to illustrate stories.

How can the victims of tragedy come to life as vulnerable humans with feelings to a professional who sees the world most of the time through a lens? A few years ago, at a conference entitled "Crime Victims and the News Media" victims of violent crime met the journalists who covered their stories. One participant noted at the end of the conference, "Once a journalist hears their simple, eloquent stories of what happened to them, he will never approach the story of a human tragedy in quite the same way."

Essentially, the photographer who is deciding whether and how to photograph a tragedy is wrestling with the dilemma of treating every subject as an end and not merely a means to an end. We can agree that powerful images of accident victims may cause some drivers to proceed more safely, but if that message often comes at the expense of an accident victim's privacy, is it a message that needs to be told?

Warren Bovée (1991), in an essay entitled "The Ends Can Justify the Means—But Rarely," offers this set of questions to help the photographer find the answer.

1. Are the means truly morally evil or merely distasteful, unpopular, etc?
2. Is the end a *real* good or something that merely *appears* to be good?
3. Is it probable that the means will achieve the end?
4. Is the same good possible using other means? Is the bad means being used as a shortcut to a good end when other methods would do?
5. Is the good end clearly greater than any evil means used to attain it?
6. Will the means used to achieve the end withstand the test of publicity?

TO ACCEPT OR NOT ACCEPT

It goes by a number of names—open source journalism and citizen journalism being among the most popular. But regardless of the label, the process is essentially the same: citizens, acting as amateur journalists without pay, submit both words and images to various Web sites. Some, such as YouTube, were established by entrepreneurs. But others are established and managed by news organizations. And, even if your local television station or newspaper doesn't have an open source site, increasingly citizens are trying to contribute their efforts to professional news organizations.

Some of those contributions have changed history. For example, amateur video aired first on local and then on national television news of African-American Rodney King being beaten by a uniformed, Caucasian police officer is credited with both riots and racial tensions in Los Angeles. Amateur video first uploaded to the Internet, and then later picked up by traditional news organizations, of Republican Senator George Allen of Virginia uttering an apparently racist remark is one of the elements credited with his electoral defeat in 2006. And then, there's the recurrent video of Midwestern tornados—taken at great personal risk by amateurs who aren't paid for their efforts and accepted by media outlets well aware that the weather garners the highest ratings during the traditional local television news show.

Before the Internet opened the possibility of "open source journalism" to thousands of bloggers and videographers, the government could and did exercise control over the media by denying access to information or battlefields or by selectively granting access or leaks to those in favor with the administration. But the Web changed all that, as *Newsweek*'s David Ansen writes in his review of the 2006 film about World War II propaganda, "Flags of our Fathers" (Ansen 2006, 71):

> What the Pentagon didn't foresee, and couldn't control was the rise of new media—the unfiltered images popping up on the Web, the mini-TV cams put in the hands of soldiers that emerge in the recent documentary, *The War Tapes*. We don't see much of the real war on network TV, but the unauthorized documentaries—*The Ground Truth, Gunner Palace* and many more—come pouring out. Just as many people think they get a straighter story from Jon Stewart's mock news reports than from traditional outlets, it's been the "unofficial media" that have sabotaged the PR wizards in the Pentagon. The sophistication of the spinners has been matched by the sophistication of a media-savvy public.

Governments also use the images of amateurs when they help. The men charged with the 2005 subway bombings in London were identified in part through the use of images passengers on the city's underground captured with their cell phones. Those images, together with sophisticated face recognition technology, became a tool of law enforcement.

The emerging ethic of open source journalism has forced some interesting compromises with the emerging ethic of the blogosphere. (For a more detailed discussion, see Chapter 10). But, open source journalism—particularly if it is managed by a more traditional news organization—faces the same ethical tests as more traditional photography. The premiums are accuracy, fairness and originality. Editors at open source cites realize that they must subject amateur content to the same journalistic standards—although not necessarily the same creative and aesthetic standards—as work by professionals. For instance, contributed video cannot be staged or re-enacted and then presented as news. Editors must be able to verify the accuracy, and sometimes the context, of citizen contributions.

STAGING PHOTOGRAPHS AND VIDEO

During a ratings period more than a decade ago, NBC's magazine show "Dateline" aired an 18-minute segment on a faulty design of General Motors pickup trucks that concluded with video of a truck exploding into flames immediately after a side-impact collision. More than 300 people had died in such collisions and the story included gripping still photographs of charred bodies pulled from accident scenes. They also produced court documents from the many suits filed against GM, including videotaped testimony from independent auto safety experts and a former GM engineer, all saying that the corporation had known about the design flaw yet had chosen to do nothing.

Calvin and Hobbes

by Bill Watterson

However, NBC did not inform viewers that, in order to ensure fire in the closing video, "sparking devices" had been mounted on the test cars by the independent testing agency the network had hired. General Motors filed a libel suit against the network, charging that the network had staged its dramatic video. In an unprecedented move, anchors Jane Pauley and Stone Phillips read a 3-minute retraction of the original "Dateline" story, admitting that the network had aired the concluding

"Your work sounds interesting." Francesca said. She felt a need to keep neutral conversation going.

"It is. I like it a lot. I like the road, and I like making pictures."

She noticed he'd said "making" pictures. "You make pictures, not take them?"

"Yes. At least that's how I think of it". That's the difference between Sunday snap-shooters and someone who does it for a living. When I'm finished with that bridge we saw today, it won't look quite like you expect. I'll have made it into something of my own, by lens choice, or camera angle, or general composition or all of those.

"I don't just take things as given; I try to make them into something that reflects my personal consciousness, my spirit. I try to find the poetry in the image."

Robert James Waller, *The Bridges of Madison County*

video even though it was staged. The NBC–General Motors confrontation proved to be the end for network news president Michael Gartner. He resigned less than a month later.

The NBC incident raises several questions. Is there a place for reenactment in the news? If so, when? How should such photos and video be labeled? The issues are not trivial, nor are they resolved. In a poll conducted by the National Press Photographers Association, the *number one ethical problem* reported by photojournalists was setup shots.

Photographer John Szarkowski (1978) writes of "mirror" and "window" photographs and his 1978 Museum of Modern Art show was entitled "Mirrors and Windows." The two types of photos are also roughly analogous to realistic and romantic photography. According to Szarkowski, window photographs should be as objective a picture of reality as the medium will allow, untouched by the bias of the lens or the photographer. On the other hand, the mirror photograph attempts to subjectively re-create the world in whatever image suits the photographer. Anything can be manipulated: light, proportion, setting, even subject.

Each type of photography has a function. A large percentage of the government-commissioned Dust Bowl–era photographs that have seared our memories of the Depression would fit into the mirror category. Photographers searched for settings, posed people and shifted props to achieve the maximum effect. On the other hand, the photos that show us the horrors of war and famine, and arouse public opinion, are windows, where the photographer captures the moment with no attempts to alter it. *The problem comes in the substitution of one for the other.* When a photograph mirrors a photographer's bias, yet is passed off as a window on reality, the viewer has been deceived.

ELECTRONIC MANIPULATION

Those who get their news from the Internet could hardly have missed it. The day after the 2005 Madrid train bombings the same photograph appeared on the front pages of a number of European newspapers—sort of. One front page displayed a photograph of the bombing with a bloody, detached limb in the foreground. Another paper displayed the same photograph, but the limb wasn't in it. Other papers cropped the photo so that only a part of the limb could be seen. Still others printed the photo in color, and some of those intensified the color of the blood with color saturation. It was the same photograph, but the electronic alternations were too obvious to ignore.

The history of photo manipulation is long, beginning with such crude drawing-board techniques as cropping with scissors and paste, darkroom techniques such as "burning" and "dodging," and, more recently, airbrushing. Today, technology allows increasingly sophisticated changes to be made to an image after it has been captured. Any person familiar with InDesign or any of many other software packages is keenly aware of how photos can be manipulated.

Technology has, in fact, made the word "photography"—literally "light writing"— obsolete, as a lighted reality no longer need exist in order for a "photograph" to be created. Photos and video are now what photography researcher Shiela Reaves (1987) has called a "controlled liquid." Writing more than two decades ago, in the infancy of computer manipulation of photography, Reaves foresaw a time photos would lose their "moral authority" while Tomlinson (1987) adds that photos could lose their legal authority as well. As a more sophisticated audience visual media, viewers will bring with them a skepticism not present in previous generations of consumers.

Most editors and photographers agree that manipulation or staging of news photos is generally more culpable than manipulation or staging of feature photos. During the 2003 war in Iraq, a photojournalist for the *Los Angeles Times* was fired for combining two similar photographs into one more aesthetically pleasing one. While the resulting photo was so similar to the "real" ones that the difference escaped the eye of the photo editor, a line had been crossed, and the photographer was dismissed.

The reason for the different standard for news photography is a presupposition that *while art may be manipulated, information may not* (Martin 1991). The problem for audiences is compounded by the fact that both advertising and non-news sections of the newspaper make frequent use of these techniques. Confusion over what is appropriate in one context and not another is bound to occur, but we suggest that the same standard of visual truth telling can and should be applied to advertising as well.

SELECTIVE EDITING

Another ethical question centers on the video editing process: whether editing itself renders a story untrue or unfair. Actually, the term "selective editing" is redundant. *All* editing is selective. The issue is who does the selecting, and what predispositions they bring to the process.

A dual standard has emerged between words and photos. The writer is allowed to reorder facts and rearrange details into an inverted-pyramid story on the rationale that the reader wants the most important facts taken out of sequence, and even out of context, and placed first in the story for more efficient reading. The result is praised as good writing and is taught in every journalism program.

However, should a photographer attempt to do the same thing with a camera—rearrange reality to make a more interesting photo or videotape—the result is called "staged." Our unwillingness to allow visual journalists the same conventions as print journalists says something fundamental about the role of visuals in the news. When a writer edits, it makes for a more readable story, and the act is applauded. When a photographer or video editor does the same thing, he or she is open to accusations of distortion.

That is because we evaluate news photos according to print standards: linear and logical. Yet video and photographs are neither. They have a quality Marshall McLuhan called "allatonceness" that we are not quite comfortable with as a technology. Just what the photographer can do with the visual truth the camera uncovers is still a topic of debate.

However, as long as readers hold the view that "Seeing is believing," that view—whether based in reality or not—becomes a promise between the media and their audiences that photographers and videographers should be hesitant to break. While many photojournalists argue that "Seeing is believing" should have never been a cultural truism (see Lester 1992), others argue that we must work within our readers' or viewers' predispositions about the truth of what they see. Steve Larson (quoted in Reaves 1991, 181) director of photography for *U.S. News & World Report,* summarized this viewer-based rationale:

> The photo is a record of a moment in time. We're on shaky ground when we start changing that. We must maintain this pact. Catching a moment in time has history. When you look at a Matthew Brady photo there is that sense "this really happened." I believe strongly that's where photography draws its power.

EYEWASH

Imagine a new government study that is released on compulsive gamblers that you are told to make into a video package for tonight's news. You might show a woman enjoying herself on a sunny afternoon at the races. While her action is taking place in public view, she might or might not be a victim of the syndrome addressed in the article, although the casual reader might infer that she is, indeed, a compulsive gambler. In this context, the photo is serving the purpose of "eyewash," decoration for a story that bears no genuine relationship to it.

Eyewash has had a brief history in the courts. A Washington, D.C., television station used a tight shot on a pedestrian facing the camera, chosen at random, to illustrate the "twenty million Americans who have herpes." The court ruled that the combination of the film and the commentary was sufficient to support an inference that the plaintiff was a victim of herpes, which she contended was not true. But in another case, a young couple photographed in a public embrace in the Los Angeles Farmer's Market had "waived their right of privacy" by their voluntary actions according to the California Supreme Court, which said that publication of their photograph merely increased the public who could have viewed the plaintiffs in their romantic pose.

While the courts have been ambiguous on the matter of eyewash, the media have created divergent policies to cover the issue. Some newspapers and television stations, for instance, will use no picture not directly related to the story. Others limit the use of file or stock footage to that which is clearly labeled. Others limit the shooting of eyewash only by insisting that it occur in public view.

The issue is exacerbated by the voracious appetite that both television and the print media have for visuals. Virtually all surveys have shown that the presence of a photo adds to the number of readers for a newspaper story, while television news consultants insist that viewers will watch "talking heads" for only a few seconds before diverting their attention elsewhere. The answer to the question "Have you got art?" often means the difference in running or killing a story. Good visuals can get a story in the coveted first slot on the nightly news or the front page of the newspaper.

Given the importance of visuals, it is not surprising that ethical lines blur. Coleman (1987) tells the story of his young son falling off a horse and breaking his arm. A photographer friend took a picture of the boy "dirty, tear-stained, in great pain, slumped in a wheelchair with his arm in a makeshift sling" on his way to the operating room. About a year later, a textbook publisher ran across the photo and wanted it as an illustration for a book on child abuse. Coleman denied the request but added that the photo could have easily been selected if he had not been easily available for the publisher to ask. The public would have been deceived by a photograph of a boy who had been a victim of nothing more than a childhood accident.

CONCLUSION

The debate over visual ethics is emotionally charged and constantly changing with technology. Simultaneously, the consumer of news photography is sometimes presented with a product too raw to be watched and at other times too polished to be believable.

The problem lies in the nature of the photojournalist's job. On a day-to-day basis, photography can be a mundane and poor-paying job. One daily newspaper made waves in the summer of 2009 when it fired its entire photography staff, hired back a few at reduced salaries and opted for reader-submitted photos to replace the rest. So when an opportunity for a gripping photo does arise the desire to break out of the daily grind can lead to excess.

Photojournalists should operate under this version of Kant's categorical imperative: *Don't deceive a trusting audience with manipulated reality and don't offend an unsuspecting audience with your gritty reality.* Fortunately, only a small percentage of photos offend, and only a small percentage of photos are staged or electronically manipulated. However, photographers are dealing with a trust that readers and viewers have placed in them. If that trust is betrayed, it will be slow to return.

Suggested Readings

BERGER, ARTHUR ASA. 1989. *Seeing is believing.* Mountain View, CA: Mayfield Publishing Co.
BERGER, JOHN. 1980. *About looking.* New York: Pantheon Books.
Journal of Mass Media Ethics. 1987, Spring–Summer. Special issue on photojournalism.
LESTER, PAUL. 1991. *Photojournalism: An ethical approach.* Hillsdale, NJ: Lawrence
    Erlbaum Associates.
———. 2003. *Images that injure.* 2nd edition. Westport, CT: Greenwood Press.
NEWTON, JULIANNE. 2000. *The burden of visual truth: The role of photojournalism in medi-
    ating reality.* Hillsdale, NJ: Lawrence Erlbaum Associates.

Cases on the Web

www.mhhe.com/mediaethics7e

"Film at 10: Handling graphic video in the news" by Sonya Forte Duhé
"Looking at race and sex: When do photographs go too far?" by Beverly Horvitt
"Faking photos: Is it ever justified?" by James Van Meter

CHAPTER 8 CASES

CASE 8-A

Daniel Pearl and the *Boston Phoenix:* Too Much of a Bad Thing?

TIMOTHY RAGONES, *WMTV*
Grand Rapids–Kalamazoo, Michigan

On January 23, 2002, *Wall Street Journal* reporter Daniel Pearl was on his way to interview an Islamic fundamentalist leader in Pakistan when he was abducted. A month later, on February 21, FBI officials received a video entitled "The Slaughter of the Spy Journalist, the Jew Daniel Pearl" confirming that Pearl's abductors had killed him. The 3-minute video included footage of Pearl confessing his Jewish roots and reading a statement denouncing U.S. foreign policy in the Middle East and Afghanistan. Pearl is then decapitated. Later, an unidentified man holds Pearl's head aloft. That image remained on screen as the National Movement for the Restoration of Pakistan Sovereignty listed demands, among them return of Pakistani prisoners to Pakistan, the delivery of U.S.-made F-16s that Pakistan paid for but which were never shipped, and an immediate end to U.S. presence in Pakistan.

U.S. news media had access to the video in the weeks after it surfaced. On Tuesday, May 14, an edited portion of the tape appeared on the "CBS Evening News." The 4.5-minute story, which was about use of the Internet to spread propaganda, showed about 30 seconds of the Pearl tape, not including the decapitation. In prefacing the story, anchor Dan Rather said, "We're about to show you edited portions of it so that you can see and judge for yourself the kind of propaganda terrorists are using in their war against the United States." Executive producer Jim Murphy noted, "[Dan and I] very, very carefully crafted this story to report what people have to know. We used very little of the video at all."

The network aired the story despite fielding calls from Secretary of State Colin Powell's office, the Justice Department, *The Wall Street Journal* and several members of Pearl's family. After the broadcast, Pearl's family accused the network of playing into the hands of terrorists by airing material that was bound to become propaganda and that spread a message of hate. Barbara Comstock, Justice Department spokeswoman, said the network had opened the door for others to use even more graphic parts of the tape.

Her fears came true on May 31, when the *Boston Phoenix,* an alternative paper that had garnered a Pulitzer Prize for criticism in 1994, posted a link to the unedited tape on its Web site. The paper had a circulation of 118,000 in the Boston area. When the link appeared, traffic on the Web site jumped to 40,000 hits. In an online note below the link, *Phoenix* publisher Stephen Mindich wrote:

> This is the single most gruesome, horrible, despicable and horrifying thing I've ever seen. If there is anything that should galvanize every non–Jew hater in the world—of whatever faith, or of no faith—against the perpetrators and supporters of those who committed this unspeakable murder, it should be viewing this video.

The *Phoenix* link connected to **Prohosters.com,** a Virginia-based Web-hosting company. Mindich said he decided to publish the link after learning that the FBI had pressured Prohosters to remove the video from one of its client sites. Prohosters said the FBI had threatened the client with legal action and objected to the government pressure on First Amendment grounds.

The *Phoenix* took another step into the controversy one week later when it published still photographs of Pearl talking to the camera and Pearl's decapitated head in the hard copy version of the paper. Warnings about the nature of the photographs, which had been available on the Web, were not included in the newsprint paper. An editorial defending the decision to run the photos noted, "The silence on this issue— the U.S. government's attempt to censor politically sensitive, yet legal content from our leading pundits and opinion makers—has been deafening." The editorial compared footage of Pearl's murder to widely disseminated images of the Nazi concentration camps, the 1986 Challenger space shuttle explosion and the 9/11 World Trade Center footage.

"Beyond its repugnance, though, it has value in reminding us, as did the September 11 footage, what anti-American terrorists are capable of. It's hard to find language strong enough to decry the impulse to keep this information from the public."

Micro Issues

1. Should CBS have aired even a portion of the tape? Justify your answer.
2. What portion of the tape, if any, should the *Phoenix* have placed on its Web site? Justify your answer.
3. Is there a morally relevant distinction between the tape of Pearl and the 9/11 World Trade Center footage?
4. In considering all the stakeholders in the decision to print the photos, how can the *Phoenix* justify its decision to the wife of Daniel Pearl? Should she be considered in the equation when making the choice whether to run the photos, or does that send the process towards "quandary ethics"?

Midrange Issues

1. Was publication of the video and the stills necessary for the *Phoenix* to accomplish one of its stated goals: educating the American public about terrorism?
2. Is posting on the Web somehow ethically distinct from publication in a tangible newspaper?
3. Does the alternative press, papers like the *Phoenix* and New York's *Village Voice,* play a professionally distinctive role in the American media mix? Do they operate under any different ethical mandates than the mainstream press? Justify your answer.
4. In the 1980s, a Pennsylvania elected official, moments from surrendering to authorities to begin a prison sentence, called a news conference where he was expected to resign his post. Instead, he surprised everyone in the room when he pulled out a gun, put it in his mouth and pulled the trigger. Video and still images were available of the suicide, and some media outlets chose to run them. In what way, if any, does that suicide differ from the Pearl case?

Macro Issues

1. Could words have adequately described what happened to Daniel Pearl? What does your answer say about the role of images in your definition of truth? Of privacy?
2. Is it ever appropriate for the government to pressure news media not to publish? Under what circumstances?
3. What is the relationship between news and propaganda? Is it appropriate for journalists to be concerned about the use others will make of their stories, particularly when that story focuses on hate?
4. How is the government's attempt to censor the tape relevant in the decision to post the tape on the Web or publish the stills?

CASE 8-B

Problem Photos and Public Outcry

JON ROOSENRAAD
University of Florida

Campus police at the University of Florida were called on a Saturday to a dorm to investigate "a large amount of blood on the floor of a women's bathroom," according to police reports. They determined that the blood "appeared to have been from a pregnancy miscarriage" and began searching the dorm area. Some time later a police investigator searching through a trash dumpster behind the dorm found bloody towels, plastic gloves, and a large plastic bag containing more towels and the body of a 6- to 7-pound female infant.

Police discovered no pulse. Rigor mortis had set in. After removing the body from the bag, the police briefly placed the body on a towel on the ground next to the dumpster. The photographer for the student paper, the *Independent Florida Alligator,* arrived at this time and photographed the body and dumpster.

Later on Saturday, the 18-year-old mother was found in her dorm bed and taken to the university's hospital. The hospital exam revealed "placenta parts and the umbilical cord in her" and she was released later in good health. A local obstetrician

Photo courtesy of the Independent Florida Alligator. *Used with permission.*

contacted about the case said that judging by the size of the infant, it was likely a miscarriage and not an abortion. The infant was determined to be about seven months developed.

The story began on the front page of the Monday issue, across the bottom of the page, under the headline "UF police investigate baby's death at dorm." It jumped inside to page 3 and was accompanied by the photo.

It was a dramatic photo, contrasting two well-dressed detectives and one uniformed policeman with the naked body and contrasting the fragile human form with the harsh metal dumpster filled with pizza and liquor boxes. The photo was played 7 by 5 inches.

The story was well written and the photo dramatic but likely offensive to many—potentially so offensive that the newspaper's staff debated most of Sunday about how to use it. The editor decided to run it, but in an unusual move she wrote an editor's column explaining why that appeared on the opinion page of the same issue. It showed a scene one might visualize in a ghetto but not on a college campus. It showed that supposedly sexually educated and sophisticated college students still need help. The editor wrote:

> Even with these legitimate reasons we did not run the picture on the front page. This is partially in response to our concern that we do not appear to be exploiting this picture to attract readers. . . . We also examined the photographer's negatives to see if there were any less graphic prints. . . . Is the message perceived by the reader worth the shock he or she experiences? After pondering what we feel is a very profound photo, we decided there is. This was a desperate act in an area of society where it is not expected. The picture shows it.

The local daily covered the story Monday in a police brief. No photo ran. It was determined that the body was from a miscarriage. The woman involved left school. The campus paper got several letters critiquing its coverage of the story. Many chose to criticize the editors for running the photo, while some praised the staff for pointing out the problem and for listing places on campus where sex and pregnancy counseling was available. Some letters did both.

An example of some of the outrage over the running of the photo by the *Alligator* came from a female student who called the coverage "the most unnecessary, tactless piece of journalism I've ever encountered." Another letter from a male student called the photo "in poor taste and extremely insensitive." The writer added, "There are times when good, sound judgment must override 'hot' copy."

Perhaps the most pointed comment came from a female writer who added 24 other names to her letter. The letter stated:

> The incident *could* have been used to remind people that they need to take responsibility for their own sexuality. The story *could* have been used as a painful reminder that there are many un-educated, naïve people out there who need help. But, unfortunately, the *Alligator* chose to sensationalize the story with a picture, completely nullifying any lesson whatsoever that might have been learned.

Micro Issues

1. Should the photographer have taken the picture? Justify your answer.
2. Is this a legitimate story, and if so, does it belong on page 1?
3. If this was the only photo available, did the paper then have to run it?
4. Various letters to the editor called the photo "unnecessary," "tactless," and "insensitive." What would you say to those charges if you were on the staff?

Midrange Issues

1. Does running the photo inside lessen any criticism of poor taste? Did its placement mitigate any ethical criticism?
2. If the staff was so unsure, was the editor correct in writing a same-day rationale for its publication?
3. Critique the reasoning stated by the editor in running the photo. What moral philosophy, if any, would lead one to agree with the action?

Macro Issues

1. Should a paper play a story and photo like this to crusade about a problem?
2. Is the perceived social value of such a picture worth more than the shock and criticism?
3. Was the writer correct in her assessment that the shock of the photo negated any good that might have been done by the story?
4. Should a campus newspaper have a different standard—of taste, play, news value—than a "regular" daily?

CASE 8-C

Manipulating Photos: Is It Ever Justified?

LEE WILKINS
University of Missouri

Author's Note: *By the decision of the* Los Angeles Times, *the photos in question in this case are not available. However, various Web sites have covered this controversy and some include the photos.*

The visual images of the 2003 war in Iraq were extraordinarily controversial. Photo editors, particularly at large media outlets, had to make decisions about hundreds of photographs every day. Sunday, March 30, was no exception. That night, *Los Angeles Times* director of photography Colin Crawford had edited about 500 photos of the war when he saw a picture from staff photographer Brian Walski. The photo depicts a group of Iraqi citizens sitting on the ground as an American soldier, armed with a rifle, stands in the foreground.

The *Times* ran the photo on Page 1, and so did sister publications the *Hartford Courant* and the *Chicago Tribune.* Thom McGuire, the *Courant*'s assistant managing editor of photography and graphics, said, "It was a great image."

But a *Courant* employee, who was looking through the images for a friend, thought he noticed a problem—what appeared to be a duplication of the Iraqi citizens in the background of the picture. He brought the problem to the attention of a copyeditor, who alerted McGuire. "After about a 600 percent magnification in Photoshop, I called Colin to ask for an investigation," McGuire said.

In Los Angeles, Crawford was disbelieving. He thought the apparent duplication of the background crowd was probably due to some sort of technical, satellite-related glitch. "He sent us 13 very good images Sunday," Crawford recalled. "We had to get information and give him the benefit of the doubt."

As it turned out, Walski had used his computer to combine elements of two photographs, taken moments apart, in order to improve the composition. Once that admission was made, Crawford fired him. All the publications that ran the composite photo ran corrections.

In his apology, Walski told other *Times* employees, "I deeply regret that I have tarnished the reputation of the *Los Angeles Times,* a newspaper with the highest standards of journalism . . . and especially the very talented and extremely dedicated photographers and picture editors and friends. . . . I have always maintained the highest ethical standards through my career and cannot truly explain my complete breakdown in judgment at this time."

Another *Times* staff photographer, Don Barletti, told the Poynter Institute's online discussion group that he recalled seeing Walski after he returned. Walski told him, "Now no one will touch me. I went from the front line of the greatest newspaper in the world, and now I have nothing. No cameras, no car, nothing."

Barletti also said he understood how the alteration might have happened. Walski had been in the desert for days under harsh conditions with little sleep and food and under enormous pressure. "He got into a zone," Barletti said. "He was on a head roll, making fantastic images, and it got out of hand. He told me that he did not plan to send the image and was just messing around. He sent it anyway . . . didn't know what he was doing, but he did it. With all that he was facing, how did he have the presence of mind? It just got out of hand."

When asked about the issue, *New York Times* photographer Vincent LaForet agreed that the breach was serious. "There is not ever a good time for such manipulation, but this is the worst time. What really differentiates us from other photographers and media is our credibility. We have a history of getting it right, accurately. . . . Our credibility is all that we have."

Micro Issues

1. How should the newspapers that ran the original photo have corrected the error?
2. Should Walski have been fired? Why?
3. Many journalists who examined the photo did not notice the problem until it was pointed out to them. Is the minor nature of the alteration relevant in the ethical discussion? Why or why not?

Midrange Issues

1. Suzanne Lainson, also commenting on the issue on the Poynter Web site, said, "Why is the culture of the photojournalist supposed to be different than that for the print, audio or video editor . . . rather than condone editing photos, perhaps we should not condone editing print, audio and video data." Evaluate this comment.
2. What should be the role of editors—in an ethical sense—in the newsroom?
3. Should employees blow the whistle on colleagues when they think there has been an ethical breach? If not, why not? If so, how should they do it?
4. How does the electronic manipulation of the persons in the background differ from the photographer simply asking the people to move to a certain location before the photo is taken? Are they equally culpable from an ethical sense?

Macro Issues

1. "People do not expect 'truth' or 'reality' from their media—today's media audience is much more aware of the doctored nature of everything they read, see and hear than we like to think. I'm sure this *LA Times* story did not come as a surprise to most people," wrote Mark Deuze. Analyze this statement. How might media organizations assure viewers and readers of the veracity of the information they publish?
2. Eric Meyer, who commented about the issue on the Poynter Web site said, "A photo is like a direct quote. You chose what to quote or what to photograph. But, when you run a direct quote or a photograph, you don't alter it to 'make it better.'" Evaluate this statement.

CASE 8-D

"Above the Fold": Balancing Newsworthy Photos with Community Standards

JIM GODBOLD, MANAGING EDITOR
Eugene Register-Guard, Eugene, Oregon

JANELLE HARTMAN, REPORTER
Eugene Register-Guard, Eugene, Oregon

Author's Note: *On November 10, 1993, a nightmare unfolded in Springfield, Oregon, a quiet town adjoining the university community of Eugene, as Alan McGuire held his 2-year-old daughter, Shelby, hostage in their house. By the end of the standoff both were dead and the media had captured some horrific photos.*

Seven children had died as a result of child abuse in Lane County, Oregon, in the 20 months prior to that day, and the media had just witnessed the eighth. Jim Godbold was the assistant managing editor of the Eugene Register-Guard *at the time. The remarks below are from an interview with him months after the event.*

Godbold: The call came over the police scanner shortly after noon. We responded to a hostage situation, a man holding someone at knifepoint in a Springfield neighborhood. We knew it was probably 20 minutes from the *Register-Guard* in the best of possible circumstances so we really scrambled. Photographer Andy Nelson and police reporter Janelle Hartman went as fast as they could to the area.

We got there when the police were trying to set up a perimeter to get people away from the area. It was real pandemonium right when Andy arrived. The situation didn't unfold for more than a few minutes before there was a burst of flame inside the house that caught the attention of the police officers, and they immediately made the decision that they were going to have to go inside.

A group of officers ran at the door, and then all of a sudden Alan McGuire, the man who was in the house, came hurtling through the front window on fire. I am not even sure if police officers knew how many people were in the house at the time. His wife had escaped from the home. She had been held at knifepoint and bound, and she had somehow gotten out and she let police know that their 2-year-old daughter, Shelby McGuire, was in the house.

Shelby was a hostage and being held at knifepoint. Police saw her and tried to set up a telephone line so they could negotiate with McGuire, but the events unfolded rapidly, and after Alan McGuire jumped through the front window, police broke down the door. Two officers hauled McGuire's flaming body to the ground and tried to douse the flames with a garden hose. Inside the house one of the officers saw Shelby McGuire sitting upright on the couch. She had a plastic grocery produce bag over her head, and it apparently had been duct-taped in some fashion, maybe around the neck.

They immediately tore the bag away. A detective picked Shelby up and sprinted out of the house with her. It was at that moment that Andy Nelson snapped his picture of one of the officers with Shelby's body in his arms, running out, two other officers standing on the side of the doorstep, another officer with a hose near Alan

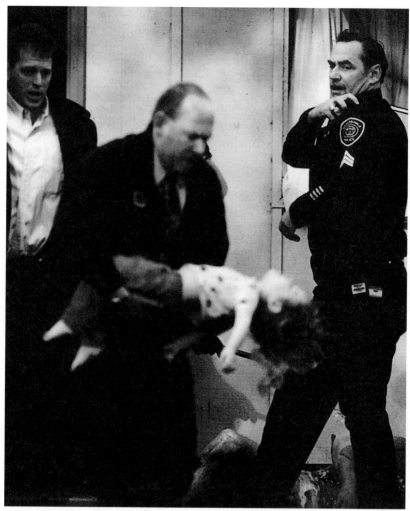

Photo courtesy of the Eugene Register-Guard. *Used by permission.*

McGuire, and Alan lying on the ground. The flame's now out, but the charred and still smoking body was present in the viewfinder as Andy snapped the picture.

At that moment the officer with Shelby McGuire, the 2-year-old, began mouth-to-mouth resuscitation on the front lawn. Andy subsequently took a photograph of that. Then they rushed both Alan and Shelby McGuire to the hospital. We did not know Shelby's condition. The police didn't respond about whether she was able to be resuscitated.

We have a standing policy at the newspaper that as a general rule we don't run photographs of dead bodies of children. That immediately triggered the kind of review that we would go through to determine where this particular incident was going to stand up on our policy, whether or not anyone was going to argue for publication or against publication.

We began to talk about the policy and the potential community reaction that we might face. The discussion was pretty brief. The photo was so compelling and the situation that it sprang from so horrifying that we began looking at the photograph and saying,

"Well, I don't know, but look at what the photo has captured." "People are going to be upset." "This is potentially a photograph of a dead 2-year-old child." "Look at the concern and the expression on the police officers' faces. This is an example of what they deal with day in and day out. They are up against this kind of domestic violence hostage situation and people don't realize that."

So, the debate was intense, and yet pretty short. We prepared a selection of pictures, and we brought those to the then-managing editor Patrick Yak and made the case that this is going to be a tough photograph for us to run. This is going to be one that we are going to have to be prepared to defend. But we believe it's that kind of exception to the rule that we look for.

The public response to the publication of the Shelby McGuire photograph was unprecedented in my 22 years in journalism and unprecedented at this newspaper. I have not come across a case, having been shown a number of them subsequently, that is of the magnitude per capita of reader response to a single photographic image. We received on the order of 450 telephone calls that began the moment people got the newspaper, which started at 6:00 a.m. First they came into our circulation department. The circulation department switchboard became overloaded and gave them the main newsroom switchboard, which didn't open until 7:30. At 7:30 when they threw the switch, all 20 of our incoming phone lines lit up, and the calls began to roll over into a holding pattern that had never been utilized by our switchboard before.

I was called at home by Al Gimmell, the corporate controller, who said, "We are inundated with telephone calls. We need some help." So I immediately came in to try to handle telephone calls, and I tried to find the time in between phone calls to call other editors in, but the calls were coming so rapidly that every time I hung up it rang again. When I picked up my voice mail messages, I had 31 unanswered messages, and that was probably 7:45 in the morning.

Photo courtesy of the Eugene Register-Guard. *Used by permission.*

The range of responses weren't monolithic, except in their anger. But the anger came from different places. For some people the anger came from a belief that we had simply stooped to a tremendously sensational graphic crime picture trying to sell newspapers. For others the anger came from the terrible sense of violation that the surviving mother and brother of Shelby McGuire would have to wake up to the morning after their ordeal and see this on the front page of the hometown newspaper.

Another component argued that this was wholly inappropriate for the kind of newspaper the *Register-Guard* has been and continues to be. That 5-year-olds and 6-year-olds were sharing the newspaper at the breakfast table, and parents were finding themselves in a position of having to explain this horrifying incident and having the question "How is the little girl?" asked again. And there was also a range of response from people who were themselves victims of domestic violence or spouses of victims or had family members who were involved in it. For them it was a combination of anger and pain.

I spoke with literally dozens of people through tears. It was an emotional response that was overwhelming and people were extremely upset by the picture. Most asked the question "Why? I need to understand why the newspaper published this picture."

We were really, I think, at a loss initially to respond to that question. I think a lot of that had to do with being in a very real sense out of touch with a substantial number of readers. The kind of reaction that we had was not anticipated by anyone in the news department.

If we were presented with a similar situation and a similar photograph today, we would absolutely not do it the way that we did it in the Shelby McGuire case. Thousands of our readers have defined for us a boundary in this community and for this newspaper that I don't think until we began to see it materialize we had any sense of exactly where it was.

Micro Issues

1. Look at the photos that accompany this text. The photo of the officer carrying out Shelby McGuire ran in full color above the fold, two-thirds of the page wide and 6 inches tall. Does a photo of that size over-sensationalize the story?
2. The photo of Sergeant Swenson's attempts to resuscitate Shelby ran below the fold in a small two-column photo. Why do you think the decision was made to run this photo smaller and lower?

Midrange Issues

1. Does the fact that Shelby died influence your decision on whether to run the photos? If so, in what way?
2. Does the fact that at least one television station and the local Springfield newspaper were there with photographers influence your decision to run the photos? If so, in what way?
3. Does the fact that seven other children had died in Lane County in less than 2 years affect your decision to run the photos? If so, in what way?

4. The biweekly *Springfield News* chose to run a front-page photo of Alan McGuire falling out of the front window of his home, his badly burned flesh still in flames. However, they covered the front page with a wrapper that read "Caution to Readers" and explained the content of the stories and photos underneath the wrapper. Critique that approach to handling the story.

5. A local television station showed a few seconds of the scene described above after warning viewers of the violent nature of the video that followed. The station got fewer than 20 complaints. How do you explain the vast difference in the reaction to the broadcast and print photos?

Macro Issues

1. What are the privacy rights of:
   a. Shelby McGuire?
   b. Shelby McGuire's mother and 4-year-old brother?
   c. Sergeant Swenson?
2. Critique the argument that these photos should be shown because they illustrate the type of tragedy that law enforcement officers are often called upon to handle.
3. Critique the argument that these photos should be shown because they illustrate the horror of domestic violence.
4. Critique the statement that "If we were presented with a similar situation and a similar photograph today, we would absolutely not do it the way that we did it in the Shelby McGuire case." In your opinion is that based on sensitivity to reader concern or caving in to reader pressure?

CASE 8-E

Horror in Soweto

SUE O'BRIEN, FORMER EDITORIAL PAGE EDITOR
The Denver Post

On September 15, 1990, freelance photographer Gregory Marinovich documented the killing, by a mob of African National Congress supporters, of a man they believed to be a Zulu spy.

Marinovich and Associated Press reporter Tom Cohen spotted the man being led from a Soweto, South Africa, train-station platform by a group armed with machetes and crude spears. Marinovich and Cohen continued to witness and report as the man was stoned, bludgeoned, stabbed, doused with gasoline and set afire.

It was one of 800 deaths in two months of factional fighting among blacks as rival organizations vied for influence in the declining days of apartheid.

The graphic photos stirred intense debate among editors. In one, the victim, conscious but stoic, lies on his back as a grinning attacker poises to plunge a knife into his forehead. In the final photo of the series, the victim crouches, engulfed in fire.

As the series was transmitted, several member editors called up to question what the photographer was doing at the scene—could he in any way have stopped the attack? In response, an advisory went out on the photo wire, saying Marinovich

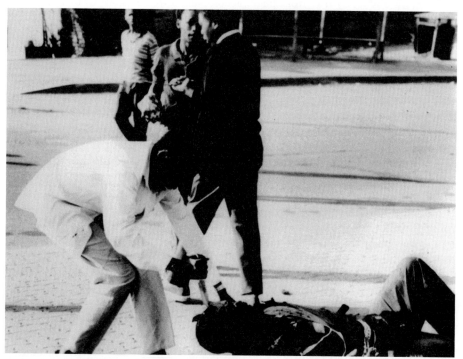

AP/WIDE WORLD PHOTOS. Used with permission.

had tried to intervene and then, when told to stop taking pictures, had told mob leaders he would stop shooting only when they "stopped hurting that man."

Decisions on what to do with the photos varied across the country, according to a survey. If any pattern emerged, it was that newspapers in competitive markets such as Denver, Minneapolis–St. Paul and New York were more likely to go with the harsh graphics.

The burning photo was the most widely used, the stabbing the least. Several editors said they specifically rejected the stabbing as too extreme. "It showed violence and animalistic hatred," said Roman Lyskowski, graphics editor for the *Miami Herald.* Another editor, who agreed that the stabbing was much more disturbing than the burning, said he recalled immolation pictures from the Vietnam era. "That's not as unusual an image as that knife sticking right out of the skull."

When the Soweto series cleared at the *Miami Herald,* the burning photo was sent to Executive Editor Janet Chusmir's home for her approval. At her direction, the immolation picture ran on the front page, but below the fold and in black and white. The detail revealed in color reproduction, Chusmir and her editors agreed, was too graphic.

At the *Los Angeles Times* and *Dallas Morning News,* however, the burning photo ran above the front-page fold—and in color.

The *St. Paul Pioneer Press* chose the stabbing for front-page color. "I look at the moment that the photo freezes on film," said News Editor Joe Sevick. "Rarely do you see a photo where a knife is about to go into somebody." The photo ran in color on the *Pioneer Press* front page, accompanied by the story Cohen had written on the attack and a longer story on the South African government's attempt, announced that day, to crack down on black-on-black violence.

In Denver, at the *Rocky Mountain News,* Managing Editor Mike Madigan wanted to run a comprehensive package on the Soweto story. The tabloid's only open page was deep in the paper, but a page 3 box referred readers to the story with a warning the photos were "horrific and disturbing." Inside, stories on the attack and government crackdown and an editor's note on Marinovich's intervention accompanied three photos: the victim being led away from the train station, the stabbing and the burning.

Most papers that ran the more challenging photos involved top management in the decision. Frequently, top editors were contacted by telephone, or came in from home, to give the photos a final go-ahead.

In most newsrooms, the burning or stabbing photos made it to the news desk for approval or rejection. But there, they sometimes were killed abruptly. "The editors at that point said no," one picture editor reported. "They would not take the heat."

Several editors deferred to the so-called breakfast test. "The question is 'Which of those photos would help tell the story without ruining everyone's breakfast?'" asked Rod Deckert, managing editor of the *Albuquerque Journal.* One editor said his paper is especially likely to de-emphasize disturbing material in the Sunday paper, which children often read with their parents. But many editors who rejected the more brutal pictures said the "breakfast test" is irrelevant. "If you're putting out a paper in New York and don't have something that's going to cause some discomfort over breakfast, then you're probably not putting out the full paper you should," said Jeff Jarvis, Sunday editor at the *New York Daily News.* "I don't think the breakfast test works for [today]."

Others cited distance tests. Some newspapers, in deference to victims' families, are less likely to use death photos from within their own circulation areas. Another editor, however, said his paper is *less* likely to run violent photos unless they are local and have a "more immediate impact on our readership."

Newspapers also differed widely on how they packaged the Soweto story. Some accompanied a photo series with the Cohen and crackdown stories, and a note on Marinovich's intervention. Some ran a single photo, often the burning, with only a cutline and a brief reference to the train-station incident in the "crackdown" story. Two respected big-city dailies, which omitted any reference to the Soweto attack in their accompanying stories, ran cursory cutlines such as "Violence continues: A boy runs away as an ANC supporter clubs a Zulu foe who was beaten, stabbed and set ablaze."

Although 41 papers used at least one of the Marinovich photos, only four—the *Charlotte Observer, Akron Beacon-Journal, Rocky Mountain News* (Denver) and *USA Today*—told the story of Marinovich's attempt to halt the attack.

Among collateral considerations at many news desks was the coverage of South African troubles that had gone before. At least one editor said the Soweto

AP/WIDE WORLD PHOTOS. Used with permission.

photos, which followed several other beating and killing photographs from South Africa that had been used earlier in the week, were "just too, too much."

With only three exceptions, editors said race did not figure in their considerations. One white editor said the fact that both attackers and victim were black deprived the series of clarity: "You don't have a sense of one side against another. You don't have a sense of right or wrong." Two editors who identified themselves as African-American, however, argued for aggressive use of the photos. Both work in communities with significant black populations. "I think black readers should be more informed about this," one said. "Across the board, black Americans don't realize what's going on with the black-on-black violence."

Front-page placement and the use of color frequently triggered reader objections, but the adequacy of cutline information and accompanying copy also appear significant. The *Albany Times Union* was flooded by phone protests and subscription cancellations. Two other papers perceiving significant reader unrest—the *Dallas Morning News* and *Los Angeles Times*—ran the burning photo in color on their front pages. But each of the three papers also ran the front-page photos with only cutline accompaniment, referring readers inside to the stories that placed the images in context.

In retrospect, *Rocky Mountain News'* Madigan said he was very pleased with the final Soweto package and readers' reaction to it.

> It wasn't so much the idea that, "Yeah, we ran these really horrific pictures and, boy, it knocked people's socks off." I don't think that was the point. I think it was more the way we handled it. Just one word or the other can make a terrific difference in whether the public starts screaming "sensationalize, sensationalize," or takes it as a thoughtful, important piece of work, which is what we were after.

Micro Issues

1. In all but the most important stories, would you support a ban on dead-body photos in your newspaper or newscast?
2. Some editors believe it is their ethical duty to avoid violating readers' sense of taste or compassion. Others argue that it is their duty to force society to face unpleasant truths, even if it means risking reader anger and rejection. Whose side would you support?
3. Many readers suspect that sensational photos are chosen to sell newspapers or capture rating points by appealing to morbid tastes. Do you believe they're right?

Midrange Issues

1. Editors sometimes justify running graphic photos by saying they can provide a "warning bell," alerting people to preventable dangers in society. What values might the Soweto photographs offer readers?
2. Is the desire to avoid offending readers an ethical consideration or a marketing consideration?
3. Is it appropriate to base editorial decisions on what readers are likely to be doing at home: to edit newspapers differently, for instance, if they are likely to be read at the breakfast table, or present newscasts differently if they are to air during the dinner hour rather than later in the evening?

4. As an editor, would you be more likely to run a photograph of someone being murdered if the event happened in your own community, or if it happened thousands of miles away and none of your readers would be likely to know the victim or his family?
5. Do you see any distinction in:
    a. whether a violent photo is run in color or black and white, or
    b. whether it is run on the front page or on an inside page?

Macro Issues

1. Is aesthetic, dramatic or photographic value ever reason enough to run a picture, regardless of how intrusive it may be or how it may violate readers' sensitivities?
2. Is it your responsibility as an editor to find out if a photographer could have saved a life by intervening in a situation rather than taking pictures of it? Is that information you need to share with your readers?
3. Is it your responsibility as an editor to find out if the presence of the camera at the scene in any way helped incite or distort an event? Is that information you need to share with your readers?
4. When dramatic photographs are printed, how important is it for readers or viewers to be told all the background of the story or situation?

CASE 8-F

Death in Print: Publication of Hurricane Katrina Photographs

ABIGAIL M. PHEIFFER
University of Missouri—Columbia

"Do we publish this photograph of a dead body?" This is one of the most difficult questions newspaper editors can face. Editors at newspapers across the nation faced this question repeatedly as they reviewed wire photographs from the coverage of hurricane Katrina destruction in Louisiana and Mississippi. This case examines the Sept. 2nd photographic coverage of this event in three newspapers—the *Los Angeles Times, Chicago Tribune,* and *St. Louis Post-Dispatch.* Specifically, the study examines whether or not they published James Nielsen's photograph provided by Getty Images. The image depicts a woman standing on a bridge, feeding her dog as a corpse floats in the water underneath her. Sept. 2nd was the fifth day of the Katrina disaster.

All of the newspapers employ a similar process for choosing wire photographs on the day prior to publication of each issue. The first step is for a few wire editors to review the entire collection of photographs provided to them by Getty Images, the Associated Press and other wire services. These editors view hundreds of photographs and narrow the options down to those that they believe have the strongest visual impact.

The second step is to have a morning or early afternoon review of this initial edit. This takes place in the form of a formal meeting of all photo editors, an informal discussion of the photos among the photo editors or a full newsroom staff meeting. At this time the photo editors consider the merits of each photograph and learn the subject matter of the stories for which they must choose photographs. Based on this analysis the initial wire photo edit is narrowed to a smaller group of photos. One editor, often the director of photography or an assistant managing editor, reviews this narrowed edit and decides which photographs he or she believes should be on the front page, also known as A1. This editor then attends an afternoon A1 meeting and makes a pitch to the top editors, usually the executive and managing editors. This pitch includes the photo representative's opinions on where a photo should run in the newspaper and why it should run there. Detailed discussions of each possible A1 photo occur and final decisions are made regarding where photos will run.

St. Louis Post-Dispatch

The *St. Louis Post-Dispatch,* a newspaper that ranks 21st nationally in circulation among American newspapers with 271,386 daily circulation and 428,601 circulation on Sunday, published six Katrina photographs. The Nielsen photograph was published on page A10 and was stripped across the top of the page at roughly 4 inches tall and 11½ inches wide. The photograph was cropped from the top and bottom, cutting out some of the water, bridge and what appears to be the base of a light post. This puts greater visual emphasis on the corpse, woman and the bag of

James Nielsen/AFP/Getty Images.

trash in the water. The front-page photograph for Sept. 2nd by Dave Martin of the Associated Press showed thousands of people boarding buses in Metairie, La., a suburb of New Orleans.

Larry Coyne, Director of Photography for the *St. Louis Post-Dispatch,* presents the photographic options for each day's edition in the A1 meeting. Coyne argued for the Nielsen photo to run on A1 but was in the minority. According to Coyne, the newspaper received many wire photographs that included dead bodies, but the publication was taking a cautious approach to running one, waiting for a photograph that was worthy of such a strong subject matter. Coyne advocated that this photograph run on the front page because it showed not only the tragedy of Katrina, but also how people were attempting to continue with their everyday lives. For him the juxtaposition of these two visual statements summarized the event and the destructive results of Katrina's power. "To get a full understanding you have to see it," Coyne said. "Until you see it, it is a figment of your imagination."

Coyne noted that there was a lively conversation in the A1 meeting regarding the Nielsen photograph, including a focus on whether or not the photograph trivialized the events of Katrina. There was concern that the photograph could offend readers because it included a corpse, but in the end the majority supported running the bus photo as the lead image because they felt it was more relevant to the stories planned for the Sept. 2nd edition.

Los Angeles Times

The *Los Angeles Times,* a newspaper that ranks 4th nationally with 843,432 daily circulation and 1,247,569 circulation on Sundays, published 15 Katrina photographs. The Nielsen photograph was published on the middle of the front page, just below the lead photo. The Nielsen photograph ran at approximately 3¼ inches tall and 5½ inches wide. The lead photograph, shot by Michael Ainsworth of the *Dallas Morning News,* showed a mob of evacuees arguing outside of the Superdome as they were boarding buses. The photo editors do work with a page designer early in the photo selection process, before a final decision is made, to determine where each photo will run. Although deference is given to the photo editor, the page designer's opinion is considered regarding where and how large the photographs will run in the publication.

Steve Stroud, the Deputy Director of Photography, represents the national, foreign and often the metro photo desks in the A1 meeting and makes the pitch for the A1 photos. Stroud states that the photo editors did consider not running the Nielsen photograph because of its graphic nature. However, the driving factor in the decision to run the image on the front page was that at the time the staff knew that at least several hundred people had died in New Orleans and there were predictions that the final body count could be in the thousands. Nielsen's work accurately represented one of the major stories that was coming out of the event on that day.

As Stroud stated, "Our role is to inform people and remind people in a way that is appropriate to the event." The Ainsworth photo was selected as the lead image because it is more active, better represents chaos and affects more people.

Chicago Tribune

The *Chicago Tribune,* a newspaper that ranks 6th nationally with 586,122 daily circulation and 950,582 circulation on Sunday, ran 17 Katrina photographs in the Sept. 2nd issue. The Nielsen photograph did not run on Sept. 2nd, but did run in a special section entitled "Special Report: Hurricane Katrina" on Sept. 4th. The image appeared on the bottom of page seven of the special section at roughly 4½ inches tall and 8½ inches wide. The image was cropped slightly from the top. The lead photograph on Sept. 2nd was a Getty Image photo by Mark Wilson that depicted crying women trying to help a relative who appeared to be fighting death outside of the New Orleans Convention Center.

Rob Kozloff, the Metro Picture Editor, was the substitute A section photo editor the week the Sept. 2nd edition was published. Kozloff believed that the Nielsen photograph was probably considered for publication in the Sept. 2nd edition, but was not one of the 15 photos that received serious consideration for A1. He stated that there were many photographs that dramatically depicted the emotion of the day. Some of these images were a better fit than the Nielsen photograph to the storylines planned for the Sept. 2nd edition. However, Kozloff felt that the image provided an accurate perspective once it was placed among many other photographs in the special section. When these images were viewed as a group they accurately represented the entirety of the Katrina disaster. According to Kozloff, Nielsen's work was intriguing because it is not clear to the viewer if the woman is aware of the body.

In all three cases these newspapers made it clear that an extensive discussion involving multiple management members is expected when an image is controversial. Each of the following questions was raised by one or more of the newspapers when deciding whether or not a photo will run and where it will run. Even though none of the newspapers had specific policies that covered the tragedy of Katrina, collectively, these questions form a set of criteria.

1. Is the image relevant to the stories that will run in the issue?
2. Is the photograph in good taste or is it too graphic?
3. Is there a compelling reason for challenging the reader with a controversial image?
4. Is the content of the image newsworthy? Does it educate the reader?
5. Does the image revictimize or embarrass the photo subjects or family members of the subjects?
6. What is the most important news story of that day?
7. Can readers tolerate the image when eating their cereal in the morning?
8. What is the tolerance level of our specific readership?
9. How technically strong is the image?
10. Is it likely that there will be a stronger image for the same topic in the future?
11. Is the image properly stating the case or is it overstating it? Is the image emblematic or gratuitous?
12. Does the event warrant use of a graphic photograph?

None of these editors mentioned selling newspapers as a criterion for deciding which image to use. The editors do consider not running controversial images or placing them inside the newspaper at a smaller size where they are not as startling to a reader.

When discussing controversial images the editors said the discussion often includes weighing the "good" of educating the public versus the "bad" of violating the privacy of the subjects in the photograph. Most of the editors indicated that they felt it was necessary to use a picture that forced the reader to confront death in order to understand the gravity of the situation in New Orleans.

The bottom line was best stated by Greg Peters of the *Kansas City Star,* when he said: "As a picture editor you learn every day and try to get smarter every day. We try to get better every day."

Micro Issues

1. Is the Nielsen photo a page 1 photo on the fifth day of the tragedy? Why or why not?
2. What story does the Nielsen photo tell?

Midrange Issues

1. Does moving a controversial photo to the inside pages of a newspaper allow the editors more latitude in what they show? Why or why not?
2. Does a warning before graphic video is shown on a local newscast give the station more latitude in what they show? Why or why not?
3. If the body had been recognizable, would that change your opinion of running the photo? If the body had been unrecognizable but naked, would that change your opinion?

Macro Issues

1. Is it important that photos pass the "breakfast test" of acceptability before being run in the paper?
2. In weighing the "good" of educating the public to the horrors of the Katrina tragedy versus the "bad" of shocking the readership, where do you stand on running this photo? When the "bad" is the invasion of privacy of the dead individuals, where do you stand on running this photo?

CASE 8-G

Digital Manipulation as Deceit? A Case Study of a *Redbook* Magazine Cover

ELIZABETH HENDRICKSON
University of Tennessee—Knoxville

The June 2003 issue of *Redbook* magazine looked at first glance like many other popular magazines on the newsstand: It featured a cover photo of a popular actress surrounded by multiple cover lines. This particular cover starred actress Jennifer Aniston, wearing a red tee shirt and blue jeans, with hands on hips. The accompanying cover line touted:

Jennifer's Secret Passion:
She opens up about making babies, Brad's beard, and the tough time that tested—
and strengthened—their love
    Plus: The key to her relaxed American Style.

A look inside the magazine credits the Aniston photograph to Barbara Green, for Image Direct/Getty Images, which indicates the cover image was not from a studio photo shoot, but rather, the photo was purchased from a stock photo agency.

While it is not uncommon for a popular magazine to utilize celebrity stock photos within its pages, it is somewhat unusual for a mainstream women's magazine to feature a stock photo of an A-list celebrity on its cover. However, what truly sets this cover apart from other competing women's titles was the public dispute between Aniston's publicist and magazine representatives that followed in the cover's newsstand wake.

According to Aniston's publicist, Stephen Huvane, the cover was procured without his consent, a tacit misstep when booking celebrities for magazine covers. But perhaps more significantly, Huvane claimed the cover photo was not one image but three different photos pieced together to make a composite photo. "The pants and her left hand with the wedding band are from one picture, her right arm, which is thicker and discolored is another, her head is from a paparazzi shot, her shirt is painted on, they changed her hair," said Huvane (Rush and Molloy 2003).

Additionally, Huvane complained that the inside photo credit gave a makeup credit, "as if she posed for a photo shoot."

A *Redbook* spokeswoman defended the cover, saying, "The only things that were altered in the cover photo were the color of her shirt and the length of her hair, very slightly, in order to reflect her current length." Moreover, *Redbook*'s then Editor-in-Chief Ellen Kunes, responded, "It's 100% her" (Rush and Molloy 2003).

While Huvane reportedly considered legal action against *Redbook* for "blatant manipulation of her [Aniston's] image," none was ultimately pursued. However, Huvane issued a statement perhaps even more damning to the magazine: that Aniston would never pose for *Redbook*. In 2003, the magazine industry considered Jennifer Aniston newsstand gold, with covers featuring the actress often being a title's top-selling newsstand issue for the year. The publicist's declaration was particularly salient given *Redbook*'s somewhat dire newsstand situation at that time.

From 2002 to 2003, *Redbook*'s single copy sales had dropped 15.2 percent to an average of 471,930 copies sold per month. It may thus seem logical to assume that the magazine was hoping to boost single copy sales with an Aniston cover.

So why did *Redbook* editors seemingly feel compelled to bypass Huvane's approval in lieu of stock photos of the star? It was likely a matter of access. Aniston's publicist manages her image, so in an effort to restrain access to his client and control exclusivity, Huvane was approving very few publicity requests in 2003. The only June 2003 magazine cover Aniston posed for was *Harper's Bazaar.*

While the case of Aniston versus *Redbook* is a recent and palpable example of digital manipulation, the matter has been lurking within the publishing industry for nearly 25 years. The February 1982 cover of *National Geographic* was perhaps the first and most infamous example, done in a pre-PhotoShop age. In order to make a photograph of the Egyptian pyramids fit onto a vertical layout, editors digitally manipulated one of the pyramids closer to another without revealing the manipulation to their readers. Another notorious instance was a 1989 cover of *TV Guide,* featuring Oprah Winfrey. In the image, Winfrey's body was superimposed onto the body of actress AnnMargret (Kim and Paddon 1999). The reason given was that no photos were available of the newly-slim Oprah for the *TV Guide* cover, so they manufactured one.

Such cases raise ethical issues within the industry as to what can and should be done with the newly evolving technology. When the tools exist to create an image that appears more attractive, more flawless and possibly, more sellable, are there ethical constraints on publishing a relatively harmless but digitally created image?

Photographic manipulation is commonly considered to be altering or tampering with a photograph, thus shifting it from its truthful, natural state. But there is no general consensus on how much manipulation is allowable before the "truth" of the photo is compromised. For instance, while certain magazine editors do not feel it is wrong to digitally take out wrinkles, undereye bags or stray hairs from a photo image, others feel it is unethical to remove background images from a photo image.

According to sources within the magazine industry, Kunes' decision was not one existing in the industry mainstream, but rather one found on the professional fringes. However, the criticism centered more on professional need for continued access to celebrities, and less on truth or on duty to the reader. As one magazine art director (Hemmel 2006) said:

> It's a perception thing, if you do that you'll never get another cover. Certain people will talk to you but you can't get a shoot with them. It's considered within the industry that if you don't shoot them they shouldn't be on your cover. A lot of times they put them on their cover because they sell. But it's just looked down upon.

Micro Issues

1. Did *Redbook* cross an ethical line when they chose to put Aniston on the cover using a stock photo?
2. If they did, indeed, piece together a photograph from more than one source as Huvane claims, did *Redbook* cross an ethical line?

3. Since an increasing number of readers know how to manipulate digital photos and likely do so on their home computers, is it still deception to manipulate photos in this more media-savvy time?

Midrange Issues

1. Are the ethical standards of photography for *Redbook* different from a news magazine such as *Time* or *Newsweek?* If so, in what way?
2. Does *Redbook* have a duty to not alter photos that occur in a news story within the magazine on a topic such as women's health? Do the rules differ for news stories and features within the same magazine or newspaper?

Macro Issues

1. Who owns the image of Jennifer Aniston? Her? Her publicist contracted to manage her image? A photographer who has a signed contract with her? A medium who buys an authorized photo of her? All of the above?
2. Write a policy that addresses photo manipulation for a magazine such as *Redbook*.

9

New Media: Continuing Questions and New Roles

By the end of this chapter, you should be able to:

- spot "old" ethical issues in their Internet incarnations.
- understand the role of copyright law in ethical decision making about Internet content.
- develop professional strategies for using the Internet as a reporting and advertising tool.
- delineate important policy issues the Internet raises for journalists and citizens.

The original journalists in America were citizens who stepped into the role of pamphleteers or publishers based on a desire to shape an emerging nation. Most of them, like Benjamin Franklin or Thomas Paine, had sources of income outside of their role as citizen journalists, and many lost money in their publishing pursuits. During the next 100 years, the role of professional journalist emerged in the new democracy and for the next century, the delivery of information was primarily considered the role of the full-time professional.

However, no formal education or license is required to be a journalist. Toward the end of the 20th century—propelled by the Internet—it became evident that the role of "journalist" no longer belonged exclusively to the trained writer working in a recognizable institutional media outlet.

And even those institutionally employed journalists today often step out of their institutional roles through their blogs—some out of passion, others by contract with their employers. Citizen journalists who have never been in a newsroom now create Web sites and write blogs whose readers rival in numbers the readers of the mainstream press and whose stories often break important national news. Videos on YouTube often receive a number of "hits" that would rank them among the top rated television programs if they had been measured by the Nielsen ratings. While the delivery methods are new, the concept is old: citizen journalists as the eyes and ears of the public. And as they point their cameras at increasingly serious topics, the results are often dramatic, as we have seen recently.

Just as the printing press came of age as an informational (and political) force with the pamphlets of Thomas Paine and others, Twitter came of age as a news medium in early 2009 when a U.S. Airways flight had to land in the Hudson River moments after takeoff from New York after birds crippled both engines. Almost as soon as the plane hit the water, Twitter messages sped the news around the world. Long before any traditional media could reach the scene, cell phones had documented the successful rescue attempts and "tweets" had spread the good news.

Later that same year, the disputed presidential Iranian presidential election showed the world the power of social networking sites as a news medium. When official media coverage of demonstrations by supporters of the defeated challenger Mir Hossein Mousavi was banned by incumbent president and alleged winner Mahmoud Ahmadinejad, the illegal video of protests went viral on sites such as Facebook despite the futile attempts of the president to shut it down. Instant Web sites popped up informing the masses of alleged irregularities in the election—something mainstream journalists were prevented from doing. But the regime couldn't stop the Internet. YouTube, Facebook and other sites had become a political force overnight.

But citizen journalism lacks one important component that traditional media had: gatekeepers. Newspapers had editors; magazines had "fact checkers" and Henry Luce's publications were legendary for the lengths they would go to for the sake of accuracy. But when John Sigenthaler, a former editor of the *Nashville Tennessean,* found himself named as a co-conspirator in the John F. Kennedy assassination in his biography in the online encyclopedia Wikipedia, he called national attention to the lack of institutional oversight of postings on Wikipedia and the difficulty he personally faced in setting the record straight. While Sigenthaler had the stature to get media attention called to the error about him and get his "official" Wikipedia entry corrected, untold numbers of factual errors race across the Internet each day where few, if any, gatekeepers exist to vouch for the accuracy of the content. And an error like the Wikipedia entry on Sigenthaler will never be chased down to all the aggregators and sites that have copied from or linked to the error.

Corrections of news stories in print or broadcast media have some permanence. On the Internet, it is possible to simply blow away the page—or even the site—that contains an error, leaving no permanent record. But with so many pages out there, and so many links, errors now persist in ways unimaginable 20 years ago. Journalists have long agreed that errors merit permanent correction. If the same professional standard is to be applied to the Internet, how might it be implemented so that readers who access the page months, or even years, later know that an error was made and be sent to the correct information?

MASS MEDIA AS AN INSTRUMENT OF FRAGMENTATION

If there was a single basic tenet of American mass media for most of our 200-plus years of existence, it would be the belief that the shared experience of consuming the daily news was crucial to informed participation in a democracy. But more than 30 years ago, Nicholas Negroponte, head of MIT's Media Lab and an early Internet guru, created a unique publication he called the *Daily Me*. Negroponte programmed his computer to develop a daily newspaper based on his information needs and desires as well as past information preferences, an experience he wrote about in the important early work *Being Digital* (1995). In a day when news was typically delivered for the masses at the pre-arranged schedule convenient to the sender, Negroponte's invention was a landmark one for its time.

Today, all of us now have the capacity to develop a *Daily Me* from the vast collection of information now on the World Wide Web. If every member of a society has access to personalized news, the implications for democracy are enormous (Sunstein 2001). According to Cass Sunstein, democracy demands two imperatives. First, people must be exposed to materials that they would not have chosen in advance and come across views that they would not have previously selected or even agree with. Second, many, or at least most, citizens should have a range of common experiences. In the absence of shared experiences, society will have a much harder time addressing social problems, Sunstein contends. Shared experience and the societal benefits of common knowledge were also at the core of the "Cultural Literacy" movement late in the last century.

Philosopher Jürgen Habermas is another advocate of this approach, arguing that one of the preconditions of a deliberative democracy is a large number of public forums where people meet by chance and begin a dialogue—none of which is possible in a society where everyone subscribes only to the *Daily Me*. Sunstein concludes that "The imagined world of the 'Daily Me' is the farthest thing from a utopian dream, and it would create serious problems from a democratic point of view."

As the "broadcast model" began to crumble for news, the same phenomenon was happening in the entertainment industry. In The *Long Tail: How the Future of Business is Selling Less of More,* Chris Anderson (2006) claims that Amazon, Rhapsody and others have made entire genres of books and music financially viable by getting around overhead problems of the traditional bookstore or music stores. He writes (2006, 5):

> The great thing about broadcast is that it can bring one show to millions of people with unmatched efficiency. But it can't do the opposite—bring a million shows to one person each. The economics of the broadcast era required hit shows— big buckets—to catch huge audiences. The economics of the broadband era are reversed. . . . There's still a demand for big cultural buckets, but they're no longer the only market. The hits now compete with an infinite number of niche markets of any size.

Wal-Mart, America's largest music retailer, stocks only 4,500 unique titles in its selection. This means that more than 99 percent of all CDs on the market are not found in the nation's largest music seller. Before its recent problems, Blockbuster carried only 3,000 of the 200,000 commercially available DVDs. Even the largest chain bookstores have only about 100,000 titles in stock out of the estimated five million English titles available. This inability to service anything other than a "hit" led to what Anderson calls "the long tail" of online distributors such as iTunes (music), Netflix (video) and Amazon (books). And making the long tail possible is the infinite storage and cataloging possibilities of Web-based suppliers.

Under the "long tail" a huge percentage of sales are of books, DVDs or CDs that will sell fewer than a handful of copies a year, yet they are a major source of income for these companies that have found a way to pass on to others the problems associated with warehousing and distribution and to focus on what they do best— offer the widest possible catalog. But even these companies will gain more virtual competitors. Netflix will give way to an Internet delivery system. Books will give way to Kindle or its competitors. Copyright law itself will yield to "digital rights management," a bundle of rights you can purchase or not when you choose your movie, book or music.

NEW TECHNOLOGIES: NEW ETIQUETTE

One of the great possibilities of the Web is to link far-flung pieces of information often across various print, audio and video platforms into a cohesive unit using embedded links and other technologies. But is unauthorized linking allowable? Is aggregating and uploading all the available news on a topic—say, the alleged marital infidelities of a figure like Tiger Woods—onto your proprietary (and perhaps user-funded) Web site allowable or is it plagiarism? All these questions were in the air when in the summer of 2009, the *Columbia Journalism Review* started a national discussion on the ethics of mainstream media crediting and linking to blogs and blogs crediting mainstream media and linking to them.

On its surface, it would appear that linking serves the same purpose as attribution—giving credit to the source of an original work you are quoting in your derivative work. It serves both a social function and a legal function and is even a fundamental part of the law of fair use. But unlike the half-sentence attribution read quickly by readers, links have the potential to carry away the reader to an entirely different Web site with no guarantee they will return to the original article. In fact, studies show that readers clicking away from a story have a low likelihood of returning to the original story.

In the *CJR* study, the Web site Gawker was found to be a particularly heavy user of borrowed material, often with little credit or links to the original source. One Gawker posting on the Church of Scientology allegedly borrowed heavily from work done by the staff of the St. Petersburg *Times* according to *CJR* Bill Grueskin. In an article entitled "Gawker's Link Etiquette (or Lack Thereof)," Grueskin found that most of the links in the Gawker article were actually to other Gawker works and the ones that did lead to the original journalism of the *Times* were buried late in the article. Grueskin noted that his own earlier research while he was at WSJ.com indicated that if a link is buried in a story where the reader has scrolled two or more screens there is a 95 percent chance they would not leave the article for the link.

In an article entitled "Dude, where's my link?" *Washington Post* writer Ian Shapira recounts how a 1,500-word story on a woman who leads seminars on how Baby Boomers can connect with the millennial generation was picked up by Gawker (Garber 2009). After much editing, it was labeled with a new headline and posted with almost no attribution to the *Post*. Shapira said he worked two "solid" days on the story and wanted not only traditional attribution, but also a link to his story and money. In the interview with *Columbia Journalism Review's* online site, Shapira proposes "a fluid blogosphere, but one where aggregators—newspapers included—are more transparent about whom they are heavily excerpting. They should mention the original source immediately. And if bloggers want to excerpt at length, a fee would be the nice, ethical gesture."

CJR's Megan Garber (2009) states that "Journalism is still in a kind of moralistic Wild West" when it comes to what constitutes fair use on the Web:

> What all this means, though, is that, as the journalistic community wanders through the desert, we need to come together to determine standards—and limits—when it comes to linking, quoting, attribution, and the like. We need, essentially, shared principles that will combine ethics with etiquette, and that will serve as benchmarks for our online behavior. Most of us, after all, want to be upstanding citizens of the digital nation.

To counter the perceived lack of rules, some mainstream media news organizations, in late 2009, began efforts to make specific news items "ungoogleable," that is, unreachable by a search engine other than the proprietary one offered for a fee by the medium. It was an effort that addressed revenue streams without full consideration of the ethical questions involved. Will locking up information behind a pay site stop allow news providers to roll back the clock and stop the free flow of information to the Web that began at the end of the last century? Or will it just send would-be readers looking elsewhere for the same information—assuming it is available at all.

In an exchange that provokes both laughter and tears, a reporter at the now defunct *Rocky Mountain News* was told by a neighbor, "Well, I'm sorry the paper is going away, but I'll still read you on the Internet." The delusional Denver resident was not the only reader to fail to understand—and appreciate—the connection between the expensive process of news gathering and the apparently free access to its result through blogs and search engines.

THE LAW LAGS BEHIND

Legal theories and case rulings have not kept pace with the technology. The courts would normally consider a photograph a concrete expression of an idea. But what happens when the photograph has been cut into pixels, the individual pixels' colors changed, the shape of the pixels reorganized—say, from a camel to an elephant—and then the resulting image, which now looks a great deal like an

Ed Stein © The Rocky Mountain News/Dist. By Newspaper Enterprise Association, Inc.

elephant and lacks a negative to indicate that it was once a camel, is downloaded onto a Web site that belongs to your news organization? Is linking to another site some form of copyright infringement? Is it like using "freelance" work in a publication? Could links constitute unjust enrichment? Or are they more like the harpsichord keys—a good idea that cannot be copyrighted although it can be used in many different ways?

Is the execution of the idea that the photograph represents the property of the photographer who shot the original image, the property of the multimedia author who took the photograph of the camel and changed it to an elephant, or the property of the news organization that ultimately distributed it in the form of electrons on a Web site? How about the designer or the content creator of the page you are linking to? Is there an express or implied contract in any of these actions? Does the creator of the elephant image owe royalties or acknowledgement to the creator of the camel?

Right now, it is unclear how the use and development of the Internet will influence these answers. Common ownership muddies the professional waters even further. Thinking about copyright has always included an element of "this came first," but that issue was defined in terms of weeks or years rather than nanoseconds.

Historically, when one medium—for example, radio—has surpassed another—say, newspapers—in an important dimension such as timeliness, both mediums have evolved to take advantage of their unique strengths. Thus, as broadcasting developed, that medium tended to emphasize immediacy while print emphasized depth. With the emergence of broadcasting as a dominant medium, journalists began to rethink the ethics of "the scoop" and to insist that accurate news reporting was more important in both a professional and ethical sense than mere speed. This same debate—the balance between accuracy and speed—is now taking place among news organizations with a substantial Internet presence.

The ability to digitize information also challenges our intuitive assumptions about a variety of things—everything from the "reality" that a picture represents to the external symbol systems that words and images together create. Digitization enables media designers to confound the external referent as never before. Students at the turn of the century will recognize that Audrey Hepburn's image has been digitized and electronically inserted into a Gap ad. But students in 2050 may not recognize the original Audrey Hepburn, may not know that she was a film star and may not be aware that she has been dead for over more than half a century at that point. They will have lost the external referent to the image and much of the ad's potency with it.

Ethical thinking combined with sound professional practice can provide some paths out of this virtual swamp. The first, and probably the most basic, maxim arises from the habits of sound professional performance. Cite the source of your information—or your electronic bytes. After all, journalists are required to note the originators of their information when reporting on documents or interviews. Multimedia designers should be subject to the same standard, just as music arrangers (as opposed to composers) or screenwriters currently are. Just as important, that source needs to be credible—even accurate. Newspapers and broadcast outlets eschew publishing rumors. Internet news—if it is to succeed as a genuine information medium—needs to consider the same standard. Just as in the days of the film *The Front Page,* scoops for the sake of scoops are ethically suspect.

If noting the originators of your information creates problems, then be willing to accept those problems as the price of using the information. Many publications require that journalists avoid sourcing their stories exclusively from the Internet; some demand confirmation of an Internet source with additional verification from non-virtual documents and in-person interviews. In an ethical sense, such professional standards allow news organizations and those who work for them to achieve two results. In the Judeo-Christian tradition, you have avoided information theft, an ethically culpable act, and fulfilled the ethical duty of beneficence, sharing credit with the originator of your information, whether that is a particular author or the source of a quote in a feature story.

In addition, you've also done your best to uphold the professional standards of accuracy and truth. In this world of bits and bytes, application of a maxim of "Cite the source of your bytes" will prejudice you to the development of original and creative work, including multiple sources. And, using your own stuff, and not someone else's, improves performance.

The second maxim that emerges from a discussion of deception is this: information that has the capacity to deceive the rational audience member as to its origin, original referent or source must be regarded as suspect. While journalistic discussion of deception has generally focused on practices used to obtain stories, we believe the concept also applies to the relationship between the journalist and his audience. The issue is whether using digitized information is intended to mislead the audience. Thus, an October 1996 cover of *Life* magazine that combined more than 400 previous covers into an image of Marilyn Monroe does not intend to deceive the audience because the editors clearly explained what they did. But lifting an image from one Web site, downloading sentences from another and combining them for your own news story without citing your original sources is an attempt to deceive both your editors and your audience.

While both plagiarism and forgery are clearly deceptive practices (Bok 1983, 218), the Web, with its nearly infinite possibilities as a source of information, has highlighted the need for journalists to take care. Even in a new era of pixels and bytes, journalists must maintain old-fashioned credibility with our audiences about the sources of our information and the means and methods of gathering that information.

SOURCES: NEW TECHNOLOGY BUT CONTINUING ISSUES

New technology often raises old ethical issues with additional permutations, and the subtleties of sourcing on the Internet don't all focus on accuracy and speed. Journalists accept that readers and viewers may better understand and evaluate news if those stories identify information sources. Identification often goes beyond a mere name and address: journalists may provide background information so audience members understand why a person or document is cited. The professional standard is that sources should be named and that journalists must have compelling reasons for withholding a source's identity. Implicit in this standard is that sources are aware that they are talking to a journalist, or that a specific document has been requested for a journalistic purpose. The Internet can confound these implicit assumptions.

First, granting anonymity requires a mutual agreement between reporter and source, not a unilateral understanding imposed on one party by the other. Anonymous sources are expected to be the exception rather than the journalistic rule. Professional mores dictate that, should a reporter decide to grant anonymity, she does not have to divulge the source's identity to editors, other supervisors or, in rare instances, the courts.

Even the traditional practice of interviewing, now considered commonplace, was controversial at its inception. The critics claimed that interviewing would destroy reporting. Critics argued that if journalists adapted this reporting technique, they would slip into a moral morass, fall prey to aggressive exploitation and manipulation and would no longer serve the public. Reporters' power grew with the use of the interview because they could select which persons to question and determine which comments to include. As the journalistic practice of the interview developed concurrently with the rise of the professional ideal of objectivity, identifying news sources became accepted professional practice (Schudson 1995, 1978).

The role sourcing plays with readers and viewers has also been questioned in mass communication research. One of the most widely accepted findings in the field is that audience members tend to disassociate the source from the message, what is known as the "sleeper" effect (Lowery and DeFleur 1988). Studies confirm that most people tend to retain the fact of what is said while forgetting the context in which they heard it. Practitioners, from Nazi master propagandist Joseph Goebbels through contemporary political consultants, have intuitively understood this human tendency to disassociate the source from the message. But readers and viewers are morally autonomous actors. Identifying news sources allows audiences to evaluate reports in terms of both content and a source's motives for divulging information.

The motives for providing and withholding information are sometimes central to political coverage, and political reporters have added an element of elasticity to the practice of anonymous sourcing. The phrase "not for attribution" means journalists may quote what is said but agree to veil the source. Thus, the attribution "a high-level White House source" may mean anyone from the president himself to cabinet officers to other, well-connected administrative appointees. The phrase "on background" means journalists should consider the information given as an aid in placing facts in context. Background information also may be used as part of a sourcing trail: journalists in possession of background information may use their knowledge to try to get other sources to provide them with the same information on the record.

Journalists continue to debate allowing sources to go "off the record" or "on deep background." A strict interpretation of these synonymous phrases means that the journalist who accepts such information may not quote the specific source and, in addition, may not use his knowledge to pry the same information from other sources. This stringent interpretation has meant that editors have instructed reporters literally to leave the room when a source asks for such anonymity. Journalists have spent time in jail rather than reveal a source's identity. Less stringent interpretations suggest that journalists who accept information off the record may not name or in any way reveal the identity of the source but may use the information itself to leverage similar or related information from other sources.

Until quite recently such agreements were arrived at through face-to-face conversation and negotiation. However, the advent of the Internet and the ability of journalists to lurk at many places on the Web have changed these dynamics. Journalists surfing for story sources or leads must be careful to identify themselves professionally on the Internet when they begin "conversing" with another Internet user. Concepts such as citizen journalism have also changed the journalist–source relationship. Citizen journalists essentially function as reporters who are most often edited by professionals. But most citizen journalism projects do not attempt to either confirm or police how citizen journalists acquire their information. In some cases, citizen journalists appear to be subject to a different set of rules than are the professionals.

Some publications, for example *The Wall Street Journal,* maintain an informal policy that requires reporters to identify themselves as reporters when they begin their Internet conversations. The reasoning behind such requirements is that people, in this instance people who are "telepresent," need to know that they are dealing with a journalist working in a professional capacity. Since journalists are well aware of the pitfalls of being deceived by a source, "wired" reporters should be more than sensitive to these problems when they become the party to the conversation with the power to deceive. Such professional identification—the Internet version of identifying yourself at the beginning of a telephone conversation—also raises additional professional issues. For example, it is possible for competitors, who also may be surfing the Net, to learn about the direction of a story or even of its specific content during the reporting process. This increases the chance that other news organizations will learn about stories or angles they have missed sometime before actual publication. While this sort of competitive consideration has always influenced journalism, the Internet makes it easier and faster to learn what other news organizations are doing.

Whether in person or through fiber optics, journalists who cover police, the courts and other areas of public life often develop informal agreements with frequent sources about when and how information may be attributed. Such relationships are necessary but risky. Many journalists have had to decide whether they will "burn a source," that is, to reveal the identity of a source who has been allowed to remain veiled in earlier stories for a particularly important story. Burning a source means terminating a relationship that worked well for both parties. It is considered a form of promise breaking. Historically, such promise keeping has been more of a one-way street. However, the capacity of sources to manipulate journalists—and hence news coverage—particularly on issues such as national security, raises important ethical questions, ones we ask you to consider in several cases in this book.

Keeping the trust between reporter and source intact is one reason that larger news organizations will often send an investigative reporter to cover a particularly sensitive story that arises on another reporter's beat. Sending an investigative reporter allows the beat reporter's sourcing agreements to remain undisturbed, ensuring a continuing flow of routine information while the investigation continues. There are significant ethical justifications for using anonymous sources. They are:

- Preventing either physical or emotional harm to a source.
- Protecting the privacy of a source, particularly children and crime victims.
- Encouraging coverage of institutions, such as the U.S. Supreme Court or the military, which might otherwise remain closed to journalistic and hence public scrutiny.

It is this final justification that is used most frequently by journalists. Reporters maintain that only when sources are allowed to remain anonymous will they provide newsworthy information that would otherwise place their careers or their physical safety at risk. While using the Internet as a reporting tool does not alter these justifications, it emphasizes the need for disclosure when working with sources in ways that nonvirtual journalists seldom encounter. The thinking may be the same, but the situation that prompts such reflection may look very different at first glance.

POLICY OPTIONS: THE ROLE OF THE PROFESSION

Unlike some media technologies such as the printing press, the Information Superhighway was initially developed by the government for political reasons. The original Internet was a computer network designed first to support the military and then, in the 1960s, reorganized to allow scientists working primarily at universities and government laboratories worldwide to communicate quickly and easily among each other. This system remained confined to the intellectual and military elite until the early 1980s, when the Internet, as we now know it, began to take shape.

This unusual history—a mass medium that was "invented" to support government policy—has made the Internet a difficult fit for both academic study and journalistic necessity. Unlike the printing press, which began as a private invention and remained private property, the Internet has historically owed a great deal to the government in both conceptual and financial terms. Because journalists never were part of the early history of Internet development, the notion of using the Internet as a profit-oriented mass medium is a very recent invention. Grafting a concept of mass communication onto a system designed for government-supported communication is fraught with the potential to raise some difficult questions.

The contemporary conceptualization of the Internet has government supporting a system that will wire and link all schools, libraries and hospitals. This proposal, which has been partially funded but will cost billions, is rooted in both practical politics and ethical theory.

The political aspects are fairly straightforward: by linking schools, hospitals and libraries, the government is supporting an infrastructure that will promote education and learning and thus strengthen the economy by providing a better-educated workforce. A better-educated workforce is also generally considered a more efficient one, thus making U.S. workers more competitive worldwide as well as driving down production costs domestically. A better-educated populace, of course, also has military implications: it enables the military to draw from a more qualified pool of recruits who are being asked to operate increasingly more complicated weapons. Thus, the reasoning goes, the federal government fulfills its constitutional responsibility to protect Americans from international as well as domestic threats by supporting a system that will promote the country's growth and development in many obvious and subtle ways.

Linking hospitals, of course, is also viewed as one way to simultaneously improve the quality of health care for many Americans while holding down medical costs. Again, the reasoning is that private, for-profit medicine would not be as likely to connect all hospitals; through government support the projected benefit can be distributed throughout American society.

This conceptualization of the Internet is also founded in ethical theory. As you may remember from the discussion of utilitarianism in Chapter 1, the notion of the greatest good for the greatest number has profound democratic implications. Wiring schools and libraries should, in theory, provide access to the Internet for every American. Indeed, some libraries in California have experimented with "Internet addresses" for the homeless. Universal access to the Internet through education also would follow Rawls's theory—it would allow the maximization of freedom (access) while protecting weaker parties (people of color, the poor) who might not have access to many other goods in U.S. society but can use the Internet as a way to better their individual and potentially collective lots in life.

Of course, journalists and journalism have not been included in this conceptualization. Yet many journalists have argued that access is only part of the picture—it does people little good to access information if they can't make sense of it. Some scholars have suggested that, as the Internet develops, journalism itself will change from a profession that primarily gathers facts—something anyone can now do on the Internet—to a profession that places those facts within a context and makes them meaningful. There is precedent for such a switch. News magazines went to contextual reporting and analysis rather than strict factual reporting in order to survive the death of the general interest magazines, as television penetrated America and delivered advertisers more cheaply than magazines. If the development of the Internet does indeed encourage newspaper development along these lines, then ethical thinking would demand that access to news coverage be distributed as widely as possible among the population and that it remain economically affordable.

That stance, of course, puts journalists at odds with all those segments of U.S. society that view the Internet as another potential profit center, including the multinational corporations for which increasing numbers of journalists now work. Insisting that affordable news become part of the policymaking that is currently swirling around the Information Superhighway would challenge the long-standing U.S. tradition of regarding journalism and government as irreconcilable adversaries. Yet ethical (and in some ways political) thinking would seem to suggest that making news coverage accessible to every American via the Internet has significant potential benefits for the individual and society at large. It also would make journalists and the government partners—a true philosophical shift in the conceptualization of a "free" press.

Finally, such a partnership would demand that journalists themselves take an active part in developing and implementing legislation that will affect their working lives. Such a change in attitude also would require a philosophical shift, one that places journalistic responsibility to political society on a plane with worker responsibility to profitable media industries.

THE MEANING OF PROFESSIONALISM

At the turn of this century, "citizen journalism" was embraced by the traditional news media. It was viewed as a way to "catch up" and "latch on" to the generation of digital natives who were leaving newspaper readership. Citizen journalism was also cost effective. Citizen journalists essentially function as reporters who may or may not be edited by professionals. But while citizen journalists often have a passionate interest in a particular public policy initiative or problem and are willing to write or blog about that single issue in great depth, they don't blog or seemingly have an interest in some of the most basic civic functions in American democracy—education, roads and highways, city councils and county commissions. Citizen journalists, in general, don't do investigative reporting. If the news agenda is to be left strictly to citizen journalists, by almost any measure, it will be not only lopsided, but also full of gaps and lacking in objectivity.

Proponents call this approach the "fifth estate," claiming that it parallels the "fourth estate" title that traditional news and opinion has carried as it served as a balance to government power. But an Internet-based fifth estate sometimes functions as an unchecked mob. For instance, when rumors that Obama-supported "death panels" would decide when the elderly would die, this outrageous assertion received so much currency on the Internet that about 24 percent of Americans said they believed it, despite facts and news reports to the contrary. The blogosphere raises questions of exactly who is a professional that extends far beyond who gets a pay check and speaks to whom and to what ideals one is loyal.

The nation has lived with a partisan press before, one so annoying that U.S. President John Adams passed a law to silence his critics. But more than two centuries later, we're left with differences in scope and immediacy. The partisan press that angered Adams, and to a lesser extent Jefferson and many presidents to come, was small and confined. Today's Internet rumor, to paraphrase Mark Twain, can circle the world before the truth's put on its shoes—sometimes with devastating results. In a story similar to the one from Denver above, one media critic related the story of a woman who, distressed by the number of errors she was seeing in her paper, told him that she had decided to drop her subscription and just read it online for free. The critic went on to make the point that by withholding from the paper her revenue, she was actually steepening the curve of editorial decline. Unfortunately by the time the average consumer realizes that professional journalism comes at a cost, it might not be available at any price at all.

Suggested Readings

ANDERSON, CHRIS. 2006. *The long tail: How the future of business is selling less of more.* New York: Hyperion.

BUGEJA, MICHAEL. 2005. *Interpersonal divide: The search for community in a technological age.* Oxford: Oxford University Press.

GODWIN, MIKE. 1998. *Defending free speech in the digital age.* New York: Times Books.

HALBERT, DEBORA J. 1999. *Intellectual property in the information age.* Westport, CT: Quorum Books.

NEGROPONTE, NICHOLAS. 1995. *Being digital.* New York: Alfred A. Knopf.

Cases on the Web

www.mhhe.com/mediaethics7e

"The witch and the woods mystery: Fact or fiction?" by Karon Reinboth Speckman

"The Napster debate: When does sharing become thievery?" by Laura Riethmiller

"Digital sound sampling: Sampling the options" by Don Tomlinson

"Cry Wolf: *Time* magazine and the cyberporn story" by Karon Reinboth Speckman

"Filmmaking: Looking through the lens for truth" by Kathy Brittain McKee

"The Madonna and the Web site: Good taste in newspaper online forums" by Philip Patterson

"The case of Banjo Jones and his blog" by Chris Heisel

CHAPTER 9 CASES

CASE 9-A

Ethics on the Internet: Abiding by the Rules of the Road on the Information Superhighway

BRUCE LEWENSTEIN
Cornell University

ComNet is a commercial online service with a wide range of options available to its subscribers, including databases, e-mail and forums for discussion. Some forums are available to all subscribers, while others are available only to registered users. In the case of JourForum, only working journalists may post or read messages. Working journalists are defined as those employed by newspapers, magazines or other legitimate publications; those whose names appear on the masthead of a regularly published magazine; those who belong to one of several professional organizations (such as the Society of Professional Journalists [SPJ] or the American Society of Newspaper Editors); or those who prove their legitimacy by presenting clips of their published work.

Subscribers to ComNet agree to abide by the service's "Rules of Behavior," which include prohibitions against objectionable or lewd language, illegal activity and "abuse of the service." Journalists signing up for JourForum are reminded of these rules and are requested to use only their true names and to limit their discussion to issues directly related to journalism. No specific statements are made about whether JourForum (or other parts of ComNet) are on or off the record. Mark Morceau is the "moderator" of JourForum—as well as its creator—and, through contractual arrangements with ComNet, the person responsible for ensuring that uses of JourForum abide by ComNet's rules.

In a new message to the JourForum, Miriam Zablonsky identifies herself as the editor of a newsletter about "alternative" medical treatments. She presents details about a new drug treatment for AIDS, including information about the research leading to the treatment. She wonders why the media has failed to cover the story.

In a response, Harry Lee, a reporter for an online magazine about medicine, suggests that the media usually cover medical stories only after they appear in medical publications such as *The New England Journal of Medicine.*

Zablonsky goes ballistic. In a long, biting, bitter message, she complains about a major medical journal that, she says, refuses to publish information about the new treatment. She calls the editor of the journal, Katherine Kelly, "a fat, sexist, lying slob." Kelly is a well-known commentator on the excesses of tabloid journalism (especially its coverage of medical topics). Her columns are often accompanied by her photo, showing a slim, stylish, beautiful woman.

A flood of messages appears, condemning Zablonsky's comments. To each one, Zablonsky responds with long, rambling diatribes about conspiracies of "them" (unspecified) out to control the world, about the deep distrust that a journalist should have toward all major institutions, and about her own unwillingness to change or even compromise her positions, no matter what information is presented to her.

At this point (less than a day after the original message from Zablonsky), Mark Morceau posts a message reminding Zablonsky of ComNet and JourForum's rules about objectionable language and abuse of the service (including posting long messages on topics that aren't germane to journalism). In addition, he asks her to apologize to Kelly and to avoid libelous statements in the future.

Zablonsky refuses, citing (among other arguments in another long, rambling message) her rights to free speech and freedom of the press.

Morceau tells Zablonsky that JourForum is not a publication, so it is not subject to rules of free press. It is, he says, more akin to a private club, which can enforce rules on its members. He points to the requirement that contributors belong to professional journalism organizations as one of the ways that JourForum maintains its limited membership. (Zablonsky once worked for a daily paper, and she maintains her membership in SPJ.)

If JourForum is a private club, responds Zablonsky, what she said isn't libelous, because the club isn't a public place or publication. Like all JourForum messages, this exchange was publicly posted so any subscriber to JourForum could view it.

The next day, Katherine Kelly joins the online discussion, threatening to sue Zablonsky, claiming that she has been libeled in a public forum. The international community of journalists with access to JourForum is so large that it cannot be considered a "private" club, she argues. Any one of those subscribers can read this forum, she reminds Zablonsky, making it equivalent to a trade paper or magazine. It is as public as any traditional publication, Kelly argues. Moreover, she says in June of 1996, a federal appeals court described online forums as one of the most important contributions to free exchange of ideas since the development of the printing press. Clearly, Kelly says, the canons of a free press—including the responsibility of avoiding libel—apply to online forums.

Cynthia Smith has been following the online discussion. She finds the issues of potential censorship, free press and free speech fascinating. She writes an article about the fracas for her own newspaper's weekly "News from Cyberspace" page. That page appears on Thursdays in the business section of the paper and in the newspaper's online edition. In her story, Smith includes quotes members of the forum from the messages those people had posted online.

When Smith's story appears, she is accused of violating the expectation many journalists had that their words in the online forum were "off the record" and would not be quoted.

Micro Issues

1. Can Zablonsky be sued for libel? Should she be sued for libel?
2. Should Smith have asked for permission to quote?
3. Does Morceau have the right to control what material appears in JourForum?

Midrange Issues

1. Does it matter if Smith's article appeared only in the traditional paper format, only in an online supplement to the newspaper or in a separate online magazine that does not have ties to a traditional-format publication?
2. Is there a moral difference between Zablonsky's potentially libelous statements and Smith's potential violation of the standards of on- and off-the-record?

Macro Issues

1. Is JourForum a public or private place? What difference would it make if any ComNet subscriber could read messages in JourForum, though only registered members could post messages there? (Compare JourForum to the floor of a convention, where members of the press are often identified with badges so that speakers know they are talking to a reporter.)
2. Under what circumstances does a reporter need to identify himself or herself? At what point do "private" conversations become open to reporting by others?
3. Are online publications subject to different rules than are traditional publications? If so, how do you distinguish between the rules that apply to publications that appear only online and those that appear in both online and offline versions? Does it matter if the online and offline versions are different or edited differently?

CASE 9-B

What Were You Linking?

PAUL VOAKES
University of Colorado

One of the oldest controversies in southern politics helped to create one of the newest controversies in media ethics.

In May 2000, the South Carolina legislature voted to remove the Confederate flag from the Capitol dome in Columbia and to have it placed behind the nearby Confederate Soldiers Monument. Activists on both sides in Alabama, Arkansas, Florida, Georgia and Mississippi were carefully monitoring the debate, expecting it would influence similar debates in their states. The National Association for the Advancement of Colored People (NAACP) was organizing a national boycott of South Carolina even after the compromise that put the "Rebel" flag behind the monument. The NAACP action included boycotting the products of several manufacturers that had recently built facilities in South Carolina. The national media were paying close attention to the story.

A few months earlier, the Associated Press had begun routinely adding URLs (Internet addresses) to its stories, which would link readers to sources of information on the World Wide Web. This practice had by now become fairly common on the Web sites of many national news organizations, but the AP's handling of its links on this particular story illustrated the ethical pitfalls that can await online journalists.

For several weeks, at the bottom of every story involving the Confederate flag controversy in South Carolina, the AP listed the Web addresses of three prominent stakeholders in the story: the NAACP, the South Carolina Heritage Coalition, and the Sons of Confederate Veterans. Surfers to the Heritage Coalition's site found the group's position on the flag issue and more: calls for "the confederate curriculum to be taught in all South Carolina public schools," for "recognition of South Carolinians as Confederate/Southern Americans for National Origin status" on government forms, for state holidays commemorating the birthdays of Confederate leaders Robert E. Lee and Jefferson Davis, and for "civil rights protection for Confederate/Southern Americans in the workplace." By providing the link to this organization, the AP had given it unprecedented access to the U.S. public.

When a news organization offers a hypertext link to another site, is it responsible in any way for the content of that site?

This wasn't the first time the question had surfaced. In 1997 the *New York Times* published a story about efforts to establish the innocence of convicted killer Charles Manson, complete with links to "Access Manson" and other sites that suggest Manson's innocence.

In the early days of online journalism, few editors thought to provide links to external Web sites as part of a news or feature story. Once editors became more enchanted by the ways in which a Web site "added value" to the printed version, links became frequently embedded in stories. By the end of the decade, a modest backlash had occurred as editors realized that (1) readers using the links were leaving the news site and quite often not returning and (2) readers may be associating the tone and views of the linked site with the provider of the original site.

In many cases, the linked Web sites simply add more detailed information or opinions to what was presented in the original story. This is often "unmediated" material that can pass directly from a source or advocate to the reader, without passing through the filters of journalists. Many Web observers and editors celebrate this capability, especially when the link goes to a site produced by a widely known, reliable organization. "I don't see that as a danger to democracy or the public interest," Jonathan Wolman of the Associated Press told the *American Journalism Review.*

But what if the journalist links readers to sites that publish more propaganda than fact or that advocate racism, violence or pornography? What if the original mission statement of the linked site might have changed since its inception—is it the job of the new story creator to check on what the sites have become in the ensuing years since the founders created the voice? What about the possibility that the site linked to had changed its original mission since the time of its founding? What if the site linked to had moved from a constitutionally expected role of "loyal opposition" to a libelous organization threatening the livelihood of the parent organization with their thinly researched opinions on cheaply produced Web sites?

News organizations have taken different approaches to the "linking" debate. Some don't link at all, except to other pages within the same site. CNN.com tries to make sure its external links are balanced to represent the major positions of a controversy. The *New York Times* says it will link to no sites that "celebrate violence," present sexual content or advocate bigotry or racism.

Other online newspapers, such as the *Chicago Tribune,* warn readers generally that by clicking on the hypertext, readers will be leaving the *Tribune*'s site. Others warn readers that such external sites "are not endorsed" by the original site. Some tell readers that information in external sites has not been checked for accuracy. In one case, the *Los Angeles Times* warned readers they might encounter "adult language" in an article about "Rage Against the Machine."

The AP has instructed its editors to use their "best news judgment" to determine which external sites to include.

As with most ethical controversies raised by fast-changing technology, consensus is lacking at this time. Most online news providers do agree on this much: linked sites do reflect on the journalistic decisions of the link provider.

Micro Issues

1. Does each reporter have a responsibility at least to "check out" every Web site his or her story links to, if only to make sure the linked site still exists?
2. Should each reporter be able to vouch for the accuracy and reliability of each linked site?
3. A significant percentage of readers who follow a link will not make it back to the newspaper's site. Is this reality a relevant factor in deciding how often to link or to whom you should link?

Midrange Issues

1. Should news organizations provide any disclaimers about links before taking readers to the linked sites? If yes, what should those disclaimers say?
2. Should mainstream news organizations link only to Web sites of established, "respectable" organizations, in order not to be associated with fringe or extremist positions? Does linking imply endorsement?
3. Who makes the call on what is respectable? Is this decision-making process a form of censorship or is it gatekeeping, or something else entirely?
4. In what way, if any, does checking the accuracy of a cited Web resource differ from checking out the veracity of an individual quoted in the story? Should the same rules apply?

Macro Issues

1. What is the media's responsibility to society in terms of expanding the "marketplace of ideas" via the Web?
2. Will the free exchange of ideas and democratic debate be enhanced, or is widespread, unchecked linking more likely to distort and discourage honest debate?

CASE 9-C

The Information Sleazeway: Robust Comment Meets the Data Robots

FRED VULTEE
Wayne State University

In detailing the *Washington Post*'s reporting of a congressional lobbying scandal that exploded in 2006, the paper's ombudsman, Deborah Howell, touched off a cyber-firestorm. Writing in her weekly column on Jan. 15, Howell noted that Republicans contended that "the *Post* purposely hasn't nailed any Democrats." On the contrary, she wrote, several stories "have mentioned that a number of Democrats . . . have gotten Abramoff campaign money." The *Post* hadn't found any Democrats in the "first tier of people being investigated," she added. "But stay tuned. This story is nowhere near over."

She was wrong. No Democrats had gotten campaign money from Jack Abramoff, the lobbyist at the center of the scandal, although he had told some of his clients to aim contributions to Democrats as well as Republicans. It was not until a week after her original column that Howell acknowledged her error and stated that the Abramoff matter, far from being bipartisan, was "a Republican scandal."

The *Washington Post* was caught flat-footed by a barrage of postings (which could only be charitably described as obscene). The postings overwhelmed one of the Web logs set up to foster public comment. In navigating the familiar journalistic terrain of correcting an error, the *Post* found itself in an unfamiliar situation where the Internet had taken the error far beyond the circulation barriers of the *Post*.

As critics on public discussion boards at washingtonpost.com took Howell to task for the error, she wrote a comment for the Web site that satisfied few and angered many: "I've heard from lots of angry readers about the remark . . . that lobbyist Jack Abramoff gave money to both parties. A better way to have said it would be that Abramoff 'directed' contributions to both parties."

Those who thought the matter was worth a more forthright admission of error were not satisfied. A torrent of comments poured in—enough of them obscenely and viciously personal that the *Post* closed the site to public comment on Thursday. When it reopened, with a much larger investment of staff time, public comments were much more carefully monitored.

The economic and social pressures on the *Post* are hardly unique. Like most metropolitan newspapers, it is losing circulation and advertisers at an alarming rate—more than three times the industry average for one accounting period a few years back (Smolkin 2005). Younger readers know its reputation but are intimidated by its bulk and more at ease with finding information they want elsewhere.

Like many other papers, the *Post* is aggressively exploring ways to put its journalistic expertise—whether in sports, business, government or international coverage—into play in interactive ways, involving almost half of *Post* staffers, with the number rising.

The ethical issue for the *Post* centers on the fact that one of the roles of a newspaper in a community is to foster public debate. Knowing that journalism is shielded by legal decisions that support the importance of uninhibited debate, how can a media outlet act as a forum for debate without exposing its own writers to scurrilous attacks?

The *Post*'s answer to the dilemma angered a number of vocal critics. The *Post*'s online editor, Jim Brady, summed up the criticism in a Feb. 12, 2006 article: "My career as a nitwitted, emasculated fascist began the afternoon of Jan. 19 when, as executive editor of the *Post*'s Web site, washingtonpost.com, I closed down the comments area of one of our many blogs" (Brady 2006). After Howell's first column, editors had removed about a hundred postings that violated the ban on profanity and personal attacks. Howell's midweek clarification only triggered a larger torrent, leading to Brady's decision to close the blog to comments—and to yet another flood of comments, this time directed at Brady.

Howell told a *Post* reporter that she had not asked for the site to be closed to commenting, saying, "I'm a First Amendment freak" (Farhi 2006). And Brady pointed to some irony in the conflict: "It was largely the reporting of the *Washington Post* that brought the Abramoff scandal to light in the first place—an inconvenient fact if one is attempting to assert that the *Post* takes its orders from the Republican White House."

Still, the string of comments on Howell's columns was closed. When comments on Post.blog resumed in February, it was with "minimal but firm rules." These rules included no personal attacks, no profanity and no posing as another writer. A profanity filter was installed, and staffers were assigned to read incoming messages, with the idea that "offensive or inappropriate" ones would be removed at once (Chandrasekaran 2006).

Micro Issues

1. Did the *Post* err in allowing readers to post uncensored messages prior to this problem?
2. Did the *Post* err in instituting profanity filters and staffers to read incoming messages after the problem?
3. How would you have handled the *Post*'s problem?

Midrange Issues

1. Should the original story of the ombudsman have been fact-checked to prevent the mistaken wording or is the copy of an ombudsman "out of bounds" for editorial control?
2. After the error was discovered and the deluge of messages began, was this a news story the *Post* should have covered?

Macro Issues

1. Is the Web site of a newspaper a forum that should be open to everyone without fear of censorship?
2. In the "marketplace of ideas" that is the modern Web log, do the normal rules of libel apply? Is a newspaper more culpable or less culpable for the content of its Web log if it fails to censor the posts?

CASE 9-D

Death Underneath the Media Radar: The Anuak Genocide in Ethiopia

DOUG MCGILL, EDITOR
The McGill Report

I first learned about the Anuak people while working as a volunteer teacher of English as a Second Language at a school in Rochester, Minn. I had a half dozen Sudanese immigrants in my ESL class, all of them refugees of the Sudan civil war and several of them "lost boys," young men separated from their families who had made their way to safe havens in the Midwest.

One of my students, a man in his late 20s named Obang Cham, was originally identified to me by the ESL school as a Sudanese refugee. But when Obang's English began to improve, and we chatted over coffee, he told me a different story. He was a member of a small tribe called the Anuak who lived primarily in remote western Ethiopia. He said that more than 1,000 Anuak lived in Minnesota, and when I asked him why they had moved here, he gave me an answer I spent another nine months working to verify before committing it to print: "The Ethiopian government is trying to kill my people."

The first thing that I discovered was the Anuak were an invisible people not only in Minnesota but in the world. Although Anuak had been immigrating to Minnesota from the early 1990s, not a single major metropolitan or local paper in the United States had written anything about them. Was it possible that not a single reporter had ever met and chatted with an Anuak before? And if they had done so, and learned the story—of an unreported African genocide no less—why had they not published anything?

According to Obang, he had fled his Ethiopian village of Dimma on foot in 1992 after Ethiopian soldiers surrounded the village and began shooting Anuak. Two dozen died in that attack, he said. Many similar attacks during the early and middle 1990s are why so many Anuak now live in Minnesota. Yet the state had absorbed the cream of the crop of the young, strong male leadership of an entire Ethiopian tribe, and their wives, without notice or knowing. The Anuak were invisible in Minnesota and the world.

On December 13, 2003, my telephone started ringing in the afternoon. One after another, Anuak men whom I'd met in the previous months told me a chilling story—that one of the periodic massacres of Anuak men, women and children was underway at that very moment.

They were having cellular telephone conversations with friends and family in their home villages and were hearing, through their cell phone connections, the sounds of the massacre—shouting and screaming, gunshots, soldiers yelling and people sobbing and crying. Some of my sources described hearing soldiers bashing down doors, yelling "Put down that phone!" followed by gunshots and then silence. I spent hours on the phone that day, gathering every detail I could. Through the cell phone connections, dozens of Anuak had heard essentially the same story over and over—that two troop trucks containing uniformed Ethiopian soldiers had arrived in town and disgorged soldiers who went from hut to hut and home to home in the village, calling out the Anuak men and boys and shooting them dead in the street. Occasionally, the soldiers were joined by non-Anuak citizens, or lighter-skinned Ethiopian "highlanders," who shouted "Today is the day of killing Anuak!" and killed their victims, usually with long spears, knives or machetes.

That evening and for several days following, I checked the wire services and the Web sites of the major daily newspapers in the United States, Europe and Africa. Not a word on the alleged massacre was published. On the Web sites of the Ethiopian embassy, the major Ethiopian newspapers and the U.S. Embassy in Addis Ababa: nothing. Finally, around Dec. 17, a small press release from the Ethiopian government came out reporting that "tribal violence" in western Ethiopia had caused up to a dozen deaths. This was nowhere near what the Anuak in Minnesota were claiming based on their knowledge from hundreds of eyewitness accounts, and the Ethiopian government was placing blame in its press releases not on the Ethiopian Army but on tribes fighting each other. I placed a call to the press spokesman at the Ethiopian embassy in Washington, Mesfin Andreas. "The deaths occurred as troops tried to stop people from killing each other," Andreas said.

On the weekend after the first phone calls came in, Anuak refugees from all over the Midwest gathered at a church in St. Paul, Minn. to discuss the crisis. I attended the meeting where I met several hundred Anuak, and interviewed maybe three dozen, only talking to people who said they had spoken directly to people on cell phones who were eyewitnesses as the massacre was happening. The stories that I heard that day were identical to the ones that I'd gotten over the telephone a week earlier. Uniformed Ethiopian soldiers had done the killing with automatic rifles, targeting Anuak men and boys for killing and Anuak women for raping, and they'd gone house to house, sometimes with a list of names in their hands, calling out specific Anuak men by name.

Hundreds—not dozens—had died.

Back at home, I called an Anuak survivor in Ethiopia. He lived in Gambella, the town where the massacre occurred. He told of seeing uniformed Ethiopian soldiers killing Anuak men on the street from the window of his home. He'd hidden under his bed as soldiers marched by his home. His own son had died in the attack. While speaking to me, he said he could still see some bodies in the streets of Gambella, and that at a mass grave on one side of the town, several hundred corpses were strewn in piles. He and other Anuak survivors had counted the corpses and noted how they had died, he said. The total was some 425 killed either by gunshots to the head or back, or by spear thrusts and machete blows.

As a former reporter for the *New York Times* for a decade, I knew I would probably have been unable to publish the story in the *Times* even with all the material I'd gathered. The main problem was, I had not actually been in Ethiopia, nor talked face-to-face with any actual eyewitnesses to the killing. Instead, my sources were a strange new breed of witness—"earwitnesses" to the sounds of a massacre and to direct eyewitness accounts of the massacre, listened to over cell phones. I was not then aware, nor am I aware today, of any report of a massacre or other crime in the media based on witness accounts of this nature. They are the creation of our present strange new world of hyper-communication.

In the end, my decision finally to publish what I'd heard, pointing a finger directly at the Ethiopian army, boiled down to my gut feelings as a journalist and my conscience as a citizen. After a week of solid reporting, interviewing dozens of Anuak in Minnesota, as well as one eyewitness in Ethiopia and the Ethiopian embassy spokesman, I felt that I knew something close enough to the truth to publish. And my conscience told me it was my duty to publish, because even up to Dec. 22, the day I finally did publish an account of the massacre, not a single news publication had done so—anywhere in the world. If I didn't publish, who would?

Within days of my story appearing on the Internet, the leaders of Genocide Watch, a nongovernmental watchdog who investigate new cases of genocide wherever they happen in the world had made enough phone calls to justify hiring an investigator and sending him to Ethiopia to check out the claims made in my article. On Feb. 25, 2004, Genocide Watch published the investigator's report, "Today is the Day of Killing Anuak," based on interviews with dozens of eyewitnesses to the massacre in Gambella (Genocide Watch 2004). The report verified all of the key claims of *The McGill Report* article, including the number of Anuak killed and the fact that uniformed Ethiopian soldiers had carried out most of the killings.

Micro Issues

1. Using a search engine, how much can you find about the genocide of the Anuak that has appeared since McGill's Web site first published the story?
2. Is it fair to say that the international attention being given to the genocide in Darfur distracted the media and the relief organizations from the situation in Ethiopia?

Midrange Issues

1. Following a trip to Ethiopia, McGill still had problems getting the mainstream media to accept the story. What does that say about how mainstream news organizations operate?
2. Is acceptance of this story by a mainstream media outlet such as the Associated Press needed to somehow "validate" the reporting done by McGill?
3. McGill has had a long career in journalism, including the *New York Times* and *Bloomberg News*. However, many "bloggers" have not had any journalism experience or training at all. Are traditional media rightfully skeptical about stories that originate in blogs? Should citizens be skeptical?

Macro Issues

1. What does this case tell you about who is a journalist in the Internet era?
2. Why do you think that a massacre of 425 people in Ethiopia wasn't reported in the mainstream media for several months after it happened? Why was it a blogger in southern Minnesota who broke the story?
3. Members of the dispersed tribal communities of Anuak e-mailed the story by McGill all over the world within days of its publication. Is the Internet a more efficient outlet for international stories such as this one?

CASE 9-E

Ownership of Information in a Digital Age: Problems and Possibilities

LEE WILKINS
University of Missouri—Columbia

In October 1995, the *New York Times* found itself under siege from a distinguished group of authors, all of whom contributed occasionally to the paper. More than 300 writers and scholars—among them Norman Mailer, Alice Walker, Garry Trudeau, Kurt Vonnegut, Barbara Raskin, Roger Rosenblatt, Ben Bagdikian and Carolyn Bird—signed a petition protesting the *Times'* newly implemented policy requiring writers to surrender syndication, electronic and other secondary rights to their work after articles were published in hard copy in the *Times*.

In an internal memorandum, the *Times* had announced it would require its free-lancers to sign "work-for-hire" contracts. It read: "The position on this is unambiguous: if someone does not sign an agreement, he or she will no longer be published in the newspaper." The writers responded that the memorandum was a historic break with publishing tradition where freelancers had been allowed to retain copyright to their own work.

What was really at issue, of course, was money. The freelancers wanted to be paid for the original publication of their efforts and for all subsequent uses—regardless of medium. The *Times,* which was struggling to develop an Internet presence and to make money from that effort, was attempting to cut both costs and subsequent legal problems by demanding copyright ownership from its freelancers.

Since the *Times,* like all other news organizations, had been unable to turn the Internet into a profit center, it sought to reduce expenses by curtailing payments to freelancers. The writers, in turn, wanted to retain their copyrights (as most of them were able to do for their books) and require each user to pay for the privilege of reproduction. Their suit was somewhat similar to issues that ultimately resulted in writers' strikes and musicians' strikes against Hollywood as the issue of pay for the aftermarket use of their work was hammered out for each of these industries once the Internet made the aftermarket a huge part of the financial reality of Hollywood.

Ultimately the courts ruled in favor of the writers. But the suit raised a fundamental question: in an Internet world, who owns—and who can profit from—a work product made up of a unique arrangement of words, notes, brush stokes, digital images, etc.?

The courts have repeatedly ruled "You can't copyright an idea." As Justice Louis Brandeis observed in *International News Service v. Associated Press,* "The general rule of law is that the noblest of human productions—knowledge, truths ascertained, conceptions and ideas—become voluntary communication to others, free as the air to common use." What can be copyrighted, however, is the particular execution of an idea. Mozart could not copyright the order of the keys on the harpsichord, but he could copyright the particular order of notes played on that instrument—the execution of an idea—in "The Magic Flute."

But when an idea is sufficiently novel and concrete to be a unique work, it does warrant protection. An entire line of cases has created a body of law about when concrete expressions of ideas can be copyrighted. The courts currently protect such concrete manifestation of ideas through contracts. A contract may be expressed through money changing hands or a promise to disclose the idea to a third party (for instance, a publisher's promise to publish a novel). The courts also protect ideas under what is called "implied contracts." A freelancer submitting an article to a magazine in the hopes that it will be published is functioning under an implied contract that the publisher will consider the article but not steal it. Closely kin to this is the legal notion of "unjust enrichment," where a person or organization attempts to enrich themselves while failing to compensate the original developer of the idea.

While the *Times* freelancers were notable for being famous and working for a high-profile medium, the legal and ethical questions are far from being isolated incidents and far from being settled in law or in practice.

Micro Issues

1. Reporters who take a salary from the *Times* are under "work for hire" contracts giving the newspaper the sole right to their work in any form for an indeterminate time. Is that custom too unilateral in favor of the employer? Should a writer, Web designer or photographer have to sign away that amount of control in exchange for a stable job?
2. Should "work for hire" be a negotiable item as a reporter, designer or photographer becomes more valuable to their medium or agency so that professional writers can maximize their income by seeking secondary markets for their work?

Midrange Issues

1. In the summer of 2009, *New York Times* bestselling author Malcolm Gladwell (*The Tipping Point, Blink, Outliers*) released a book of his essays written for *The New Yorker* magazine, where he has been a staff writer since 1996. If his relationship with the prestigious publication gained him fame and an audience, does Gladwell have an ethical obligation to share in the profits of the essay collection with *The New Yorker?* If he uses his staff position in his book jacket biography, does he owe them anything?
2. Conversely, can *The New Yorker* use Gladwell's fame to advertise the quality of writers one might come across in their publication? Do you want to fall back on the language of his contract? What role does loyalty play in your answers? Does loyalty work both ways here?

Macro Issues

1. Is the legal notion that you cannot copyright an idea an obsolete notion? Is it time to give ideas the same legal protection as the concrete expression of them? If so, how would that work?
2. Over half a century ago, the courts discovered a "right to publicity" in a case where baseball players were cleared to sign with as many trading card companies as they wished—something Major League Baseball had prohibited. Does a journalist enjoy the same right? Can he or she take her notoriety from working at *Newsweek,* the *New York Times,* etc. and turn it into a stint on CNN or Fox News without compensating their original employer? What *prima facie* duties from Ross are at play here?

CASE 9-F

Sending the Wrong Message about Doing the Right Thing

NAOMI WEISBROOK
University of Missouri

On July 20, 2007, Black Entertainment Television introduced a short cartoon video entitled *Read a Book*. The cartoon encourages life skills including reading, maintaining good hygiene, responsible parenting and wise use of money in what appears to be a public service announcement. These messages are incorporated into the lyrics and sung by the cartoon rapper D'Mite. D'Mite bears a striking resemblance to Lil' Jon, at the time the reigning king of crunk, a subgenre of hip hop. Keeping with the style of crunk music, the video's lyrics are repetitive and filled with obscenities and the N-word. An uncensored version circulated on YouTube while a cleaner version was shown on BET.

The song was the brainchild of Bomani D'Mite Armah, an educator who works with young people in the Washington D.C. area. He composed the song "Read a Book" because, "If crunk is what's in, I'll do crunk" (Harris 2007). After Armah circulated his song on MySpace for a while, it made it to BET's President of Entertainment Reginald Hudlin, who contacted Armah about making the song into a video (Martin 2007).

In addition to the obscenities, the video contains potentially offensive images, including women shaking their behinds with the word "BOOK" stamped across their pants. There is also an image of a book being loaded as a cartridge in an automatic weapon.

The video immediately created buzz on the Internet, generating more than one million hits and 4,000 comments on YouTube. Some comments praised the video: "[This video is] satirically presenting how the rap has degenerated into nothing but violent and sexual messages when it originally it [sic] was meant to convey important messages of black culture. So while the video shows both violent and sexual images it paradoxically is trying to send a positive message of how to lead a better life (ROBOFISH)."

Others were critical. When CNN anchor Tony Harris interviewed Tyree Dillihay, the video's director, Harris pointedly began the interview by asking, "You proud of this?" (Harris 2007). On his Rainbow PUSH coalition Web site, Jesse Jackson (2007) released a statement condemning "Read a Book," saying, "'Read a Book' heaps scorn on positive values and (un)intentionally celebrates ignorance. The narrator is obviously illiterate, unkempt and disrespectful. So who takes his advice seriously?"

Much of the controversy centers on exactly what the video is trying to say. According to Armah, "The message behind the song was secondary to the idea of parodying this style of music." In the same interview, Armah jokes that a friend told him that to write a crunk song the authors must be repetitive, aggressive and "curse as often as possible" (Martin 2007).

However, to someone unfamiliar with crunk music, the satire might be lost. Greg Forde, a African-American parent featured in CNN coverage of "Read a

Book," points out that "the thing with satire, really clever satire, is that it speaks to a point, but you still realize it's satire. People who are not in our community are not going to see this as satire" (Harris 2007).

To those who don't recognize the satire, the video just appears to be methodically cataloging negative perceptions of African-Americans. In fact, according to the *Los Angeles Times,* "Most of the discussion centers on the negative stereotypes of African-Americans, rather than the language" (Braxton 2007). The negative stereotypes include gun use, men sitting on the porch drinking "40s" (40 oz. bottles of alcohol), drive-bys, irresponsible spending on decorative tire rims, negligent parenting and poor hygiene.

But, the video contains positive references to African-American history: There are images of historical figures such as Martin Luther King and the covers of several books such as *The Color Purple* and Maya Angelou's *I Know Why the Caged Bird Sings.*

Bomani Armah said he hopes people will get two messages from his song: that crunk music is ridiculous and that kids should read books. Armah says that he gets e-mails from kids thanking him for validating that getting an education is cool. Parents have told him that their kid picked up a book after listening to his song.

Micro Issues

1. BET claims on its Web site to provide "contemporary entertainment that speaks to young Black adults from an authentic, unapologetic viewpoint of the Black experience." Is it fulfilling that promise with *Read a Book?* Why or why not?
2. Critique the specific words and images used in this video, finding it on the Web if possible. What ethical values are dominant in *Read a Book?* Does it succeed in promoting those values?

Midrange Issues

1. Promoting literacy is a "good" cause. In fact, it's a non-contentious good cause; there is no pro-ignorance lobby to counter the message. Given the universal approval of the idea of literacy does a campaign promoting it have greater creative latitude or must it take greater caution?
2. For satire to work it must have a reference point, which often means dealing in stereotypes to make a point. Should satire be used in a pro-social way such as a Public Service Announcement? How would your answer change if the cause were Planned Parenthood? A ballot issue that has deeply divided the community?

Macro Issues

1. The *Read a Book* campaign is an example of strategic communication for a cause. When Yoplait puts pink tops on its product to support breast cancer research, this is another example of "cause-related marketing." Critique the concept of cause-related marketing.
2. How does the fact that this message was intended for children change the rules about what is allowable and what is ethically questionable? Do the responsibilities and duties of the message creators change for this particular audience?

CASE 9-G

Looking for Truth Behind the Wal-Mart Blogs

PHILIP PATTERSON
Oklahoma Christian University

When you think of blogging, the image of a lone person passionately pounding out a late-night journal hoping to gain a few loyal readers comes to mind. But if you're Wal-Mart, the largest retailing chain in the world, you can afford a little professional help, and that's precisely what the corporation did on at least two blogs until Wal-Mart's public relations firm was forced to reveal the ruse.

Before the admission, rumors had been circulating about the authenticity of the blogs. In an article on www.cnnmoney.com entitled "Corporate Blogging: Wal-Mart's Fumbles," *Fortune* senior writer Marc Gunther (2006) broke the story in the mainstream press with this posting:

> A blog praising Wal-Mart called "Wal-Marting Across America," ostensibly created by a man and a woman traveling the country in an RV and staying in Wal-Mart parking lots, turned out to be underwritten by Working Families for Wal-Mart, a company-sponsored group organized by the Edelman public relations firm. Not cool.

The couple, it turns out, were Laura St. Claire, a freelance writer and an employee at the U.S. Treasury Department and Jim Thresher, a staff photographer at the *Washington Post.* And Wal-Mart, far from being the lucky beneficiary of a blog that found happy Wal-Mart employees at every stop, was shown to be behind the trip and was paying for the couple's support, including money for renting the RV, gas and fees for writing the blog (Gogoi 2006). And behind Wal-Mart was Edelman, a nationally recognized PR firm as a part of their "Working Families for Wal-Mart" campaign.

As bloggers expressed their outrage at the ruse, Edleman CEO Richard Edelman issued an apology on his personal blog. "I want to acknowledge our error in failing to be transparent about the identity of the two bloggers from the outset. This is 100 percent our responsibility and our error, not the client's" he wrote (Gogoi 2006).

But the happy RVing couple was not the only phony Wal-Mart blog. Two days after Gunther's article, cnnmoney.com exposed the practice on their Web site, in an unsigned article entitled "PR Firm Admits It's Behind PR Blogs." In that article, the following information was posted:

> A public relations firm has revealed that it is behind two blogs that previously appeared to be created by independent supporters of Wal-Mart. The blogs Working Families for Wal-Mart and subsidiary site Paid Critics are written by three employees of PR firm Edelman, for whom Wal-Mart is a paid client, according to information posted on the sites Thursday. Before Thursday, the authors of the blogs were not disclosed. But Web critics had been skeptical of claims that the blogs were grass-roots efforts, and pushed for greater transparency.

Employees of the Edelman public relations firm were eventually revealed as the source of blogs on two more sites that produced favorable stories about

Wal-Mart and sought to debunk its critics. In mid-October of 2006, the following message appeared on www.forwalmart.com:

> In response to comments and emails, we've added author bylines to blog posts here at forwalmart.com. The site has been updated, but readers may have to refresh the page for the new information.

By clicking on the single name byline of "Miranda," the reader would find the following information: "Miranda Grill works for Edelman. One of her clients is Working Families for Wal-Mart." The same message appeared on the www.paidcritics .com site, whose tagline is ironically, "Exposing the Paid Critics" in a posting entitled "A CHANGE TO PAIDCRITICS.COM" written by "Brian." A click on Brian's byline yielded the following information: "Brian McNeill works for Edelman. One of his clients is Working Families for Wal-Mart."

According to their Web site (www.edelman.com), the Edelman public relations firm claims 2,220 employees in 46 offices worldwide and billed $305 million in fees in fiscal year 2006. They were named "Large PR Agency of the Year" by *PR Week US* in 2006. The "welcome" page on the Edelman Web site contains the following description over the signature of Daniel J. Edelman, Founder and Chairman, and Richard Edelman, President and CEO:

> We were the first firm to apply public relations to building consumer brands. We invented the media tour, created litigation and environmental PR, were the first to use a toll-free consumer hotline and the first to employ the Web in crisis management. That's just the beginning. Today we're on a mission: to make public relations the lead discipline in the communications mix, because only public relations has the immediacy and transparency to build credibility and trust.

There was no mention of the Wal-Mart incident under "Latest Headlines" on the Edelman Web site in the week after the story broke.

Micro Issues

1. Should Edelman have acknowledged the problem on their Web site before the *Fortune* magazine reporter broke the story? Should they have responded afterwards?
2. How common do you think Wal-Mart's actions are? Is it possible that "grassroots" fan sites are actually paid for by celebrities or their publicists, for instance?
3. If Wal-Mart is right that its critics are "paid," does that justify paying a public relations firm to say good things about Wal-Mart?

Midrange Issue

1. In the "marketplace of ideas" is there any place for this type of "stealth" public relations?
2. How does this differ from "viral marketing," where companies try to generate "buzz" about products to bypass traditional advertising media to reach the public with a message, often paying agents in the process?
3. How does this differ from "product placement" in television or movies, where the audience is not informed if a product manufacturer paid to be on the screen?

Macro Issues

1. Upon hearing of Thresher's involvement, the *Post*'s executive editor demanded that he pay back any money he received for the trip and remove his photographs from the blog (Gogoi 2006). Should there be any other penalties for his actions? Does it make a difference if he is on his own time during the trip? Does it make any difference if every posting represents his true opinion?

2. Critics called for greater transparency in the blogs. Edelman claims to use "transparency to build credibility and trust." What does transparency mean in public relations? Is it different from transparency in journalism? Was Edelman transparent in its dealings on these two Web sites?

3. Barbara Ehrenreich in her book *Nickel and Dimed* writes a very different story about the plight of Wal-Mart workers. To get the story, she took a job in a Wal-Mart and attempted to live on the income they paid. Her bestselling book was highly critical of the way Wal-Mart treats its employees. Is her work, for which she received royalties, any different than the paid Wal-Mart bloggers? If so, in what way? Is Ehrenreich a journalist? Is it the role of journalism to put pressure on corporations such as Wal-Mart?

10

The Ethical Dimensions of Art and Entertainment

By the end of this chapter you should be able to:

- understand the link between aesthetics and excellent professional performance.
- explain Tolstoy's rationale for art and apply it to issues such as stereotyping.
- understand the debate over the role of truth in popular art.

In the last century, the primary use of media shifted from distributing information to providing entertainment and popularizing culture. In this chapter, we examine the ethical issues from the field of aesthetics. We will apply these principles, plus some findings from social science, to the art and entertainment industries, focusing on the responsibilities of both creators and consumers of entertainment.

AN ANCIENT MISUNDERSTANDING

Plato didn't like poets. His reasoning was straightforward: poets, the people who dream, were the potential undoing of the philosopher king. They were rebels of the first order, insurrectionists on the hoof, and he banned them from the Republic.

Plato's skepticism is alive today. Few weeks elapse without a news story about an artist or entertainment program that has offended. You are probably familiar with at least some of the following:

- The very public feud between David Letterman and Sarah Palin in the summer of 2009 over a joke Letterman made about Palin's daughter.
- Attempts to ban books, even classics such as *Catcher in the Rye* or *Lady Chatterley's Lover,* from public or school libraries for being too sexually explicit.

Recently, Harry Potter was the focus of the most successful and the most unsuccessful attempts to ban a book.

- The controversy over government funding of art that some claim is obscene.
- Calls by conservatives and liberals to boycott television networks and their advertisers over allegedly objectionable content.
- The furor over rappers, television producers and filmmakers whose homophobic, misogynistic and sometimes clever content offend many while earning nominations for the industry's top awards.
- The public outcry and political posturing that followed Don Imus's statements about the Rutgers' women's basketball team in 2007.

Like Plato long ago, those who would restrict the arts do so because they mistrust the power of the artist to link emotion and logic in a way that stimulates a new vision of society, culture or individuals.

OF TOLSTOY AND TELEVISION

Tolstoy was the sort of artist Plato would have feared. In his famous essay, "What Is Art?", Tolstoy (1960) argued that good art had one dominant characteristic: it communicated the feelings of the artist to the masses in the way in which the artist intended.

> To evoke in oneself a feeling one has once experienced and having evoked it in oneself then by means of movements, lines, colors, sounds or forms expressed in words, so to transmit that feeling that others experience the same feeling—that is the activity of art. . . . Art is a human activity consisting in this, that one may consciously by means of certain external signs, hand on to others feelings he has lived through, and that others are infected by these feelings and also experience them.

Tolstoy's standard was so demanding that he rejected the works of both Shakespeare and Beethoven as being incapable of being understood by the masses. Tolstoy's rationale is particularly pertinent to photographers and videographers who, through their visual images, seek to arouse emotion as well as inform. Haunting pictures of starvation from the Third World have launched international relief efforts. Televised images of Katrina's victims spurred the resignation of some of FEMA's top officials—and affected the 2006 election. Award-winning dramas such as the play *Angels in America,* the AIDS quilt, movies such as *Philadelphia* (in which Tom Hanks won an Academy Award for his portrayal of an AIDS victim) and obituaries of famous artists who have succumbed to AIDS have all aroused both our intellects and our emotions about the disease. They invite action. Television and film documentaries have made viewers more aware of the plight of the mentally ill and homeless, raised important public policy questions and occasionally made us laugh, through a unity of purpose and craft.

Such work reminds readers and viewers of the moral power of art by putting us in touch with characters and situations sometimes more complex than our own lives. By thinking about these fictional characters, we enlarge our moral imaginations.

Calvin and Hobbes

by Bill Watterson

CALVIN AND HOBBES © Watterson. Dist. By
UNIVERSAL UCLICK. Reprinted with permission.
All rights reserved.

    Unfortunately, Tolstoy's assertion that great art is defined by how it is understood by an audience also includes a genuine dilemma. Even if given Tolstoy's life experiences, many readers could not articulate the deep truths about human nature Tolstoy wrote about in *War and Peace*. Worse yet, it is nearly impossible to sell those insights to a sometimes lukewarm public, or to produce them on demand for an hour a week, 36 weeks a year. The result is popular art that loses its critical edge and takes shortcuts to commonplace insight. In fact, some mass communication scholars have argued that the unstated goal of popular art is to reinforce the status quo; popular culture, they say, blunts our critical-thinking abilities.

What Is Art?

Philosophers, sociologists and artists have debated the meaning of art for hundreds of years. Prior to the Industrial Revolution, art was something only the well educated paid for, produced and understood. Mozart had to capture the ear of the Emperor to get a subsidy to write opera. Such "high" or "elite art" provided society with a new way to look at itself. Picasso's drawings of people with three eyes or rearranged body parts literally provided Western culture with a new way of seeing. Michelangelo's paintings and sculpture did the same thing in the Renaissance.

But patronage had disadvantages. The patron could restrict both subject matter and form, a reality depicted in the film *Amadeus* where the Emperor informed Mozart that his work, *The Marriage of Figaro,* had "too many notes." Gradually artists discovered that if they could find a way to get more than one person to "pay" for the creation of art, artistic control returned to the artist. The concept of "popular art" was born.

Scholars disagree about many of the qualities of elite and popular art; some even assert that popular art cannot truly be considered art. While both kinds of art are difficult to define, the following list outlines the major differences between popular and elite art and culture:

1. Popular art is consciously adjusted to the median taste by the artist; elite art reflects the individual artist's vision.
2. Popular art is neither abstruse, complicated nor profound; elite art has these characteristics.
3. Popular art conforms to majority experience; elite art explores the new.
4. Popular art conforms to less clearly defined standards of excellence, most often linked to commercial success; elite art is much less commercially oriented, and its standards of excellence are consistent and integrated.
5. Popular artists know that the audience expects entertainment and instruction; elite artists seek an aesthetic experience.
6. The popular artist cannot afford to offend its target audience; the elite artist functions as a critic of society, and his or her work challenges and sometimes offends the status quo.
7. Popular art often arises from folk art; elite art more often emerges from a culture's dominant intellectual tradition.

Today, mass media have become the primary cultural storytellers of the era. Nearly half a century ago, Ellul (1965) argued that in a modern society storytelling is an inevitable and desirable tool to stabilize the culture. This "propaganda of integration" is not the deliberate lie commonly associated with propaganda but the dissemination of widely held beliefs to the culture at large. Aesop's fables and the early *McGuffey Readers* influenced generations of Americans with subtle (or not) messages that reinforced the social structure. This is precisely where the entertainment media get their power—not in the overt messages but in the underlying assumptions that (if unchallenged) will become widely held societal values. For instance, entertainment content can reinforce the status quo by constantly depicting certain social groups in an unflattering and unrepresentative way, presenting a distorted picture of reality. Groups as disparate as Muslims and evangelicals have chafed under depictions (or omissions) that reinforce cultural stereotypes despite evidence to the contrary.

At least some such distortion is the natural outcome of compression. Just as substances such as rubber change form when compressed, so do media messages. Given only 15 seconds to register a message in a commercial, an advertising copywriter will resort to showing us the presumed stereotype of a librarian, a mechanic or a pharmacist. Using stereotypes as a form of mental shorthand is a natural way media work and was noted as early as 1922 by Walter Lippmann in *Public Opinion.* Lippmann said that we are all guilty of "defining first and seeing second."

Soon, we expect reality to imitate art. Mass communicators know the power of stereotypes and deeply held notions and use them. According to Tony Schwartz (1973), advertising messages are often constructed backward. The communicator actually starts with what the receiver knows—or believes he knows—and then constructs a message that fits within that reality. Schwartz calls it hitting a "responsive chord." Time is saved in plucking the chords already deeply held by the public rather than challenging stereotypes. So pimps are African-American, terrorists are Middle Eastern and no one challenges the unstated assumptions. The audience gets the idea of a pimp or a terrorist, but notions of racism and worse have been planted as well. While these images suit the artist's purposes, they are problematic.

TRUTH IN ART AND ENTERTAINMENT

No question in the field of aesthetics is more thoroughly debated with less resolution than the role of truth in art. Most philosophers seem to agree that artists are not restricted to telling the literal truth. Often artists can reveal a previously hidden or veiled truth, providing a new way of looking at the world or understanding human nature that rings deeply true.

But just how much truth should the audience expect from entertainment? And how entertaining should the audience expect truth to be? There are several opinions. At one point on the continuum is the argument that there is no truth requirement at all in art. At another point on the continuum is the belief that there must be one accepted truth for all.

Compounding the problem is that often the audience doesn't care when the lines of truth and entertainment are blurred. Jon Stewart and Stephen Colbert each host nightly satirical newscasts aired on the Comedy Central. Surveys show that these fake news shows are actually a main source of news content for young people in the 18 to 30 age bracket. The fact the shows feature interviews with real political figures, include "real" news footage of actual events and have the license to be satirical rather than fair and balanced seems to be of no consequence to the demographic attracted to the shows. An exchange between Stewart and Tucker Carlson, host of CNN's "Crossfire," during the 2004 campaign shows the tension between traditional news and satirical news in the following sidebar:

When "Fake News" Calls out "Journalism"

Jon Stewart, host of Comedy Central's "The Daily Show," has always insisted that he is a comedian and that he reports "fake news." Stewart follows a long tradition of news being incorporated into entertainment programming, beginning with Orson Wells's 1939 radio play *War of the Worlds* and continuing through today's "Saturday Night Live" newscast.

What makes Stewart unique is that his "fake news" programs often incorporate actual news video and direct quotes from authors, newsmakers and political officials. Multiple polls have documented that young people between the ages of 18 to 30 get "some" or "most" of their public affairs information from Stewart. He has won both an Emmy and a Peabody Award, given for programming that raises important public issues.

At the same time, Stewart continues to work as a comedian and has hosted the Academy Awards, a night that perennially yields television's highest ratings. So, when Stewart appeared on "Crossfire," Carlson, his bosses and his audience believed they were booking a comedian. But Stewart was far from funny. Instead, Stewart lambasted Carlson, "Crossfire" and the television news media in general for doing bad political theater rather than their jobs. In a curious way, the media's reduction of the complexities of a presidential campaign to a "horserace" complete with each party and hundreds of journalists for both old and new media alike playing a daily game of "gotcha" with the candidates, had made a show like Stewart's which ridiculed the process not only popular but quite possibly necessary. Among the comments on the night in question were the following (transcript found at: transcripts.cnn.com when accessed on October 27, 2006):

STEWART: "But the thing is that this—you're doing theater, when you should be doing debate, which would be great."

CARLSON: "You had John Kerry on your show and you sniff his throne and you're accusing us of partisan hackery?"

STEWART: "Absolutely. . . . What is wrong with you? . . . You know, the interesting thing I have is, you have a responsibility to the public discourse, and you fail miserably."

CARLSON: "You need to get a job at a journalism school, I think."

STEWART: "You need to go to one. The thing that I want to say is, when you have people on for just knee-jerk, reactionary talk . . . "

CARLSON: "Wait. I thought you were going to be funny. Come on. Be funny."

STEWART: "No. No. I'm not going to be your monkey. . . . I watch your show every day. And it kills me."

CARLSON: "I can tell you love it."

STEWART: "It's so—oh, it's so painful to watch. You know, because we need what you do. This is such a great opportunity you have here to actually get politicians off of their marketing and strategy."

CARLSON: "Is this really Jon Stewart? What is this, anyway?"

STEWART: "Yes, it's someone who watches your show and cannot take it anymore. I just can't. And come work for us, because we, as the people . . . "

CARLSON: "How do you pay?"

STEWART: "The people—not well. . . . But you can sleep at night."

Should there be a truth standard in art? The tendency of the status quo to impose a specific moral "truth" on the masses has been common to many cultures and political systems across the ages. In *The Republic* Plato had Socrates argue against allowing children to hear "casual tales . . . devised by casual persons." The Third Reich burned books deemed unsuitable for reading. In the United States, the battle historically has raged over library books. Classics such as *Huckleberry Finn, Of Mice and Men, The Grapes of Wrath* and *The Merchant of Venice* are but some of the long-revered and award-winning works that now face censorship by various school systems. The American Library Association reports that incidents of book banning now reach more than 1,000 instances annually, with little legal intervention. The U.S. Supreme Court has not heard another book-banning case since allowing a lower court ruling to stand in 1982.

Protests began early in the history of television. The 1951 show "Amos n' Andy" was condemned by the National Association for the Advancement of Colored People for depicting "Negroes in a stereotyped and derogatory manner." In the 1960s the United Church of Christ successfully challenged the license renewal of WLBT in Jackson, Mississippi, on the grounds that the owners had blatantly discriminated against African-Americans.

In the latter half of the 20th century, a variety of special-interest groups used more subtle methods to influence entertainment programming. Some, such as the Hispanic advocacy group Nosotros, worked closely with network bureaucracies, previewing potentially problematic episodes of entertainment programs, often altering program content before it reached the airwaves. Not all protests involve censoring a program. Some want to make sure that programming airs, such as advocacy groups who lobby advertisers and affiliates to ensure the airing of certain shows or inclusion of certain controversial characters in prime time.

New York Times television critic Jack Gould framed the problem of artistic accountability in the early days of these advocacy groups arguing that such agreements held

> "latent dangers for the well-being of television as a whole. An outside group not professionally engaged in theatre production has succeeded in imposing its will with respect to naming of fictional characters, altering the importance of a leading characterization and in other particulars changing the story line" (Montgomery 1989, 21).

And for the artist trying to create in the medium, network attempts to "balance" competing advocacy-group interests had come close to recreating the patronage system, albeit a far more sophisticated one with government as the patron.

Today, advocacy groups represent only one such problem. Take product placement. When popular television programs such as "Heroes" include ads for specific car models or computers—in the case of Heroes, the Nissan Rogue and various Apple devices—then there is some indication that the creative process has been tweaked, if not warped, by commercial demands.

The struggle over content becomes even more acute when governmental sponsorship is at stake. Some argue that because tax dollars are extracted from all, the programs they fund should be acceptable to all. Federal support for programs such as the National Endowment for the Arts (NEA) has been repeatedly questioned in

Congress. Conservatives objected to funding artists such as photographer Robert Mapplethorpe, whose blend of homoerotic photos and traditional Judeo-Christian symbols offended many. Eventually, the criticism was a factor in the resignation of one of the NEA's directors, John E. Frohnmayer.

The government also censors directly. On multiple occasions Infinity Broadcasting was fined several hundred thousand dollars for disc jockey Howard Stern's on-air profanity and offensive racial slurs. Stern protested that the FCC's action amounted to an enforcement of political correctness. But others noted that Stern most often castigated disadvantaged people and groups. By 2006, Stern had left terrestrial radio and its rules for satellite radio, where he found a fat payday, artistic freedom and a much smaller audience.

In 2006 with the Broadcast Decency Enforcement Act Congress raised the fine for a single count of indecency from $27,500 to $325,000. Because of the potential liability for crippling fines, producers of live programming such as the Grammy awards and the Oscars were forced to put a delay on the broadcast to bleep out indecent language or nudity.

COP TV: ENTERTAINMENT, INFOTAINMENT OR NEWS?

In his ingenious Academy Award–winning script, *Network,* the late writer-director Paddy Chayefsky envisioned a time when the lines would be blurred between entertainment and news, rendering them indistinguishable. However, Chayefsky was wrong in one detail. News did begin to take on the look of entertainment (as he predicted it would, to great satirical effect) but he did not predict that entertainment would also begin to look like news with the two meeting somewhere in the middle.

Consider these television shows: "America's Most Wanted," in which the audience is encouraged to help by calling in tips for police; "Unsolved Mysteries," with its focus on the criminal and the paranormal; "Inside Edition," a voyeuristic look at stories dubbed "too hot to handle" for traditional network news; and others of the same breed, including "A Current Affair," "Hard Copy," "COPS," "Rescue 911" and any number of other spin-offs. And then came YouTube, where virtually no event was outside the range of cameras and videos shot by amateurs often found their way on to the mainstream media.

In what genre do these shows belong? When "America's Most Wanted" follows a bounty hunter on an illegal trip into Mexico to bring home a nationally known fugitive is it news or entertainment? Which set of standards of truth should the producer of that show (and others like it) operate under—the artistic license of entertainment or the more rigorous truth standard of news?

Currently, dozens of such pseudo-news shows are in production simultaneously. From arrests to court trials to public confrontations, very little escapes our fascination. Dubbed "infotainment" by critics, these shows are hot with television programming executives and audiences alike. Such programming provides relief from reruns of situation comedies and the sameness of game shows and draws large ratings. When produced by syndicators, the shows are prepackaged with ads embedded in them, making them attractive to station owners.

But there is the downside. A man who agreed to appear on the "Jenny Jones Show" on the premise of meeting someone who had a crush on him later murdered the would-be lover who was male—a fact that was not revealed until the moment the showed taped. After a highly publicized trial, the television show was exonerated of any blame in the murder, but public opinion was clearly divided on the show's culpability. CNN's Nancy Grace faced an avalanche of criticism when a guest on her show committed suicide the day after an extremely confrontational interview.

The blending of facts and entertainment is not restricted to the small screen. Films such as *Ray, Walk the Line, The Alamo, Nixon, Hoffa* and *Thirteen Days* reflect a particular artistic vision based on fact. *Hoffa* director Danny DeVito sought to make an entertaining film of the major facts of the controversial missing labor leader's life, but took symbolic liberties with many events and people. DeVito justified his changes on the "Today" show by saying what he sought was entertainment—"not sitting down and reading a book."

Based-on-reality films and reality-based television shows differ in format and content but they are alike in invoking the license allowed entertainment programming while retaining the authority of fact—a risky combination. By blending information and entertainment, the possibility for abuse of an unsuspecting audience exists. To understand how this happens, we look to the theory of "uses and gratifications." Phrased simply, the theory says audience members will use the media to gratify certain wants and needs. People bring something to the message, and what they bring affects what they take away.

For example, seeking news and information is a common use of the media, with an expected gratification of getting information necessary for living one's life from traffic to weather to news about government. Entertainment is another common media use, with its own gratification of laughter, crying or any other emotion evoked by entertainment media.

Infotainment keeps the look of news yet airs the content of lowbrow entertainment juxtaposing traditional uses and gratifications. With a look of authority (an anchor's desk, a courtroom, a police precinct) and the hype of their importance (e.g., "200 lives saved so far!"), these shows appear to be useful for acquiring information. However, by invoking their license as entertainment, such shows are free to bypass accuracy, fairness, balance and other standards normally associated with news and to focus on more sensational elements to gather larger ratings.

Consequently, infotainment, while fundamentally flawed, gets widely accepted as fact. *New York Times* columnist A. M. Rosenthal (1989) compared airing these tabloid television shows to buying news programming "off the shelf." Stations should add the disclaimer, "We did not put this stuff in the bottle, whatever it is," Rosenthal added.

REALITY TELEVISION: OXYMORON, PROFIT CENTER AND USING THE AUDIENCE

They eat cow's lips, let their families pick their mates and routinely lie about their financial and physical assets. They are Americans with talent. They are "Jon and Kate Plus 8." It's all part of the reality television craze that has made strong inroads into prime-time entertainment programming. The craze began with the wildly successful "Survivor" series, which ran first as a summer replacement show and garnered ratings that impressed network executives. "Survivor" quickly spawned other reality shows, among them "Amazing Race," "Danger Island," "Wife Swap," "The Osbornes," "Fear Factor" and "American Idol," to name a few.

Why the rush to reality programming? Ratings and money. For three decades, traditional network television programming lost audience share to cable television, TiVo and the Internet. At their height, the original three American networks, ABC, CBS and NBC, could count on attracting approximately 90 percent of American homes with televisions on any given evening; the rest tuned in a few fledgling independents playing reruns. Today, the audience for five broadcast networks (including Fox and CW) has plunged to less than half of all households, with the number slipping every season.

Then traditional cable outlets such as HBO, TNT and USA got into original scripted programming, cutting further into the audience for scripted entertainment, often sweeping the industry's awards along the way. The reason for the immediate artistic success was a matter of sheer economics: it was easier to program a few hours of quality television a week than to try to program three hours every night as the traditional networks have done for years.

Compounding the problem, those who continued to watch the traditional networks were an older demographic not popular with advertisers. For the networks, reality television was a chance to pull viewers away from cable and computers and back to their programming at a cost lower than scripted television series. Not only did reality shows draw viewers, but the audience they drew centered on 18- to 49-year-olds, a ratings bonanza in the preferred demographic and a potent inducement to produce more reality programming.

Reality programming was not only popular, but cheap to produce. There was little need to pay writers, and the actors who populated them worked for scale or prizes. Unlike the "CSI" and "Law and Order" franchises where the popularity of the show caused cast salaries to skyrocket, pay was never an issue for producers of reality programming, which was cheaper and more watched than even the ubiquitous evening news magazines such as "Dateline."

But there was a price to pay. The shortsighted view of using cheaply produced reality programming to garner ratings has had consequences. Quality shows such as "ER" and "Chuck" were expensive to produce and it often took time to find an audience sufficient to sustain these shows. What the producers hoped for was a chance to air enough episodes—typically 60 or more—to make it to the lucrative syndication market and DVD, where they live on for years and produce a sizable return on the initial investment.

By eating up entire chunks of the network schedule, reality television pushed many quality shows into an early retirement and kept many more out of production. The result now is fewer quality programs in syndication and fewer producers of quality shows able to get their product into the schedules of the major networks now infatuated with reality. Quality writers fled to the movies or the cable channels willing to try scripted television. The light-viewing months of the summer were once a time when networks took some chances on genre-defining shows to see if they could find an audience. Now that season is given over to reality television that turns immediate profits with no regard for the future.

If they didn't add to the nation's intellect, reality shows have added to American slang. Getting "voted off the island" became a catch phrase for everyone from politicians to news journalists. "You're fired" entered the American vernacular from "The Apprentice" starring Donald Trump.

The "new" reality television was really a second pass at the genre. The first attempt took place in the 1950s with quiz shows such as "21" and "The $64,000 Question." These shows were enormously popular and, as it turned out, could be rigged. Popular contestants were given the answers to general-knowledge questions beforehand. What the audience saw was a scripted contest with the winner predetermined. Winners came back from week to week and some gained a national following. Not surprisingly, the predetermined winner was the one the producers believed would sustain the ratings or increase them. The quiz show scandals, as they are referred to in media history, were followed by congressional hearings, ruined careers and even legislation.

The new reality shows suffered from some of the same problems. When it was discovered that those who advanced on one or more popular reality shows had actually been determined in advance, it became national news. Soon after, audiences learned that participants in the various reality shows were not always novices to the medium but were often recruited from ranks of fledgling actors. Furthermore, the notion of spontaneity, crucial to getting the audience to believe the premise of the reality show, was false. The producers of shows such as "Survivor," "Joe Millionaire" and the like most often shot hundreds of hours of video with a predetermined "story line" to edit into an allegedly spontaneous program.

Some reality shows were based on legally questionable premises, such as the series that proposed to capture men hiring prostitutes—the reality of "johns"— or cop shows that allowed media to capture arrests inside homes only to be successfully sued for invasion of privacy later. Some shows seemed notable for their complete lack of a moral compass or made us more like voyeurs than traditional viewers. "Temptation Island" put couples and relationships in physical and emotional jeopardy for the entertainment of the audience. But, still, America watched even as lives were altered irreparably.

In June of 2009, a record 10.6 million people tuned into the TLC show "Jon and Kate Plus 8" to learn that Jon and Kate Gosselin were calling it quits after 10 years of marriage, including several years that were documented on television. The concept was a reality series of two parents and their eight children on a $1.1 million Berks County, PA home built in part with television funds. At the time of their divorce, papers filed by the couple indicated that they had long lived separate lives, including the possibility that they had been misleading the public about their marriage for up to two years before the filing—a claim disputed by the lawyers as mere "legalese." In an interview with *People* magazine, Kate didn't blame the ubiquitous cameras for the failure of the marriage, saying that the divorce would have happened with or without the television show, which was consistently one of the top shows for the TLC network.

Reality television raises an important ethical question: what constitutes reality? As you'll remember from Chapter 1, definitions of truth and the relationship between truth and reality have changed throughout the millennia. Reality television is a lot like the computer-generated matrix in the film *The Matrix*. Reality shows used participants for its purposes, and along the way, a lot of people in the matrix world of reality TV were entertained.

The early part of this century has been a scary time, and watching Joe Millionaire bungle his relationships is a lot easier than taking the chance of going out on a first date. However, that scary first date has the chance of turning into something wonderful or awful—neither outcome one that Joe Millionaire had to face. Truth in relationships matters because it's how people form connections. Reality television was people, inside a box, having a planned and edited experience. That planning wasn't about truth. It wasn't even particularly personal. Just like in the matrix world, it was a code.

AESTHETICS IS AN ATTITUDE

Artists see the world differently. While most people perceive only what is needful, the artist works with what some have called an "enriched perceptual experience." This aesthetic attitude is one that values close and complete concentration of all the senses. An aesthetic attitude is a frankly sensual one, and one that summons both emotion and logic to its particular ends.

For example, the theatre audience knows that Eugene O'Neill's plays are "merely" drama. But they also provide us with an intense examination of the role of family in human society—an experience that is both real and personal to every audience member. Such intense examination is what gives the plays their power to move.

The makers of mediated messages, whether they are the executive producers of a television sitcom or the designers of a newspaper page, share this aesthetic impetus. These mass communicators are much like architects. An architect can design a perfectly serviceable cube-like building, one that withstands the elements and may be used for good ends. But great buildings—St. Paul's Cathedral in London or Jefferson's home at Monticello—do more. They are tributes to the human intellect's capacity to harmoniously harness form and function.

In fact, philosophers have argued that what separates the commonplace from the excellent is the addition of an aesthetic quality to what would otherwise be a routine, serviceable work. These qualities of excellence have been described as:

- An appreciation of the function realized in the product.
- An appreciation of the resulting quality or form.
- An appreciation of the technique or skill in the performance.

These three characteristics of aesthetic excellence characterize excellence in mass communication as well.

Take the newspaper weather page. *USA Today* literally recalibrated the standard from tiny black and white agate type to a colorful full page. They understood what the late political columnist Molly Ivins knew: when people aren't talking about football, they talk about the weather. They devoted more space to it and printed it in color. They added more information in a more legible style and form. In short, they gave newspaper weather information an aesthetic quality. While much about *USA Today* has been criticized, its excellent weather page has been copied.

Although mass-communication professionals are infrequently accused of being artists, we believe they intuitively accept an aesthetic standard as a component of professional excellence. As philosopher G. E. Moore (1903, 83) noted in *Principia Ethica:*

> Let us imagine one world exceedingly beautiful. Image it as beautiful as you can; put into it whatever on this earth you most admire: mountains, rivers, the sea, suns and sunsets, stars and moon. Imagine these all combined in the most exquisite proportion so that no one thing jars against another, but each contributes to increase the beauty of the whole. And then imagine the ugliest world you can possibly conceive. Imagine it just one heap of filth, containing everything that is most disgusting to you for whatever reason, and the whole, as far as may be, without one redeeming factor. . . . Supposing (all) that quite apart from the contemplation of human beings; still it is irrational to hold that it is better that the ugly world exist than the one which is beautiful.

Substitute film, compact disc, poem, news story, photograph or advertising copy for Moore's word "world" and we believe that you will continue to intuitively agree with the statement. While we may disagree on what specifically constitutes beauty in form and content, the aesthetic standard of excellence still applies.

Philosopher John Dewey (2005) noted, "Aesthetic experience is a manifestation, a record and celebration of the life of a civilization, a means of promoting its development, and is also the ultimate judgment upon the quality of a civilization." In an interview on the PBS series "The Promise of Television," commentator Bill Moyers (1988) said:

> The root word of television is vision from afar, and that's its chief value. It has brought me in my stationary moments visions of ideas and dreams and imaginations and geography that I would never personally experience. So, it has put me in touch with the larger world. Television can be a force for dignifying life, not debasing it.

Though Moyers' comments were made specifically about television, the same argument can be made for a good book, a favorite magazine, music or a film. And whether the media are a force for dignifying humanity or debasing it is largely in the hands of those who own and work in them.

Suggested Readings

CALVERT, CLAY. 2000. *Voyeur nation: Media, privacy and peering in modern culture.* Boulder, CO: Westview Press.

JENSEN, JOLI. 2002. *Is art good for us?* Lanham, MD: Rowman & Littlefield, Publishers.

MEDVED, MICHAEL. 1992. *Hollywood vs. America.* New York: HarperCollins Publishers.

MONTGOMERY, KATHRYN C. 1989. *Target: Prime time. Advocacy groups and the struggle over entertainment television.* New York: Oxford University Press.

POSTMAN, NEIL. 1986. *Amusing ourselves to death: Public discourse in the age of television.* New York: Penguin Books.

Cases on the Web

www.mhhe.com/mediaethics7e

"How to remember Malcolm X" by Dennis Lancaster

"Beavis and Butthead: The case for standards in entertainment" by Philip Patterson

"Joe Klein and the authorship of 'Primary Colors'" by Lee Wilkins

"'Bamboozled': Truth (or prophesy) in satire" by Lee Wilkins

"Truth in filmmaking: Removing the ugliness from 'A Beautiful Mind'" by Philip Patterson

"Playing hardball: The Pete Rose–Jim Gray controversy" by Ben Scott

"How much coverage is appropriate? The case of the highly paid athlete" by Matt Keeney

"Up for debate: NBC news logo decorates 'The West Wing'" by Reuben Stern

CHAPTER 10 CASES

CASES 10-A

When Radio Comedy Crosses the Line: Trouble at the BBC

BRIAN SIMMONS
Portland State University

Sometimes, what you think is funny someone else finds offensive. It is one thing when that occurs in private conversation, but what happens when it goes out over the airwaves to an audience of several hundred thousand people across Great Britain? What happens when it generates more than 38,000 complaints, including condemnations by members of Parliament and the Prime Minister?

On October 18, 2008, the BBC aired "The Russell Brand Show," featuring popular British comedians Russell Brand and Jonathan Ross. The show included a pre-recorded segment in which the two left messages on the answering machine of a well-known British actor, 78-year-old Andrew Sachs. Before leaving the messages, Brand said, "What Andrew doesn't know is that I've slept with his granddaughter," Georgina Baillie, an exotic dancer going by the name of "Voluptua" with the dance troupe "The Satanic Sluts." Over the course of four different messages, Brand described his sexual encounters with Baillie and in the background of one message Ross can be heard yelling, "He fucked your granddaughter!" They end with a mocking apology set to song and Brand's wise-cracking marriage proposal to Baillie.

A week later, the British tabloid *The Mail on Sunday* reported the incident, noting that Brand and Ross might face prosecution for the act. Soon thereafter, complaints began pouring into the BBC totaling 38,000, the second highest amount ever received for a single broadcast. Baillie said she felt betrayed by Russell and called for the two to be fired. Several Members of Parliament condemned the two radio personalities for their actions and the BBC for allowing the program to air. Even British Prime Minister Gordon Brown called the incident "clearly inappropriate and unacceptable."

Brand issued an apology for the prank calls, but referred to the comedy bit as "funny." The BBC also apologized for the incident, stating that the telephone calls were "grossly offensive" and "a breach of editorial standards." Brand ultimately resigned from the BBC and Ross was suspended without pay for 12 weeks, an experience he described as "fun." In addition, two BBC administrators who were familiar with the show's content before it aired and gave their permission to it resigned.

Oddly, in an interview three months later Georgina Baillie said, "I think its way out of proportion what's happened and I don't hate either one of them—I don't at all." And Andrew Sachs, after originally complaining to the BBC, dropped the matter quickly.

A complicating factor in all of this is that the BBC is publicly funded through a license fee paid by those owning television sets. The BBC's mandate is to inform and entertain, and the organization is always trying to balance the two directives in appropriate manners. Some Members of Parliament believe that the BBC's funding obligates it to a higher standard of programming while others disagree.

How does the story end? At press time Andrew Sachs was still working occasionally as an actor on a British TV series. Russell Brand is furthering his career with acting projects in the United States and Great Britain. Jonathan Ross still hosts his "Friday Night with Jonathan Ross" program for the BBC. And Georgina Baillie reportedly is still dancing with "The Satanic Sluts."

Micro Issues

1. Are you offended by Brand and Ross' actions? If so, why?
2. Who was hurt by these actions?
3. Georgina Baillie ultimately said it was no big deal. Andrew Sachs ultimately dropped the matter? Do their actions change your views of this?
4. Does the fact that the phone calls were pre-recorded change the way you see this incident?

Midrange Issues

1. Who should accept responsibility for this? Brand and Ross? The BBC administrators who knew about the content but allowed it to air?
2. Does the fact that the BBC receives public funding play into any assessments of this incident's propriety?
3. What, if any, are the differences between Brand and Ross's *legal* right to do what they did and the *ethical* implications of what they did?
4. Do you think that if the same incident occurred in America the reaction would be identical?

Macro Issues

1. More than 30,000 people joined a Facebook group supporting Brand and Ross, many because they believe that the two are simply being entertaining. Are entertainers relieved of ethical responsibilities if they are "just giving the audience what they want"?
2. Though Great Britain understands freedom of speech differently than does the United States, such freedom is still cherished and defended. Where ought the right to free speech end when it comes to entertainment programs such as Brand and Ross's?

CASE 10-B

Hardly Art

MITO HABE-EVANS
University of Missouri—Columbia

Hardly Art is an independent record label, a sister label started in 2007 by Sub Pop Records in Seattle. Sub Pop started in 1987 and was among the pioneers of the grunge rock scene, including releasing the first album by Nirvana before the group moved to the major label Geffen/DGC.

Despite its fan popularity, Sub Pop floundered economically. The growing commercial success of alternative music in the 1990s meant that major labels competed with Sub Pop to sign talent. According to a biography of the label on its Web site, the financial woes of Sub Pop were due in part to "unwise spending on meals and travel" among other line items as they sought to grow the business in an increasingly crowded market. Eventually, financial troubles led Sup Pop to sell 49 percent of its ownership to Warner Bros. Records in exchange for a cash infusion (Sub Pop 2008).

The typical business model used by record labels, both independent and major, is one where the label signs a contract with the artist for a set number of albums, fronts the money and resources for recording, producing, manufacturing, distribution, touring and promotion, and the artist earns royalties from recording sales—all of which pay back the music company for its initial investment (Albini 1993). In Sub Pop's case, sales weren't enough to recoup the initial investment—particularly after the smaller label began competing against larger, better funded labels.

Major labels, on the other hand, are able to recover their investment by keeping artists' royalties small. Often, artists remain indebted, even after modest success. David Hesmondhalgh (1999) describes the logic of the music industry as "towards internationalization, because of the economies which accrue to very big, as opposed to moderate, sales: the costs of development, marketing and recording are high; marginal costs for reproducing each copy are very small." Support from major labels—when it comes at all—has turned into survival of the fittest where the commercialization of music mandates that only those artists who make music that attracts the widest possible audience will be supported by the music industry once signed. This is especially true when artists who have signed into multi-album deals and remain in debt to the label must find a way to fulfill their contractual obligations and make enough money to get out of debt.

The emergence of independent record labels has been a response to a lack of support for smaller, less commercially digestible music. These labels value artistic autonomy for musicians, yet must try to balance this with the need to be financially viable. Whereas profit is not the independent record label's sole motivation, it must still be conscious of not losing money in order to survive as a business.

Sub Pop launched Hardly Art as a sister label with a new business model based on a net profit split of 40/60 between the label and the band as opposed to the system of royalties typically used in the industry. All the costs must first be recouped, but once they are, the band sees a much higher percentage of the profit. Because both parties involved have a vested interest in keeping the costs down, they work together to decide what extra activities such as touring and promotions are worth the extra spending. Instead of multi-album deals that bind the band and the label, they work using a one-off project model, which allows for spontaneous releases by small bands. Sarah Moody, the general manager of Hardly Art, says, "as for why we went with this particular model, a large part of it had to do with being artist-friendly, especially to bands just starting out, and a smaller part had to do with seeing whether or not it would be a financially viable venture,"

As of now, with six releases under its belt, Hardly Art is not yet a fully profitable operation, but Moody believes that once the last few months are accounted for, two of their projects will be fully recouped or nearly so. She notes that the first couple of projects carried the additional burden to not being able to share advertising expenses with others, increasing their total budget. She sees this expense as declining on a per project basis after more projects are launched employing the same marketing infrastructure. "There are plenty of other opportunities offered to our bands along the way to help out, " Moody says, "whether it's touring, licensing opportunities, and the like . . . so while getting our artists into the black is at the forefront, everyone understands that there has to be a modicum of patience involved."

Micro Issues

1. What are the values that the Sub Pop approach brings to artistic expression? Are any of these values ethical in nature?
2. How important, in an ethical sense, should the freedom to create be to artists? To those who make their work available to others? To music lovers?

Midrange Issues

1. Using the concepts of stakeholder and stockholder theory from the media economics chapter, analyze the ethical implications of the Sub Pop approach.
2. Evaluate whether and to what extent independent music, films, etc., have to consider the dictates of popular culture in their efforts.
3. What is independent music? Is it simply entertainment? Long-lasting art? Business? A blend of the three? How are your answers—in an ethical sense—changed by the way you define "indy" efforts?

Macro Issues

1. Might ownership and profit-sharing structures like this be workable in other areas of the mass media, for example in the creation of advertising or public relations agencies or news organizations? Would you be willing to work for an organization with this sort of business model?
2. Evaluate the ethical claims in the following statement by Moody: "I'd like to think that another goal of the label is to create an environment in which the artists feel comfortable and informed, and feel as though they could make a career of it—as opposed to slinging out random records left and right in an attempt to turn a profit. We view it as much more of a partnership with our bands."

CASE 10-C

Schindler's List: The Role of Memory

LEE WILKINS
University of Missouri—Columbia

In 1982 director Steven Spielberg purchased the rights to Australian novelist Thomas Keneally's retelling of the story of the "Schindler Jews," a group of about 1,100 Krakow, Poland, residents who survived the Holocaust because Czech businessman Oskar Schindler was willing to cajole, bribe and bully the Nazis for their lives. Today, Schindler, a Roman Catholic by birth, is known in Israel as a "righteous person"; he is the only Nazi buried in Jerusalem's Mount Zion cemetery.

By 1992 when Spielberg began work on the film, both he and the world had changed. Bosnia was in the midst of "ethnic cleansing," as were nations in Africa and in the Far East, such as Nepal. Some polls indicated that more than half of the U.S. teenagers living in that decade had never heard of the Holocaust; about 23 percent of the U.S. public at the time maintained the gassing of 6 million Jews plus 5 million other "undesirables" in Germany and its occupied territories never happened.

"I think the main reason I wanted to make this film was as an act of remembrance," Spielberg told the film editor of the *Atlanta Journal-Constitution.* "An act of remembrance for the public record. Maybe it won't be seen by millions of people who see my other movies, but it might be the kind of movie shown one day in high schools. I also wanted to leave this story for my children. I wanted to leave them a legacy of their Jewish culture."

What Americans, as well as Spielberg's children, will see is a 3-hour-and-15-minute examination of the conscience of Oskar Schindler, who entered World War II on the side of the Nazis, intending to make a profit. He hires Jews to work in his enamelware factory because they work for less than slave wages. Initially, he befriends the Nazis and the SS to help expedite his purchase and takeover of the plant. Later, after the Nazis have first ghettoized and then attempted to exterminate the Jewish population of Krakow, Schindler uses his personal charm, his connections and most of his war-amassed wealth to have "his" Jewish workers first labeled as essential to the German war machine and later moved from Germany and into Czechoslovakia for safekeeping. None of the bombs manufactured at Schindler's plant ever exploded.

Spielberg shot the film in black and white on location in Poland. Much of the movie has a documentary feel; cinematography is at eye level. It was often Spielberg himself who focused the handheld camera. Hitler appears only once—in a photograph on someone's desk. And, by centering on Schindler, Spielberg captured the conscience of an uneasy hero.

As Keneally's book indicates, Oskar Schindler was a complex man. He managed to maintain outward friendships with many Nazis whom he despised. He was a sensualist who enjoyed good food, expensive possessions and carnal knowledge of women who were not his wife. Spielberg's film, which was rated "R," depicted all of this, including scenes of lovemaking that involved full, frontal nudity and more distant shots of concentration camp existence in which Jewish inmates were required to run naked in front of their guards to determine who remained well enough to work and who was sick enough to be murdered.

Perhaps the most disturbing element of the film was Spielberg's portrait of the violence embedded in Hitler's "final solution" and of the banality of evil (Hannah Arendt's phrase used to describe convicted war criminal Adolph Eichmann) that individual human beings can come to represent. That sundered humanity is symbolized by Amon Goeth (played by Ralph Fiennes), the amoral and, some have suggested, sociopathic commandant of the labor camp from which many of the people who worked for Schindler survived. Whether it is the Nazis hunting the Jews who remain in hiding in the Krakow ghetto or Goeth's random murder of the men and women who lived in his camp as before-breakfast sport, the violence in the film is devastating not just for its brutality but also for its casualness.

When Spielberg's mother told him making "*Schindler's List* would be good for the Jews," Spielberg responded that "it would be good for all of us."

Critics, who had a difficult time accepting that the same man who directed *Jurassic Park* could also produce *Schindler's List* in the same year, praised the film for its aesthetic qualities and for its retelling of the story of the Holocaust in such a powerful fashion. The film also brought Spielberg multiple Oscars, an award that had eluded him despite his enormous popular success. After the film's release, President Bill Clinton said that every American should see it.

Writing in the *Washington Post,* Rita Kempley saw more than a superficial resemblance between Schindler and Spielberg. "And Schindler, played with élan by [Liam] Neeson, is really a lot like Spielberg himself," she wrote, "a man who manages to use his commercial clout to achieve a moral end."

Micro Issues

1. Should a film like *Schindler's List* receive the same "R" rating as films such as *Road Trip*?
2. What is the appropriate role of a film critic for films such as *Schindler's List*? Should different standards be used to evaluate this film than some other Spielberg successes, such as *E.T.* or *Jaws*?
3. Would you allow a child under 17 to see this film?

Midrange Issues

1. Should news accounts focus on events such as the ethnic cleansing in Bosnia with the goal of changing public opinion?
2. Are docudramas that focus on social issues such as spouse abuse or child molestation the appropriate mechanism to engage the public in debate or discussion about such serious questions?
3. Some people have argued that certain historical events, such as the Holocaust or the recent genocide in Rwanda, should never be the subject of entertainment programming because entertainment can never capture the true horror of what has happened. How would you evaluate such an assertion?

Macro Issues

1. Compare the moral development of Oskar Schindler with that of the main characters in a film such as *Gandhi*.

2. John Dewey wrote about "funded memory," by which he meant how a culture remembers and reconstructs its own history. What is the role of entertainment programming in funded memory? What should be the role of news programming in such cultural constructions?

3. Tolstoy argues that good art communicates the feelings of the artist to the masses in such a way that others may experience the same feeling as the artist. How does this film accomplish that purpose?

CASE 10-D

Naomi Campbell: Do Celebrities Have Privacy?

LEE WILKINS
University of Missouri—Columbia

Supermodel Naomi Campbell is an international celebrity. Campbell was discovered in London's Covent Garden when she was only 15 and soon became one of the best paid and most often photographed supermodels, earning more than $1 million a year. Her worldwide celebrity was helped, in part, because of her physical image; a native of the United Kingdom, Campbell is black. She was often the focus of media coverage in both Britain and the United States and, in the years after her discovery, developed a reputation for being a prima donna—irritable and manipulative. She was dropped by her agency in 1993, although she was later reinstated, and she was once arrested for assaulting her personal assistant. These stories about Campbell were news.

Campbell often sought the media spotlight. And, like many models, among them Britain's Kate Moss, Campbell was rumored to use drugs—specifically cocaine, which depresses the appetite and hence helps with weight control. Campbell publicly denied any drug addiction on multiple occasions, including in 1997 when she had been rushed to a hospital in Gran Canaria following an alleged drug overdose. After that incident, she told Britain's *The Daily Telegraph,* "I didn't take drugs." Then, in February 2001, London's *Daily Mirror,* one of Britain's most widely read tabloids, published a photograph of Campbell leaving a Narcotics Anonymous meeting in King's Road, Chelsea, a wealthy London neighborhood. The article that appeared with the photograph included details of the meeting she attended.

Campbell sued in British courts—not for libel but for invasion of privacy. The suit was the first brought under laws governing the European Union (EU), which includes in its charter protection of individual privacy under the Human Rights Convention. Britain is a member of the EU. Campbell's attorneys reasoned that the EU statutes, which are more specific about privacy than legal precedent in either Britain or the United States, gave them the best chance of winning the suit.

Speaking later, Campbell said the *Mirror* photograph and articles made her feel as if she had been raped. She characterized the article as "very damaging." However, things got more complicated when the case actually went to Britain's High Court. During that proceeding, Campbell maintained that she was not a drug addict and denied that she had been receiving therapy for some years. She did admit that she was "notorious for tantrums."

In its ruling in March 2002, the High Court awarded Campbell £3,500 (about $6,000) in damages and ordered that the newspaper pay additional court costs equal to about $110,000 (£70,000). The judge in the case noted that even celebrities were entitled to some privacy. "Although many aspects of the private lives of celebrities and public figures will inevitably enter the public domain, in my judgment it does not follow that even with self-publicists every aspect and detail of their private lives are legitimate quarry for the journalist." The judge noted that Campbell's attendance at the Narcotics Anonymous meeting and the details of her therapy clearly related to her physical and mental health and therefore met the standard of "sensitive personal data."

However, the judge also noted that the public clearly had an interest in knowing that Campbell had been misleading them by her denials of drug addiction. "Clearly *The Mirror* was fully entitled to put the record straight and publish that her denials of drug addiction were deliberately misleading. She might have been thought of and, indeed, she herself seems to be, a self-appointed role model to young black women." The judge also noted, "I am satisfied she lied when making denials about her drug addiction."

News organizations in Britain generally treated the ruling as a victory, noting that the small damage award served as much as a rebuke to Campbell than as a punishment to the often invasive tabloids. Campbell, too, seemed to regret many aspects of the suit. She said the case had left her unable to sleep. "I didn't expect it to be the way it's blown up like this. . . . Recovery is something that takes time. You feel that you're getting better in the right direction. I wasn't hiding. But first of all an addict had to admit to themselves that they have a problem before they can admit it to anybody else. That is the first step."

Piers Morgan, editor of the *Mirror,* characterized the judgment as ". . . derisory. . . . This is a case that should never have been brought. It is quite clear that the judge thought we had every right to say she was a drug addict. We have every right to tell the public that she was having treatment. The only thing we couldn't do—and this was what the whole case came down to—was say she was going to Narcotics Anonymous."

Micro Issues

1. If Campbell had admitted her drug addiction when first asked, would it have been ethical to publish the story?
2. Was it appropriate for other media outlets—the mainstream press in both Britain and the United States—to publish the *Mirror* photo and story details once the *Mirror* had published them?
3. Are the details of Campbell's drug treatment ethically distinct from the fact that she is in treatment? Justify your answers in terms of ethical theory.

Midrange Issues

1. How should Campbell's character influence media coverage of her, particularly her private life?
2. Are celebrities morally distinct from other categories of people when it comes to privacy issues? Would you make the same or a different argument for public officials?
3. Is there something more invasive about a photograph of Campbell leaving the meeting than a story that recounted the event? Was a photograph necessary for a journalistic purpose?
4. Should there be different standards for the tabloid press than for more mainstream media? If there are different standards, how do you account for them?

Macro Issues

1. In a commentary that ran after the court decision was announced, British journalist Kim Fletcher noted: "There is more at stake here than the right to write about what famous people do in their own time. The fear is that lawyers will extend the notion of what can be regarded as confidential—conversations between business colleagues, tax discussions—to prevent newspapers gaining and publishing information that may be of greater significance and more in the public interest than a model's drug addiction." Analyze and evaluate this statement based on ethical theory.

2. How do you believe this case would have been resolved in the United States, had Campbell chosen to sue there? Is your analysis based on legal precedent? On ethical theory? Which is more appropriate in privacy cases?

3. How does your reasoning apply to the coverage of Michael Jackson's death, particularly his drug use and the charges—none of which were proved in court—of child molestation?

CASE 10-E

Hate Radio: The Outer Limits of Tasteful Broadcasting

BRIAN SIMMONS
Portland State University

Trevor Van Lansing has what some would call the greatest job in the world. He is employed by KRFP-AM, an all-talk-format radio station in a large city in the West. His program airs weekdays from 3:00 p.m. to 7:00 p.m., and he is currently rated number one in his afternoon drive-time slot. Van Lansing is, quite simply, the most popular radio personality in the market. He is also the most controversial.

Each afternoon Van Lansing introduces a general topic for discussion and then fields calls from listeners about the topic. However, Lansing's topics (and the calls from his listeners) revolve around a recurring theme: the world as viewed by a Caucasian, Anglo-Saxon Protestant who also happens to be vocal, uncompromising and close-minded.

A sampling of his recent programs typifies his show. On Monday, Van Lansing discusses a woman in a small Indiana town who quits her job in a convenience store to go on welfare because there is more money to be made on the federal dole than in the private sector. Says Van Lansing, "All these irresponsible whores are the same. They get knocked up by some construction worker, then expect the taxpayers to pay for them to sit around the house all day and watch Oprah Winfrey."

Callers flood the airwaves with equally combative remarks in support of and opposition to Van Lansing's comments. On Tuesday, the topic of racial discrimination (always a Van Lansing favorite) comes up. According to Van Lansing, "Those Africans expect us Americans to make up for two hundred years of past mistakes. Forget it. It can't be done. If they are so keen on America, let them compete against Caucasians on an equal basis without the 'civil rights crutch.'"

When one African-American caller challenges Van Lansing's thinking, the host responds, "Why don't you tell your buddies to work for what they get like us Caucasians? All you do anyway is steal from the guys you don't like and then take their women."

Wednesday finds Van Lansing lashing out against education: "The problem with today's schools is that our kinds are exposed to weird thinking. I mean, we tell our kids that homosexuality is okay, that we evolved from a chimp, and that the Ruskies are our friends. It all started when we elected women to school boards and started letting fags into the classroom. It's disgusting."

Thursday features an exchange between Van Lansing and an abortion-rights activist. At one point they are both shouting at the same time, and the airwaves are peppered with obscenities and personal attacks. By comparison, Friday is calm, as only a few irate Jews, women, and Mormons bother to call in.

Critics have called Van Lansing's program offensive, tasteless, rude, racist, obscene and insensitive. Supporters refer to the program as enlightening, refreshing, educational and provocative. The only thing everyone can agree on is that the show is a bona fide moneymaker. Van Lansing's general manager notes that the station's ratings jumped radically when he was hired, and that advertising revenues have tripled.

In fact, Van Lansing's popularity has spawned promotional appearances, T-shirts, bumper stickers and other paraphernalia, all designed to hawk the station. "Sure, Trevor is controversial, but in this business that's good," says KRFP's general manager.

"Van Lansing is so good that he will make more money this year than the president of the United States. Besides, it's just a gimmick."

Does Van Lansing see a problem with the content and style of his program? "Look," he says, "radio is a business. You have to give the audience what they want. All I do is give them what they want. If they wanted a kinder, gentler attitude, I would give it to them." He continues, "Don't get mad at me. Thank God we live in a country where guys like me can express an opinion. The people who listen to me like to hear it straight sometimes, and that's what the First Amendment is about, right?"

Finally, Van Lansing points out that if people are really offended by him, they can always turn the dial. "I don't force these people to listen," he pleads. "If they don't like it, let them go somewhere else."

Others disagree. The National Coalition for the Understanding of Alternative Lifestyles, a gay- and lesbian-rights group, calls Van Lansing's show "reprehensible." "Trevor Van Lansing is hiding behind the First Amendment. What he says on the air isn't speech; it's hate, pure and simple," says the group's director. "His program goes well beyond what our founders intended."

Adds a representative of the National Organization for Women: "Van Lansing is perpetuating several dangerous stereotypes that are destructive, sick and offensive. Entertainment must have some boundaries."

Micro Issues

1. Would you be offended by Van Lansing's program? If so, why?
2. Would Van Lansing's program be less offensive if the station aired another talk show immediately after his that featured a host holding opposite views?
3. How are the lyrics of rapper Eminem like or unlike Van Lansing's rants? Is an artist subject to different restrictions?

Midrange Issues

1. Who should accept responsibility for monitoring this type of program? Van Lansing? The radio station, KRFP? The FCC? The courts? The audience?
2. What, if any, are the differences between Van Lansing's *legal* right to do what he does and the *ethical* implications of what he does?
3. Legal scholar Mari Matsuda (1989) has called for a narrow legal restriction of racist speech. She notes, "The places where the law does not go to redress harm have tended to be the places where women, children, people of color, and poor people live" (Matsuda 1989, 11). She argues that a content-based restriction of racist speech is more protective of civil liberties than other tests that have been traditionally applied. Could such an argument be applied to entertainment programming?

4. In the current American media landscape, talk radio is supposedly the stronghold of the right while the majority of major daily newspapers are supposedly controlled by the left. Does the evidence validate this widely held assumption? Is democracy well-served by this arrangement of entire media systems leaning to one side of the political spectrum?

Macro Issues

1. Are entertainers relieved of ethical responsibilities if they are "just giving the audience what they want"? Do Van Lansing's high ratings validate his behavior, since many people are obviously in agreement with him?
2. How does Van Lansing's narrow view of the world differ from a television situation comedy that stereotypes blondes as dumb, blue-collar workers as bigoted, etc.?
3. Van Lansing says that it's great that a guy like him can have a radio show. Is tolerance one of the measures of a democracy? If so, are there limits to tolerance, and who draws those lines?
4. Supreme Court Justice William O. Douglas has said, "If we are to have freedom of mind in America, we must produce a generation of men and women who will make tolerance for all ideas a symbol of virtue." How should democratic societies cope with unpopular points of view, particularly as expressed through the mass media?

CASE 10-F

Do You Really Want to Hurt Me? Michael Riedel and Theater Criticism

BRYAN M. VANDEVENDER
University of Missouri

> *There's a bitchiness in the theatre. There's that guy on* The (New York) Post.
>
> William Goldman, playwright

Michael Reidel is arguably the most hated man in New York City—or at least the stretch of town that runs from 42nd to 51st streets. Riedel covers the Broadway theatre scene for *The New York Post*. His bi-weekly column offers commentary on the theatre industry and its climate. He reports on show openings and closing, makes value judgments of the plays he sees and predicts which will win awards. His column appears in the Arts/Entertainment section of the paper. Simply put, Michael Riedel critiques the theatre. Whether he is a theater critic is up for debate.

Meryl Cordon of *New York Magazine* described Riedel's column as "mean, often funny, always dishy . . . ruthlessly vitriolic." While a certain level of cynicism is not uncommon in theater reviews, critics generally direct it at the play on stage. Riedel, however, focuses his attention on drama offstage. The shows that have technical difficulties, financial difficulties, conflicts of interest, conflicts of ego or creative team infighting are the shows that make it into his column.

For instance, Riedel chided Tony Award winner Bernadette Peters for missing several preview performances in 2003 during the musical revival of *Gypsy*. A picture of the actress's face on a milk carton accompanied the article. In 2004, Riedel targeted Alfred Molina, the British film actor who headlined director David Leveaux's revival of *Fiddler on the Roof.* The columnist quipped that Molina's Tevye "seems to have been reared on Wonder Bread." In the same article, he described the show's direction as "Episcopalian" and "not Jewish enough."

These comments earned the writer a blow to the face from Leveaux. Says Riedel, "I'm a wimp when it come to physical violence, but give me a keyboard and I'll kill ya." Perhaps this is why Meryl Gordon entitled her *New York Magazine* piece "Assassin."

Theater insiders credit Riedel with ending the run of the 2004 musical, *Taboo.* Conceived and scored by pop icon Boy George, the musical wove together two independent stories: Boy George's rise to fame and the life of Leigh Bowery, a London fashion designer and performance artist with whom George was acquainted. The musical was set in Bowery's underground, gay club, Taboo, and boasted a colorful cast of freaks, Goths and transvestites and Boy George himself in the role of Leigh Bowery. Former daytime talk show host Rosie O'Donnell served as the musical's producer. Having seen the London production, O'Donnell invested $10 million and single-handedly brought *Taboo* to New York.

However, the production's backstage discord quickly became Riedel's cause. Between Sept. 17, 2003, and Jan. 6, 2004, Riedel dedicated nine columns to *Taboo.*

He reported that O'Donnell had purchased a $190,000 ad for the play in the *New York Times* and alleged that the ad had failed to generate adequate advance ticket sales. In response to a quote that the show would win a Tony, Riedel wrote, "Well, that's a nice show of confidence, Rosie, but don't you think you'd better figure out a way to sell some tickets first?"

In October, Riedel reported that O'Donnell hired a director-choreographer friend to consult on *Taboo* prior to its first performance. Riedel wrote, "Translation: Rosie's lost faith in her original choreographer . . . and is muscling him aside . . . bringing in a show doctor is a dramatic move that is always interpreted as a sign that the show is in trouble." Five days later, Riedel recounted a behind-the-scenes spat between O'Donnell and actor Raul Esparaza over the producer giving the actor unwelcome direction. Riedel accused O'Donnell of micromanaging and claimed that both she and the actor suffered from inflated egos. The next month, Riedel reported that O'Donnell wanted to replace the show's director. "Iceberg, dead ahead," was his comment.

During the fracas, Boy George wrote Riedel a letter the columnist reprinted. In part, the letter read, "I must applaud you on your ability to sneak under the cracks of the theater doors and find people willing to betray those they work with and disrespect the hard work of everyone from producers to leading actors, ensemble and crew. . . . Michael, you work in an industry that relies on your singular good nature, and you are among an elite few who seemingly decide the future of a Broadway show."

The closing of a Broadway play results not only in lost art, but also lost jobs and lost revenue. The theater is not as resilient as television or film. Its financial foundations are not nearly as strong, and it cannot be discovered later when the audience rents a DVD or watches reruns. Theater is ephemeral. It has no reliable "aftermarket." While film can record the work, it cannot recreate the art, the jobs lost or the original financial investment. As theater owner and producer Rocco Landesman notes, "It's a brutal business. It's a harsh business. It's the kind of business that unless you love the project or love the show, you're not going to get involved because the risk/reward is terrible."

Micro Issues

1. Define the ethical obligations of a critic. Do they differ from that of a columnist or an investigative reporter? If so, how?
2. Should a critic be held accountable for the visuals such as the Peters photo that accompany his work?
3. Justify in ethical terms Riedel's decision to reprint George's letter.

Midrange Issues

1. Should the standards of criticism in New York—whether of music, theater or restaurants—differ from those in your home town? If so, why? If not, why not?
2. Should columnists be edited differently than news journalists?

Macro Issues

1. Analyze the role of journalism in covering any industry that produces jobs and profits. To whom, and for what, are journalists responsible?
2. Much of what Riedel wrote could be considered backstage gossip. Compare the ethical implications of this approach for readers with that of magazines such as *Us Weekly* or Web sites such as Gawker.
3. Should journalists be more cautious in their reporting on artistic performances that cannot be reproduced—such as theater or live concerts—than other forms of popular art? Is there a distinctive sort of potential harm involved in negative coverage of such events?

11

Becoming a Moral Adult

By the end of this chapter you should:

- **know the stages of moral development as described by Piaget and Kohlberg.**
- **understand the ethics of care.**
- **understand the stages of adult moral development.**

INTRODUCTION

Graduation is not the end of the educational process; it is merely a milestone marking the beginning of a new era of learning. College studies should not only equip you for entry into or promotion within the workforce but also equip you to be a lifelong learner.

The same is true about moral development. There is no "moral graduation," marking you as an upright person capable of making right choices in life's personal and professional dilemmas. It's a lifelong process of steps—some of which you've taken; others lie ahead. Where you are now is a function of both age and experience, but the person you are now is not the person you will be 10 years from now. In a decade, you'll have added insight. Growth may, and probably will, change your decisions. This process is not only inevitable but also desirable.

This chapter is designed to provide you with an overview of some psychological theories of moral development. It attempts to allow you to plot your own development not only in terms of where you are but also in terms of where you would like to be.

BASIC ASSUMPTIONS ABOUT MORAL DEVELOPMENT: THE RIGHTS-BASED TRADITION

People can develop morally just as they can learn to think critically (Clouse 1985). Scholars base this assertion on the following premises.

First, *moral development occurs within the individual.* Real moral development cannot be produced by outside factors or merely engaging in moral acts. People develop morally when they become aware of their reasons for acting a certain way.

Second, *moral development parallels intellectual development.* Although the two may proceed at a slightly different pace, there can be little moral development until a person has attained a certain intellectual capacity. For this reason, we exempt children and people of limited mental ability from some laws and societal expectations. While you can be intelligent without being moral, the opposite is not likely.

Third, *moral development occurs in a series of universal, unvarying and hierarchical stages.* Each level builds on the lower levels, and there is no skipping of intermediate stages. Just as a baby crawls before walking and babbles before speaking, a person must pass through the earlier stages of moral development before advancing to the later stages.

Fourth, *moral development comes through conflict.* As moral development theorist Lawrence Kohlberg notes (1973, 13), "A fundamental reason why an

CALVIN AND HOBBES © Watterson. Dist. By UNIVERSAL UCLICK. Reprinted with permission. All rights reserved.

individual moves from one stage to the next is because the latter stages solve problems and inconsistencies unsolvable at the present developmental stage." Just as a baby learns strategies other than crying to get its needs met, the developing moral being learns more complex behaviors when older, more elementary strategies no longer work.

The two most cited experts in the field of moral development did their work decades and continents apart yet came to remarkably similar conclusions. Jean Piaget conducted his research in Switzerland in the 1930s by watching little boys play marbles, and Lawrence Kohlberg studied Harvard students in the 1960s. They are often called "stage theorists" for their work in identifying and describing the stages of moral development.

THE WORK OF PIAGET

Piaget watched as boys between the ages of 3 and 12 played marbles, and he later tested his assumptions about their playground behavior in interviews. The box on the next page presents the basics of Piaget's theory.

The children under ages 5 to 7 didn't really play a game at all. They made up their own rules, varied them by playmate and game and delighted in exploring the marbles as tactile objects. Their view of the game was centered exclusively on what each child wanted.

The younger boys (ages 7 and 8) did follow the rules and played as if violations of the rules would result in punishment. The boys believed the rules were timeless, handed down from some "other," and that "goodness" came from respecting the rules. Boys in this stage of moral development believed "Right is to obey the will of the adult. Wrong is to have a will of one's own" (Piaget 1965, 193).

Children progressed to the next stage of moral development about age 11 when the boys began to develop notions of autonomy. They began to understand the reasoning behind the rules (i.e., fair play and reciprocity) that were the foundation of the rules themselves. Children in this stage of moral development understood that the rules received their power from the group, not some outside authority.

These children had internalized the rules and the reasons behind them. Understanding the rules allowed the boys to rationally justify violating them. For example, children in this stage of moral development allowed much younger children to place their thumbs inside the marble circles, a clear violation of the rules. But the younger boys' hands were smaller and weaker, and by allowing them a positional advantage, the older ones had—in contemporary language—leveled the playing field. They had ensured fairness when following the rules literally would have made it impossible.

Although Piaget worked with children, it is possible to see that adults often demonstrate these stages of moral development.

Take the videographer whose primary motivation is to obtain a great shot, regardless of the views of those he works with or his story subjects. This journalist

Piaget's Stages of Moral Development

EARLY DEVELOPMENT (before age 2)

- Interest in marbles is purely motor (e.g., put the marbles in your mouth).

FIRST STAGE—egocentrism (years 3–7)

- Children engage in "parallel play"; there is no coherent set of rules accepted by all.
- The moral reasoning is "I do it because it feels right."

SECOND STAGE—heteronomy (years 7–8)

- Children recognize only individual responsibility; obedience is enforced through punishment.
- Each player tries to win.
- Rules are regarded as inviolate, unbreakable and handed down from outside authority figures, usually older children.

- The children do not understand the reason behind the rules.

THIRD STAGE—autonomy (begins about age 11)

- Children internalize the rules; they understand the reasons behind them.
- They develop an ideal of justice and are able to distinguish between individual and collective responsibility.
- They ensure fair play among children.
- Children can change the rules in responses to a larger set of obligations.
- Authority is internal.
- Children understand universal ethical principles that transcend specific times and situations.

operates within an egocentric moral framework that places the primary emphasis on what "I" think, "my" judgment, and what's good for "me."

Beginning journalists, the ones who find themselves concerned with the literal following of codes of ethics, may be equated with the heteronomy stage of development. This journalist knows the rules and follows them. She would never accept a freebie or consider running the name of a rape victim. It's against organizational policy, and heteronymous individuals are motivated largely by such outside influences.

Just as the boys at the third stage of moral development were more willing to alter the rules to ensure a fair game for all, journalists at the final stage of moral development are more willing to violate professional norms if it results in better journalism. The journalist at this stage of moral development has so internalized and universalized the rules of ethical professional behavior that he or she can violate some of them for sound ethical reasons.

However, people seldom remain exclusively in a single stage of moral development. New situations often cause people to regress temporarily to a previous stage of moral development until enough learning can take place so that the new situation is well understood. Perhaps the immediacy of the Internet or the power of social networking sites caused such a regression in some at first. But in any case, such regression would not include behaviors that would be considered morally culpable under most circumstances, for example, lying or killing, even despite the new context.

THE WORK OF KOHLBERG

Harvard psychologist Lawrence Kohlberg mapped six stages of moral development in his college-student subjects. The accompanying box outlines Kohlberg's stages of moral development, divided into three levels.

Kohlberg developed a lengthy set of interview questions to allow him to establish which stage of moral development individual students had achieved. He asserted that only a handful of people—for example, Socrates, Gandhi, Martin Luther King or Mother Teresa—ever achieved the sixth stage of moral development. Most adults, he believed, spend the greater portion of their lives in the two conventional stages where they are motivated by society's expectations.

Doing right, fulfilling one's duties and abiding by the social contract are the pillars upon which the stages of Kohlberg's work rest. Under Kohlberg's arrangement, justice—and therefore morality—is a function of perception; as you develop, more activities fall under the realm of duty than before. For instance, reciprocity is not even a concept for individuals in the earliest stage, yet it is an essential characteristic of people in upper stages of moral development. Conversely, acting to avoid punishment is laudable for someone who is young, yet might not be praiseworthy for someone who is older. The further up Kohlberg's stages students progressed, the more they asserted that moral principles are subject to interpretation by individuals and subject to contextual factors.

Kohlberg's stages are descriptive and not predictive. They do not anticipate how any one individual will develop but suggest how most will develop. Kohlberg's formulation has much to recommend it to journalists, concerned as they are with concepts such as free speech, the professional duty to tell the truth and their obligations to the public and the public trust. However, Kohlberg's work was not without its problems. At least two aspects of his research troubled other moral development theorists.

Many scholars have argued that any general theory of moral development should allow people who are not saints or religious leaders to attain the highest stages of moral development. While perhaps only saints can be expected to act saintly most of the time, history is replete with examples of ordinary people taking extraordinary personal or professional risk for some larger ethical principles. Some felt that Kohlberg's conception—unlike Piaget's—was too restrictive.

Still more troubling was that in repeated studies, men consistently scored higher than women on stages of moral development. This gender bias in Kohlberg's work prompted discussion about a different concept of moral development founded on notions of community rather than in the rights-based tradition. It is called the ethics of care.

The Six Moral Stages of Kohlberg

LEVEL 1: PRECONVENTIONAL

Stage 1: Heteronymous morality is the display of simple obedience.

Stage 2: Individualism is the emergence of self-interest. Rules are followed only when they are deemed to be in one's self-interest and others are allowed the same freedom. Reciprocity and fairness begin to emerge, but only in a pragmatic way.

LEVEL 2: CONVENTIONAL

Stage 3: Interpersonal conformity is living up to what others expect, given one's role (e.g., "brother," "daughter," "neighbor," etc.). "Being good" is important and treating others as you would have them treat you becomes the norm.

Stage 4: Social systems is the recognition that one must fulfill the duties to which one has agreed. Doing one's duty, respect for authority and maintaining the social order are all goals in this level. Laws are to be upheld unilaterally except in extreme cases where they conflict with other fixed social duties.

LEVEL 3: POSTCONVENTIONAL

Stage 5: Social contract and individual rights is becoming aware that one is obligated by whatever laws are agreed to by due process. The social contract demands that we uphold the laws even if they are contrary to our best interests because they exist to provide the greatest good for the greatest number. However, some values such as life and liberty stand above any majority opinion.

Stage 6: Universal ethical principles self-selected by each individual guide this person. These principles are to be followed even if laws violate those principles. The principles that guide this individual include the equality of human rights and respect for the dignity of humans as individual beings regardless of race, age, socioeconomic status or even contribution to society.

PARALLEL ASSUMPTIONS ABOUT MORAL DEVELOPMENT: THE ETHICS OF CARE

The psychologists who developed the ethics of care disagree with at least two of the fundamental assumptions underlying Piaget and Kohlberg. First, they say, moral development does not always occur in a series of universal, unvarying and hierarchical stages. Second, moral growth emerges through understanding the concept of community, not merely through conflict. The rights-based scholars believe that moral development emerges from a proper understanding of the concept "I." Proponents of the ethics of care say that moral development arises from understanding the concept of "we."

Carol Gilligan (1982) provides the clearest explanation of the ethics of care. Gilligan studied women deciding whether to have abortions. As she listened, she learned that they based their ethical choices on relationships. The first thing these women considered was how to maintain a connection. Gilligan argued that the moral adult is the person who sees a connection between the "I" and the "other." The women spoke in a "different voice" about their ethical decision making.

For example, Gilligan presented the women with Kohlberg's classic ethical dilemma: the case of the desperate man and the greedy pharmacist. In this scenario, a man with a terminally ill spouse doesn't have enough money to purchase an expensive and lifesaving drug. When he explains the situation to the pharmacist, the pharmacist refuses to give him the medication.

Under Kohlberg's system, it would be ethically allowable for a man at the highest stages of moral development to develop a rationale for stealing the drug, an act of civil disobedience for a greater good. However, women made this particular choice less often. Instead, they reasoned that the most ethical thing to do was to build a relationship with the pharmacist, to form a community in which the pharmacist viewed himself or herself as an active part. In that situation, the women reasoned, the pharmacist ultimately would give the man the drug in order to maintain the connection.

Gilligan proposed that the women's rationale was no more or less ethically sophisticated than that expected under Kohlberg's outline. However, it was different, for it weighed different ethical values. Whether those values emerged as the result of how women are socialized in Western culture (an assertion that has often been made about Gilligan's work) or whether they merely reflected a different kind of thinking still remains open to debate. For our purposes, the origin of the distinction— and whether it is truly gender-linked—is not as important as the content.

Gilligan's notion of moral development is not neatly tied into stages. Her closest theoretical counterpart is probably the theory of communitarianism (see Chapter 1 for a description) with its emphasis on connection to community and its mandate for social justice.

If you were to carve stages from Gilligan's work, they would resemble:

- **First**—an ethic of care where the moral responsibility is for care of others before self.
- **Second**—an acknowledgment of the ethic of rights, including the rights of self to be considered in ethical decision making.
- **Third**—a movement from concerns about goodness (women are taught to believe that care for others is "good" while men are taught that "taking care of oneself" is good) to concerns about truth.

A complete sense of moral development, Gilligan observed, requires the ability "to [use] two different moral languages, the language of rights that protects separations and the language of responsibilities that sustains connection" (Gilligan 1982, 210).

Contemporary journalists have struggled with the issues of connection. Since much of our profession is based on an understanding of rights as outlined in various legal documents, ethical reasoning for journalists almost always assumes a rights-based approach. (You probably took this ethics course along with or immediately after a media law course, for example.) This historical rights-based bias, however, has led journalists into some of their more profound errors, including arrogance toward sources and readers and an unwillingness to be genuinely accountable to anyone.

If journalism as a profession is to mature ethically (or even survive economically), it must see itself as the vehicle to help people become the citizens they can be and to help reconnect and sustain communities that have become increasingly fragmented.

In 1992, deadly riots rocked the streets of Los Angeles in the wake of a police brutality trial (look up "Rodney King" for information on this historic event). In a *Newsweek* essay the next week entitled "Whose Values?", Joe Klein wrote:

> Television brought the nation together in the '50s; there were evenings when all of America seemed glued to the same show—Milton Berle, "I Love Lucy" and yes, "Ozzie and Harriet." But cable television has quite the opposite effect, dividing the audience into demographic slivers. . . . Indeed, if you are a member of any identifiable subgroup—black, Korean, fundamentalist, sports fan, political junkie—it's now possible to be messaged by your very own television and radio stations and to read your own magazines without having to venture out into the American mainstream. The choices are exhilarating, but also alienating. The basic principle is centrifugal: market segmentation targets those qualities that distinguish people from each other rather than emphasizing the things we have in common. It is the developed world's equivalent of the retribalization taking place in Eastern Europe, Africa and Asia. (Klein 1992, 21–22)

In the late 1990s, a movement called "civic journalism" mushroomed as an attempt to return journalism to what touched the everyday lives of people. Despite having a fatal flaw in the lack of a central definition for what constituted "civic journalism," its advocates did have a noble goal of bringing people back together and fostering a sense of community using the media as a primary tool in the process. To that end, the movement was a laudable one and is missed today.

DEVELOPING AS AN ETHICAL PROFESSIONAL

In the 1970s, James Rest, a psychology professor at the University of Minnesota, took Kohlberg's schema of moral development and used it to create a paper-and-pencil test to measure moral development among various professions. In the ensuing years, the test, called the Defining Issues Test (DIT), has been administered to more than 40,000 professionals, among them doctors, nurses, dentists, accountants, philosophers and theologians, members of the U.S. Coast Guard, surgeons, veterinarians, graduate students, junior high students, prison inmates and others. Those taking the test read four to six scenarios and are then asked to make a decision about what the protagonist should do, and then to rate the factors that influenced that decision. Because the test is based on Kohlberg's work, test takers who rely on universal principles and who consider issues of justice score well. Most people who take the DIT score in the range of what Kohlberg would have called conventional moral reasoning—stages 3 and 4 of his scale.

Wilkins and Coleman (2005) asked journalists to take the DIT and compared journalists' scores to those of other professionals. Journalists do well on the DIT, scoring below only three other professions: philosophers/theologians, medical students and practicing physicians. Because the single biggest predictor of a good score on the DIT is education, and journalists as a group have less formal education than the three professions with scores "above" them, the findings are significant. Other professions, for example orthopedic surgeons, scored lower than journalists on the test. In a follow-up study (Coleman and Wilkins 2006), public relations professionals also did well on the DIT.

The scenarios on the DIT are not directed at any particular profession but rather determine how people think about "average" moral questions. When journalists are presented with scenarios that deal directly with journalism, for example, problems involving the use of hidden cameras or whether to run troubling photographs of children, they score even better. In these tests, journalists often score in the fourth and fifth stage of Kohlberg's moral development schema. In an interesting side note, scholars found that having a visual image, such as a photograph, of some of the stakeholders in an ethical dilemma elevates ethical reasoning.

Other scholars have studied journalists' ethical decision making. Investigative reporters make moral judgments about the subjects of their stories, even though when they talk about their work they are reluctant to drop their professional objectivity (Ettema and Glasser 1998). Another study found that journalists who have been sued for invasion of privacy don't often think about the ethical issues their reporting creates (Voakes 1998). This leads to an indirect but plausible conclusion that solid ethical thinking may keep journalists out of court.

Finally, research shows that journalists do agree on what constitutes "good work" in their profession—an emphasis on truth telling, taking a role as government watchdog, investigative reporting and treating the subjects with dignity. However, journalists believe that the single biggest threat to continuing professional excellence is the increasing pressure to make a profit. Journalists are out of joint with a mission that includes the competing interests of public service and profit making (Gardner et al. 2001). How that tension is resolved is the essential question facing news operations today.

WHERE DO YOU GO FROM HERE?

Perry (1970) postulates that one of the major accomplishments of college students is to progress from a simple, dualistic (right versus wrong) view of life to a more complex, mature and relativistic view. Perry states that students must not only acknowledge that diversity and uncertainty exist in a world of relativism but also make a commitment to their choices (i.e., career, values, beliefs, etc.) out of the multiplicity of "right" choices available.

Unlike physical development, moral development is not subject to the quirks of heredity. Each individual is free to develop as keen a sense of equity as any other individual, yet not all reach their full potential. Kohlberg (1973) claims we understand messages one stage higher than our own. Through "aspirational listening"—picking a role model on a higher level—you can progress to a higher stage of moral development. This observation is not new. In fact, Aristotle suggested that virtues could be learned by observing those who possess them.

This book uses the case study method. Often in case studies, it is the reasoning behind the answer rather than the answer itself that is the best determiner of moral growth (Clouse 1985). *An important part of moral development is the recognition that motive, not consequence, is the critical factor in deciding whether an act is ethical.*

Elliott (1991) illustrates the difference in the following scenario. Imagine a situation where you are able to interview and choose your next-door neighbor. When you ask Jones how she feels about murder, she replies she doesn't kill because if she got caught she would go to jail. When you interview Smith, he says he doesn't kill people because he believes in the sanctity of life. It takes little reflection to decide which neighbor you would prefer. Elliott concludes: "Ethics involves the judging of actions as right or wrong, but motivations count as well. Some reasons for actions seem better or worse than others" (1991, 19).

To the above quote we might add: "and some justifications are more deeply rooted in centuries of ethical thought than others." The goal of this book—and probably one of the goals your professor had for this class—is to ensure that your choices are not merely "right," as that's a debate for the ages, but to ensure that your choices are grounded in the ethical theories that have stood the test of time and are not subject to the vagaries of current popular thought. The work of Kohlberg and Piaget suggests that your journey is not finished, but that you *have* started. And with the set of tools you have now acquired, you have an excellent chance of reaching your destination.

Suggested Readings

BELENKY, MARY F., et al. 1988. *Women's ways of knowing: The development of self, voice and mind.* New York: Basic Books.

COLES, ROBERT. 1986. *The moral life of children.* New York: Atlantic Monthly Press.

ETTEMA, JAMES, and THEODORE GLASSER. 1998. *Custodians of conscience: Investigative journalists and public virtue.* New York: Columbia University Press.

GARDNER, H., MIHALY CSIKSZENTHMIHALYI, and WILLIAM DAMON. 2001. *Good work: When excellence and ethics meet.* New York: Basic Books.

GILLIGAN, CAROL. 1982. *In a different voice: Psychological theory and women's development.* Cambridge, MA: Harvard University Press.

LEVINSON, DANIEL J. 1978. *Seasons of a man's life.* New York: Alfred A. Knopf, Inc.

WILKINS, LEE, and RENITA COLEMAN. 2005. *The moral media.* Mahwah, NJ: Lawrence Erlbaum Associates.

Bibliography

Albini, S. (1993). The problem with music. The Baffler, vol 5. Retrieved November 14, 2008, from Negativland Web site: **http://www.negativland.com/albini.html.**

Alderman, E. and Kennedy, C. (1995). *The right to privacy.* New York: Alfred A. Knopf, Inc.

Allossery, P. (2000, January 21). Benetton sparks controversy again: Series of magazine ads attack death penalty. *Financial Post,* p. C3.

Anderson, C. (2006). *The long tail: How the future of business is selling less of more.* NewYork: Hyperion.

Ansen, D. (2006, October 23). "Inside the hero factory." *Newsweek,* pp. 70–71.

APME. (2009). *The Associated Press Statement of News Values and Principles.* Retrieved September 10, 2009, from **http://www.apme.com/news/news_values_statement.shtml.**

Arendt, H. (1970). *The human condition.* Chicago: University of Chicago Press.

Aristotle. *The Nicomachean ethics.* Book II 4–5 (1973). Trans. by H. Rackham. Ed. by H. Jeffrey. Cambridge, MA: Harvard University Press.

Associated Press. (2009). *Associated Press to build news registry to protect content.* Retrieved September 10, 2009, from **http://www.ap.org/pages/about/pressreleases/ pr_072309a.html.**

Auletta, K. (1991). *Three blind mice: How the TV networks lost their way.* New York: Random House.

Axelrod, R. (1984). *The evolution of cooperation.* New York: Basic Books.

Bagdikian, B. H. (1990). *The media monopoly.* (3rd ed.). Boston: Beacon Press.

Baker, S. and Martinson, D. (2001). "The TARES test: Five principles of ethical persuasion." *Journal of Mass Media Ethics, 16*(2 & 3), pp. 148–175.

Belenky, M., et al. (1988). *Women's ways of knowing: The development of self, voice and mind.* New York: Basic Books.

Bennett, L. (1988). *News: The politics of illusion.* Longman: New York.

Benoit, W. (1999). *Seeing spots: A functional analysis of Presidential television advertisements.* Westport, CT: Praeger.

Berger, A. (1989). *Seeing is believing.* Mountain View, CA: Mayfield Publishing Co.

Berger, J. (1980). *About looking.* New York: Pantheon Books.

Bianco, R. (2003, November 5). "Cowardly CBS unfair to viewers, not Reagans." *USA Today,* p. D1.

Bok, S. (1978). *Lying: Moral choice in public and private life.* New York: Random House.

_____. (1983). *Secrets: On the ethics of concealment and revelation.* New York: Vintage.

Booth, C. (1999, November 15). "Worst of times." *Time,* pp. 79–80.

Borden, S. (2009). *Journalism as practice: MacIntyre, virtue ethics and the press.* Burlington, VT: Ashgate Publishing.

Boulware, J. (2006, October 15). "Everybody's watching." *American Way,* pp. 98–104.

Bovée, W. (1991). "The end can justify the means—but rarely." *Journal of Mass Media Ethics, 6,* pp. 135–145.

Brady, J. (2006, February 12). "Blog rage." *Washington Post,* p. B1.

Braxton, G. (2007, August 24). "Right words to inspire reading?" *The Los Angeles Times.* Retrieved from **http://www.latimes.com.**

Brooks, D. E. (1992). "In their own words: Advertisers and the origins of the African-American consumer market." (A paper submitted to the Association for Education in Journalism and Mass Communications), Montreal, Canada, August 5–8.

Bryant, G. (1987, Spring–Summer). "Ten-fifty P.I.: Emotion and the photographer's role." *Journal of Mass Media Ethics,* pp. 32–39.

Buckner, J. (2000, January 30). "Horrific photo forces us to face a painful past." *Charlotte Observer,* p. 3C.

Bugeja, M. (2005). *Interpersonal divide: The search for community in a technological age.* Oxford: Oxford University Press.

Calvert, C. (2000). *Voyeur nation: Media, privacy and peering in modern culture.* Boulder, CO: Westview Press.

Carey, J. W. (1989, Autumn). "Review of Charles J. Sykes' Profscam." *Journalism Educator,* p. 48.

Carr, D. (2008, October 20). "Jim Cramer retreats along with the Dow." *New York Times.*

Cassier, E. (1944). *An essay on man.* New Haven, CT: Yale University Press.

Chaffee, P. (2006). "How the *Times* sells genocide." **www.pulitzer.org.**

Chandrasekaran, R. (2006). "Comments resuming in *Post*.blog." *Washington Post.* Retrieved February 17, from **http://www.Poynter.org.**

Chester, G. (1949). "The press–radio war: 1933–1935," *Public Opinion Quarterly,* pp. 252–264.

Chow, Sher-Min (2005, March 22). *Rodeo Houston rope in records.* Retrieved from **http://www.khou.com/news/rodeo/stories.**

Christians, C. (1986). "Reporting and the oppressed." In D. Elliott (ed.). *Responsible journalism* (pp. 109–130). Newbury Park, CA: Sage Publications, Inc.

Christians, C. G. (2010). "The ethics of privacy." In Christopher Meyers (ed.), *Journalism ethics: A philosophical approach* (pp. 203–214). Oxford: Oxford University Press.

Christians, C. G., Ferré, J. P., and Fackler, M. (1993). *Good news: Social ethics and the press.* New York: Longman.

Christians, C., Glasser, T., McQuail, D., and Nordenstreng, K. (2009). *Normative theories of the media: Journalism in democratic societies.* Champagne, IL: University of Illinois Press.

Christians, C., Rotzoll, K., and Fackler, M. (1987). *Media ethics: Cases and moral reasoning.* (2nd ed.). New York: Longman.

Christians, C., Rotzoll, K., Fackler, M., McKee, K., and Woods, R., (2005). *Media ethics: Cases and moral reasoning.* Boston: Pearson Education, Inc.

Clegg, A. (2005). "Dove gets real." **www.brandchannel.com.**

Clouse, B. (1985). *Moral development.* Grand Rapids, MI: Baker Book House.

CNN Transcripts. Retrieved October 27, 2006, from **http://transcripts.cnn.com.**

Coleman, A. D. (1987, Spring/Summer). "Private lives, public places: Street photography ethics." *Journal of Mass Media Ethics,* pp. 60–66.

Coleman, R. and Wilkins, L. (2006, August). *The moral development of public relations practitioners.* Presented at AEJMC, San Francisco, CA.

Coles, R. (1986). *The moral life of children.* New York: Atlantic Monthly Press.

Collins, S. (2008, October 8). "CNBC banking on Jim Cramer." *Los Angeles Times.*

Costello, A. (2004). "Chad/Sudan: A question of genocide." From PBS "Frontline." **www .pbs.org.**

Cramer, J. (2008, October 8). Today Show.

Cramer, J. (2008, May 11). Mad Money.

Cramer, J. (2008, March 17). Street Signs.

Cramer, J. (2008, September 29). Mad Money.

Cranberg, G., Bezanson, R., and Soloski, J. (2001). *Taking stock.* Ames, IA: Iowa State University Press.

Crouse, T. (1974). *The boys on the bus: Riding with the campaign press corps.* New York: Ballantine.

Cunningham, B. (2003, July/August). "Re-thinking objectivity." *Columbia Journalism Review,* pp. 24–32.

Davies, J. C. (1963). *Human nature in politics.* New York: John Wiley & Sons.

Deuze, M. (2008). "The changing nature of news work: Liquid journalism and monitorial citizenship." *International Journal of Communication, 2,* pp. 848–865.

Dewey, J. (2005/1932). *Art as experience.* New York: Penguin Putnam Inc.

Dionne, E. J. (1991). *Why Americans hate politics.* New York: Simon & Schuster.

_____. (1996). *They only look dead.* New York: Simon & Schuster.

Doyle, M. (2003, March 26). "Photos of POWs raise legal questions." *Star Tribune* (Minneapolis), p. 10A.

Dyck, A. (1977). *On human care.* Nashville: Abingdon.

Elliott, D. (1986). "Foundations for news media responsibility." In D. Elliott (ed.), *Responsible journalism* (pp. 32–34). Newbury Park, CA: Sage Publications, Inc.

_____. (1991, Autumn). "Moral development and the teaching of ethics." *Journalism Educator,* pp. 19–24.

Ellul, J. (1965). *Propaganda* (K. Kellen and J. Lerner, Trans.). New York: Alfred A. Knopf.

Etcoff, N., Orbach, S., Scott, J., and D'Agostino, H. (2004, September). "The real truth about beauty: A global report" Dove.

Ettema, J. and Glasser, T. (1998). *Custodians of conscience: Investigative journalists and public virtue.* New York: Columbia University Press.

Fallows, J. (1996). *Breaking the news: How the media undermine American democracy.* New York: Pantheon.

Fancher, M. (2004, April 18). "Powerful photograph offered chance to tell an important story." *Seattle Times,* p. A1.

Farhi, P. (2006, January 28). "Deluge shuts down *Post* blog." *Washington Post,* p. A8.

Farzad, R. (2005, October 31). "The mad man of wall street." *BusinessWeek.*

Feldstein, D. (2005a, February 27). "The big business of rodeo." *Houston Chronicle,* p. A1.

Feldstein, D. (2005b, April 10). "Is rodeo's spending justified?" *Houston Chronicle,* p. B1.

Feldstein, D. (2005, November 4). Personal communication with the author.

Fenwick, A. (2009, September 18). "ACORN's family tree: Was the Baltimore video journalism? Does it matter?" *Columbia Journalism Review.* Retrieved September 19, 2009, from **http://www.cjr.org.**

Festinger, L. (1957). *A theory of cognitive dissonance.* Stanford, CA: Stanford University Press.

Fischer, C. T. (1980). "Privacy and human development." In W. C. Bier (ed.), *Privacy: A vanishing value?* (pp. 37–46). New York: Fordham University Press.

Fitzpatrick, K. and Bronstein, C. (2006). *Ethics in public relations: Responsible advocacy.* Thousand Oaks, CA: Sage.

Fletcher, G. P. (1993). *Loyalty: An essay on the morality of relationships.* New York: Oxford University Press.

Fort Worth Star-Telegram unsigned column. (2003, March 26). "Painful images." *Fort Worth Star-Telegram,* Metro, p. 14.

Frazier, M. (2008, October 6). "Pressure is on to recycle water filters." *New York Times.* Retrieved November 13, 2008, from **http://www.nytimes.com**

Friedman, M. (1970, September 13). "The social responsibility of business is to increase its profits." *The New York Times Magazine,* p. 13.

Fry, D. (ed.). (1983). *The adversary press.* St. Petersburg, FL: The Modern Media Institute.

Fuss, P. (1965). *The moral philosophy of Josiah Royce.* Cambridge, MA: Harvard University Press.

Gans, H. (1979). *Deciding what's news: A study of CBS Evening News, NBC Nightly News, Newsweek and Time.* New York: Vintage.

Garber, M. (2009, August 3). "Dude, where's my link?: Ian Shapira, fair use and 'the death of journalism (Gawker Edition).'" *Columbia Journalism Review.* Retrieved from **http://www.cjr.org/behind_the_news/dude_wheres_my_link.php?page+all.**

Gardner, H., Csikszenthmihalyi, M., and Damon, W. (2001). *Good work: When excellence and ethics meet.* New York: Basic Books.

Genocide Watch (2004, February 24). "Today is the day of killing Anuaks." **www .genocidewatch.org.**

Gert, B. (1988). *Morality, a new justification of the moral rules.* New York: Oxford University Press.

Gilligan, C. (1982). *In a different voice: Psychological theory and women's development.* Cambridge, MA: Harvard University Press.

Godwin, M. (1998). *Defending free speech in the digital age.* New York: Times Books.

Goffman, E. (1959). *The presentation of self in everyday life.* New York: Anchor.

Gogoi, P. (2005, August 17). "From reality TV to reality ads." **www.businessweek.com.**

Gogoi, P. (2006, October 17). "Wal-Mart vs. the blogosphere." **www.businessweek.com.**

Gormley, D. W. (1984). "Compassion is a tough word." *Drawing the Line,* pp. 58–59. Washington, DC: American Society of Newspaper Editors.

Gough, P. (2006, March 28). " 'Mad' man adds insight to CNBC money news." *The Hollywood Reporter.*

Graham, B. and Weisman, J. (2003, March 24). "Display of 5 POWs draws firm rebuke." *Washington Post,* p. A1.

Grcic, J. M. (1986). "The right to privacy: Behavior as property." *Journal of Values Inquiry, 20,* pp. 137–144.

Grunig, L., Toth, E., and Hon, L. (2000). "Feminist values in public relations." *Journal of Public Relations Research, 12*(1), pp. 49–68.

Gunther, M. (2006, October 18). "Corporate blogging: Wal-Mart fumbles." Retrieved from **www.cnnmoney.com.**

Gurevitch, M., Levy, M., and Roeh, I. (1991). "The global newsroom: Convergences and diversities in the globalization of television news." In P. Dalhgren and C. Sparks (eds.), *Communication and citizenship.* London. Routledge.

Gutwirth, S. (2002). *Privacy and the information age.* Lanham, MD: Rowman & Littlefield Publishers, Inc.

Hadley, C. (2006). Personal interview with case study author.

Haiman, F. (1958). "Democratic ethics and the hidden persuaders." *Quarterly Journal of Speech, 44,* pp. 385–392.

Halberstam, D. (2001). *War in a time of peace.* New York: Scribner.

Halbert, D. J. (1999). *Intellectual property in the information age.* Westport, CT: Quorum Books.

Hamilton, A. (2003, March 25). "5 GIs held in Iraq, shown on Arab TV." *The Dallas Morning News,* p. 1A.

Hammargren, R. (1936). "The origin of the press-radio conflict," *Journalism Quarterly, 13,* pp. 91–93.

Hanson, K. (1986). "The demands of loyalty." *Idealistic Studies, 16,* pp. 195–204.

Harris, T, (Producer). (2007, September 1). *CNN Newsroom.* Atlanta: Cable News Network.

Hart, A. (2003, July/August). "Delusions of accuracy." *Columbia Journalism Review,* p. 20.

Hemmel, P. (2006, June 11). Personal interview with author.

Hendrickson, E. and Wilkins, L. (2009). "The wages of synergy." *Journalism Practice, 3*(2), pp. 3–21.

Hesmondhalgh, D. (1999). Indie: The institutional politics and aesthetics of a popular music genre. *Cultural Studies, 13*(1), pp. 34–61.

Hess, S. (1981). *The Washington reporters.* Washington, DC: The Brookings Institution.

Hickey, N. (2001, November–December). "The cost of not publishing." *Columbia Journalism Review.*

Hickey, N. (2003, July/August). "FCC: Ready, set, consolidate." *Columbia Journalism Review,* p. 5.

Hixson, R. F. (1987). *Privacy in a public society.* New York: Oxford University Press.

Hobbes, T. (1958). *The Leviathan* (Reprints from 1651). New York: Bobbs-Merrill.

Hodges, L. W. (1983). "The journalist and privacy." *Social Responsibility: Journalism, Law, Medicine, 9,* pp. 5–19.

———. (1986). "Defining press responsibility: A functional approach." In D. Elliott (ed.), *Responsible journalism,* (pp. 13–31). Newbury Park, CA: Sage Publications, Inc.

Hollifield, C. A. and Becker, L. B. (2009). *Clash of cultures: The effects of hypercompetition on journalistic ethics and professional value.* Presented to the International Conference on the Basics of Journalism, Eichstatt, Germany.

Horn, B. (2004, January 10). "Any more questions?" *Dallas Morning News,* p. C-2.

Hortsch, D. (2003, March 30). "Photos of dead and POWs raise thorny questions." *The Oregonian,* p. C1.

House, D. (2003, March 30). "Worth a thousand words." *Fort Worth Star-Telegram Weekly Review,* p. 3.

Houston Livestock Show and Rodeo (2005). *Economic impact.* Retrieved from **http://www.hlsr.com.**

Houston Livestock Show and Rodeo (2005). *Frequently asked questions: Houston Livestock Show and Rodeo scholarships.* Retrieved from **http://www.hlsr.com.**

Houston Livestock Show and Rodeo (2005). *HLSR homepage.* Retrieved from **http://www.hlsr.com.**

Houston Livestock Show and Rodeo (2005). *Ticket availability.* Retrieved from **http://www.hlsr.com.**

Jackson, J. L. (2007, August 23). "PUSH speaks out after release of rap video 'Read a Book.'" Retrieved April 14, 2009, from **http://www.rainbowpush.org.**

Jamieson, Kathleen Hall (1983). *The interplay of influence: Mass media and their publics in news, advertising, politics.* Belmont, CA: Wadsworth Publishing.

Jamieson, K. H. (1992). *Dirty politics.* New York: Oxford University Press.

_____. (2000). *Everything you think you know about politics . . . and why you're wrong.* New York: Basic Books.

Jensen, J. (2002). *Is art good for us?* Lanham, MD: Rowman & Littlefield, Publishers.

Journal of Mass Media Ethics. (1987, Spring–Summer). Special issue on photojournalism.

Kaid, L. L. (1992). "Ethical dimensions of political advertising." In R. E. Denton (ed.), *Ethical dimensions of political communication* (pp. 145–169). New York: Praeger.

Kenworthy, T., Willing, R., and Cauchon, D. (2003, March 28). "TV coverage takes toll on families of POWs." *USA Today,* p. 9A.

Kim, G. and Paddon A. (1999, September). "Digital manipulation as new form of evidence of actual malice in libel and false light cases." *Communications and the Law, 21,* p. 3.

Klein, J. (1992, June 8). "Whose values?" *Newsweek,* pp. 19–22.

Koehn, D. (1998). *Rethinking feminist ethics.* New York: Routledge.

Kohlberg, L. (1973). "The contribution of developmental psychology to education." *Educational Psychologist, 10,* pp. 2–14.

Kovach, B. and Rosenstiel, T. (2007). *The elements of journalism: What newspeople should know and the public should expect.* New York: Three Rivers Press.

Kozloff, R. (2005). Interview by case study author.

Kristof, N. (2005, November 22). "Sudan's department of gang rape." *New York Times,* p. 23.

Kristof, N. (2006, March 7). "Where killers roam, the poison spreads." *New York Times,* p. 19.

Lacy, S. (1989, Spring). "A model of demand for news: Impact of competition on newspaper content." *Journalism Quarterly,* pp. 40–48, 128.

Lebacqz, K. (1985). *Professional ethics: Power and paradox.* Nashville: Abingdon Press.

Ledford, J. (2005). Interview by case study author.

Lee, S. T. (2005). "Predicting tolerance of journalistic deception." *Journal of Mass Media Ethics* 20(1), pp. 22–42.

Leiss, W., Kline, S., and Jhally, S. (1986). *Social communication in advertising: Person, products and images of well being.* New York: Methuen Publications.

Lester, P. (1991). *Photojournalism: An ethical approach.* Hillsdale, NJ: Lawrence Erlbaum Associates.

_____. (1992). *Photojournalism: An ethical approach.* Hillsdale, NJ: Lawrence Erlbaum and Associates.

_____. (1996). *Images that injure.* Westport, CT: Greenwood Press.

_____. (2003). *Images that injure.* Westport, CT: Greenwood Press.

Levinson, D. J. (1978). *Seasons of a man's life.* New York: Alfred A. Knopf, Inc.

Linsky, M. (1986). *Impact: How the press affects federal policymaking.* New York: W. W. Norton.

Lippmann, W. (1922). *Public opinion.* New York: Free Press.

_____. (1982). *The essential Lippmann.* Cambridge, MA: Harvard University Press.

Los Angeles Daily News. (2005, November 8). "If only real debates were this exciting," **www.dailynews.com**

Lowery, S. and DeFleur, M. (1988). *Milestones in mass communication research* (2nd ed.). New York: Longman.

Lubrano, G. (2003, March 31). "Images of POWs—and questions." *San Diego Union-Tribune,* p. B1.

Madison, J., Hamilton, A., and Jay, J. *The Federalist papers.*

Mad Money Disclaimer. (2008). CNBC. Retrieved from CNBC: **http://www.cnbc.com/id/17362458/.**

Manly, L. (2005, October 3). "U.S. network TV shows turn props into dollars." *International Herald Tribune,* pp. A14, 16.

Martin, E. (1991). "On photographic manipulation." *Journal of Mass Media Ethics, 6,* pp. 156–163.

Martin, M. (2007, September 17). "Man behind BET's 'Read a Book' responds to critics." *Tell Me More @ NPR News.* Interview streamed from **http://www.npr.org.**

Marx, G. T. (1999). "What's in a name." *The Information Society, 15*(2), pp. 99–112.

Marx, G. (2009, September 18). "Seeds of discontent: What does the ACORN story mean for the mainstream media?" *Columbia Journalism Review.* Retreived September 19, 2009, from **http://www.cjr.org.**

Matsuda, M. (1989). "Public response to racist speech: Considering the victim's story." *Michigan Law Review, 87,* pp. 2321–2381.

May, William F. (2001). *Beleaguered rulers: The public obligation of the professional.* Westminster: John Knox Press.

McChesney, R. (1991). *Rich media, poor democracy: Communication politics in dubious times.* Champaign-Urbana: University of Illinois Press.

_____. (1997). *Corporate media and the threat to democracy.* New York: Seven Stories Press.

McCluskey, C. (2009, August 29–30). "At best plagiarism, at worst outright theft: *Courant* covers towns with other papers' reporting." *Journal Inquirer.*

Medved, Michael. (1992). *Hollywood vs. America.* New York: HarperCollins Publishers.

Merrill, J. C. (1974). *The imperative of freedom: A philosophy of journalistic autonomy.* New York: Hastings House.

Meyers, C. (2003). "Appreciating W.D. Ross: On duties and consequences." *Journal of Mass Media Ethics, 18*(2), pp. 81–97.

Mill, J. S. (1859). *On liberty.*

Mills, C. W. (1956). *The power elite.* New York: Oxford University Press.

Mills, K. (1989, Winter). "When women talk to women." *Media and Values,* p. 12.

Molotch, H. and Lester, M. (1974). "News as purposive behavior: On the strategic use of routine events, accidents and scandals." *American Sociological Review, 39,* pp. 101–112.

Montgomery, K. C. (1989). *Target: Prime time. Advocacy groups and the struggle over entertainment television.* New York: Oxford University Press.

Moore, G. F. (1903). *Principia ethica.*

Moyers, B. (1988). Quoted in "The promise of television," episode 10. Produced by PBS.

Mundow, A, (2000, January). "Ad men walking—Benetton is facing its biggest advertising backlash yet, with a new campaign about Death Row." *The Irish Times,* p. 61.

National Association of Broadcasters. (1985). *Radio: In search of excellence.* Washington, DC: NAB.

Negroponte, N. (1995). *Being digital.* New York: Alfred A. Knopf.

Nelkin, D. (1987). *Selling science: How the press covers science and technology.* New York: W. H. Freeman.

Neuffer, E. (2003, March 24). "Airing of POW footage blasted." *The Boston Globe,* p. A19.

Neville, R. C. (1980). "Various meanings of privacy: A philosophical analysis." In W. C. Bier (ed.), *Privacy: A vanishing value?* (pp. 26–36). New York: Fordham University Press.

Newsom, D., Turk, J. V., and Kruckeberg, D. (1996). *This is PR: The realities of public relations.* Belmont, CA: Wadsworth.

Newton, Julianne (2000). *The burden of visual truth: The role of photojournalism in mediating reality.* Hillsdale, NJ: Lawrence Erlbaum Associates.

Niles, R. (2009). "What are the ethics of online journalism?" *Online Journalism Review.* Retrieved September 10, 2009, from **http://www.ojr.org.**

O'Toole, J. (1985). *The trouble with advertising.* New York: Times Books.

Oldenquist, A. (1982). "Loyalties." *Journal of Philosophy, 79,* pp. 73–93.

Orwell, G. (1949). *1984.* San Diego: Harcourt, Brace, Jovanovich.

Pasternak, J. (2003, March 24). "Treatment of POWs is said to violate treaty." *Los Angeles Times,* p. 4.

Patterson, P. (1989). "Reporting Chernobyl: Cutting the government fog to cover the nuclear cloud." In L. M. Walters, L. Wilkins and T. Walters (eds.), *Bad Tidings: Communication and Catastrophe.* Mahway, NJ: Lawrence Erlbaum Associates.

Perry, W. (1970). *Forms of ethical and intellectual development in the college years.* New York: Holt, Reinhart & Winston.

Pfanner, E. (2005, October 3). "Product placements cause a stir in Europe." *International Herald Tribune,* pp. A14–15.

Piaget, J. (1965). *The moral judgment of the child.* Translated by Marjorie Gabain. New York: Free Press.

Picard, R. (1988). *The ravens of Odin: The press in the nordic nations.* Ames, IA: Iowa State University Press.

Plaisance, P. L. (2002). "The journalist as moral witness: Michael Ignatieff's pluralistic philosophy for a global media culture." *Journalism: Theory, Practice & Criticism, 3*(2), pp. 205–222.

Plato. *The republic.*

Pojman, L. (1998). *Ethical theory: Classical and contemporary readings.* Belmont, CA: Wadsworth Publishing Co.

Postman, N. (1986). *Amusing ourselves to death: Public discourse in the age of television.* New York: Penguin Books.

Powell, T. F. (1967). *Josiah Royce.* New York: Washington Square Press, Inc.

Privacy Implications of Online Advertising Full Committee. (2008, July 9). Retrieved from **http://commerce.senate.gov/public/index.cfm?FuseAction=Hearings.Hearing& Hearing_ID=e46b0d9f-562e-41a6-b460-a714bf370171.**

Radin, M. J. (1982). "Property and personhood." *Stanford Law Review, 34*(5), pp. 957–1015.

Rainey, J. (2006, September 14). "Local leaders urge owner of the *Times* to avoid cuts." Retrieved from **www.latimes.com.**

Rainville, R. and McCormick, E. (1977). "Extent of racial prejudice in pro football announcers' speech." *Journalism Quarterly, 54,* pp. 20–26.

Rawls, J. (1971). *A theory of justice.* Cambridge, MA: Harvard University Press.

Reaves, S. (1987, Spring–Summer). "Digital retouching: Is there a place for it in newspaper photography?" *Journal of Mass Media Ethics,* pp. 40–48.

_____. (1991). Personal correspondence to the author quoted in digital alteration of photographs in consumer magazines. *Journal of Mass Media Ethics, 6,* pp. 175–181.

Reid, T. and Doran, J. (2003, March 24). "Mistreating prisoners is a war crime, says Bush." *The Times* (London), p. 2.

Ricchiardi, S. (2009). "Share and share alike; once considered unthinkable, content-sharing arrangements are proliferating rapidly, often uniting newspapers long seen as bitter rivals." *American Journalism Review. 31.1*(February–March), 28(8).

Rieder, R. (1999, November/December). "A costly rookie mistake." *American Journalism Review,* p. 6.

Robinson, M. and Sheehan, G. (1984). *Over the wire and on TV.* New York: Basic Books.

R0B0F1SH. *Read a Book (Dirty Version).* Comment posted.

Rosen, J. (2000). *The unwanted gaze: The destruction of privacy in America.* New York: Random House.

Rosenthal, A. M. (1989, October 10). "Trash TV's latest news show continues credibility erosion." Syndicated column by *New York Times* News Service.

Ross, W. D. (1930). *The right and the good.* Oxford, England: Clarendon Press.

_____. (1988). *The right and the good.* Hackett: Indianapolis, IN.

Royce, J. (1908). *The philosophy of loyalty.* New York: Macmillan.

Rush, G. and Molloy, J. (2003, May 16). "Cut and cover." *New York Daily News,* p. D1.

Russell, B. (ed.). (1967). *History of Western philosophy.* New York: Touchstone Books.

Sabato, L. J. (1992). *Feeding frenzy: How attack journalism has transformed American politics.* New York: Free Press.

Salmon, F. (2006, March 27). "Blood money." Retrieved from **www.democracynow.org.**

Sandel, M. J. (1982). *Liberalism and the limits of justice.* Cambridge, MA: Harvard University Press.

Schoeman, F. D., (ed.). (1984). *Philosophical dimensions of privacy: An anthology.* Cambridge, MA: Harvard University Press.

Schudson, M. (1978). *Discovering the news.* New York: Basic Books.

_____. (1984). *Advertising: The uneasy persuasion.* New York: Basic Books.

_____. (1995). *The power of news.* Cambridge, MA: Harvard University Press.

Schwartz, T. (1973). *The responsive chord.* Garden City, NY: Anchor Press.

Seabrook, J. (2003, July 7). "The money note." *New Yorker,* p. 46.

Seelye, K. (2006, October 5). "Publisher is fired at *Los Angeles Times.*" Retrieved from **www.nytimes.com.**

Shaw, D. (1999, December 20). "Journalism is a very different business—Here's why." *Los Angeles Times,* p. V3.

Smith, C. (1992). *Media and apocalypse.* Westport, CT: Greenwood Press.

Smolkin, Rachel (2005, April/May). "Reversing the slide." *American Journalism Review*

Society of Professional Journalists. (2009). *SPJ Code of Ethics.* Retrieved September 10, from **http://www.spj.org/ethicscode.asp.**

Sorkin, A. R. (2008, September 30). "What goes before a fall? On Wall Street, reassurance." *New York Times.*

Spencer, J. (2001, October 1). "Decoding bin Laden." *Newsweek.*

Stanard, A. (2006, October 12). "Facebook privacy charges raise student ire." Retrieved from **www.detnews.com.**

Sterngold, J. (2006, November 6). *San Francisco Chronicle.*

Stone, I. F. (1988). *The trial of Socrates.* Boston: Little, Brown and Co.

Story, L. and Stone, B. (2007, November 30). "Facebook users protest online tracking." *New York Times.*

Sub Pop Records (2008) The Sub Pop Story, Retrieved November 14, 2008, from Sub Pop Records Web site: **http://www.subpop.com/artists/sub_pop.**

Sunstein, C. (2001). *Republic.com.* New Haven: Princeton University Press.

Swanberg, W. A. (1972). *Luce and His Empire.* New York: Charles Scribner's Sons.

Szarkowski, J. (1978). *Mirrors and windows.* New York: Museum of Modern Art.

Thomas, B. (1990, January 19). "Finding truth in the age of 'infotainment.'" *Editorial Research Reports.* Washington, DC: Congressional Quarterly, Inc.

Thorson, E., Duffy, M., and Schumann, D. (2007). "The Internet waits for no one." In D. W. Schumann and E. Thorson (eds.), *Internet Advertising: Theory and Research* (pp. 3–14). New York: Routledge.

Tolstoy, L. N. (1960). *What is Art?* (Almyer Maude, Trans.). New York: MacMillan Publishing Company, p. 96.

Tomlinson, D. (1987). "One technological step forward and two legal steps back: Digitalization and television news pictures as evidence in libel." *Loyola Entertainment Law Journal, 9,* pp. 237–257.

Toronto Star unsigned column (2003, March 23). "A note to readers about photos." *Toronto Star.* p. A2.

Toulmin, S. (1988). "The recovery of practical philosophy." *The American Scholar,* Summer, p. 338.

Unilever Corporation (2005). Retrieved from **www.campaignforrealbeauty.com.**

Voakes, P. S. (1998). "What were you thinking? A survey of journalists who were sued for invasion of privacy." *Journalism and Mass Communications Quarterly, 75*(2), pp. 378–393.

Vonnegut, K. (1952). *Player piano.* New York: Dell Publishing Co.

Ward, Stephen J. (2004). *The invention of journalism ethics.* Montreal: McGill-Queens University Press.

Weaver, D. H., Beam, R. A., Brownlee, B. J., Voakes, P. S., and Wilhoit, G. C. (2007). *The American journalist in the 21st century: U.S. news people at the dawn of a new millenium* (LEA's Communication Series). Mahwah, NJ: Lawrence Erlbaum & Assoc.

Weiss, A. (2006). "*New York Times* probed on Sudan ad insert." Retrieved from **www.forward.com.**

Weinberg, S. (1995, Nov/Dec.). "ABC, Philip Morris and the infamous apology." *Columbia Journalism Review,* pp. 29–37.

Werhane, Patricia (2006). "Stockholder ethics in health care." Presented to the Association of Applied and Professional Ethics, February 2006. San Antonio, Texas.

Wilkins, L. (1987). *Shared vulnerability: The mass media and American perception of the Bhopal disaster.* Westport, CT: Greenwood Press.

Wilkins, L. and Christians, C. (2001). "Philosophy meets the social sciences: The nature of humanity in the public arena." *Journal of Mass Media Ethics, 16*(2,3), pp. 99–120.

Wilkins, L. and Coleman, R. (2005). *The moral media.* Mahwah, NJ: Lawrence Erlbaum and Associates.

Williams, B. (2009). "The ethics of political communication." In L. Wilkins and C. G. Christians (eds.), *Handbook of Mass Media Ethics.* New York and London: Taylor & Francis.

Winslow, D. (2004). "Peter Turnley's photo-essays to debut in *Harper's Magazine.*" **www.digitaljournalist.org.**

Woodward, K. (1994, June 13). "What is virtue?" *Newsweek,* pp. 38–39.

Index

A

Access, 62
Accuracy, 35, 41–42
Activism, 88–89
Advertising, 12, 70–73, 98
    Advertorials, 90–93
    Advocacy in, 1, 2, 59–60, 63, 79–81
    Behavioral, 55–56, 123
    Criticisms of, 56
    Defenses of, 56
    Honesty and, 63, 90–93
    Political, 145–146, 150–152
    Sincerity in, 61, 62
    Target marketing, 55, 63–64, 70–73
    See also deception
    See also public relations
Advocacy, 61, 90–93, 176–178, 268–269
Aesthetics, 284–285
Aggregation, 38–39
al-Jazeera, 156, 166, 169
Aristotle, 7–9, 16, 101
Associated Press, 39
Audience, 149
Authenticity, 61

B

Bacon, Francis, 15
Balance theory, 57–58
BBC, 287–288
Beneficence, 12
Benetton, 79–81
Bentham, Jeremy, 10

Bernays, Edward, 65
Bill of Rights
    See also Constitution
Blair, Jayson, 31–32
Blogs, 255–257, 270–271
Bok, Sissela, 4–7, 33–34
Bonding announcements, 198–200
Book banning
    See censorship
Borden, Sandra, 16
Boston Herald, 19–21
Boyd, Gerald, 33
Bragg, Rick, 33
Brandeis, Louis, 125
Bribery, 183
Bryant, Kobe, 142–143

C

Capital punishment, 79–81
Care, ethics of, 308–310
Case study method, 17–20
Categorical imperative, 9–10, 79–81
    See also Kant
Caveat emptor, 58, 59
CDs, 186
Celebrity
    See privacy
Censorship, 273–274, 279, 287–288
Character, 153–154
Cheney, Richard, 124
Chicago Tribune, 237–238
Children, 64
Christians, Clifford G., 26, 127, 158